THE
American Patriot's
ALMANAC

OTHER BOOKS BY WILLIAM J. BENNETT

THE
American Patriot's
ALMANAC

WILLIAM J. BENNETT
AND JOHN T. E. CRIBB

THOMAS NELSON
Since 1798

NASHVILLE   DALLAS   MEXICO CITY   RIO DE JANEIRO   BEIJING

To the families of the American soldier,

families who, for love of country,

have sacrified in countless ways.

Published in Nashville, Tennessee, by Thomas Nelson. Thomas Nelson is a registered trademark of Thomas Nelson, Inc.

Illustrations: Clint Hansen/Scott Hull Associates

Thomas Nelson, Inc., titles may be purchased in bulk for educational, business, fund-raising, or sales promotional use. For information, please e-mail SpecialMarkets@ThomasNelson.com.

Page design: Walter Petrie

Editorial staff: Joel Miller and Thom Chittom

Library of Congress Cataloging-in-Publication Data

Bennett, William J. (William John), 1943–
    The American patriot's almanac / by William J. Bennett and John Cribb.
        p. cm.
    Includes bibliographical references.
    ISBN 978-1-59555-267-9
    1. United States—History—Anecdotes. 2. Patriotism—United States—History—Anecdotes.
3. United States—Biography—Anecdotes. 4. United States—History—Miscellanea. 5. Almanacs, American. I. Cribb, John T. E. II. Title.
E179.B53 2008
973—dc22   2008032262

Printed in the United States of America

09 10 11 12 QW 5

CONTENTS

THE AMERICAN PATRIOT

Patriotism means "love for country." The word comes from the Latin *pater*, meaning "father." Loving your homeland is just as natural as loving your father or mother—after all, your country nourishes you, protects you, and in many ways makes you who you are. Just as it's a virtue to honor your parents, it's a good and admirable thing to honor the land you call home.

Patriotism involves all sorts of ties and attachments. We love our country because it's the place where family and friends live. We love it because it's where we have so many things in common with others: the language we speak, the history we share, the holidays we celebrate, the government we elect, even the sports teams we cheer and television programs we watch. The land itself stirs deep feelings—as the song "America" goes, "I love thy rocks and rills, thy woods and templed hills."

In America patriotism involves even more. From its beginnings the United States was founded on a set of ideals. Freedom of thought and speech. Equality before the law. The right to worship God as we please. The dignity of each individual. Such ideals, more than anything else, make us one nation indivisible. They're the glue that holds our society together. American patriotism is largely about some shining principles and the spirit it takes to make them work.

Why should we be patriots? In part, simply out of gratitude. No other country has ever offered so much opportunity to learn, to grow, to make a living, to make a mark. We should not forget that. We Americans are so good at critiquing our own nation, so determined to make it better, that sometimes we neglect to acknowledge all that is wonderful about it. Let us not commit the sin of ingratitude for so many blessings.

We should love our country because of its achievements. The United States has brought freedom to more people than any other nation in history. It has welcomed millions to its shores. It offers its citizens one of the highest standards of living in the world. If the United States is not worth loving, then no country is.

Our nation's founding principles of liberty and equality are among humanity's noblest aspirations. As long as the United States is a place dedicated to those principles, then to be an American patriot is to love something noble and good. By loving America, we lift our own sights.

To love something is to stand up for it. September 11, 2001, reminded us that there will always be tyrants, bullies, and madmen who hate American ideals and want to destroy our country. As President Harry Truman once said, freedom "calls for courage and endurance, not only in soldiers, but in every man and woman who is free and who is determined to remain free." Our country needs patriots who will stand fast for America.

Some folks view patriotism as something quaint and even embarrassing, an awkward sentiment out of step with modern times. A couple of years after 9-11, an Associated Press story told readers that the war against terror had brought "fallout—patriotism, paranoia, propaganda, and plotting." But treating patriotism as a downside only encourages those who want to knock America down. Actor James Cagney, playing Broadway legend George M. Cohan, summed it up in the 1942 movie *Yankee Doodle Dandy*: "It seems it always happens. Whenever we get too high-hat and too sophisticated for flag-waving, some thug nation decides we're a pushover all ready to be blackjacked. And it isn't long before we're looking up, mighty anxiously, to be sure the flag's still waving over us."

There will always be some people ready to paint America as a place not worthy of special love or respect. A few years ago, a well-known American filmmaker went abroad and told an audience that they were "stuck with being connected to this country of mine, which is known for bringing sadness and misery to places around the globe." This country needs patriots to debunk such America-bashing. It's true that, at times, the United States has fallen short of its ideals. As the late Senator Daniel Patrick Moynihan put it, "Am I embarrassed to speak for a less-than-perfect democracy? Not one bit. Find me a better one. Do I suppose there are societies that are free of sin? No, I don't. Do I think ours is on balance incomparably the most hopeful set of human relations the world has? Yes, I do. Have we done obscene things? Yes, we have. How did our people learn about them? They learned about them on television and in the newspapers." For all its errors, this much is true of the American record: it's a mostly good and hopeful story. It's the story of a great country that's done great things. When the roll of nations is called, the American record stands tall.

Patriotism doesn't mean obnoxious boasting. It's not about bragging that our country is the best in the world, but it *does* involve taking pride in our country's achievements, sticking up for its principles, supporting its efforts, and cheering it on at times. It means offering respect to our nation and its institutions.

To love something is to try to make it as good as it can possibly be. The United States will always need patriots willing to work to improve it. In this land of plenty, we're often distracted by easy entertainments and shopping aisles full of the latest fashions and gadgets. This country needs citizens who remember that America is about much more than the good life, patriots who are willing to strive for our best ideals.

Patriotism doesn't mean blind loyalty. It isn't knee-jerk agreement with the president or the political party to which we belong. Nobody wants the United States to be a republic of sheep. We need, in James Madison's words, a nation of "loving critics" who use their free minds and free wills to examine the country's actions closely and raise concerns when necessary. Sometimes the debate gets noisy. American patriotism can be rough-and-tumble. That's okay, as long as it's all for the good of the country.

In the early nineteenth century, naval hero Stephen Decatur gave a famous toast: "Our country! In her intercourse with foreign nations, may she always be in the right, but our country, right or wrong!" That almost hits the mark, but not quite. Carl Schurz, a German immigrant who served as a Union general in the Civil War and later as a U.S. senator, improved Decatur's toast: "Our country right or wrong—when right to be kept right, when wrong to be put right."

Patriotism brings obligations. It involves actions, not just feelings. Claiming patriotism while shirking the duties that come with it is no better than telling your parents how much you love them and then looking the other way when they need your help. Yes, patriotism can mean flying the flag and marching in parades on the Fourth of July. It also means getting to the polls on Election Day. Reading, listening, and discussing so as to make informed judgments about current issues. Offering your services to community and civic groups. Obeying the laws. Learning about the nation's history. Knowing something about the Constitution. Helping your neighbors. It's usually not that hard to be a patriot. But it does require some effort.

Occasionally, being a patriot means putting national interest before self. Here is when patriotism can be a hard virtue to live up to—when it involves sacrifice. The people who founded this nation did it. The signers of the Declaration of Independence, for example, were mostly wealthy men who could have gone on living comfortable lives with the status quo. But they put their fortunes, their safety, and their sacred honor on the line for something greater than themselves.

Americans who serve in the armed forces frequently put national interest before their own. They're often men and women who love their country more than self. As one young American from Virginia who enlisted in the Marines to fight terrorism put it, "How can I live here, have all the things we have, and *not* give something back?" These pages include several stories about heroes in uniform. This is not to romanticize battle. "I know war as few other men now living know it, and nothing to me is more revolting," General Douglas MacArthur said. For good reason, the eagle on the Great Seal of the United

States faces the talon clutching an olive branch, a sign of peace, rather than the talon clutching arrows. Nevertheless, it is crucial to remember and honor those patriots who have fought for America when necessary. Without them, we would not have a country.

The stories, symbols, heroes, and famous words in this book are important because they help tell us who we are as Americans. They remind us that we're all a part of this wonderful common enterprise called the United States. The long winter at Valley Forge. The Tomb of the Unknown Soldier. The Wright Brothers at Kitty Hawk. Neil Armstrong and Buzz Aldrin planting a flag on the moon. These events and images are part of what Abraham Lincoln called the "mystic chords of memory" that unite us as a people and connect us with the past we all share. They help us understand the ideals we stand for and appreciate how hard it has been to preserve them. They help us know our country better and love it more.

Every American has a claim on the contents of this book. Many of us don't have ancestors who were in this country when it was founded, but we're *all* heirs to that founding, even the most recent arrivals. That's one of the great things about the United States. As others have observed, you can move to Italy or Japan and live there for years and still never be considered a "true" Italian or Japanese. But in this country, it doesn't take long for newcomers to become every bit as "American" as someone whose family has been here for generations. President Ronald Reagan said that he "always believed that this anointed land was set apart in an uncommon way, that a divine plan placed this great continent here between the oceans to be found by people from every corner of the earth who had a special love of faith and freedom." All American patriots, whatever their blood lines, are descendants of the spirit of 1776.

At the end of the Constitutional Convention of 1787, a Philadelphia lady asked Benjamin Franklin, "Well, Doctor, what have we got—a republic or a monarchy?" Franklin replied, "A republic, if you can keep it." It takes a nation of patriots to keep a republic. Especially this republic. The United States, with all its might, isn't likely to be conquered from the outside anytime soon. If American liberty loses its luster, the dimming will come from within. It will be due to our own lack of attention and devotion. Without patriotism, there cannot be a United States. It falls upon us—upon you and me—to take care of this miraculous American democracy, to make it work, to *love it.*

JANUARY

ON JANUARY 1, 1863, Abraham Lincoln signed the Emancipation Proclamation, which declared all slaves in Confederate territory to be free. The proclamation stated that, as of that day, "all persons held as slaves within any State, or designated part of a State . . . in rebellion against the United States, shall be then, thenceforward, and forever free."

Those words changed the Civil War from a fight to save the Union into a battle for human freedom. They meant that the United States was finally facing the fact that it could not tolerate the evil of slavery if it really believed that all people had the right to life, liberty, and the pursuit of happiness. With the Emancipation Proclamation, the U.S. started down the path of becoming a truly great nation, one that could try to live up to the soaring ideals on which it was founded.

Lincoln signed the proclamation in his office on New Year's Day afternoon. A handful of advisors joined him for the historic occasion. The president dipped a pen in ink but then put it down because his hand was trembling. He'd been shaking hands for hours at a reception, he explained, and his arm felt "almost paralyzed." He worried that a shaky signature might prompt critics to claim that he hesitated. "I never, in my life, felt more certain that I was doing right than I do in signing this paper," he told those looking on.

Flexing his arm and taking up the pen again, he carefully wrote his name. Lincoln signed most government documents as *A. Lincoln*. For the Emancipation Proclamation, he wrote his name in full. "That will do," he said, looking up and smiling.

With the passing of time, the text of the original Emancipation Proclamation has faded, and its paper has yellowed. But the signature of Abraham Lincoln stands forth bold, bright, and clear.

The Emancipation Proclamation is reprinted on page 331.

AMERICAN HISTORY PARADE

1752   Betsy Ross, said to have sewed the first American flag, is born in Philadelphia.

1863   Abraham Lincoln issues the Emancipation Proclamation.

1892   Ellis Island begins processing immigrants in New York Harbor.

1902   The first Rose Bowl is played in Pasadena, California (Michigan defeats Stanford 49-0).

1928   The first air-conditioned office building opens in San Antonio, Texas.

ON THIS DAY IN 1777, George Washington's army was busy fighting the British in the Second Battle of Trenton, New Jersey. While Washington fought, another great patriot was hard at work behind the scenes, aiding the American cause. You may never have heard of Haym Salomon, but he was one of the heroes of the American Revolution. In fact, if not for Patriots like Salomon, there would never have been a United States.

Born in Poland, Salomon immigrated to New York City in 1772 and soon became a successful merchant and banker. He joined the Sons of Liberty, a Patriot group, and when war broke out, he helped supply American troops. The British arrested him in 1776 and flung him into prison. After a while they released him, and he went straight back to aiding the Patriots.

The British arrested Salomon again in 1778. This time they decided to be rid of him. They sentenced him to be hanged as a rebel, but he escaped and fled to Philadelphia.

Once again Salomon went into business as a banker, and he continued to devote his talents and wealth to the Patriot cause. American leaders frequently turned to him for help in raising funds to support the war. Salomon risked his assets by loaning the government money for little or no commission. He helped pay the salaries of army officers, tapped his own funds to supply ragged troops, and worked tirelessly to secure French aid for the Revolution.

After the war the young nation struggled to get on its feet. When the republic needed money, Salomon helped save the United States from financial collapse.

The years following the Revolution took a toll on Haym Salomon's business. At the end of his life, his wealth was gone. In fact, he died impoverished. He had poured much of his fortune into the service of his country.

AMERICAN HISTORY PARADE

1777   George Washington's army fights the Second Battle of Trenton, New Jersey.

1788   Georgia becomes the fourth state to ratify the U. S. Constitution.

1882   John D. Rockefeller forms the Standard Oil Trust, a giant oil monopoly.

1942   During World War II, Japanese forces capture Manila, the capital of the Philippines.

1974   President Richard Nixon signs legislation limiting highway speeds to 55 miles per hour to conserve gas.

ON THIS DAY IN 1959, Alaska became the first new state to enter the Union since Arizona, forty-seven years before. It's by far the largest state—more than twice as large as Texas and almost a fifth as large as all the rest of the states put together. Nearly a third of Alaska lies north of the Arctic Circle, and its mainland stretches almost to Asia, coming within 51 miles of Russia. One of Alaska's islands, Little Diomede Island, lies only two and a half miles from Russia's Big Diomede Island, with the International Date Line running between them.

Here are a few more state statistics:

Largest	**Alaska** (663,267 sq. mi.)
Largest in Lower 48	**Texas** (268,581 sq. mi.)
Largest east of the Mississippi*	**Michigan** (96,716 sq. mi.)
Smallest	**Rhode Island** (1,545 sq. mi.)
Smallest west of the Mississippi**	**Hawaii** (10,931 sq. mi.)
Most coastal shoreline	**Alaska** (33,904 mi.)
Least coastal shoreline	**Pennsylvania** (89 mi.)
Most populated	**California** (approx. 37,000,000 people)
Least populated	**Wyoming** (approx. 500,000 people)
Most densely populated	**New Jersey** (1,135 people per sq. mi.)
Least densely populated	**Alaska** (1.1 people per sq. mi.)
First to enter union	**Delaware** (Dec. 7, 1787)
Latest to enter union	**Hawaii** (Aug. 21, 1959)

* Area figures include land and water. Georgia is the largest state east of the Mississippi in terms of land, with 57,906 square miles.

** In the Lower 48, Arkansas (53,179 sq. mi.) is the smallest state to lie entirely west of the Mississippi River. Louisiana (51,840 sq. mi.) lies mostly west of the Mississippi.

AMERICAN HISTORY PARADE

1777   A Patriot army under General George Washington defeats the British in the Battle of Princeton, New Jersey.

1870   Construction on the Brooklyn Bridge begins.

1947   Congressional proceedings are televised for the first time as part of the 80th Congress's opening ceremonies and are broadcast in a few cities.

1959   Alaska becomes the forty-ninth state.

JANUARY 4 is the feast day of Elizabeth Ann Seton, the first American-born saint.

Elizabeth was born in New York City on August 28, 1774. She grew up in a well-to-do family and married William Seton, a wealthy young New York shipping merchant. Elizabeth had five children, enjoyed a privileged social position, and devoted herself to several charitable activities.

In 1803, her world came crashing down around her. William's shipping business went bankrupt, and he developed tuberculosis. They sailed to Italy in search of a healthier climate, but William soon died. While waiting for passage back to the United States, Elizabeth stayed with an Italian family and was deeply impressed with their devout Catholic faith.

Elizabeth returned to New York with little money. She soon made a decision that made her life even harder—she decided to become a Catholic. It was a time in American history when Catholics often suffered great prejudice. Rejected by family and friends, she struggled to support her children.

A rector in Baltimore heard of her plight and invited her to establish a school for girls there. In 1808, Elizabeth embarked on a remarkable new life. Settling in Baltimore, she started the Paca Street School, the country's first Catholic elementary school. A year later she founded the Sisters of Charity of St. Joseph's, a religious community of women devoted to teaching and serving the poor. As the community grew, it opened schools and orphanages in New York and Philadelphia.

Elizabeth Seton died on January 4, 1821. By then the Sisters of Charity were spreading across the country. Today Seton's legacy includes thousands of sisters who work in hundreds of schools, hospitals, and social service centers throughout the world. In 1975, the Roman Catholic Church declared Elizabeth Ann Seton a saint.

AMERICAN HISTORY PARADE

1821   Elizabeth Ann Seton dies in Emmitsburg, Maryland.

1885   Dr. William W. Grant of Davenport, Iowa, performs what is thought to be the first succussful appendectomy in the United States.

1896   Utah becomes the forty-fifth state.

2004   *Spirit*, a robotic rover, lands on Mars to explore the planet.

2007   Nancy Pelosi of California becomes the first female Speaker of the House.

THE FIRST WEEK OF JANUARY 1892 saw the opening of a new U.S. immigration station on Ellis Island in New York Harbor. A 15-year-old lass from Ireland named Annie Moore entered the United States and history when she passed through its doors, becoming the first immigrant to be processed there. Over the next 62 years, 12 million more would follow, making Ellis Island the most famous entry point in America.

Ferryboats full of eager immigrants who had just crossed the Atlantic on sailing vessels or steamships docked at Ellis Island. There passengers disembarked to be screened by doctors and immigration officers. If they were in good health and their papers in order, they were allowed into the United States. Over the years, 98 percent of all those examined at Ellis Island were admitted into the country. More than 40 percent of all U.S. citizens can trace their ancestry through those immigrants.

Ellis Island closed as an immigration station in 1954. In 1990 it reopened as the Ellis Island Immigration Museum. Ferries that take visitors to the Statue of Liberty make stops at the museum.

Ellis Island was named for Samuel Ellis, a colonist who owned the island in the late eighteenth century. Today the name reminds us that America has been a beacon of hope for the world—as Abraham Lincoln called it, "the last best hope of earth"—and that the United States has taken in more people seeking new lives than any other nation in history.

AMERICAN HISTORY PARADE

1781   A British force led by Benedict Arnold burns Richmond, Virginia.

1914   Henry Ford, head of the Ford Motor Company, introduces a wage of five dollars a day in his automotive factories.

1925   Nellie T. Ross becomes the first woman governor when she succeeds her late husband as governor of Wyoming.

1933   Construction begins on the Golden Gate Bridge in San Francisco.

AS A YOUNG MAN, Samuel Morse set out to become a famous painter. His ambition was "to rival the genius of a Raphael, a Michelangelo, or a Titian." He studied at the Royal Academy in London and won acclaim by painting portraits of men such as President James Monroe and the Marquis de Lafayette.

In 1832, onboard a ship crossing the ocean, Morse heard another passenger describe how electricity could pass instantly over any length of wire. He began to wonder: Could messages be sent over wires with electricity? He rushed back to his cabin, took out his drawing book, and began to sketch out his idea for a telegraph.

He knew little about electricity, but he learned as he went. He used a homemade battery and parts from an old clock to build his first models. He developed a code of long and short electrical impulses—"dots" and "dashes"—to represent letters. His invention raised the interest of Alfred Vail, a machinist who became his partner.

On January 6, 1838, the inventors were ready to test their device over two miles of wire at the Vail family ironworks in New Jersey. Vail's father scribbled *A patient waiter is no loser* on a piece of paper and handed it to his son. "If you can send this and Mr. Morse can read it at the other end, I shall be convinced," he said. A short time later, his words came out on the receiving end.

On May 24, 1844, an amazed crowd in the Supreme Court chambers in Washington, D.C., watched Samuel Morse demonstrate his telegraph by sending a message over a wire to Baltimore, 35 miles away. In Morse code, he tapped out a quote from the Bible: *What hath God wrought!*

Soon telegraph lines linked countries and continents, and the world entered the age of modern communication.

AMERICAN HISTORY PARADE

1759 George Washington and Martha Dandridge Custis are married.

1838 Samuel Morse conducts a successful demonstration of his telegraph near Morristown, New Jersey.

1912 New Mexico becomes the forty-seventh state.

1942 The Pan American Airways *Pacific Clipper* arrives in New York City to complete the first round-the-world trip by a commercial airplane.

CONNECTICUT PATRIOT ISRAEL PUTNAM, born January 7, 1718, was a successful farmer and tavern keeper at the outset of the Revolutionary War. He had already seen more than his share of fighting. During the French and Indian War, he had been captured by Indians and would have been burned alive if a French officer had not intervened at the last minute. He took part in campaigns against Fort Ticonderoga and Montreal, and in 1762 survived a shipwreck off Cuba during a mission against Havana.

On April 20, 1775, Putnam and his son Daniel were plowing in a field in Brooklyn, Connecticut, when a messenger galloped into the village with news that the British had fired on the American militia at Lexington, Massachusetts. At once Putnam mounted a horse to spread the alarm in neighboring towns and consult with local leaders. Then came news of fighting at Concord, and a call for "every man who is fit and willing" to come to their countrymen's aid.

Without stopping to rest or even change the checkered farmer's frock he'd been wearing when he left his plow, Putnam rode through the night to Cambridge, Massachusetts, near Boston, to join colonial soldiers there. By the time he reached his destination, he'd ridden 100 miles in 18 hours.

Two months later, Putnam commanded troops at Bunker's Hill (Breed's Hill), where he reportedly told his men, "Don't fire until you see the whites of their eyes!" Like the ancient Roman Cincinnatus, who also left his plow standing in a field when called to duty, Putnam never hesitated when his country needed him.

A monument to Israel Putnam at Brooklyn, Connecticut, reads: "Patriot, remember the heritages received from your forefathers and predecessors. Protect and perpetuate them for future generations of your countrymen."

AMERICAN HISTORY PARADE

1718   Israel Putnam, American patriot, is born in Salem Village, Massachusetts.

1782   The Bank of North America, the first U.S. commercial bank, opens in Philadelphia.

1789   The first presidential election is held as Americans vote for electors who, a month later, choose George Washington as the nation's first president.

1800   Millard Fillmore, the thirteenth U.S. president, is born in Locke, New York.

1927   Commercial transatlantic telephone service between New York and London is inaugurated.

1999   President Bill Clinton's impeachment trial begins in the Senate on charges of perjury and obstruction of justice (he is later acquitted).

ON JANUARY 8, 1815, Andrew Jackson and his band of "half-horse, half-alligator" men whipped the British in the Battle of New Orleans, the last major battle of the War of 1812.

General Jackson, known to his troops as "Old Hickory" because of his toughness, had been placed in charge of defending the port city. As the British approached, he frantically threw up earthworks and assembled an extraordinary army of some 5,000 men. He had volunteers from New Orleans, including Creole aristocrats, tradesmen, and laborers. His forces also counted Tennessee and Kentucky militia, as well as Free Negroes, Spanish, French, Portuguese, Italians, and Indians.

Jackson even had help from Jean Lafitte, the infamous, French-born gentleman pirate. The British had offered Lafitte money and a command in the Royal Navy if he would help them attack New Orleans. Lafitte turned them down and offered his pirates to the American side. Jackson, needing every man he could get, said yes.

The British, who ridiculed the American defenders as "dirty shirts," came at Old Hickory at daybreak with more than 8,000 troops. As the main attack began, they fired a rocket. Old Hickory remained calm. "Don't mind those rockets," he said. "They are mere toys to amuse children."

As the redcoats advanced, the Americans took aim with rifles and artillery. "Boys, elevate them guns a little lower!" Jackson ordered as he directed cannon fire.

The battle turned into a rout. About 2,000 British soldiers were killed, wounded, or captured. The American toll was just 13 dead and 58 wounded or missing.

Several weeks later, news arrived that American and British negotiators had signed a peace treaty in Ghent, Belgium, two weeks *before* the battle. Still, the victory electrified Americans, filled them with confidence, and gave them a hero who would go on to become the nation's seventh president.

AMERICAN HISTORY PARADE

1790   President George Washington delivers the first State of the Union address in New York City.

1815   U.S. forces led by General Andrew Jackson defeat the British in the Battle of New Orleans.

1918   President Woodrow Wilson outlines his fourteen points for peace after World War I.

1935   Rock 'n' roll king Elvis Presley is born in Tupelo, Mississippi.

1964   President Lyndon B. Johnson declares war on poverty.

1987   The Dow Jones Industrial Average closes above 2,000 for the first time.

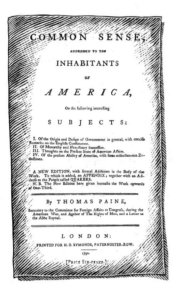

ON JANUARY 9, 1776, Thomas Paine published *Common Sense*, a pamphlet that set the American colonies afire with a longing for independence.

Paine was born in England to a poor family and received little schooling. For several years he drifted from job to job—corset maker, seaman, schoolteacher, customs collector, tobacco seller—without success. His prospects were few when he met Benjamin Franklin, then living in London, who suggested he go to America. Sailing across the Atlantic, Paine caught a fever and was carried ashore half dead in Philadelphia. Once recovered, letters of recommendation from Franklin helped him get a job as a magazine writer.

It has been said that Paine "had more brains than books, more sense than education, more courage than politeness, more strength than polish." But he could work magic with pen and paper. In *Common Sense* he made bold arguments that Americans should demand their freedom. "The birthday of a new world is at hand," he insisted. He attacked the idea that people must live under a king, and urged a break from Britain.

"O ye that love mankind! Ye that dare oppose, not only the tyranny, but the tyrant, stand forth!" he wrote. "Every spot of the old world is overrun with oppression. Freedom hath been hunted round the globe. Asia, and Africa, have long expelled her. Europe regards her like a stranger, and England hath given her warning to depart. O! [America] receive the fugitive, and prepare in time an asylum for mankind."

Paine's words sounded like a trumpet blast through the colonies. Thousands snatched up the pamphlet and decided that he was right. As Thomas Edison, one of America's great geniuses, wrote 150 years later, "We never had a sounder intelligence in this Republic. . . . In *Common Sense* Paine flared forth with a document so powerful that the Revolution became inevitable."

AMERICAN HISTORY PARADE

1776   Thomas Paine publishes *Common Sense* in Philadelphia.

1788   Connecticut becomes the fifth state to ratify the Constitution.

1861   The Union merchant ship *Star of the West* is fired on in Charleston harbor as it attempts to resupply Fort Sumter, marking the first shots of the Civil War.

1913   Richard Milhous Nixon, the thirty-seventh U.S. president, is born in Yorba Linda, California.

MANY AMERICAN COLONISTS started each year by opening the latest edition of their favorite almanac. The most famous was *Poor Richard's Almanack*, published by Benjamin Franklin from 1733 to 1758, while he was a printer in Philadelphia. Readers appreciated the almanac's weather predictions, astronomical data, and agricultural information. But they especially loved its humor, verses, and practical advice, all dispensed by the pen of "Poor" Richard Saunders, a fictional astrologer whom Franklin invented to be the editor of his publication.

Some of Poor Richard's proverbs—such as "A penny saved is a penny earned" and "Early to bed and early to rise, makes a man healthy, wealthy, and wise"—are still quoted today. Many of the aphorisms came from earlier writers, ranging from Greek to English, but were often "Americanized" for Franklin's readers.

A few more proverbs from Poor Richard:

- With the old Almanack and the old year Leave thy old vices, tho'ever so dear.
- He that riseth late must trot all day, and shall scarce overtake his business at night.
- Well done is better than well said.
- People who are wrapped up in themselves make small packages.
- Little strokes fell great oaks.
- If a man could have half his wishes, he would double his troubles.
- One today is worth two tomorrows.
- He that by the plow would thrive,
  Himself must either hold or drive.
- Laziness travels so slowly that Poverty soon overtakes him.

AMERICAN HISTORY PARADE

1753   Poor Richard predicts "wind and falling weather, then very cold" for the second week of January.

1861   Florida secedes from the Union.

1901   A drilling derrick near Beaumont, Texas, strikes oil, creating a huge gusher and signaling the beginning of American oil history.

1946   A radar beam from a U.S. Army laboratory at Belmar, New Jersey, bounces off the moon and returns to Earth in 2.4 seconds.`

ALEXANDER HAMILTON was born January 11 in either 1755 or 1757—the exact year is uncertain. An orphan from the Caribbean island of Nevis, he rose with astounding speed to become an aide-de-camp to George Washington, a hero of the Revolutionary War, and a member of the Constitutional Convention. As the first secretary of the treasury, he helped build the new nation's financial systems. As a leader of the Federalist Party, he helped create our political system. He was never president of the United States, but he shaped the new American nation as few other Founding Fathers did.

Because he argued for a strong central government, Hamilton is often seen as an anti-democratic figure. But he could write as memorably of natural law and human rights as any of the Founders. "The sacred rights of mankind are not to be rummaged for among old parchments or musty records," he wrote. "They are written, as with a sunbeam, in the whole volume of human nature, by the hand of the Divinity itself and can never be erased or obscured by mortal power."

One of Hamilton's greatest contributions was to help persuade Americans to accept the Constitution. With James Madison and John Jay, he wrote *The Federalist Papers*, a series of brilliant newspaper essays urging the Constitution's ratification. Many people predicted that the new plan for government would not work. But Hamilton believed his countrymen should put aside their differences and give it a try. "The system, though it may not be perfect in every part, is, upon the whole, a good one," he reminded them. "I never expect to see a perfect work from imperfect man." If not for Hamilton's brilliant arguments and efforts, the thirteen former colonies might have gone their separate ways.

AMERICAN HISTORY PARADE

1755   Founding Father Alexander Hamilton is born in the West Indies.

1785   Congress relocates from Trenton, New Jersey, to New York City, the nation's new temporary capital.

1861   Alabama secedes from the Union.

1908   President Theodore Roosevelt declares the Grand Canyon a national monument.

JOHN HANCOCK, born January 12, 1737, was a Boston merchant and one of the richest men in America at the time of the Revolution. A fiery Patriot, he never hesitated to risk his wealth for the cause of independence. The British considered him a dangerous traitor and reportedly put a price of £500 on his head.

Hancock served as president of the Continental Congress and was the first to sign the Declaration of Independence in 1776. He signed in bold letters and, according to legend, remarked as he wrote, "There! His Majesty can now read my name without glasses. And he can double the reward on my head!"

John Hancock and his fellow Patriots knew they were signing their own death warrants should the Revolution fail. Yet they pledged, as the Declaration states, "our lives, our fortunes, and our sacred honor" so that America might be free.

AMERICAN HISTORY PARADE

1737   John Hancock is born in Braintree, Massachusetts.

1773   The first public museum in America is established in Charleston, South Carolina.

1906   The Dow Jones Industrial Average closes above 100 for the first time.

1915   Congress establishes Rocky Mountain National Park.

1932   Hattie W. Caraway of Arkansas becomes the first woman elected to the U.S. Senate.

THE WINTER OF 1777–78 brought dark days to the American Revolution. The British had captured Philadelphia, the colonies' largest city, and settled into snug quarters there for the season. George Washington's battered army, meanwhile, limped to a bleak hillside in Pennsylvania and set about making winter camp. The name of the place was Valley Forge.

The coming weeks saw unimaginable suffering. The Americans lived in crude log huts that did little to keep out rain or snow. The army dressed in rags. Some soldiers had no shoes except strips they had cut from their precious blankets to wrap around their feet. At night they lay on the frozen ground, or stayed up until morning crowding around their fires to keep from freezing to death. At one point Washington wrote, "We have this day no less than 2,873 men in camp unfit for duty because they are barefooted and otherwise naked."

There was almost never enough food. Men lived for whole days at a time on nothing but flour and water baked on hot stones. Disease swept through the camp, leaving an army of skeletons shivering in the biting winds.

But the Patriot spirit never broke. Somehow, in the midst of misery, the troops managed to march, drill, and train themselves to fight. "If we can just live through this winter," they told themselves, "we can win our freedom."

The Americans had arrived at Valley Forge with perhaps 12,000 men. By the time the snows of winter melted, only 8,000 remained—8,000 who had survived on little but loyalty, courage, and resolve. It was a tougher army that marched away from Valley Forge, an army ready to fight.

AMERICAN HISTORY PARADE

1778 At Valley Forge, the Patriot army attends to the construction of makeshift hospitals for the sick.

1794 President Washington approves a measure adding two stars and stripes to the flag to represent Vermont and Kentucky.

1910 In an early radio demonstration, opera star Enrico Caruso is broadcast live from the Metropolitan Opera in New York.

1990 Douglas Wilder of Virginia is sworn in as the nation's first elected black governor.

DURING THE LONG WINTER OF 1777–78, when the Patriot army camped at Valley Forge, George Washington shared the hardships suffered by his men. He spent much of his time rounding up food, begging the Continental Congress for supplies, and bolstering the troops' spirits. His presence kept the army from disintegrating.

Tradition holds that one cold day, Isaac Potts, a Quaker farmer who lived near Valley Forge, was walking through the woods when he heard a low, solemn voice. Stealing quietly in its direction, he found a riderless horse tied to a sapling. The farmer crept nearer and through the trees saw a lone man on his knees in the snow.

It was General Washington. Tears marked his face as he bowed his head and asked God to look after his men.

At home that evening the farmer told his wife of the encounter. "All will be well, Martha," he said. "If there is anyone the Lord will listen to, it is this brave man. I have seen General Washington on his knees. Our independence is certain."

AMERICAN HISTORY PARADE

1639   Three Connecticut towns adopt the Fundamental Orders, one of the earliest constitutions in the colonies.

1784   The Continental Congress ratifies the Treaty of Paris, officially ending the Revolutionary War.

1914   Henry Ford introduces a moving assembly line for cars, reducing production time from more than 12 hours to about 90 minutes.

1943   Franklin D. Roosevelt becomes the first U.S. president to travel by airplane while in office, when he flies to a wartime conference in Casablanca, Morocco.

THE REVEREND MARTIN LUTHER KING JR., born January 15, 1929, was one of the most gifted leaders the country has known. Never was that more evident than on a cold winter night in 1956 in Montgomery, Alabama. King had left his wife and baby at home to attend a meeting at a nearby church. As the meeting wound down, someone rushed in with terrible news: "Your house has been bombed."

King raced home and saw that the bomb had exploded on his front porch. By now the house was full of people. He pushed his way inside and found his family safe.

Outside, however, trouble was stirring. An angry crowd was gathering and wanted revenge against whoever had done this. Several people carried guns and broken bottles. They hurled insults at arriving policemen. The situation was about to spin out of control. That's when King stepped onto his porch.

Silence fell over the crowd.

King told them in a calm voice that his family was all right. "I want you to go home and put down your weapons," he said. He told them violence would not solve their problems; it would only harm their cause. He reminded them of the teachings of the Bible: "We must meet hate with love."

Then something remarkable happened. "Amen," someone said. "God bless you," others called. The crowd, which a moment ago had been on the verge of violence, began to drift apart. A night that had been heading toward chaos came to a quiet, if uneasy, close.

Dr. King spent his life meeting adversity with courage and love and reminding his fellow Americans that "we must forever conduct our struggle on the high plane of dignity and discipline." Good words to remember on this day.

AMERICAN HISTORY PARADE

1844 The University of Notre Dame receives its charter from the Indiana legislature.

1892 The rules of basketball are first published in Springfield, Massachusetts.

1967 In Los Angeles, the Green Bay Packers defeat the Kansas City Chiefs 35–10 in the first Super Bowl.

1929 Martin Luther King Jr. is born in Atlanta, Georgia.

2006 *Stardust*, a NASA spacecraft, returns to Earth with the first dust ever retrieved from a comet.

IN JANUARY 1943, while World War II raged in Europe and the Pacific, the U.S. military began to manage the war effort from the Pentagon, its newly finished headquarters in Arlington, Virginia. The gigantic edifice, which sits on the bank of the Potomac River outside of Washington, D.C., still serves as the nerve center of the Department of Defense. It is one of the largest office buildings in the world.

Before the Pentagon's construction, the different parts of the War Department (as the Defense Department was called) were headquartered in scattered offices. Ground was broken in September 1941 and construction completed in only sixteen months at a cost of $83 million. The war had caused a shortage of steel, so engineers dredged 680,000 tons of sand and gravel from the Potomac and turned it into reinforced concrete for the building.

Virtually a city unto itself, the Pentagon covers 29 acres. It has 3.7 million square feet of space, three times the floor space of the Empire State Building. The U.S. Capitol building could fit into any one of its five wedge-shaped sections. About 26,000 people work at the Pentagon.

The five-sided building is designed in the form of five concentric rings. Despite its huge size and 17.5 miles of corridors, the Pentagon is one of the world's most efficient office buildings. It takes only seven minutes to walk between any two points in the structure.

During the September 11, 2001, terrorist attacks, a hijacked jetliner slammed into the Pentagon, blowing a gaping hole in one side and killing 189 people. Construction crews worked around the clock for a year to repair the outer ring before the first anniversary of the attacks.

AMERICAN HISTORY PARADE

1920   Prohibition begins, outlawing the sale of liquor, as the Eighteenth Amendment goes into effect.

1944   General Dwight D. Eisenhower assumes command of the Allied invasion force that later invades northern Europe from England during World War II.

1953   Chevrolet introduces the Corvette at New York City's Waldorf-Astoria Hotel.

1991   The Persian Gulf War begins as the United States and allied nations launch Operation Desert Storm to drive Saddam Hussein's Iraqi forces out of Kuwait.

ON JANUARY 17, 1781, Patriots under Brig. Gen. Daniel Morgan defeated a British force under Lt. Col. Banastre Tarleton at the Battle of Cowpens in South Carolina, a crucial victory in the American Revolution.

Morgan was a rough-and-tumble fellow. As a young man in Virginia, he had worked as a wagoner, driving supplies to settlers west of the Blue Ridge Mountains. During the French and Indian War, while driving wagons for the British, he managed to offend a British officer, who struck him with the flat of his sword. Morgan responded by decking the officer and was sentenced to 500 lashes. In later years, he liked to say that the British miscounted and gave him only 499, and that they still owed him one.

During the Revolution, Morgan fought at Quebec and Saratoga. In 1780, he headed south to help fight the British in the Carolina backcountry.

Tarleton, a brilliant commander, was determined to destroy Morgan's army. He once declared that "these miserable Americans must be taught their places!" The Americans viewed Tarleton as a butcher because his troops had been known to slaughter men who tried to surrender.

When Morgan realized that Tarleton was on his trail, he sent word to local militia: meet at the Cowpens, a frontier pasturing ground. The night before the battle, "the Old Wagoner" moved among his troops, bucking them up and showing them the whipping scars on his back. By dawn he had perhaps 1,500 men carefully placed on the field.

Tarleton's fearsome dragoons charged straight into a trap. The Americans managed to surround the attackers, killing or capturing most of Tarleton's 1,050 men. Tarleton himself managed to escape. But the battle was a staggering blow to the British—"a devil of a whipping," as Morgan put it—and helped turn the tide of the war.

AMERICAN HISTORY PARADE

1706   Benjamin Franklin is born in Boston.

1781   A Patriot army led by General Daniel Morgan wins a decisive victory over the British at Cowpens, South Carolina.

1806   Thomas Jefferson's daughter Martha gives birth to James Madison Randolph, the first child born in the White House.

1893   American sugar planters led by Sanford B. Dole overthrow Hawaii's Queen Liliuokalani.

1917   The United States buys the Virgin Islands from Denmark for $25 million.

1994   A magnitude 6.7 earthquake strikes Southern California, killing at least 61 people.

JANUARY 18 • "LIBERTY AND UNION, NOW AND FOR EVER, ONE AND INSEPARABLE!"

JANUARY 18 is the birthday of Daniel Webster, born in 1782 in Salisbury (now Franklin), New Hampshire, and remembered as one of the greatest orators of his day. Perhaps his grandest moment came in January 1830, a time of growing discord between North and South. Webster, representing Massachusetts in the U.S. Senate, rose to dispute an argument by Robert Hayne of South Carolina, who asserted that states had greater sovereignty than the federal government—an argument that implied that states were free to secede if they wished. Webster's passionate but reasoned defense of the Union is considered one of the greatest speeches in the Senate's history. Generations of schoolchildren memorized the closing words of his address:

When my eyes shall be turned to behold for the last time the sun in heaven, may I not see him shining on the broken and dishonored fragments of a once glorious Union; on states dissevered, discordant, belligerent; on a land rent with civil feuds, or drenched, it may be, in fraternal blood! Let their last feeble and lingering glance rather behold the gorgeous ensign of the republic, now known and honored throughout the earth, still full high advanced, its arms and trophies streaming in their original lustre, not a stripe erased or polluted, not a single star obscured, bearing for its motto, no such miserable interrogatory as "What is all this worth?" nor those other words of delusion and folly, "Liberty first and Union afterwards"; but everywhere, spread all over in characters of living light, blazing on all its ample folds, as they float over the sea and over the land, and in every wind under the whole heavens, that other sentiment, dear to every true American heart—Liberty and Union, now and for ever, one and inseparable!

AMERICAN HISTORY PARADE

1782   Statesman and orator Daniel Webster is born in Salisbury, New Hampshire.

1911   The first landing of an aircraft on a ship takes place aboard the USS *Pennsylvania* in San Francisco harbor.

1919   The post–World War I peace conference begins in Paris, ultimately resulting in the Treaty of Versailles, which sets the terms for the end of the war.

1966   Robert C. Weaver becomes the first black cabinet member as head of the Department of Housing and Urban Development.

IS IT COLD OUTSIDE? Today begins the fifth week of winter. In Anchorage, Alaska, the average high for January 19 is 22° F. The average low is 9° F. In Honolulu, Hawaii, the average high for today is 77° F, and the average low is 62° F. It's a big country, with lots of weather. Here are a few U.S. weather records.

Lowest recorded temperature: -80° F, Prospect Creek, Alaska, Jan. 23, 1971

Coldest spot (lowest average yearly temperature): Barrow, Alaska, 9.3° F

Highest recorded temperature: 134° F, Death Valley, California, July 10, 1913

Warmest spot (highest average yearly temperature): Key West, Florida, 78.2° F

Driest spot (lowest average yearly rainfall): Death Valley, California, 1.63 in.

Wettest spot (greatest average yearly rainfall): Mt. Waialeale, Kauai, Hawaii, 460 in.

Most rainfall in 24 hrs: 43 in., Alvin, Texas, July 25–26, 1979

Most snow in 24 hrs: 76 in., Silver Lake, Colorado, April 14–15, 1921*

Maximum snow depth: 451 inches, Tamarack, California, March 11, 1911

Strongest recorded wind: 231 mph, Mount Washington, New Hampshire, April 12, 1934

Largest hailstone: 7 inches in diameter, 18.75 inches in circumference, Aurora, Nebraska, June 22, 2003

Most tornadoes: Tornado Alley, the wide belt stretching through the central U.S., especially Texas, Oklahoma, Kansas, Nebraska, and Iowa.

* A reported 77 inches of snow fell in 24 hours on January 11–12, 1997, in Montague, New York. Due to the way measurements were taken, however, the National Weather Service ruled that it was not a new national record.

AMERICAN HISTORY PARADE

1807   Confederate general Robert E. Lee is born at Stratford Hall, Virginia.

1861   Georgia secedes from the Union.

1953   Seventy percent of homes with a TV watch Lucy Ricardo (Lucille Ball) give birth to a son on *I Love Lucy*.

1955   Dwight D. Eisenhower gives the first presidential news conference filmed for TV.

1977   Snow falls in Miami for the first and only time.

EVERY FOUR YEARS, following a presidential election, the nation holds an inauguration to install the president. The ceremony takes place at noon on January 20, usually outside the U.S. Capitol in Washington, D.C.

The highlight comes when the president elect takes the oath of office. Every president since the nation's founding has taken the exact same oath. The Constitution (Article II, Section 1) states the words that must be recited:

"I do solemnly swear (or affirm) that I will faithfully execute the office of President of the United States, and will to the best of my ability, preserve, protect and defend the Constitution of the United States."

George Washington is said to have added the words "So help me God" when he took the oath, and other presidents have done the same.

Thomas Jefferson was the first president to hold his inauguration in Washington, D.C., which did not become the U.S. capital until 1800. After his second inauguration, he rode by horseback from the Capitol building to the President's House accompanied by well-wishers and band music. That procession began the tradition of the Inaugural Parade, which today proceeds from the Capitol down Pennsylvania Avenue to the White House.

During the nation's early history, Inauguration Day was March 4. In 1933 the Twentieth Amendment changed the date to January 20 to speed the changeover of administrations.

Other countries sometimes suffer bloodshed as governments rise and fall. In America, power flows smoothly from one elected leader to the next. As Ronald Reagan said during his 1981 inaugural address, "Few of us stop to think how unique we really are. In the eyes of many in the world, this every-four-year ceremony we accept as normal is nothing less than a miracle."

AMERICAN HISTORY PARADE

1801   John Marshall is appointed chief justice of the United States.

1892   The first official basketball game takes place at a YMCA gymnasium in Springfield, Massachusetts.

1937   Franklin D. Roosevelt, beginning his second term, becomes the first president to be inaugurated on January 20.

1949   Harry Truman's inauguration is the first to be televised.

1981   Moments after the presidency passes from Jimmy Carter to Ronald Reagan, Iran releases 52 Americans held hostage for 444 days.

BECAUSE JANUARY 20, the constitutionally prescribed date for presidential inaugurations, fell on a Sunday in 1985, Ronald Reagan's public inaugural ceremony for his second term was moved to January 21. Due to bad weather, the ceremony was held in the Capitol Rotunda, the first time the oath of office was taken there.

Like many presidents, Reagan swore the oath with a Bible opened to scripture he chose. Here are some examples of Scripture passages used by various presidents.

Theodore Roosevelt, 1905–"But be doers of the word, and not hearers only, deceiving yourselves. For if anyone is a hearer of the word and not a doer, he is like a man who looks intently at his natural face in a mirror." *James* 1:22–23

Woodrow Wilson, 1917–"God is our refuge and strength, a very present help in trouble. . ." *Psalm 46*

Franklin D. Roosevelt, 1933, 1937, 1941, 1945–"If I speak in the tongues of men and of angels, but have not love, I am a noisy gong or a clanging cymbal . . ." 1 *Corinthians* 13

Gerald Ford, 1974–"Trust in the LORD with all your heart, and do not lean on your own understanding. In all your ways acknowledge him, and he will make straight your paths." *Proverbs* 3:5–6

Jimmy Carter, 1977–"He has told you, O man, what is good; and what does the LORD require of you but to do justice, and to love kindness, and to walk humbly with your God?" *Micah* 6:8

Ronald Reagan, 1981, 1985–"If my people who are called by my name humble themselves, and pray and seek my face and turn from their wicked ways, then I will hear from heaven, and will forgive their sin and heal their land." 2 *Chronicles* 7:14

AMERICAN HISTORY PARADE

1789   The first novel by an American writer published in America, *The Power of Sympathy* by William Hill Brown, is printed in Boston.

1950   Former State Department official Alger Hiss is convicted of perjury regarding allegations that he was a spy for the Soviet Union.

1954   The first nuclear-powered submarine, USS *Nautilus*, is launched at Groton, Connecticut.

1977   President Jimmy Carter pardons almost all Vietnam War draft evaders.

"MY DEAREST FRIEND," wrote Abigail Adams on January 22, 1797, "We have had this day something very like a snow storm. It has banked some though not very deep. . . ." So ran one of hundreds of letters she penned to her husband, John, during their 54-year marriage.

When John began to aid the Patriot cause, Abigail stood beside him, even though rebellion threatened his livelihood as a lawyer. When he was asked to serve in the Massachusetts Assembly, she made ready to share whatever dangers would come, though it meant the king might consider her family traitors.

While John was in Philadelphia at meetings of the Continental Congress, Abigail stayed home in Quincy, Massachusetts, to run their farm. She tended the garden and orchards, looked after the livestock, sold milk and butter, and taught their children (one of them, John Quincy, a future president). When war came to Massachusetts, Abigail traded for food since American money was worthless. She took refugees into her house and calmed her children as gunfire sounded across the hills.

While John worked in Congress, she wrote to him almost daily, encouraging him, keeping up his spirits, giving advice, and sending him war news from New England.

Twice Abigail saw John cross the sea to represent the new American government abroad. It meant years of being apart. When John grew so miserable he could not go on without her, she sailed to Europe to join him.

When John became the second president, Abigail worked by his side, giving her counsel, helping him with his papers and speeches, and entertaining dignitaries. She opened the brand-new White House, which at that time was an unfinished mansion in a swamp.

When we count this nation's blessings, it is good to remember that without women like Abigail Adams, there would never have been a United States.

AMERICAN HISTORY PARADE

1797 Abigail Adams writes to John, in Philadelphia, giving him news of home.

1939 The uranium atom is split for the first time using a cyclotron at Columbia University in New York City.

1944 In World War II, the Allies launch an offensive in central Italy with a hard-fought amphibious landing at Anzio Beach.

1973 The Supreme Court hands down a decision in *Roe v. Wade*, legalizing abortion.

1997 The Senate confirms Madeleine Albright as the nation's first female secretary of state.

ON JANUARY 23, 1849, Elizabeth Blackwell became the first woman in the United States to receive a medical degree when she graduated from New York's Geneva Medical College.

Blackwell had emigrated with her family from England to the U.S. at age eleven after her father's sugar refinery business failed. A few years later her father died, and she took up teaching to help support the family. The idea to become a doctor came from a dying friend. "If I could only have been treated by a lady doctor, my worst sufferings would have been spared me," she told Elizabeth. "Promise me you will at least think about it."

It was a time when most people thought women incapable of such work. More than two dozen medical schools rejected Blackwell before she was finally accepted by Geneva Medical College. She arrived on campus to discover that her admission had been something of a jest. Evidently the faculty had allowed the all-male student body to vote on her application, thinking they would never accept her. Many students thought it was a practical joke, and voted yes.

Once enrolled, Blackwell earned the admiration of her professors and classmates. She ended up graduating with top honors.

In 1851, Blackwell opened her own practice in New York City. At first most doctors shunned her, and few patients came to see her. A few years later, her sister and another female friend, who had also become doctors, joined her to open the New York Infirmary for Women and Children (now the New York Downtown Hospital). The institution served the poor and established a medical school that graduated hundreds of female doctors and nurses.

By the time Blackwell died in 1910, thousands of American women had followed in her footsteps. Today, about half of the doctors graduating from U.S. medical schools are women.

AMERICAN HISTORY PARADE

1849   Elizabeth Blackwell becomes the first woman in America to receive a medical degree.

1855   The first permanent bridge over the Mississippi River opens in what is now Minneapolis, Minnesota.

1957   The Wham-O toy company begins manufacturing aerodynamic plastic discs, now known as Frisbees.

1964   The Twenty-fourth Amendment, barring the poll tax in federal elections, is ratified.

1973   President Nixon announces an accord has been reached to end the Vietnam War.

ON JANUARY 24, 1848, a carpenter named James Marshall discovered gold in northern California, setting off the grandest gold rush in American history.

Marshall made his discovery while building a sawmill on the south fork of the American River for wealthy landowner John Sutter. He spotted some shining flecks in the water, scooped them up, and declared, "Boys, by God, I believe I've found a gold mine."

He took the nuggets to Sutter, who tried to keep the discovery quiet out of fear his land would be overrun. But word leaked out, especially after newspaper publisher and merchant Samuel Brannan bought all the shovels he could find and then paraded the streets of San Francisco waving a bottle of gold and yelling, "Gold, gold, gold from the American River!" He resold his shovels at a handsome profit.

The news filtered back east. After President Polk announced an "abundance of gold" that could "scarcely command belief," the stampede was on. By 1849, tens of thousands of Forty-niners were headed for California. The *New York Herald* reported that "in every Atlantic seaport, vessels are being filled up, societies are being formed, husbands are preparing to leave their wives, sons are parting with their mothers, and bachelors are abandoning their comforts; all are rushing head over heels toward the El Dorado on the Pacific."

They traveled overland and by sea, from the U.S. and around the world. As far away as China, California became known as *Gum Shan*—the Mountain of Gold. In about a year San Francisco grew from a hamlet to a city of 25,000.

A lucky few struck it rich in the gold fields. Most did not. Sutter himself died bankrupt after fortune-seekers invaded his lands. But the gold rush spurred the development of the West. By 1850, California contained enough people to become the thirty-first state.

AMERICAN HISTORY PARADE

1848   James W. Marshall discovers gold at Sutter's Mill in northern California, sparking a gold rush.

1922   Christian Nelson of Onawa, Iowa, receives a patent for the Eskimo Pie.

1950   Percy Spencer, who never graduated from grammar school, receives a patent for the microwave oven.

1984   The first Apple Macintosh computers go on sale—and revolutionize the personal computer industry.

IN 1873, the French novelist Jules Verne published *Around the World in Eighty Days*, in which Englishman Phileas Fogg wins a bet that he can circle the world in eighty days. Sixteen years later, intrepid *New York World* reporter Nellie Bly decided to beat Fogg's fictional trip, something never done before.

On November 14, 1889, carrying a crocodile gripsack, she boarded the *Augusta Victoria* and steamed across the Atlantic. Reaching England, she made a quick detour to France to meet Verne himself. "Good luck, Nellie Bly," he toasted her. Then it was on by mail train to Brendisi, Italy, where she sent a hurried cable to her editors before sailing for the Suez Canal.

The *World* published daily reports on its feminine Phileas Fogg's progress. "Can Jules Verne's great dream be reduced to actual fact?" it asked. The whole country followed the attempt to "girdle the spinning globe."

Nellie raced on. On the boat to Egypt, two men proposed marriage. In Ceylon she impatiently waited five days for a ship. In Singapore she bought a monkey. En route to Hong Kong, a monsoon filled passengers' cabins with water. Another storm hit as she steamed across the Pacific. The ship's crew posted a sign: "For Nellie Bly, We'll win or die!"

Nearing San Francisco, she heard rumors of a smallpox quarantine onboard ship. She jumped on a tugboat and headed for land. Blizzards had stranded locomotives in the mountains, so she hopped on a train taking a southern route and dashed across the continent.

On January 25, 1890, cannons boomed and crowds cheered as Nellie arrived in Jersey City. She looked at her watch: 72 days 6 hours 11 minutes—she'd beaten Phileas Fogg by a week. "Father Time Outdone!" the *World* trumpeted. Around the globe, young Nellie Bly became a symbol of the American can-do spirit.

AMERICAN HISTORY PARADE

1890   Nellie Bly completes her 72-day around-the-world trip.

1915   Alexander Graham Bell makes a call from New York to San Francisco, inaugurating transcontinental telephone service.

1937   *The Guiding Light* debuts on radio; it later moves to TV, becoming the longest-running drama ever broadcast.

1959   American Airlines inaugurates transcontinental jet flights with the Boeing 707, the first successful commercial jet airliner.

1961   President John F. Kennedy holds the first live televised presidential news conference.

THE MARINES TURNED HIM DOWN. They said he was too small. The Army paratroopers said no too. But Audie Murphy was used to setbacks. The son of Texas sharecroppers, he had helped raise his ten siblings after their father deserted them and their mother died. When the U.S. entered World War II, he was determined to fight. The Army finally accepted him in the infantry a few days after his eighteenth birthday.

He fought in the invasion of Sicily, and then in Italy at Salerno, at Anzio, and in the mountains as the Allies pushed to Rome. On January 26, 1945, in eastern France, 250 Germans and six tanks attacked his unit. Ordering his outnumbered men to fall back, Murphy climbed onto a burning tank destroyer and used its machine gun to hold off the enemy. Then, though wounded, he organized a counterattack. For his courage the military awarded him the Medal of Honor.

It wasn't the only time he threw himself in harm's way. Before he turned twenty-one, Murphy had become the most decorated American combat soldier of World War II, earning twenty-four medals from the U.S. government, three from France, and one from Belgium.

After the war, Murphy became an actor, making more than forty movies. He starred in *To Hell and Back*, based on his autobiography, and in *The Red Badge of Courage*. Still, his life wasn't easy. For years he battled post-traumatic stress disorder. He died in a plane crash in 1971 and is buried in Arlington National Cemetery.

"The true meaning of America, you ask?" Murphy once said. "It's in a Texas rodeo, in a policeman's badge, in the sound of laughing children, in a political rally, in a newspaper. . . . In all these things, and many more, you'll find America. In all these things, you'll find freedom. And freedom is what America means to the world."

AMERICAN HISTORY PARADE

1784   Benjamin Franklin writes to his daughter that the turkey would be a better national symbol than the bald eagle.

1837   Michigan becomes the twenty-sixth state.

1861   Louisiana secedes from the Union.

1945   Audie Murphy, the most decorated U.S. combat soldier of WWII, is wounded while holding off a German attack in eastern France.

1970   Navy Lt. Everett Alvarez Jr., the first American aviator shot down over North Vietnam, spends his 2,000th day as a prisoner of war.

ON JANUARY 27, 1838, when he was almost twenty-nine years old, Abraham Lincoln delivered an address before the Young Men's Lyceum in Springfield, Illinois, entitled "The Perpetuation of Our Political Institutions." In his speech he argued that liberty could not survive without reverence for laws, a theme prompted in part by the recent murder of an abolitionist by a mob in Alton, Illinois.

Let every American, every lover of liberty, every well-wisher to his posterity, swear by the blood of the Revolution, never to violate in the least particular the laws of the country, and never to tolerate their violation by others. As the Patriots of Seventy-six did to the support of the Declaration of Independence, so to the support of the Constitution and laws, let every American pledge his life, his property, and his sacred honor. Let every man remember that to violate the law is to trample on the blood of his father, and to tear the character of his own, and his children's, liberty. Let reverence for the laws be breathed by every American mother to the lisping babe that prattles on her lap. Let it be taught in schools, in seminaries, and in colleges. Let it be written in primers, spelling books, and in almanacs. Let it be preached from the pulpit, proclaimed in legislative halls, and enforced in courts of justice. And, in short, let it become the political religion of the nation; and let the old and the young, the rich and the poor, the grave and the gay, of all sexes and tongues, and colors and conditions, sacrifice unceasingly upon its altars.

AMERICAN HISTORY PARADE

1785   Georgia becomes the first state to charter a state-supported university, the University of Georgia.

1838   Abraham Lincoln addresses the Young Men's Lyceum in Springfield, Illinois.

1880   Thomas Edison receives a patent for his electric incandescent lamp.

1888   The National Geographic Society is founded in Washington, D.C.

1967   Astronauts Gus Grissom, Edward White, and Roger Chaffee die in a fire aboard their *Apollo I* spacecraft at Cape Canaveral, Florida.

1973   The Paris Peace Accords officially end the Vietnam War.

DISASTER STRUCK America's space program on January 28, 1986, shortly after the space shuttle *Challenger* lifted off from its launchpad at Cape Canaveral, Florida. Seventy-three seconds into its flight, *Challenger* suddenly disintegrated into a ball of fire. Millions of Americans watched their televisions in horror as the shuttle fell to the ocean, killing the seven crew members. Among the astronauts was Christa McAuliffe, who had spent months training to become the nation's first teacher in space. An investigation concluded that the explosion was caused by a faulty O-ring seal in one of the shuttle's solid-fuel rockets.

It was not the first or last tragedy for the space program. On January 27, 1967, astronauts Gus Grissom, Edward White, and Roger Chaffee were in their command module at Cape Canaveral, conducting a preflight test for the first *Apollo* manned mission, when one of them reported, "Fire—I smell fire." Seconds later, flames swept through the capsule. Technicians rushed to get the hatch open, but the heat and smoke drove them back. The three crew members perished.

On February 1, 2003, the shuttle *Columbia* disintegrated in flames over Texas as it headed for a landing at Cape Canaveral. All seven astronauts aboard died. Debris rained down over hundreds of square miles in Texas and Louisiana.

Scores of American astronauts have risked their lives to lead the world into space. Those who perished were pulling us into the future, and we'll continue to follow them. As President Reagan noted after the *Challenger* disaster, "We will never forget them, nor the last time we saw them . . . as they prepared for the journey and waved goodbye and 'slipped the surly bonds of earth' to 'touch the face of God.'"

AMERICAN HISTORY PARADE

1878   The first commercial telephone exchange is installed in New Haven, Connecticut, serving 21 subscribers with eight lines.

1915   Congress creates the U.S. Coast Guard.

1916   Louis D. Brandeis is appointed to the Supreme Court by Woodrow Wilson, becoming the high court's first Jewish member.

1934   America's first ski lift opens in Woodstock, Vermont—a tow rope pulled by a Model T engine.

1986   The space shuttle *Challenger* explodes 73 seconds after liftoff from Cape Canaveral.

JANUARY 29 IS THE BIRTHDAY OF WILLIAM McKINLEY, the twenty-fifth U.S. president, who was born in 1843 in Niles, Ohio. If you ever have the good fortune to see a $500 bill, you'll find him pictured on it. McKinley was the last veteran of the Civil War to serve as president. He also holds the unfortunate distinction of being one of four presidents to be assassinated. Who were the others? Read on.

Who was the first president born outside the thirteen original states? *Abraham Lincoln*, in Kentucky

Who was the first president born west of the Mississippi? *Herbert Hoover*, in Iowa

Who was the first president born in the twentieth century? *John F. Kennedy*, 1917

Who was the tallest president? *Abraham Lincoln*, 6'4"

Who was the shortest? *James Madison*, 5'4"

Which presidents were father and son? *John Adams* and *John Quincy Adams*; *George H. W. Bush* and *George W. Bush*

Which presidents were grandfather and grandson? *William Harrison* and *Benjamin Harrison*

Which president never married? *James Buchanan*

Which president was born on the Fourth of July? *Calvin Coolidge*, 1872

Which presidents died on the Fourth of July? *Thomas Jefferson*, 1826; *John Adams*, 1826; *James Monroe*, 1831

Which presidents were assassinated? *Abraham Lincoln*, 1865; *James Garfield*, 1881; *William McKinley*, 1901; *John F. Kennedy*, 1963

Which survived assassination attempts? *Andrew Jackson, Theodore Roosevelt, Franklin D. Roosevelt, Harry Truman, Gerald Ford, Ronald Reagan*

Other than the four assassinated, which four presidents died in office? *William Harrison*, 1841; *Zachary Taylor*, 1850; *Warren Harding*, 1923; *Franklin D. Roosevelt*, 1945

AMERICAN HISTORY PARADE

1843   William McKinley, the twenty-fifth U.S. president, is born in Niles, Ohio.

1861   Kansas becomes the thirty-fourth state.

1900   The American League is organized in Philadelphia with eight baseball teams.

1936   The first five inductees into baseball's Hall of Fame, including Ty Cobb and Babe Ruth, are named in Cooperstown, New York.

1944   The USS *Missouri*, the Navy's last battleship, is launched in New York City.

FRANKLIN DELANO ROOSEVELT, BORN JANUARY 30, 1882, entered politics because he was a man of ambition and because he wanted to serve his country. His plans were almost cut short while vacationing at Campobello Island in New Brunswick, Canada, in 1921 when he came down with what, at first, seemed to be a cold. He lost his appetite, his back began to ache, and his left leg went numb. A few days later, he couldn't stand. At age thirty-nine Roosevelt was diagnosed with polio. Paralyzed from the waist down, he watched as the muscles of his legs began wasting away.

Roosevelt was determined to beat the disease. For months he crawled from room to room in his house and dragged himself hand over hand up the stairs, gritting his teeth but never asking for help. Every day, he strapped steel braces onto his legs and tried hobbling on crutches to the end of his long driveway. Through rigorous exercise he developed tremendous upper body strength. "Maybe my legs aren't so good," he said, "but look at those shoulders." Despite his efforts, he never again walked without aid.

He did, however, make it to the White House, where he led the nation through the Great Depression and World War II. President Roosevelt worked with such vigor that millions of Americans never realized the full extent of his disability. Once someone asked him how he had so much perseverance. He smiled and answered, "If you have to spend two years in bed trying to wiggle your big toe, everything else seems easy."

Roosevelt knew that our trials often make us stronger. "The only thing we have to fear is fear itself," he told Americans during the Depression. The thirty-second U.S. president did his best to live by those words.

AMERICAN HISTORY PARADE

1798   A brawl erupts in the U.S. House when Matthew Lyon of Vermont spits on Roger Griswold of Connecticut after an exchange of insults.

1835   In the first presidential assassination attempt, Richard Lawrence, a mentally ill man, tries to shoot Andrew Jackson in the U.S. Capitol.

1847   The California town of Yerba Buena is renamed San Francisco.

1862   The Union ironclad USS *Monitor* is launched at Greenpoint, New York.

1882   Franklin Delano Roosevelt, the thirty-second president, is born in Hyde Park, New York.

1933   The first episode of *The Lone Ranger* is broadcast on radio station WXYZ in Detroit.

SINCE JANUARY 1946, U.S. dimes have carried an image of President Franklin Delano Roosevelt. The U.S. Mint issued the coin less than a year after Roosevelt's death. Before 1946, U.S. dimes carried images of female figures representing Liberty.

The Roosevelt Dime was issued in part to honor FDR's efforts in establishing the National Foundation for Infantile Paralysis (now known as the March of Dimes), which was founded to help defeat polio. Roosevelt and others urged Americans to send dimes to the foundation to fight the dreaded disease.

The back of the Roosevelt Dime shows three emblems: an olive branch, a torch, and an oak branch. The olive branch (left of the torch) stands for peace. The torch, which is an image of the one held by the Statue of Liberty, stands for freedom. The oak branch stands for safety, security, and strength.

Soon after the coin's release, controversy erupted when people noticed the tiny letters "JS" beneath Roosevelt's neck. Rumors spread that a Communist agent at the Mint had placed the letters there to honor the Soviet dictator Joseph Stalin. In truth, the initials belong to John Sinnock, the coin's designer.

AMERICAN HISTORY PARADE

1950   President Truman announces he has ordered development of the hydrogen bomb.

1958   The United States enters the Space Age with the launch of its first satellite, *Explorer I.*

1961   Ham the Chimp becomes the first chimpanzee in outer space when he blasts off from Cape Canaveral, Florida, aboard a Project Mercury rocket.

1990   McDonald's opens its first fast-food restaurant in Moscow, symbolizing a triumph of capitalism over Communism following the end of the Cold War.

Twelve Great Reasons to Love a Great Country

Why should Americans love their country? Here are a dozen good reasons to be grateful and proud to live here.

1. **The United States was the first nation in history created out of the belief that people should govern themselves.** As James Madison said, this country's birth was "a revolution which has no parallel in the annals of human society." The U.S. Constitution is the oldest written national constitution in operation. It has been a model for country after country as democracy has spread across the continents.

2. **America really is the land of the free.** There are large parts of the world where people can't say what they think, learn what they'd like, or even dress the way they want. There are places where people spend years in jail or disappear if they question their rulers. Less than half of the world's population lives in countries where people are truly free. In this nation, as George Washington put it, the love of liberty is interwoven with every ligament of American hearts.

3. **No other country has done a better job of establishing equal rights for all citizens.** Certainly there have been times when the United

States has fallen tragically short of its founding principles. But especially in recent decades, no country has worked harder to eliminate discrimination and protect the rights of minorities. There are plenty of nations where people's ethnicity, religion, or gender define them as second-class citizens. In contrast, America has been a pioneer in striving toward the ideal that all are created equal.

4. **This is the place where dreams can come true.** U.S. newspapers are full of stories that read almost like fairy tales: the son of a laborer who grows up to be a doctor, the stay-at-home mom who turns a hobby into a flourishing business, the immigrant who becomes a movie star and governor. The United States has long been the country people flock to for the chance to make better lives. No other country has built a sturdier ladder for people to climb to success.

5. **We enjoy one of the world's highest standards of living.** Americans live longer, have better health, and enjoy safer and more comfortable lives than the vast majority of the world's people. Ours is one of the most prosperous nations in history. U.S. companies provide some of the best jobs in the world. They have also built countless hospitals, libraries, and parks; created great universities; filled museums with works of art; found cures for diseases; and improved human life in countless ways.

6. **No other country has welcomed and united so many people from so many different shores.** From its beginnings, the U.S. has been the world's great melting pot. Never before have so many people from different backgrounds, races, nationalities, and religions lived and worked together so peacefully. In no other nation has the spirit of cooperation and brotherhood accomplished more than it has in the United States.

7. **The U.S. military is the greatest defender of freedom in the world.** Twice in the twentieth century, the United States led the way in saving the world from tyranny—first from the Axis Powers, then from Soviet totalitarianism. Throughout history, other superpowers have used armies to conquer territory and build empires by force. America, with its unrivaled military, has chosen a different course. The United States has liberated more people from tyranny than any other nation in history.

8. **America is a world leader in scholarship and invention.** The United States is home to the world's finest collection of universities and research institutions. Name just about any subject—from ancient philosophy to quantum physics—and chances are good that leading authorities work here. The record of American inventions and discoveries goes on and on, from the mechanical reaper to the microchip. American medical research facilities are among the best in the world. The United States leads the world in space exploration. The computer revolution started here.

9. **Americans are among the most generous people on earth.** The United States has built the most extraordinary collection of charitable, philanthropic, and civic organizations in the world, and this country is the planet's largest source of humanitarian aid. American government programs and private giving constitute one of the greatest efforts to help people in history. In 2007, Americans donated more than $300 billion to charities. When disasters strike overseas, Americans are among the first to offer help and support.

10. **The United States is the world's greatest marketplace for the free exchange of ideas and information.** In some countries, governments shut down newspapers and broadcast stations they don't like, and

limit access to the Internet. Freedom of expression and freedom of the press are bedrock principles of American democracy. The staggering volume of information traded here every day—via books, newspapers, magazines, the Internet, TV, and radio—makes this country the liveliest center of thought and debate in history.

11. **This nation possesses an amazing capacity for self-renewal.** Time and again, Americans have been able to address the country's problems and flaws. Think of those Americans at Philadelphia in 1787 who devised the most miraculous political document in history just as the young nation seemed to be falling apart. Or Americans in the Civil Rights movement prodding the country to right the wrongs of segregation. The American people have a genius for self-correction. Sometimes it takes a while, but in the end we find our way.

12. **America is a nation that looks to God for guidance.** It was founded to be a place where all are free to worship, or not to worship, as they please. Never before have so many different religions, creeds, and beliefs coexisted so peacefully in one country. Amid this diversity, the vast majority of Americans draw strength from faith in God's goodness and wisdom. In God We Trust is our national motto, and we have never had a president who has been reluctant to say, "Let us pray."

FEBRUARY

ON FEBRUARY 1, 1960, four black college freshmen from North Carolina A&T State University sat down at a lunch counter in an F. W. Woolworth's store in Greensboro, North Carolina, and asked to be served. They were told no—the counter was for white people only. The four sat quietly until the store closed, and the next day they came back. Again they were refused service. Again they sat quietly at the counter until the store closed, and returned the next day.

The four students—Franklin McCain, Joseph McNeil, Ezell Blair Jr., and David Richmond—knew they were running a risk of being arrested, beaten, or worse. Across the South, black people were supposed to stay away from whites-only restaurants, drinking fountains, and restrooms. But the four freshmen were determined to challenge segregation.

By day four, the store was still refusing to serve them, and many people were stopping by to heckle or stare. But there were also hundreds showing up to support their silent protest.

As word of the sit-in spread, black students in towns across the South began politely asking to be served at whites-only lunch counters. Whenever police arrested them, more protestors stepped forward to sit in their place.

The sit-ins gradually had an effect. In July 1960, Woolworth's decided to integrate its stores. Across the South, racial barriers gradually began to fall. The sit-ins helped bring about the Civil Rights Act of 1964, which banned the segregation of public facilities.

The Greensboro Four, as the four brave young Americans came to be known, had helped make the United States a more just place. "This is my country," said Joseph McNeil, who later served in the Air Force in Vietnam. "I not only fought for it; I fought for the chance to make it right."

AMERICAN HISTORY PARADE

1790   The U.S. Supreme Court convenes for the first time, in New York City.

1861   Texas secedes from the Union.

1893   Thomas Edison completes the world's first movie studio in West Orange, New Jersey.

1960   Four black college students begin a sit-in protest at a Woolworth's lunch counter in Greensboro, North Carolina, where they'd been refused service.

2003   The space shuttle *Columbia* disintegrates during reentry, killing all seven crew members.

FEBRUARY 2 IS GROUNDHOG DAY, a holiday that, like so many American traditions, has roots in customs brought here by immigrants. Weather lore holds that if a groundhog emerges from his burrow on this day and sees his shadow, he will be frightened back into his home, and winter will last for six more weeks. But if it's an overcast day, and he doesn't see his shadow, spring will come early.

Why February 2? The day falls about halfway between the winter solstice (beginning of winter) and spring equinox (beginning of spring). Many ancient cultures observed rituals that marked the midseason. They also watched for the reappearance of hibernating animals, such as bears and badgers, as a natural sign that winter was coming to an end.

Early Christians observed February 2 as Candlemas, the day on which priests blessed candles and distributed them to the faithful. A superstition arose that if the weather was fair on Candlemas, the second half of the winter would be cold and stormy. "If Candlemas Day is bright and clear, there'll be two winters in the year," an old Scottish saying ran. In Germany, it was said that if Candlemas Day was bright enough to make a hedgehog cast a shadow, he would go back into hibernation until the spring equinox, meaning six more weeks of cold.

Many of Pennsylvania's early settlers were Germans, and they brought the custom with them. By 1887, Groundhog Day had become an official celebration in the town of Punxsutawney. Every year, a groundhog named Punxsutawney Phil is pulled from his heated burrow so he can look for his shadow and predict the weather. Punxsutawney Phil is the nation's most famous forecaster, but other groundhogs, such as General Beauregard Lee near Atlanta and Staten Island Chuck in New York City, help keep the tradition going strong.

AMERICAN HISTORY PARADE

1653   New Amsterdam, later to become New York City, is incorporated.

1848   The Treaty of Guadalupe Hidalgo ends the Mexican War.

1876   Baseball's National League is formed with eight teams.

1887   The first official Groundhog Day is observed in Punxsutawney, Pennsylvania.

1940   Frank Sinatra gets his big break when he debuts with the Tommy Dorsey Orchestra in Indianapolis.

IN THE EARLY HOURS OF FEBRUARY 3, 1943, the U.S. Army troopship *Dorchester* steamed through the icy waters of "torpedo alley" some one hundred miles off the coast of Greenland. The ship, carrying more than 900 men, was having a rough go of it. Winter winds screeched across the North Atlantic, and heavy seas pounded the bow. Beneath the frenzied surface lurked a German submarine.

At 12:55 a.m. a torpedo ripped into the *Dorchester*'s side, and immediately the ship started to sink. Desperate soldiers rushed topside, stumbling toward lifeboats and jumping overboard.

Amid the confusion, four Army chaplains worked quietly and methodically, calming the soldiers, directing them toward lifeboats, and handing out life jackets. When they ran out, they took off their own life jackets and put them on other men.

They were four chaplains of different faiths: Jewish rabbi Alexander Goode, Catholic priest John Washington, and Protestant ministers George Fox and Clark Poling. They had joined the U.S. Army to tend to the spiritual needs of the troops. Now, in this hour of urgent need, they put their courage and faith to work so others might live.

As the ship slid beneath the surface, soldiers in the lifeboats took one last look at the *Dorchester*. They saw the four chaplains standing on deck, arms linked, praying.

Rescue ships plucked 230 men from the sea, but 672 died in the freezing Atlantic. The four chaplains were not among the survivors.

"They were always together," one of the soldiers later said. "They carried their faith together." The four chaplains died as they lived, serving their country, their fellow men, and God.

AMERICAN HISTORY PARADE

1690   Massachusetts authorizes the first paper currency issued in America.

1913   The Sixteenth Amendment, authorizing a federal income tax, is ratified.

1917   The United States breaks off diplomatic relations with Germany after a German submarine sinks the liner *Housatonic* off the coast of Sicily.

1943   The Army transport ship *Dorchester* sinks after being hit by a German torpedo.

1959   Rock stars Buddy Holly, Ritchie Valens, and J. P. "The Big Bopper" Richardson are killed when their chartered plane crashes in Iowa.

FREDERICK DOUGLASS was born a slave near Easton, Maryland, in February 1818 (the exact date is uncertain). A story from his youth sums up his courage in many ways. When he was sixteen years old, his master hired him out to a farmer named Edward Covey, who had a reputation for cruelty to slaves. Covey often whipped his new field hand until Douglass was, in his own words, "broken in body, soul, and spirit."

One day Covey began to tie Douglass with a rope, intending to beat him again. "At this moment—from whence came the spirit, I don't know—I resolved to fight," Douglass later recalled. He grabbed Covey by the throat and held off his blows. The two men fell to wrestling and rolling in a barnyard until finally Covey quit. Striking a white man could bring severe punishment, but Covey told no one of the fight—he did not want people to know he could not control a 16-year-old slave. He never tried to whip the boy again. "My long-crushed spirit rose," Douglass remembered. "The day had passed forever when I could be a slave."

Douglass eventually escaped to the North, where he became one of the nation's most eloquent voices decrying the evils of slavery. After the Civil War he continued to write and speak for the rights of black Americans. Though often a fiery critic of his country, he was also a patriot who was determined to make it a better place. "No nation was ever called to the contemplation of a destiny more important and solemn than ours," he wrote. He spent his life working for an America that offered "justice for all men, justice now and always, justice without reservation or qualification except those suggested by mercy and love."

AMERICAN HISTORY PARADE

1789   The Electoral College chooses George Washington to be the first U.S. president.

1826   *The Last of the Mohicans* by James Fenimore Cooper is published.

1861   Six Southern states form the Confederate States of America.

1932   The first Winter Olympics in the United States open in Lake Placid, New York.

1945   Franklin Roosevelt, Winston Churchill, and Joseph Stalin meet at Yalta in the Crimea to discuss the post-WWII world.

JULIA WARD HOWE, a writer, lecturer, and antislavery reformer, was visiting a Union army camp near Washington, D.C., during the Civil War when she heard soldiers singing the song "John Brown's Body," which began with the words "John Brown's body lies a-moldering in the grave." A clergyman who accompanied her suggested she write new lyrics to the tune. Howe went back to the Willard Hotel in Washington, and then, as she told it:

> I went to bed and slept as usual, but awoke the next morning in the gray of the early dawn, and to my astonishment found that the wished-for lines were arranging themselves in my brain. I lay quite still until the last verse had completed itself in my thoughts, then hastily arose . . . searched for an old sheet of paper and an old stub of a pen which I had had the night before, and began to scrawl the lines almost without looking.

Howe submitted her verses—which began "Mine eyes have seen the glory of the coming of the Lord: He is trampling out the vintage where the grapes of wrath are stored"—to the *Atlantic Monthly*, which accepted them and paid her a fee of four dollars. The magazine printed the lyrics on the first page of its February 1862 issue under the title "Battle Hymn of the Republic."

The song quickly became a favorite of the Union army. In the decades since, in times of war and peace, it has remained one of America's most-loved hymns.

AMERICAN HISTORY PARADE

1846   The *Oregon Spectator*, the first newspaper on the Pacific Coast of the United States, is published in Oregon City.

1883   The Southern Pacific Railroad opens a transcontinental "Sunset Route" from New Orleans to San Francisco.

1918   First Lieutenant Stephen W. Thompson of the 1st Aero Squadron becomes the first aviator in the U.S. military to win a victory over an enemy aircraft when he shoots down a German plane over Saarbrücken during World War I.

1937   President Franklin Roosevelt proposes increasing the number of Supreme Court justices, leading critics to charge that he is trying to "pack" the court with justices to his liking.

RONALD WILSON REAGAN, BORN FEBRUARY 6, 1911, in Tampico, Illinois, became the nation's fortieth president at a time when many said that America's best days were behind us, that the future would be one of fewer opportunities. He spent much of his presidency (1981–89) reminding Americans, again and again, that this country is still a land of boundless potential, a beacon of freedom and hope for the world.

History is a ribbon, always unfurling. History is a journey. And as we continue our journey, we think of those who traveled before us . . . and we see and hear again the echoes of our past: a general falls to his knees in the hard snow of Valley Forge; a lonely president paces the darkened halls and ponders his struggle to preserve the Union; the men of the Alamo call out encouragement to each other; a settler pushes west and sings a song, and the song echoes out forever and fills the unknowing air. It is the American sound. It is hopeful, big-hearted, idealistic, daring, decent, and fair. That's our heritage, that's our song. We sing it still. For all our problems, our differences, we are together as of old. We raise our voices to the God who is the author of this most tender music. And may He continue to hold us close as we fill the world with our sound—in unity, affection, and love—one people under God, dedicated to the dream of freedom that He has placed in the human heart, called upon now to pass that dream on to a waiting and hopeful world.

— Ronald Reagan,
second inaugural address

AMERICAN HISTORY PARADE

1788   Massachusetts becomes the sixth state to ratify the Constitution.

1862   The Union wins its first major victory in the Civil War, with the capture of Fort Hood on the Tennessee River.

1899   The Senate ratifies the treaty ending the Spanish-American War.

1911   Ronald Reagan, the fortieth U.S. president, is born in Tampico, Illinois.

1971   *Apollo 14* astronaut Alan Shepard hits three golf balls on the moon.

FEBRUARY 7 IS THE BIRTHDAY of Laura Ingalls Wilder, born in 1867 in an area then known as the "Big Woods" of western Wisconsin. "I was born in a log house within four miles of the legend-haunted Lake Pippin in Wisconsin," she wrote. "I remember seeing deer that my father had killed, hanging in the trees about our forest home. When I was four years old we traveled to the Indian Territory, Fort Scott, Kansas, being our nearest town. My childish memories hold the sound of the war whoop and I see pictures of painted Indians.

"I was a regular little tomboy, and it was fun to walk the two miles to school," she recalled, although she also confessed, "My education has been what a girl would get on the frontier. . . . I never graduated from anything and only attended high school two terms."

After moves to Minnesota and Iowa, Laura's family established a homestead claim near De Smet, South Dakota, where she grew up and married Almanzo Wilder. "It was there I learned to do all kinds of farm work with machinery," she recalled. "I have ridden the binder, driving six horses. And I could ride. I do not wish to appear conceited, but I broke my own ponies to ride. Of course they were not bad but they were broncos. . . . And, believe me, I learned how to take care of hens and make them lay."

Later, in Mansfield, Missouri, Laura began writing down memories of her pioneer life. During the Great Depression, she asked her daughter Rose, a writer, to look at her manuscript, written in pencil on lined school tablets. Rose helped her turn portions into a novel, and in 1932, when Laura Ingalls Wilder was sixty-five years old, *Little House in the Big Woods* was published. *Little House on the Prairie* and other books followed, turning the former pioneer into one of America's most beloved authors.

AMERICAN HISTORY PARADE

1795   The Eleventh Amendment, which clarifies federal judicial powers, is ratified.

1812   The last of the New Madrid earthquakes, a series of violent quakes that changes the course of the Mississippi River, occurs near New Madrid, Missouri.

1867   Laura Ingalls Wilder is born near Pepin, Wisconsin.

1964   The Beatles arrive in New York for their first U.S. tour and an appearance on *The Ed Sullivan Show*, touching off Beatlemania.

1984   Space shuttle *Challenger* astronauts Bruce McCandless and Robert Stewart take the first untethered spacewalk.

THIS DAY IN 1693 saw the birth of the College of William and Mary, one of the nation's oldest colleges. At the request of Virginia colonists, King William III and Queen Mary II granted a charter that established "a certain place of universal study, a perpetual college of divinity, philosophy, languages, and the good arts and sciences . . . to be supported and maintained, in all time coming."

Americans have long recognized the importance of a strong university system. By the time of our nation's founding, a handful of institutions of higher learning had already been established. The following are the oldest U.S. colleges (with the year in which each institution became a bachelor's degree-granting institution):

Harvard University	**Cambridge, Massachusetts**	1636
College of William and Mary	**Williamsburg, Virginia**	1693
Yale University	**New Haven, Connecticut**	1701
Princeton University	**Princeton, New Jersey**	1746
Columbia University	**New York City, New York**	1754
University of Pennsylvania	**Philadelphia, Pennsylvania**	1757
Brown University	**Providence, Rhode Island**	1764
Rutgers University	**New Brunswick, New Jersey**	1766
Dartmouth College	**Hanover, New Hampshire**	1769

In the United States today there approximately 2,500 four-year institutions and 1,670 two-year institutions serving approximately 18 million students. It is the finest system of colleges and universities in the world.

AMERICAN HISTORY PARADE

1693   The College of William and Mary, second oldest college in the United States, is chartered.

1870   The Fifteenth Amendment, guaranteeing voting rights regardless of race, is ratified.

1910   The Boy Scouts of America is founded in Washington, D.C.

1922   President Warren G. Harding has a radio installed in the White House.

1971   The NASDAQ, the world's first electronic stock market, begins operation.

1978   Senate debates are broadcast on radio for the first time.

ON FEBRUARY 9, 1950, during a speech in Wheeling, West Virginia, Senator Joseph McCarthy of Wisconsin waved a piece of paper in the air and claimed that he had a list of Communists who had infiltrated the U.S. State Department. It was a time of heightened Cold War tensions. Communism had robbed millions around the world of their freedom. McCarthy's shocking claim hit a nerve with the American people.

Over the next few years, the opportunistic McCarthy accused hundreds of Americans of Communist activities. He usually had little evidence, but that didn't stop him. He hauled public officials and others before his Congressional subcommittee and tried to browbeat them into acknowledging Communist affiliations. The accusations and investigations spread. Thousands of people, from librarians to actors to clergymen, fell under suspicion. McCarthy's reckless tactics trampled rights and ruined reputations.

There were many who recognized the dangers of "McCarthyism." The Senate's only woman, Maine's Margaret Chase Smith, stood tall. The Constitution, she told fellow senators, speaks of "trial by jury instead of trial by accusation." Veteran newsman Edward R. Murrow reminded Americans that "we cannot defend freedom by *deserting* it at home." In one hearing, Boston attorney Joseph Welch skewered McCarthy: "Have you no sense of decency, sir? At long last, have you left no sense of decency?"

The more Americans saw of McCarthy's bullying, the less they liked him. Behind the scenes, President Eisenhower successfully urged the Senate to censure him, and McCarthy fell into disrepute.

Decades later, we now know that the Soviet Union did, in fact, recruit Americans to be spies during the Cold War. One of the tragedies of McCarthy's tactics was that he undermined *legitimate* efforts to counter Communism. Ronald Reagan would later say that he used a shotgun where a rifle was called for. The episode is a reminder that threats to liberty deserve serious responses, not showmanship.

AMERICAN HISTORY PARADE

1773   William Henry Harrison, the ninth U.S. president, is born in Charles City County, Virginia.

1825   The House of Representatives elects John Quincy Adams president after no candidate receives a majority of electoral votes.

1942   Daylight saving time (then called "war time") goes into effect to conserve fuel during World War II.

1943   American troops recapture Guadalcanal in the southwest Pacific.

1950   Sen. Joseph McCarthy charges that Communists have infiltrated the State Department.

EVERY DAY, MILLIONS OF CHILDREN across the country and around the world cuddle up with their favorite teddy bears. How did toy bears come to be so popular, and how did they come to be called "teddy"? Credit Teddy Roosevelt, our twenty-sixth president, as well as a political cartoonist and some resourceful entrepreneurs.

In 1902 Roosevelt, an avid outdoorsman, went on a bear-hunting trip in Mississippi. The president was a good hunter, but on this particular trip, he had terrible luck. For several days, he never even saw a bear.

Finally one of his guides cornered a small black bear, wounded it, and tied it to a tree. Then he called for the president to come shoot it. Teddy the sportsman resolutely refused. He had eagerly shot grizzly bears in the Wild West, but he had no interest in taking unfair advantage of a terrified, trapped animal.

When *Washington Post* cartoonist Clifford Berryman heard the story, he drew a picture of the president turning away in disgust from the idea of shooting the helpless bear. The nation loved the fact that their president had spared the poor creature, and in no time it became the story of "Teddy's bear."

By early 1903, two Russian Jewish immigrants named Morris and Rose Michtom were making and selling stuffed "Teddy bears" in their Brooklyn shop. (One of the Michtoms' original stuffed bears can be seen at the Smithsonian's National Museum of American History in Washington, D.C.) About the same time, toy company FAO Schwarz of New York City began selling plush teddy bears made in a German toy factory. A worldwide craze began, which shows no sign of ebbing more than a century later.

AMERICAN HISTORY PARADE

1763   The Treaty of Paris ends the Seven Years' War (the French and Indian War).

1861   Jefferson Davis receives word that he has been chosen to be president of the Confederate States of America.

1903   Teddy bears begin appearing in stores early this year.

1942   Glenn Miller receives the first-ever gold record for selling 1.2 million copies of "Chattanooga Choo Choo."

1967   The Twenty-fifth Amendment, dealing with presidential disability and succession, is ratified.

ON FEBRUARY 11, 1933, President Herbert Hoover designated Death Valley in California and Nevada as a national monument (later re-designated as a national park). One of the valley's unique characteristics is that it contains the lowest spot in the United States, 282 feet below sea level. Here's the rundown on U.S. extreme points, in altitude and around the compass.

Highest point - Mount McKinley, Alaska	20,320 ft.
Highest point outside Alaska - Mount Whitney, California	14,494 ft.
Lowest point - Death Valley, California	- 282 ft.
Northernmost point - Point Barrow, Alaska	71° 23' N
Northernmost point outside Alaska - Northwest Angle, Montana	49° 23' N
Southernmost point - Ka Lae, Hawaii	18° 55' N
Southernmost point outside Hawaii - Key West, Florida	24° 33' N
Easternmost point - West Quoddy Head, Maine*	66° 57' W
Westernmost point - Cape Wrangell, Attu Island, Alaska**	172° 27'E
Westernmost point outside Alaska - Cape Alava, Washington	124° 44' W

* Since Alaska's Aleutian Islands stretch into the Eastern Hemisphere, Semisopochnoi Island, Alaska, has the easternmost U.S. longitudinal coordinates at 179° 46' E.

** Amatignak Island, Alaska, has the westernmost longitudinal coordinates at 179° 06' W.

AMERICAN HISTORY PARADE

1752   Pennsylvania Hospital, the first hospital in the United States, opens in Philadelphia.

1809   Robert Fulton patents his steamboat.

1812   Massachusetts governor Elbridge Gerry signs a law that redraws district lines in his party's favor, thus giving rise to the term "gerrymandering."

1861   President-elect Abraham Lincoln leaves Springfield, Illinois, for Washington, D.C., saying, "I now leave, not knowing when, or whether ever, I may return"—he never does.

1933   President Hoover designates Death Valley as a national monument.

FEBRUARY 12 IS THE BIRTHDAY OF ABRAHAM LINCOLN, born in 1809 in a log cabin near Hodgenville, Kentucky. Long before he became president, Lincoln's friends and acquaintances called him "Honest Abe."

When he was a boy in Indiana, he borrowed a book about George Washington from a neighbor, Josiah Crawford. After rainwater ruined it, he went straight to Crawford, owned up to what had happened, and spent three days in Crawford's cornfield working to pay for the book.

When Lincoln was a young storekeeper in New Salem, Illinois, he accidentally shortchanged a customer by six and a quarter cents. As soon as he discovered the error, he closed the shop and walked six miles to pay the money back.

Lincoln's store was not a success. He and his partner, William Berry, went into debt trying to make a go of it. The store "winked out" anyway, as Lincoln put it, and left him owing a great deal of money, especially after Berry died. He could have done what so many others in similar situations did—simply head west for new frontiers and leave the debt behind. But he resolved to stay. For a young man of his means, it was a large burden. He called it, with grim humor, his "national debt." It took him several years, but he paid it all back.

His reputation as a lawyer caused people to say, "He'll be fair and square." One time he forced a law partner to give back half the fee the man had charged a client. "That money comes out of the pocket of a poor, demented girl," he said, "and I would rather starve than swindle her."

It is no coincidence that one of our most beloved presidents was a man who held himself to the highest standards of truthfulness.

AMERICAN HISTORY PARADE

1809   Abraham Lincoln, the sixteenth U.S. president, is born near Hodgenville, Kentucky.

1909   The National Association for the Advancement of Colored People (NAACP) is founded.

1973   Hanoi begins to release American POWs following the end of the Vietnam War.

1999   The Senate acquits President Bill Clinton on charges of perjury and obstruction of justice.

2001   The *NEAR* (*Near Earth Asteroid Rendezvous*) spacecraft touches down on Eros, marking the first landing on an asteroid.

THE LINCOLN MEMORIAL, which stands beside the Potomac River in Washington, D.C., is not only one of the nation's most beloved monuments but also one of its most widely publicized, by virtue of the fact that it appears on the back of every penny and five-dollar bill. The cornerstone of the majestic temple, built of white Colorado marble in the style of a flat-roofed Greek temple, was laid in February 1915. The monument was dedicated in 1922, fifty-seven years after Lincoln died.

The thirty-six Doric columns surrounding the monument symbolize the thirty-six states in the Union at the time of Lincoln's death. Inside, a colossal statue of a seated Lincoln, carved from blocks of white Georgia marble, looks east toward the Washington Monument and Capitol Building. The statue by Daniel Chester French, nineteen feet high and weighing 175 tons, is the second most famous sculpture in America, after the Statue of Liberty. (Look at a penny with a magnifying glass, and you can see a tiny representation of the statue engraved in the monument's center.)

Two of Lincoln's most famous speeches, the Gettysburg Address and his second inaugural address, are inscribed on the memorial's walls. Above the solemn figure of Lincoln, visitors can read these words emblazoned in stone:

IN THIS TEMPLE
AS IN THE HEARTS OF THE PEOPLE
FOR WHOM HE SAVED THE UNION
THE MEMORY OF ABRAHAM LINCOLN
IS ENSHRINED FOREVER

AMERICAN HISTORY PARADE

1635   Boston Public Latin School, the nation's oldest public school, is founded.

1795   The University of North Carolina, the first state university to open its doors in the new United States, begins operating.

1826   The American Temperance Society, the first national organization to advocate prohibition, is founded.

1935   Bruno Richard Hauptmann is found guilty of murder in the kidnapping and death of Charles and Anne Lindbergh's infant son.

2000   Charles Schulz's last *Peanuts* comic strip runs the day after the cartoonist dies at age seventy-seven.

FOSSILS REVEAL THAT THEY'VE GROWN as a wildflower in America for more than 35 million years. George Washington bred them and named a variety after his mother. The White House has a famous garden full of them, where presidents often welcome distinguished guests and heads of state.

As Ronald Reagan once noted, "We lavish them on our altars, our civil shrines, and the final resting places of our honored dead." And, of course, millions of people give them today, Valentine's Day. They are Americans' favorite flower and loved the world over.

For all these reasons, in 1986 Congress and President Reagan proclaimed the rose the national flower of the United States.

"Americans have always loved the flowers with which God decorates our land," Reagan said in his proclamation. "More often than any other flower, we hold the rose dear as the symbol of life and love and devotion, of beauty and eternity. For the love of man and woman, for the love of mankind and God, for the love of country, Americans who would speak the language of the heart do so with a rose."

AMERICAN HISTORY PARADE

1849   James Polk becomes the first president to be photographed in office.

1859   Oregon becomes the thirty-third state.

1912   Arizona becomes the forty-eighth state.

1946   ENIAC (Electronic Numerical Integrator and Computer), the first general-purpose electronic computer, is unveiled at the University of Pennsylvania.

1962   Millions tune in to watch First Lady Jacqueline Kennedy host the first televised tour of the White House.

SUSAN B. ANTHONY was born on February 15, 1820, in an age when women in the U.S. and the rest of the world were considered inferior to men. Most colleges weren't open to women. Many restaurants had signs saying "No Females Allowed." Husbands by law controlled their wives' property and any money they might earn. Women could not hold most jobs and public offices, or even vote.

Anthony spent most of her life trying to right those injustices. She founded women's rights groups and wrote books, pamphlets, and articles. She crossed the country again and again to give speeches in town halls, schoolhouses, barns, sawmills, log cabins—anyplace where people would listen. Crowds sometimes shouted her down or pelted her with rotten eggs. Newspapers called her names. Mobs burned her effigies. But Anthony would not give up.

On Election Day 1872, she showed up at a poll in Rochester, New York, and cast a vote for president. Two weeks later, a marshall knocked on her door with a warrant for her arrest. At trial the judge prohibited her from speaking on her own behalf and ordered the jury to find her guilty of voting illegally. The court fined Anthony $100. "I will never pay a dollar of your unjust penalty," she replied. And she didn't.

Anthony died in 1906. Fourteen years later, the Nineteenth Amendment to the Constitution finally gave women the right to vote.

Today the U.S. is a world leader in women's rights. In no other country do women enjoy more freedom and opportunity. And in the struggle for equal rights, no name deserves more honor than that of Susan B. Anthony.

AMERICAN HISTORY PARADE

1764   St. Louis, Missouri, is founded as a French fur-trading post.

1799   Pennsylvania authorizes the first printed election ballots in the United States.

1820   Women's suffrage leader Susan B. Anthony is born in Adams, Massachusetts.

1898   The USS *Maine* blows up in Havana Harbor, touching off the Spanish-American War.

1933   President-elect Franklin D. Roosevelt narrowly escapes an assassination attempt in Miami.

NO MORE. That was President Thomas Jefferson's answer to the rulers of the Barbary States of North Africa. For centuries, the Barbary States had licensed pirates to attack merchant ships in the Mediterranean. The pirates not only captured booty but also held crews for ransom or sold them in the market as slaves.

European nations and the young United States had been paying the Barbary rulers huge sums of money to "protect" their ships from the pirates. It was an extortion racket, pure and simple.

When Jefferson became president, he refused to pay the tribute. The Bashaw of Tripoli declared war, and other Barbary rulers soon followed. In response, Jefferson sent Navy ships to the region.

In late 1803 the USS *Philadelphia* ran aground off Tripoli's harbor, and the Tripoli pirates captured it. So on February 16, 1804, young Lt. Stephen Decatur launched a raid to keep the Tripolitans from using the ship. Disguising themselves as Maltese sailors, Decatur and his men—who included several U.S. Marines—sailed into Tripoli harbor, boarded the *Philadelphia*, attacked its crew, set the ship ablaze, and sailed away. The great British admiral Horatio Nelson reportedly called the exploit "the most bold and daring act of the age."

The next year, a motley army of U.S. Marines, sailors, and Greek and Arab mercenaries struck again. They marched 500 miles across the Libyan Desert to take the coastal town of Derna, with help from three U.S. warships. From this victory, the Marines' Hymn takes the line "to the shores of Tripoli," and Marine officers still wear Mameluke swords shaped like Arab scimitars.

By the summer of 1805, the Bashaw of Tripoli had had enough. Thomas Jefferson's willingness to stand up to the Barbary rulers and their pirates had triumphed in America's first war on terror in the Middle East.

AMERICAN HISTORY PARADE

1804   Lt. Stephen Decatur leads a daring naval raid into Tripoli harbor to burn the U.S. frigate *Philadephia*, which had fallen into the hands of the Barbary pirates.

1852   Henry and Clement Studebaker found a wagon-making business in South Bend, Indiana, that eventually becomes a famous automobile manufacturer.

1937   Wallace H. Carothers, a research chemist for Du Pont, receives a patent for nylon.

1945   American troops recapture the Bataan Peninsula in the Philippines almost three years after the infamous Bataan Death March.

ON FEBRUARY 17, 1817, the first public gas streetlight in the United States was lit in Baltimore, Maryland. Artist Rembrandt Peale brought the idea of gas lighting to the city. He had learned about it during a visit to England, and on his return had displayed a "Ring of Fire" gas-powered light in his Baltimore museum. The success of that experiment led to the idea of lighting U.S. city streets and the founding of the country's first gas company, the Gas Light Company of Baltimore.

Here are a few other firsts in the U.S.A.

First	City	Date
Municipal subway	Boston, MA	opened 1897
Movie theater	Los Angeles, CA	opened 1902
Gas station	Pittsburgh, PA	opened 1913
Traffic light	Cleveland, OH	installed 1914
Licensed radio station	Detroit, MI	1920 (station 8MK)
Shopping mall	Kansas City, MO	built 1922
Motel	San Luis Obispo, CA	opened 1925
Air-conditioned office building	San Antonio, TX	opened 1928 (21 stories)
Drive-in movie theater	Camden, NJ	opened 1933
Parking meter	Oklahoma City, OK	installed 1935
City parking garage	Welch, WV	opened 1941

AMERICAN HISTORY PARADE

1801   The U.S. House of Representatives breaks an electoral tie between Thomas Jefferson and Aaron Burr, choosing Jefferson to be the third U.S. president.

1817   The first public gas streetlight in the United States is lit in Baltimore, Maryland.

1864   The Confederate *H. L. Hunley* becomes the first submarine to sink a warship, the USS *Housatonic*, but goes down after the attack.

1968   The Naismith Memorial Basketball Hall of Fame opens to the public in Springfield, Massachusetts.

"I AM PILING UP MANUSCRIPT in a really astonishing way," Mark Twain wrote his family in 1883. "I believe I shall complete, in two months, a book which I have been fooling over for seven years. This summer it is no more trouble to me to write than it is to lie." The book, published on February 18, 1885, turned out to be *The Adventures of Huckleberry Finn*. Young Huck's raft trip down the Mississippi River with the runaway slave, Jim, remains one of the most captivating images of freedom in American literature.

This second night we run between seven and eight hours, with a current that was making over four mile an hour. We catched fish, and talked, and we took a swim now and then to keep off sleepiness. It was kind of solemn, drifting down the big still river, laying on our backs, looking up at the stars, and we didn't ever feel like talking loud, and it warn't often that we laughed, only a little kind of a low chuckle. . . .

Every night we passed towns, some of them away up on black hillsides, nothing but just a shiny bed of lights, not a house could you see. The fifth night we passed St. Louis, and it was like the whole world lit up. . . . I used to slip ashore, towards ten o'clock, at some little village, and buy ten or fifteen cents' worth of meal or bacon or some other stuff to eat; and sometimes I lifted a chicken that wasn't roosting comfortable, and took him along. Pap always said, take a chicken when you get a chance, because if you don't want him yourself you can easy find somebody that does, and a good deed ain't ever forgot. . . .

We shot waterfowl, now and then, that got up too early in the morning or didn't go to bed early enough in the evening. Take it all around, we lived pretty high.

> — Chapter XII,
> *The Adventures of Huckleberry Finn*

AMERICAN HISTORY PARADE

1735   The first opera performed in America, *Flora*, or *Hob in the Well*, is presented in Charleston, South Carolina.

1841   The first continuous filibuster begins in the Senate and lasts until March 11.

1885   Mark Twain's *The Adventures of Huckleberry Finn*, the great American novel, is published.

1977   The first space shuttle, *Enterprise*, takes its maiden test flight, attached to the top of a Boeing 747.

ON FEBRUARY 19, 1942, in what is now considered to be one of the worst mistakes of his presidency, Franklin Delano Roosevelt signed Executive Order 9066, which cleared the way for the internment of tens of thousands of people of Japanese descent.

The order came ten weeks after the Japanese attack on Pearl Harbor. Up and down the West Coast, posters appeared declaring that "all persons of Japanese ancestry, both alien and non-alien, will be evacuated." Some 110,000 Japanese-Americans were uprooted and moved inland to internment camps in remote locations scattered across seven states. Nearly two-thirds of these "evacuees" were American citizens.

Security concerns prompted the drastic step—the U.S. government worried that people of Japanese ancestry might be spying for Japan. Mexico and Canada took similar actions. But the ugly truth is that hysteria and racism were also at work. Many Americans, with images of burning ships and dead sailors at Pearl Harbor seared in their minds, looked at Japanese-Americans and saw the enemy.

Many internees spent two and a half years in the camps, which were hastily constructed miniature cities, full of wooden barracks and surrounded by barbed wire. After the war, they faced the task of rebuilding their lives.

In no way can the internment camps be compared with Nazi concentration camps or Stalin's *Gulag*, where millions died. But the terrible fact remains that loyal Americans who had done no wrong lost their property and, temporarily at least, their liberty. It's an ugly blot on our nation's history.

In 1988, President Reagan signed a law that offered a national apology to Japanese-Americans and $20,000 to each person who had been interned in the camps.

AMERICAN HISTORY PARADE

1807　Former vice president Aaron Burr is arrested in Alabama on suspicions that he is scheming to establish an independent republic.

1847　The first rescuers reach the Donner Party, a band of California-bound settlers stranded by snow in the Sierra Nevada Mountains.

1878　Thomas Edison receives a patent for the phonograph.

1942　President Franklin D. Roosevelt signs an executive order authorizing the internment of Japanese-Americans.

1945　U.S. Marines begin a horrific struggle for the Pacific island of Iwo Jima.

THOSE WORDS SENT MARINE LIEUTENANT COLONEL JOHN H. GLENN on his way as his Atlas rocket lifted off from Cape Canaveral and roared into the sky on February 20, 1962. They came from fellow *Mercury* astronaut Scott Carpenter, on the ground. Tom O'Malley, General Dynamics Corporation project director, added his prayer: "May the good Lord ride with you all the way."

The young test pilot could hear none of this encouragement over the sound of his engines as *Friendship* 7 thundered into space on the U.S.'s first attempt to send a man into orbit. The mission went well until, after watching his first sunset in space, Glenn realized that the automatic control system was failing, causing the spacecraft to drift. He calmly switched to a manual system and took command of the capsule, guiding it along at about 17,500 miles per hour.

During the second orbit, a flight controller on the ground noticed a heart-stopping signal: a sensor monitoring the spacecraft's landing system indicated that its heat shield might have come loose. Without it, the capsule would burn to a cinder when it reentered the earth's atmosphere. The ground team decided that the craft's retrorockets, which were designed to be jettisoned before reentry, would be left on to help keep the heat shield in place.

The temperature outside *Friendship* 7 rose to 9500° F as it slammed into the atmosphere. The capsule entered the communications blackout zone—a brief period when the heat made radio contact impossible. The world held its breath while the spacecraft plummeted. Would the shield hold? Finally, after what seemed an eternity, Glenn's steady voice crackled through the static: "My condition is good, but that was a real fireball, boy!"

John Glenn had spent five hours in space and circled the earth three times. Americans were headed toward a new frontier.

AMERICAN HISTORY PARADE

1809   The Supreme Court rules that the power of the federal government is greater than the power of state governments.

1839   Congress outlaws dueling in the District of Columbia.

1862   Willie Lincoln, Abraham Lincoln's son, dies at the White House of typhoid fever.

1942   Lt. Edward "Butch" O'Hare becomes the Navy's first flying ace of World War II after shooting down five Japanese bombers headed for the USS *Lexington*.

1962   John Glenn becomes the first American to orbit the earth.

A FRIEND AND POLITICAL ALLY of Thomas Jefferson asked the retired president to give some advice to his young son, Thomas Jefferson Smith, who had been named after Jefferson. A little more than a year before he died, Jefferson composed a letter to be given to Smith when he was old enough to appreciate it. He enclosed some practical advice, such as "Pride costs us more than hunger, thirst and cold," and "When angry, count ten before you speak. If very angry, a hundred." But the most moving part of the letter consists of the following "few words":

Monticello, February 21, 1825

This letter will, to you, be as one from the dead. The writer will be in the grave before you can weigh its counsels. Your affectionate and excellent father has requested that I would address to you something which might possibly have a favorable influence on the course of life you have to run, and I too, as a namesake, feel an interest in that course. Few words will be necessary, with good dispositions on your part. Adore God. Reverence and cherish your parents. Love your neighbor as yourself, and your country more than yourself. Be just. Be true. Murmur not at the ways of Providence. So shall the life into which you have entered, be the portal to one of eternal and ineffable bliss. And if to the dead it is permitted to care for the things of this world, every action of your life will be under my regard. Farewell.

AMERICAN HISTORY PARADE

1848   Former president John Quincy Adams suffers a stroke on the floor of the U.S. House, and dies two days later.

1878   The first telephone directory is issued in New Haven, Connecticut.

1885   The Washington Monument is dedicated.

1965   African American leader Malcolm X is shot and killed by three members of the Nation of Islam in New York City.

1972   Richard Nixon becomes the first U.S. president to visit China.

GEORGE WASHINGTON WAS BORN ON FEBRUARY 22, 1732, in Westmoreland County, in eastern Virginia. In three crucial ways he shaped our nation. First, he led American forces during the fight for independence. Second, he presided over the writing of our Constitution. Third, he served as our first president.

At times, it was Washington's character alone that seemed to hold the fledgling United States together. He became a symbol of what Americans were struggling for, risking his life and fortune to lead his countrymen to liberty.

During one battle of the Revolution, at Monmouth in New Jersey, the American troops were in confused flight and on the verge of destruction when General Washington appeared on the field. Soldiers stopped in their tracks and stared as the tall, blue-coated figure spurred his horse up and down the line, halting the retreat. The young Marquis de Lafayette remembered the sight for the rest of his life, how Washington rode "all along the lines amid the shouts of the soldiers, cheering them by his voice and example and restoring to our standard the fortunes of the fight. I thought then, as now, that never had I beheld so superb a man."

The general turned his army around. The fighting raged until sundown, and that night the British took the chance to slip away. Washington's very presence had stopped a rout and turned the tide of battle.

It was not the only time. Again and again, Americans turned to Washington. He was, as biographer James Flexner called him, the "indispensable man" of the American founding. Without George Washington, there may never have been a United States.

AMERICAN HISTORY PARADE

1732   George Washington is born in Westmoreland County, Virginia.

1819   Spain cedes Florida to the United States.

1879   Frank Woolworth starts a retail revolution when he opens his first "five cents store" in Utica, New York.

1924   Calvin Coolidge delivers the first presidential radio broadcast from the White House.

1980   The U.S. Olympic hockey team wins a stunning victory over the Soviets, 4-3, at Lake Placid, New York.

ON THE MORNING OF FEBRUARY 19, 1945, some 70,000 U.S. Marines began to swarm onto a tiny island in the northwest Pacific called Iwo Jima—a name that means "Sulfur Island" in Japanese. Twenty-one thousand Japanese defenders lay waiting for them, burrowed into volcanic rock in hundreds of underground fortifications.

The Japanese plan was simple: fight to the death. The goal of each defender: kill ten Americans before being killed.

On the southern tip of the island stood Mount Suribachi, a 550-foot volcano. From its flanks, Japanese guns could crisscross Iwo Jima with deadly fire.

With bullets and shells screeching around them, wave after wave of Marines hit the beach. "I just didn't see how anybody could live through such heavy barrages," one officer remembered. The Americans rarely saw their hidden enemy, while the Japanese had every U.S. soldier in their sights. The Marines fought forward, inch by inch.

On the morning of February 23, 1945, U.S. troops all over the island were elated by the sight of a small American flag flying atop Mount Suribachi—the Marines had gained the summit. Later that afternoon, five Marines and a Navy hospital corpsman raised a larger flag.

By the time the fighting finally ended, some 6,800 Americans had died capturing Iwo Jima's eight square miles. More than 21,000 Japanese were dead.

Today a giant bronze statue near Arlington National Cemetery, outside of Washington, D.C., depicts one of the most famous images from American history: the Marines raising the U.S. flag atop Mount Suribachi. The Marine Corps War Memorial is dedicated to all Marines who have given their lives in defense of the United States. An inscription on its base reads: "Uncommon Valor was a Common Virtue."

AMERICAN HISTORY PARADE

1836   The siege of the Alamo begins in San Antonio, Texas.

1847   U.S. troops under General Zachary Taylor defeat Mexican general Santa Anna at the Battle of Buena Vista.

1861   President-elect Abraham Lincoln arrives secretly in Washington, D.C., amid reports of assassination plots.

1945   U.S. Marines fighting on Iwo Jima raise the American flag atop Mount Suribachi.

1954   Schoolchildren in Pittsburgh receive the first injections of a polio vaccine developed by Dr. Jonas Salk.

"I AM TOO OLD!" protested John Quincy Adams, congressman and former president of the United States, when admirers asked him to argue a case before the U.S. Supreme Court.

The situation was this. In 1839 the Spanish schooner *Amistad* left Havana, Cuba, for another Cuban port, carrying fifty-three African slaves. Under the leadership of an African named Cinque, the captives revolted, killed the captain, and seized the ship. They demanded to be taken back to Africa, but the *Amistad*'s navigator tricked them and sailed toward Long Island, New York. A U.S. Navy vessel took the ship into custody and brought it to Connecticut.

Spain demanded that the U.S. return the *Amistad* and its human cargo as the property of Spain. The administration of President Martin van Buren agreed. But Cinque and his comrades—supported by American abolitionists—insisted that they were not "property" at all, but human beings who had been kidnapped in Africa.

Now the dispute was going to the U.S. Supreme Court, and the abolitionists wanted John Quincy Adams, known as "Old Man Eloquent," to help argue their case. Adams worried he was too rusty. He had not been in a courtroom in decades. But he finally agreed.

On February 24, 1841, a nervous Adams began presenting his argument to the justices. His voice faltered at first, but his cause brought him confidence. He pointed to a framed document on the wall. "The moment you come to the Declaration of Independence, that every man has a right to life and liberty, as an inalienable right, this case is decided. I ask nothing more on behalf of these unfortunate men than this Declaration."

The Court ruled that since the transatlantic slave trade had been banned, the Africans were free men. Old Man Eloquent won his case. For payment, he received a handsomely bound Bible from the Africans—and profound satisfaction at having struck a blow for liberty.

AMERICAN HISTORY PARADE

1803   The Supreme Court, in *Marbury v. Madison*, affirms its power as the final interpreter of constitutional issues.

1841   John Quincy Adams begins two days of arguments before the U.S. Supreme Court in the *Amistad* case.

1868   President Andrew Johnson becomes the first president to be impeached by the House of Representatives (the Senate later acquits him).

1871   For the first time since the Civil War, the South gains full representation in Congress with the seating of the Georgia delegation.

1991   In the Persian Gulf War, a U.S.-led coalition begins a ground campaign against Iraq.

A SEA CAPTAIN FROM SALEM, MASSACHUSETTS, named William Driver first called the U.S. flag "Old Glory." In 1824, when Driver turned twenty-one, his mother and several young ladies sewed a large American flag for his merchant ship. The captain was delighted with the birthday gift. "I name thee Old Glory!" he declared when he saw it unfolding on the breeze. In the 1820s and '30s, he flew it on his ship during his sea voyages.

In 1837 Driver left the sea and moved to Nashville, Tennessee, taking his precious flag with him. On Washington's birthday, the Fourth of July, and St. Patrick's Day (which happened to be Driver's birthday), he proudly hung Old Glory from a rope stretched across his street.

With the coming of the Civil War, Driver grew worried that Confederates might seize his flag, so he hid it by sewing it inside a bed comforter. The war divided the Driver family, as it did so many others. Captain Driver was a staunch Union man, but his two sons fought for the Confederacy, and one was killed at the Battle of Perryville, Tennessee.

On February 25, 1862, Nashville became the first Southern state capital to fall to Union troops. When the soldiers entered the city, Driver ripped open the comforter's seams, carried Old Glory to the capitol building, climbed its tower, and raised his beloved banner. After hearing the story, Americans adopted the nickname Old Glory for the U.S. flag.

Today Driver's original Old Glory resides at the Smithsonian Institution in Washington, D.C., where it has been carefully preserved.

AMERICAN HISTORY PARADE

1836   Inventor Samuel Colt patents his revolver.

1862   Captain William Driver flies Old Glory after Union troops enter Nashville.

1870   Hiram R. Revels, a Mississippi Republican, becomes the first black U.S. senator when he is sworn in to complete the unexpired term of Jefferson Davis, former president of the Confederacy.

1901   J. P. Morgan forms U.S. Steel, the world's first billion-dollar company.

1933   The USS *Ranger*, the first U.S. Navy ship designed and built as an aircraft carrier, is launched at Newport News, Virginia.

THE NAME WILLIAM FREDERICK CODY, born this day in 1846 in Scott County, Iowa, may not ring a bell. But chances are you know Cody's nickname, Buffalo Bill.

Cody left home at age eleven, after his father died, and cut a fearless path across the Western frontier. Cowboy, teamster, fur trapper, gold miner, Pony Express rider, Civil War soldier, cavalry scout, Indian fighter—he did it all. He earned his nickname while hunting buffalo to supply meat for railroad work crews—reportedly killing more than 4,000 buffalo in 18 months. A few years later, when he served as a scout for Army troops fighting Indians, the government awarded him the Congressional Medal of Honor for valor in action.

In 1872 Cody decided to take advantage of his growing fame and began a long career as a showman. His "Buffalo Bill's Wild West" spectacular toured the country with hundreds of cowboys, cowgirls, and Indians—including sure-shot Annie Oakley and Sitting Bull—as well as live buffalo and cattle. The show's mock shoot-outs and round-ups thrilled audiences. Cody even toured Europe and performed for the queen of England. "Buffalo Bill has come, we have seen, and he has conquered," a British newspaper reported. By the turn of the twentieth century, Cody was perhaps the most famous American of his day.

Buffalo Bill was, in some ways, a man of contradictions. He was an Indian fighter, but also pushed for Indian rights. He hunted buffalo, but later supported their conservation. He loved the frontier, but in promoting it helped it disappear. "The West of the old times, with its strong characters, its stern battles and its tremendous stretches of loneliness, can never be blotted from my mind," he wrote. "Nor can it, I hope, be blotted from the memory of the American people."

AMERICAN HISTORY PARADE

1846   Frontiersman and showman William Frederick "Buffalo Bill" Cody is born near Le Claire, Iowa.

1917   President Wilson learns of the Zimmermann Telegram, a coded German message suggesting an alliance between Germany and Mexico, a communication that hastens the U.S. entry into World War I.

1919   The Grand Canyon becomes a national park.

1993   Islamic terrorists explode a bomb in the garage of New York's World Trade Center, killing six people.

ON THIS DAY IN 1776, the newly established Continental Navy was at sea on its first operation, an expedition to the Bahamas to capture some badly needed munitions. The flagship of the little fleet flew a new ensign presented by Christopher Gadsden of South Carolina: a yellow banner emblazoned with a coiled rattlesnake and the legend "Don't Tread on Me."

The rattlesnake was a favorite emblem during the Revolutionary War. In December 1775, Benjamin Franklin published an essay in the *Pennsylvania Journal* under the pseudonym "An American Guesser" in which he ruminated on the symbol.

"I observed on one of the drums belonging to the marines now raising, there was painted a Rattle-Snake, with this modest motto under it, 'Don't tread on me,'" Franklin wrote. He noted that the rattlesnake's "eye excelled in brightness that of any other animal, and that she has no eye-lids. She may therefore be esteemed an emblem of vigilance. She never begins an attack, nor, when once engaged, ever surrenders. She is therefore an emblem of magnanimity and true courage."

Today the rattlesnake image remains popular with many military units. U.S. Navy ships currently fly a Navy Jack with a rattlesnake and the Don't Tread on Me slogan as a symbol of vigilance during the war on terrorism.

AMERICAN HISTORY PARADE

1827   Revelers dance through the streets of New Orleans, marking the beginning of the city's famous Mardi Gras celebrations (Mobile, Alabama, claims the first Mardi Gras celebration, in 1703).

1860   In New York City, Abraham Lincoln gives his Cooper Union speech, which helps him gain national recognition as an opponent of the spread of slavery.

1951   The Twenty-second Amendment, limiting presidents to two terms, is ratified.

1991   President George H. W. Bush announces the end of the Persian Gulf War, an overwhelming U.S. and allied victory against Iraq's Saddam Hussein.

ON THIS DAY IN 1969, Airman First Class John Levitow was lying in a hospital bed, his body covered with forty shrapnel wounds, trying to piece together exactly how he had ended up there. Meanwhile, seven Air Force buddies in South Vietnam were telling themselves they wouldn't be alive if not for Levitow's courage.

Four days earlier, the eight men had flown a night combat mission over South Vietnam aboard an AC-47 gunship, dropping magnesium flares to illuminate enemy positions on the ground. Each flare had a safety pin. Twenty seconds after the pin was pulled and the flare was tossed out a cargo door, it would ignite to 4,000° Fahrenheit, lighting up the countryside.

In the fifth hour of the mission, a Vietcong mortar hit the plane, blasting a hole through a wing and nearly wrenching the gunship out of the sky. Levitow, wounded in the back and legs, had just dragged a bleeding crewmate away from the open cargo door when he saw a smoking flare roll across the floor amid ammunition canisters. Its pin had been pulled.

Levitow tried to grab the flare, but it skidded away. In desperation, he threw himself on top. Hugging it to his chest, he dragged himself to the plane's rear, leaving a trail of blood, and hurled the flare through the door. An instant later it burst into a white-hot blaze, but free of the aircraft.

Levitow recovered and went on to fly twenty more combat missions. In 1970 he received the Medal of Honor, an award he accepted with humility. "There are many people who have served, who have done things that have been simply amazing and never been recognized," he said—a good reminder that the U.S. military has no shortage of heroes.

AMERICAN HISTORY PARADE

1827   The Baltimore and Ohio Railroad, the first commercial railroad in the United States to carry passengers and freight, is incorporated.

1849   The steamship *California*, carrying gold-seekers, arrives in San Francisco from New York, marking the beginning of regular steamboat travel between the East and West Coasts.

1854   Opponents of slavery meet in Ripon, Wisconsin, and agree to form a new political group, which later becomes the Republican Party.

1932   The last Ford Model A (the successor to the Model T) rolls off the factory line.

FLAGS OF THE REVOLUTIONARY WAR

American troops fought under no single flag during the Revolution. The war was conducted with relatively little central direction, and many militiamen held their strongest loyalties for the state or region from which they hailed. So it's not surprising that soldiers brought all sorts of banners to the field. Navy ships were more likely to carry flags than troops on land, since seagoing vessels had an ancient tradition of flying standards.

Most Revolutionary War flags disappeared long ago, and historians don't have much reliable information about what many of them looked like. A few have survived, though. Some famous examples follow. They are among our earliest symbols of unity and dedication to freedom.

RATTLESNAKE FLAG

The rattlesnake was a favorite American emblem during the Revolution because it struck with deadly force if provoked. The legend "Don't Tread on Me" usually accompanied the image. This flag, known as the First Navy Jack, is believed to have flown aboard Navy ships in the early days of the republic. U.S. Navy vessels fly it today as an emblem of vigilance during the war on terrorism. Another version, known as the Gadsden Flag because it was promoted by Col. Christopher Gadsden of South Carolina, features a coiled rattlesnake emblazoned on a yellow banner.

Washington's Cruisers Flag

This flag, a green pine tree on a white field, was carried by a squadron of warships that George Washington outfitted during the Revolution. The pine had long been a symbol of New England.

Bunker Hill Flag

This flag, a blue banner with a white field in the upper left corner, is said to have been carried by Americans at the Battle of Bunker Hill on June 17, 1775. It was basically a modified British maritime flag with a New England pine tree added to the white field, which also carried the red cross of St. George—a traditional symbol of England.

Fort Moultrie Flag

South Carolinians under the command of Col. William Moultrie raised one of the earliest flags of American liberty in 1776 on Sullivan's Island while defending Charleston from British attack. The flag was the dark blue of the soldiers' uniforms and bore a white crescent like the silver crescents on their caps. Today's South Carolina flag still uses the crescent.

Green Mountain Boys Flag

Soldiers from New England known as the Green Mountain Boys reportedly flew this green flag at the Battle of Bennington in New York, about ten miles from Bennington, Vermont, on August 16, 1777. The stars were arranged on a blue field in a somewhat random fashion but still symbolized the unity of the thirteen colonies fighting for freedom.

Rhode Island Regiment Flag

Rhode Island troops carried this white flag at the battles of Brandywine, Trenton, and Yorktown. Its stars on a blue field, signifying national unity, may have influenced the design of the American flag. The anchor is an early Christian symbol of hope.

Washington's Commander-in-Chief Flag

The Commander in Chief's Personal Flag traveled with George Washington wherever he went during the Revolutionary War. It probably dates to 1775. Its thirteen white stars have six points, rather than the five points in the Stars and Stripes flag. The original is kept at Valley Forge, where it flew at Washington's headquarters during the winter of 1777–78.

The Guilford Courthouse Flag

Revolutionary War flags came in all shapes and sizes. This one, carried by North Carolina militiamen at the Battle of Guilford Courthouse in North Carolina on March 15, 1781, was an early form of the Stars and Stripes. It used blue stars with eight points on a white field along with red and blue stripes.

Cowpens Flag

On January 17, 1781, the Third Maryland Regiment carried this flag at the Battle of Cowpens, South Carolina, a turning point in the war in the South. The original is enshrined at the state capitol in Annapolis, Maryland.

MARCH

THE UNITED STATES created the world's first national park on March 1, 1872, when President Ulysses S. Grant signed legislation setting aside Yellowstone National Park in Wyoming. Before the century was out, the country had four more parks—General Grant (now Kings Canyon), Sequoia, and Yosemite in California, and Mount Rainier in Washington. By that time the idea of preserving stretches of wilderness was spreading to other countries.

Today the United States has the finest, most extensive system of national parks in the world. From the Thaddeus Kosciuszko National Memorial in Philadelphia (1/50 of an acre) to the Wrangell–St. Elias National Park and Preserve in Alaska (13 million acres), the National Park Service administers more than 84 million acres. The system includes about 400 parks, historic places, monuments, battlefields, preserves, and more. As the conservationist J. Horace McFarland observed, "The parks are the nation's pleasure grounds and the nation's restoring places. . . . [They] are an American idea. . . . These great parks are, in the highest degree, as they stand today, a sheer expression of democracy."

Yellowstone, which lies mostly in the northwest corner of Wyoming but spills into Idaho and Montana, covers some 2.2 million acres that boast natural wonders such as petrified forests and bubbling pools of colored mud called *paint pots*, as well as wildlife such as elk, bison, and grizzly bears. The park contains more hot springs and geysers than any other area in the world.

In the first part of the nineteenth century, hunters and trappers returned from the region describing a place of "fire and brimstone" with boiling mud and trees made of rock, accounts at first dismissed as myths. After the Civil War, several expeditions confirmed the stories. Their reports of a surreal, spectacular landscape convinced the government to preserve the area as a giant public park.

AMERICAN HISTORY PARADE

1781   The Articles of Confederation go into effect.

1803   Ohio becomes the seventeenth state.

1845   President Tyler signs a Congressional resolution annexing the Republic of Texas.

1867   Nebraska becomes the thirty-seventh state.

1872   Yellowstone becomes the world's first national park.

1932   Charles and Anne Lindbergh's infant son is kidnapped from their home near Hopewell, New Jersey.

1961   President Kennedy establishes the Peace Corps.

SAM HOUSTON LIVED A LIFE as big as Texas. Born on March 2, 1793, near Lexington, Virginia, he moved to the Tennessee frontier with his family at age thirteen and soon struck out on his own. He lived for a while with the Cherokee . . . taught in a one-room schoolhouse . . . fought the Creek Indians under Andrew Jackson . . . studied law and was elected to Congress . . . became governor of Tennessee . . . organized a Texas army and defeated General Santa Anna at the Battle of San Jacinto . . . became the first president of the Republic of Texas . . . worked to have Texas admitted to the United States . . . represented Texas in the U.S. Senate . . . and served as governor of Texas.

His finest moment came toward the end of his life, as the Civil War approached, and a secession convention voted to take Texas out of the Union. Houston opposed the move with every fiber of his soul. He took to the hustings to warn scornful crowds that secession would bring only disaster. In one town, when an armed man threatened him, the 68-year-old Houston stared him down, declaring, "Ladies and gentlemen, keep your seats. It is nothing but a fice [a small dog] barking at the lion in his den."

His efforts weren't enough. Texas legislators demanded that Governor Houston swear loyalty to the Confederacy. "In the name of my own conscience and manhood . . . I refuse to take this oath," he wrote, knowing it meant the end of his career.

Supporters offered to take up arms to fight for control of the statehouse, but Houston turned them down. He did not want to cling to office by spilling the blood of fellow Texans. Brokenhearted, he retired to private life. It was for this final act of public service that John F. Kennedy would later make Sam Houston a hero in his book *Profiles in Courage*.

AMERICAN HISTORY PARADE

1793   Sam Houston is born near Lexington, Virginia.

1807   Congress outlaws the importation of slaves.

1836   The Republic of Texas declares its independence from Mexico.

1877   Republican Rutherford B. Hayes is declared president by an electoral commission over Democrat Samuel J. Tilden in a disputed election.

1917   Puerto Rico becomes a U.S. territory and its inhabitants U.S. citizens.

1949   *The Lucky Lady II*, a B-50 Superfortress, becomes the first plane to fly nonstop around the world, refueling four times in the air along the way.

ON THIS DAY IN 1776, George Washington's Patriot army was in the final stages of pulling off one of the biggest surprises of the Revolutionary War, thanks to a bookseller named Henry Knox.

The opening phase of the war found the British in control of Boston. The Patriots had not been able to break the redcoats' hold on the port, and George Washington was running out of time since the enlistment terms of many of his men would soon expire.

Henry Knox, who had owned the London Book Store in Boston and read all he could on military subjects, especially artillery, made an unlikely suggestion. Three hundred miles away, at Fort Ticonderoga in New York, lay the answer to the Patriots' problem: cannons. If the Patriots could somehow get the heavy artillery to Boston—an idea that made several officers shake their heads—they could drive the British out. With Washington's blessing, Knox hurried to Ticonderoga; chose 59 big guns; loaded them onto sleds pulled by horses, oxen, and men; and headed south.

Day after day, they skidded along snow-covered trails. They lurched through mud and mountainous drifts, heaved up rough hills and down steep valleys. Crossing the frozen Hudson River, the ice cracked and a huge gun broke through. Somehow the men pulled it out. In late February the "noble train of artillery" reached Boston.

During the first few days of March, Washington's army made a big racket to distract the enemy while they moved the guns into place. Early one morning, a sleepy British sentry blinked in disbelief through the dawn mists toward Dorchester Heights, where Knox's cannons, as if appearing out of nowhere, aimed straight at him. The British, realizing they could no longer hold the city, soon boarded their fleet and sailed away. Henry Knox's long haul had saved Boston. It was the first major victory of the Revolutionary War.

AMERICAN HISTORY PARADE

1776   The Patriot army prepares to occupy Dorchester Heights outside of Boston.

1820   Congress passes the Missouri Compromise, admitting Maine as a free state and Missouri as a slave state.

1845   Florida becomes the twenty-seventh state.

1863   In need of soldiers to fight in the Civil War, Congress passes a conscription act that results in the first wartime draft in the United States.

1931   "The Star-Spangled Banner" is adopted as the national anthem.

2005   Adventurer Steve Fossett becomes the first person to fly a fixed-wing aircraft around the world alone without stopping or refueling.

WHEN ABRAHAM LINCOLN gave his second inaugural address at the U.S. Capitol on March 4, 1865, the end of the Civil War was in sight. Sherman had cut through the South, and Grant was slowly tightening the Union vise around Lee's army at Petersburg. Yet Lincoln did not speak of triumph. Instead, he turned to the task of healing a broken nation. He reminded his listeners that the war would end the evil of slavery, and suggested that it was God's will that both North and South pay for that evil. He urged his countrymen to maintain their faith in God's wisdom as they began to "bind up the nation's wounds."

Lincoln's second inaugural address, like his Gettysburg Address, is inscribed on an inner wall of the Lincoln Memorial.

. . . Fondly do we hope, fervently do we pray, that this mighty scourge of war may speedily pass away. Yet, if God wills that it continue until all the wealth piled by the bondsman's two hundred and fifty years of unrequited toil shall be sunk, and until every drop of blood drawn with the lash shall be paid by another drawn with the sword, as was said three thousand years ago, so still it must be said "the judgments of the Lord are true and righteous altogether."

With malice toward none, with charity for all, with firmness in the right, as God gives us to see the right, let us strive on to finish the work we are in, to bind up the nation's wounds, to care for him who shall have borne the battle, and for his widow, and his orphan—to do all which may achieve and cherish a just and lasting peace, among ourselves, and with all nations.

AMERICAN HISTORY PARADE

1789   The U.S. Constitution goes into effect as the first session of Congress meets in New York City.

1791   Vermont becomes the fourteenth state.

1829   The White House is overrun with partygoers when Andrew Jackson holds an "open house" to celebrate his inauguration.

1837   The Illinois legislature grants a city charter to Chicago.

1865   Abraham Lincoln delivers his second inaugural address.

1933   Frances Perkins, secretary of labor in Franklin D. Roosevelt's administration, becomes the first woman to serve in the Cabinet.

BOSTON, MASSACHUSETTS, seethed with resentment in 1770. London had imposed taxes on the colonists even though they had no voice in Parliament, and the king had sent troops to Boston to keep an eye on the unruly Americans.

On the night of March 5, a crowd began to taunt some British guards at the royal Customs House, brandishing clubs and calling them "lobsters." The soldiers fixed bayonets onto their muskets, and the mob responded by pelting them with trash, oyster shells, and snowballs. With their backs to the Customs House, and feeling hemmed in, the frightened soldiers opened fire on the crowd. When the smoke cleared, five colonists lay dead or dying.

News of the "Boston Massacre" raced through the colonies. Boston's Paul Revere, a silversmith, soon engraved a powerful—but exaggerated—print that depicted the killings as a slaughter. Samuel Adams distributed the image as part of his battle cry for American liberty.

Samuel's cousin, John Adams, was asked to defend the soldiers at trial, a job no one else wanted. Determined to prove that every man had a right to a fair trial in an American courtroom, Adams took the case, a move that aroused "a clamor and popular suspicions and prejudices" against him. Adams argued that the unruly colonists had provoked the soldiers, and that hanging the redcoats would disgrace Massachusetts's name in history. The jury found six of eight accused soldiers not guilty and convicted two of manslaughter, for which, as punishment, they were branded on their thumbs.

John Adams's show of fairness in the trial eventually won him much respect. He later called it "one of the best pieces of service I ever rendered my country."

AMERICAN HISTORY PARADE

1770   British soldiers fire on colonists in what becomes known as the Boston Massacre.

1933   President Franklin D. Roosevelt declares a "bank holiday," closing U.S. banks for four days to keep panicked depositors from withdrawing all their money.

1946   In a speech at Westminster College in Fulton, Missouri, Winston Churchill declares that an "Iron Curtain" has fallen across Eastern Europe, trapping millions behind it in Communist states.

1963   Country music star Patsy Cline dies in a plane crash near Camden, Tennessee.

STORM WINDS OF TYRANNY BLEW across Texas in early 1836. In those days the region was a part of Mexico, where General Santa Anna had seized power and made himself dictator. Texans weren't willing to submit to his rule, so Santa Anna marched north with an army.

In San Antonio a small band gathered to make their stand at the Alamo, an old Spanish mission turned into a fort. They were tough characters, men who had settled a wild frontier. With them was the famous Davy Crockett from Tennessee.

The Mexican army arrived and demanded the Alamo's surrender. The Texans answered with a cannon shot. Santa Anna ordered a red flag raised, a signal meaning "We will take no prisoners."

Colonel William Travis, commander of the Alamo, dispatched messengers bearing appeals for reinforcements. "Our flag still waves proudly from the walls," he wrote. "I shall never surrender nor retreat . . . Victory or death!"

Only 32 men made their way through the enemy lines to join the Texans at the Alamo. That brought the number of defenders to about 189. The Mexican army, meanwhile, swelled to perhaps 5,000.

Legend says that Travis called his men together, drew a line in the dust with his sword, and announced that those who wanted to stay and fight should step over the line. Every man but one crossed over.

The attack came early the next morning, on March 6, 1836. For a while, the Texans managed to hold the Mexican army back, but soon Santa Anna's soldiers swarmed over the walls. All of the Alamo's defenders were killed.

The Texans weren't finished. On April 21, troops commanded by Sam Houston attacked and broke Santa Anna's army. "Remember the Alamo!" was their battle cry—a cry that still reminds Americans of unyielding courage and sacrifice for freedom.

AMERICAN HISTORY PARADE

1836   A Mexican army overwhelms the defenders of the Alamo.

1857   The Supreme Court rules in its infamous *Dred Scott* decision that blacks are not citizens and that Congress cannot prohibit slavery in U.S. territories.

1896   Charles King tests his "horseless carriage" in Detroit, becoming the first person to drive a car in Motor City.

1930   Clarence Birdseye begins to sell prepackaged frozen food in Springfield, Massachusetts.

1951   Julius and Ethel Rosenberg go on trial for spying for the Soviet Union during World War II.

BY 1965 A CENTURY HAD PASSED since the end of the Civil War, but in some parts of the South, blacks still lacked the right to vote. Literacy tests, registration requirements, and other barriers hindered them on Election Day. Hoping to draw attention to the problem, civil rights workers planned to march more than fifty miles from Selma, Alabama, a town where blacks had suffered much violence and discrimination, to Montgomery, the state capital.

On Sunday, March 7, 1965, about 600 protesters began their march. They had barely started when they met a line of state troopers and policemen, some on horseback, who ordered the crowd to turn back. When the marchers held their ground, the police attacked with tear gas, bullwhips, and billy clubs, driving the activists back into Selma.

The nation was shocked by televised images of "Bloody Sunday," as the brutal assault came to be known. The Reverend Martin Luther King Jr. immediately called on civil rights activists to converge on Selma for another march.

On March 21, after even more bloodshed, some 3,200 marchers left Selma again, this time under the protection of the National Guard. With King leading the way, they walked along Highway 80 through rain and chilly weather, camping out at night and singing hymns of freedom. By the time they reached the capital on March 24, thousands more had joined them. "In a real sense this afternoon, we can say that our feet are tired, but our souls are rested," King told a swelling crowd the next day. "I stand before you this afternoon with the conviction that segregation is on its deathbed in Alabama."

He was right. The Selma-to-Montgomery march opened many eyes to the need for change. Later that year, President Lyndon Johnson signed into law the Voting Rights Act, which helped ensure voting rights for all citizens.

AMERICAN HISTORY PARADE

1876   Alexander Graham Bell receives a patent for the telephone.

1897   In Battle Creek, Michigan, Dr. John Kellogg serves the world's first cornflakes to patients in hopes that a better diet will help cure some of their ailments.

1926   The first successful transatlantic radio-telephone conversation takes place, between New York City and London.

1933   Businessman Charles Darrow of Atlantic City, New Jersey, trademarks the board game Monopoly.

1945   U.S. troops cross the Rhine River at Remagen, establishing the first Allied bridgehead in Germany during World War II.

1965   Police attack peaceful civil rights demonstrators trying to march from Selma to Montgomery, Alabama.

IN 1887, six-year-old Helen Keller spent this day getting to know her new teacher, Anne Sullivan, who had arrived at the Keller household in Alabama less than a week before.

Helen was not two years old when she came down with an illness that robbed her of sight and hearing for the rest of her life. For the next few years she grew up, as she later wrote, "wild and unruly, giggling and chuckling to express pleasure; kicking, scratching, uttering the choked screams of the deaf-mute to indicate the opposite."

Then Anne Sullivan arrived from Boston and moved in with Helen's family, determined to help the girl break out of her lonely world of darkness and silence. With painstaking determination and love, Anne taught Helen to spell words with her fingers, then to read and write braille. Eventually, Helen learned to speak. Anne devoted much of the rest of her life to her student. With her help, Helen grew up to:

- graduate from prestigious Radcliff College with honors;
- give lectures around the globe and write books that sold the world over;
- star in a movie about her own life;
- meet with every president from Grover Cleveland to Lyndon Johnson;
- receive countless awards, from France's Legion of Honor to the U.S. Presidential Medal of Freedom; and
- swim, ride horses and bicycles, play chess, go camping, and ride in an open-cockpit airplane.

Americans loved Helen Keller for her unconquerable spirit. "Life," she once wrote, "is either a daring adventure or nothing."

AMERICAN HISTORY PARADE

1796   The U.S. Supreme Court rules on the constitutionality of a congressional act for the first time when it upholds a carriage tax in *Hylton v. United States*.

1817   The New York Stock Exchange is formally chartered.

1965   The first U.S. combat troops arrive in South Vietnam when Marines land near Da Nang to secure an air base.

1983   In a speech in Florida, President Ronald Reagan refers to the Soviet Union as an "evil empire," signaling that he is determined to stand fast against Communist totalitarianism.

ON MARCH 9, 1862, the age of modern naval warfare began with the first battle between two ironclad vessels, the Union's *Monitor* and the Confederacy's *Virginia*.

The *Virginia* was originally a wooden U.S. frigate called the *Merrimack* that had been scuttled near Norfolk, Virginia. The Confederates raised the *Merrimack*, covered its hull with slanting iron plates, and renamed it the *Virginia*. The result looked like a floating barn roof with ten cannons sticking out of the sides and a smokestack on top.

On March 8 the clumsy *Virginia* steamed into combat against five wooden Union ships blockading the port of Norfolk. The *Virginia* quickly sank the USS *Cumberland* and USS *Congress*, and drove the USS *Minnesota* aground. The Union ships' cannonballs glanced off the *Virginia*'s iron sides with "no more effect than peas from a pop-gun," as one observer put it.

When news of the Union disaster reached Washington, Abraham Lincoln's secretary of war worried the *Virginia* would sink the whole Union fleet, then "come up the Potomac River and disperse Congress, destroy the Capitol and public buildings."

But the next day, when the *Virginia* chugged out of its berth, it met a surprise. The Union navy had rushed its own experimental ironclad to the scene. The *Monitor* rode low in the water and had just one revolving turret housing two big guns. It looked like a "tin can on a shingle." But it was every bit as tough as the *Virginia*.

The ironclads locked in battle, pounding away with their guns. Neither could puncture the other's iron shell. After more than three hours, the battered ships both turned and limped away.

Each side considered the battle a draw, but overall it was a Northern victory in that the *Virginia* failed to break the Union blockade. When admirals around the world heard of the battle, they realized that the age of tall-masted wooden warships had come to a close.

AMERICAN HISTORY PARADE

1847   U.S. forces land near Vera Cruz and lay siege to the city during the Mexican War.

1862   The first battle between two ironclad ships, the Union *Monitor* and the Confederate *Virginia* (formerly the *Merrimack*), takes place at Hampton Roads, Virginia.

1916   Mexican raiders led by Pancho Villa attack Columbus, New Mexico, killing 18 people.

1945   U.S. bombers drop incendiary bombs on Tokyo, engulfing much of the city in a firestorm.

1964   The Ford Motor Company produces the first Mustang.

ALEXANDER GRAHAM BELL had two great passions: helping the deaf and inventing. He was born in 1847 in Scotland, where his father taught the art of public speaking and helped deaf people learn to speak. When Alexander was a young man, his family immigrated to Canada, and he soon moved south to Boston, Massachusetts, where he opened a school for teachers of the deaf.

In Boston, Bell grew fascinated with the idea of developing a way to send voices over telegraph wires. He became fast friends with a young mechanic named Thomas Watson, who helped him with his experiments.

For months, the two tinkered with electric currents, switches, and reeds. March 10, 1876, brought one of the great moments in the history of invention. Bell was hard at work in his laboratory, preparing to test a new transmitter he had recently designed, when he spilled some battery acid on his clothes. "Mr. Watson, come here! I want you!" he called. Watson rushed from another room to Bell's side, not with alarm, but with excitement. He had heard Bell's call on their instrument. It was the first time words had ever traveled over a wire. Alexander Graham Bell had just given the world the telephone.

The next year, the young inventor launched the Bell Telephone Company, which grew into one of the world's largest corporations. But Bell had little interest in business. He spent the rest of his life coming up with new ideas and finding ways to help the deaf. He became a proud U.S. citizen in 1882 and is still remembered as one of America's greatest inventors.

AMERICAN HISTORY PARADE

1785   Thomas Jefferson is appointed minister to France, succeeding Benjamin Franklin.

1864   Abraham Lincoln promotes Ulysses S. Grant to commander of all Union armies.

1876   Alexander Graham Bell succeeds in sending words over a telephone wire.

2000   The Nasdaq Composite closes at 5048.62, an all-time closing high that precedes the end of the dot-com boom of the 1990s.

ON MARCH 11, 1960, NASA launched *Pioneer 5*, one of its first efforts to explore interplanetary space. The spacecraft orbited the sun between Earth and Venus and provided the first map of the magnetic field between planets.

Since that time, NASA has sent dozens of unmanned probes into deep space, giving humans our first glimpses of the solar system's far reaches. Famous interplanetary probes include:

Launch	Mission	Achievements
1962	*Mariner 2*	**First spacecraft to successfully fly by and gather data on another planet (Venus)**
1964	*Mariner 4*	**First to transmit close-up photos of another planet (Mars)**
1972	*Pioneer 10*	**First to investigate Jupiter and exit the planetary system**
1975	*Viking 1 & 2*	**First to land safely on another planet (Mars)**
1977	*Voyager 1*	**Studied Jupiter and Saturn; *Voyager 1* is now the most distant man-made object in the universe**
1977	*Voyager 2*	**Studied Jupiter and Saturn; first spacecraft to visit Uranus and Neptune**
1989	*Galileo*	**Studied Jupiter's atmosphere and its moons**
1996	*Mars Pathfinder*	**Landed a rover on Mars in 1997 to explore its surface**
1997	*Cassini*	**First spacecraft to orbit Saturn**
2003	*Mars Exploration Rover*	**Landed two rovers on Mars in 2004**
2005	*Deep Impact*	**First probe to explore a comet's interior**
2006	*New Horizons*	**En route to study Pluto and its moons**

AMERICAN HISTORY PARADE

1888   One of the worst blizzards in U.S. history hits the Northeast, killing some 400 people.

1918   The first U.S. cases of the Spanish flu are reported, an epidemic that kills 600,000 Americans and tens of millions worldwide.

1941   President Roosevelt signs the Lend-Lease Bill, which provides war supplies to countries fighting the Axis Powers.

1960   NASA launches *Pioneer 5*, one of the first probes to explore the solar system.

2002   Two columns of light beam skyward from ground zero in New York City in tribute to victims of the September 11, 2001, attacks.

ON MARCH 12, 1947, President Harry Truman went before Congress to request $400 million to help Greece and Turkey resist Communist-led rebels bent on overthrowing their governments. The president laid out a policy that became known as the Truman Doctrine—a pledge that the United States would help nations struggling to resist anti-democratic forces. Truman's words still resonate, and are still important:

> At the present moment in world history nearly every nation must choose between alternative ways of life. The choice is too often not a free one.
>
> One way of life is based upon the will of the majority, and is distinguished by free institutions, representative government, free elections, guarantees of individual liberty, freedom of speech and religion, and freedom from political oppression.
>
> The second way of life is based upon the will of a minority forcibly imposed upon the majority. It relies upon terror and oppression, a controlled press and radio, fixed elections, and the suppression of personal freedoms.
>
> I believe that it must be the policy of the United States to support free peoples who are resisting attempted subjugation by armed minorities or by outside pressures. . . .
>
> The seeds of totalitarian regimes are nurtured by misery and want. They spread and grow in the evil soil of poverty and strife. They reach their full growth when the hope of a people for a better life has died. We must keep that hope alive.
>
> The free peoples of the world look to us for support in maintaining their freedoms.
>
> If we falter in our leadership, we may endanger the peace of the world—and we shall surely endanger the welfare of our own nation.

AMERICAN HISTORY PARADE

1755   The first known use of a steam engine in the United States takes place at a New Jersey copper mine, where it is used to pump water from the mine.

1912   Juliette Gordon Low founds the Girl Scouts of the U.S.A. in Savannah, Georgia.

1923   The first motion picture with sound recorded on film is demonstrated in Los Angeles; it shows people dancing to music but has no dialogue.

1933   In the first of his radio "fireside chats," President Franklin Delano Roosevelt urges Depression-weary Americans to have faith in U.S. banks.

1947   President Harry Truman establishes the Truman Doctrine.

ON MARCH 13, 1639, the oldest institution of higher learning in the United States was named for Puritan minister John Harvard, one of the school's earliest and greatest benefactors.

Historians know little about John Harvard's life. The son of a London butcher, he was born in 1607 near the Surrey end of London Bridge, and as a young man he received his education at Emmanuel College, part of the University of Cambridge. By the 1630s, his father and most of his family had died of the plague. His inheritance made him a well-to-do member of England's middle class.

Faced with religious persecution, Harvard joined the wave of Puritans emigrating to America for a better life and chance to worship freely. In 1637 he and his wife, Ann, arrived in New England and became inhabitants of Charlestown, Massachusetts. That same year, he became a teaching elder of the First Church of Charlestown, a position that required him to explain scripture and give sermons.

But John Harvard did not last long in the New World. A little more than a year after his arrival, he died of consumption. On his deathbed he bequeathed £779 (half his estate) and a collection of about four hundred books to a college that had been founded in 1636 in Newtown (now Cambridge, Massachusetts).

It was a generous gift, one that helped launch the fledgling college on its mission to educate students in a classical curriculum and Puritan theology. In 1639 the Massachusetts General Court decided to name the school Harvard College in honor of the minister. Today the name Harvard is a good reminder that many of this country's finest universities trace their roots to churches and clergymen who realized that without educated citizens, America could not thrive.

AMERICAN HISTORY PARADE

1639   Harvard College is named for one of its first benefactors, clergyman John Harvard.

1868   The Senate begins the impeachment trial of President Andrew Johnson.

1928   The St. Francis Dam gives way on a reservoir 40 miles northwest of Los Angeles, killing at least 450 people.

1930   Clyde W. Tombaugh and fellow astronomers at Lowell Observatory in Flagstaff, Arizona, announce the discovery of a ninth planet, later named Pluto.

IN EARLY 1783, the infant United States faced a crisis. The Revolutionary War was practically over, but the army had not been paid. Soldiers who had fought for years were in desperate need of money. Congress had no funds, and rumors spread that it would send the men home without pay.

By mid-March, the threat of violence filled the air. Officers encamped at Newburgh, New York, talked of mutiny against the government. George Washington, realizing the country verged on disaster, sat at his desk on March 14 and wrote an address urging his men to have patience.

The next day, when the general strode into the hall where his officers had gathered, a hush fell over the room. These men had come to love their commander in chief during the war, but now they looked at him with resentful eyes.

Washington began to speak. He urged his men to have patience. He promised to do everything he could to secure their pay. He asked them to consider the safety of their new country, and begged them not to "open the flood gates of civil discord."

He paused. His men stared uneasily.

Washington produced a letter from a congressman explaining difficulties the government faced. He started to read, stumbled over the words, stopped. Then he pulled from his pocket something the men had never seen him use before—spectacles.

"Gentlemen, you must pardon me," he said softly. "I have grown gray in the service of my country, and now find myself growing blind."

The hardened soldiers fought back tears as they suddenly recalled Washington's own sacrifices. Later, when the general left the room, they voted to give Congress more time. As Thomas Jefferson later observed, "The moderation and virtue of a single character probably prevented this Revolution from being closed, as most others have been, by a subversion of that liberty it was intended to establish."

AMERICAN HISTORY PARADE

1743   America's first recorded town meeting takes place at Faneuil Hall in Boston.

1783   George Washington writes his Newburgh Address, urging the army not to revolt over a lack of pay.

1794   Eli Whitney patents the cotton gin.

1923   Warren G. Harding becomes the first president to file an income tax report.

1950   The FBI's "Ten Most Wanted" list debuts.

1951   United Nations forces, led by U.S. troops, recapture Seoul during the Korean War.

SHORTLY AFTER WORLD WAR I ENDED, twenty officers of the American Expeditionary Forces met in Paris with orders to confer on how the Army could improve troop morale. One of the officers, Lt. Col. Theodore Roosevelt Jr., son of President Theodore Roosevelt, suggested an idea that had already crossed many of the men's minds: an organization in which veterans could stay in touch, help each other, and work together after the fighting was over.

The officers wasted no time putting the idea into action. On March 15, 1919, about one thousand U.S. soldiers gathered in Paris for the very first meeting of the American Legion.

Today the Legion is the nation's largest veterans' organization, with nearly 3 million members. Men and women may join if they have served honorably in the U.S. armed forces during times of hostilities, such as World War II, the Korean War, Vietnam War, Persian Gulf War, and Iraq War.

The Legion's purpose is partly to help veterans continue friendships formed during military service. It also gives members a way to keep serving their country. The American Legion has built parks and playgrounds, donated equipment to hospitals and fire halls, sponsored Boy Scout troops and youth baseball leagues, promoted the study of the Constitution in schools, and much more.

For God and Country is the American Legion motto. The organization has nearly 15,000 posts worldwide. There is probably one near you, and your community is almost certainly a better place for it.

AMERICAN HISTORY PARADE

1767   Andrew Jackson, the seventh U.S. president, is born in the Waxhaw area of South Carolina.

1781   British troops win a Pyrrhic victory at Guilford Courthouse, North Carolina, a battle that helps push them to Yorktown.

1820   Maine becomes the twenty-third state.

1892   In New York State, voting machines are first authorized for use in elections.

1916   U.S. troops under General John J. Pershing cross the Mexican border in pursuit of Pancho Villa.

1919   The American Legion is founded in Paris.

THE AGE OF ROCKETS BEGAN ON MARCH 16, 1926, when Robert H. Goddard launched the world's first liquid-fuel rocket at a farm in Auburn, Massachusetts.

Goddard had become fascinated with the idea of space travel as a boy when he read H. G. Wells's science fiction classic *War of the Worlds*. As a student and then a physics professor, he experimented with different rocket designs. His work went virtually unnoticed. In fact, the most publicity he received was when the *New York Times*, hearing of his theory that someday a rocket might reach the moon, printed a jeering editorial declaring that Dr. Goddard "seems to lack the knowledge ladled out daily in high schools."

Goddard kept at his work. For nearly twenty years he tried experiment after experiment. None of the rockets he built would fly. Then came the cold March day in 1926 when he drove to his aunt Effie's farm, set up a ten-foot-tall rocket he had dubbed Nell, and lit the fuse.

For an instant the missile did nothing, then suddenly screeched off the pad, shot 41 feet into the air at 60 miles per hour, and thumped down in a cabbage patch 184 feet away. The flight lasted only two and a half seconds, but it was two and a half seconds that ultimately led human beings into outer space.

In the following years Goddard kept developing his rockets, shooting them higher and faster. He continued to work in relative obscurity. Not until after his death in 1945 did the world realize his achievements. Rockets based on Goddard's work eventually carried men to the moon.

Today Robert Goddard is remembered as the father of modern rocketry. NASA's Goddard Space Flight Center in Greenbelt, Maryland, is named in his honor.

AMERICAN HISTORY PARADE

1751   James Madison, the fourth U.S. president, is born in Port Conway, Virginia.

1802   Congress authorizes the establishment of the U.S. Military Academy at West Point.

1850   *The Scarlet Letter* by Nathaniel Hawthorne is published.

1926   Robert H. Goddard launches the world's first liquid-fuel rocket.

1968   U.S. troops shoot hundreds of unarmed civilians in the village of My Lai during the Vietnam War.

1995   Astronaut Norman Thagard becomes the first American to visit the Russian space station *Mir*.

SAINT PATRICK, A FIFTH-CENTURY MISSIONARY born in Roman Britain, became the patron saint of Ireland by spreading Christianity throughout the Emerald Isle. For centuries the Irish have set aside a day to remember him. But the version of St. Patrick's Day that Americans know, which celebrates all things Irish with parades, parties, and "putting on the green," was invented chiefly in our own country.

And no wonder. Some 36 million Americans claim Irish ancestry—almost nine times as many people as the population of Ireland itself.

Irish settlers, many of them indentured servants, brought the custom of remembering Saint Patrick to the American colonies. Boston held its first observance in 1737. In New York City, Irish soldiers in the British army held a parade on St. Patrick's Day 1762. During the Revolutionary War, George Washington allowed his troops camped at Morristown, New Jersey, many of whom were of Irish descent, to have a holiday on March 17, 1780.

In the nineteenth century, as millions more Irish immigrants arrived, including those fleeing the Great Potato Famine, St. Patrick's Day observances became more widespread. Over time the day became less a remembrance of the saint himself, and more a way to remember Irish heritage, often with flair (as in Chicago, where the city dyes the Chicago River green).

From Davy Crockett to Bing Crosby, Americans with Irish roots have shaped our history and culture. By some estimates, one-third to one-half of American troops in the Revolutionary War were of Irish descent, as were 9 of the 56 signers of the Declaration of Independence. As many as 19 presidents, including Andrew Jackson, John F. Kennedy, and Ronald Reagan, have had Irish ancestors. If the United States is the world's melting pot, the broth has a wee bit o' the taste of Irish stew.

AMERICAN HISTORY PARADE

1737   The Charitable Irish Society of Boston holds the first public celebration of St. Patrick's Day in the American colonies.

1776   Threatened by Patriot cannons on Dorchester Heights, the British evacuate Boston.

1898   The USS *Holland*, the first practical submarine, conducts a trial run off Staten Island.

1958   The United States launches its second satellite, *Vanguard I* (still in orbit as of 2008).

1959   The USS *Skate* becomes the first submarine to surface at the North Pole.

ON MARCH 18, 1959, Dwight D. Eisenhower signed the Admission Act, a statute that cleared the way for Hawaii to become the fiftieth state.

According to tradition, the name *Hawaii* was bestowed long ago by Polynesian settlers in honor of their chief Hawaii-loa, who is said to have led them to the islands. All of the states' names are rooted in history. Here are a few more name origins:

Alabama – after the Alabama River and Alabama tribe that once lived in the area; *Alabama* may mean "plant gatherers," from the Choctaw words *alba* (plant) and *amo* (to gather)

Alaska – from the Aleut word *alyeska*, meaning "great land"

Arizona – perhaps from a Basque word meaning "good oak tree"

Arkansas – from a Quapaw tribe word meaning "downstream people" or "people of the south wind"

California – thought to be named by early Spanish explorers after a legendary gold-laden island described in a sixteenth-century Spanish book

Colorado – from the Spanish word *colorado* ("colored red"), a name explorers gave to the Colorado River, which flows through canyons of red stone

Connecticut – from the Indian word *quinnehtukqut*, meaning "long river place" or "beside the long tidal river"

Delaware – for Sir Thomas West, Lord De La Warr, the Virginia colony's first governor

Florida – named by Spanish explorer Ponce de León, who discovered the peninsula around April 2, 1513, and called it *La Florida* in honor of Pascua Florida, the Spanish Feast of the Flowers at Easter time

Georgia – in honor of King George II of England

AMERICAN HISTORY PARADE

1766 After months of protests by American colonists, Britain repeals the Stamp Act.

1818 Congress approves pensions for Revolutionary War vets ($20 per month for officers, $8 per month for soldiers).

1834 The first railroad tunnel in the United States opens for business, the Staple Bend Tunnel in western Pennsylvania.

1837 Grover Cleveland, the only U.S. president to serve two nonconcurrent terms, is born in Caldwell, New Jersey.

1925 The Tri-State Tornado, the deadliest tornado in U.S. history, kills some seven hundred people in Missouri, Illinois, and Indiana.

SOMETIMES PRINTED WORDS affect history. One of those times came in March 1852 with the publication of *Uncle Tom's Cabin*, a novel Harriet Beecher Stowe wrote to call attention to the evils of slavery.

The book hit America like an earthquake. Written at a time when the Fugitive Slave Law lacerated consciences throughout the North, it created unforgettable characters such as poor Eliza, the young slave woman who races across the frozen Ohio River toward freedom, clutching her infant at her breast. Stowe took care to depict Southern slave owners with charity. She showed them trapped in a system they did not devise. The worst villain of the book is the vicious plantation owner Simon Legree, a transplanted Yankee. Even so, many Southerners reacted with rage. The book was banned in many Southern communities.

In our time "Uncle Tom" has become a term of abuse, referring to a black man who is obsequious toward whites. But Stowe's Uncle Tom is a dignified, courageous man who suffers a beating until he dies rather than give up the whereabouts of two runaway slaves. The story moved millions of Americans, especially evangelicals of the North, and helped convince them that slavery in the United States must end. In England, Queen Victoria wept over the book.

It is said that when Abraham Lincoln met Harriet Beecher Stowe in 1862, during the Civil War, he said, "So you're the little woman who wrote the book that started this great war!" Certainly, *Uncle Tom's Cabin* did not start the Civil War, but it did much to help end slavery in America. The book has been translated into dozens of languages and has sold millions of copies. Since its publication, it has never been out of print.

AMERICAN HISTORY PARADE

1831   Edward Smith steals $245,000 from the City Bank in downtown New York, the first recorded bank robbery in American history.

1916   The first U.S. air combat mission begins as the First Aero Squadron takes off from Columbus, New Mexico, in an expedition to catch Pancho Villa.

1952   The one millionth Jeep, originally produced as a "general purpose" vehicle for the U.S. Army, is manufactured.

1979   The U.S. House begins televising its day-to-day business on C-SPAN.

2003   An American-led coalition launches a war against Iraqi dictator Saddam Hussein, with air strikes on Baghdad.

WAVES OF JAPANESE TROOPS assaulted the Philippine Islands at the outset of World War II, steadily overpowering Filipino and American defenders. The U.S. forces commanded by General Douglas MacArthur fought back but were short on supplies and vastly outnumbered. Surrender was inevitable.

MacArthur received personal instructions to proceed to Australia without his soldiers, where he could organize a counterattack. He refused to leave his hungry, desperate men behind until President Roosevelt issued an order he could not ignore. The heartbroken general slipped past the Japanese navy by boat and plane to reach Australia. Once there, on March 20, 1942, he made a solemn pledge to his men back in the Philippines: "I shall return."

In April, unable to hold out any longer, some 75,000 American and Filipino troops on the Bataan Peninsula surrendered to the Japanese—the largest mass surrender in American history. The captors beat and murdered many POWs during the infamous 65-mile Bataan Death March to prison camps. American and Filipino soldiers on nearby Corregidor Island fared no better. The Japanese also imprisoned thousands of American and other Allied civilians living in the Philippines, and for months assumed no responsibility for feeding them.

By the summer of 1942, the United States had launched a counteroffensive. For two and a half years, Allied forces fought their way across the Pacific, island by island. On October 20, 1944, MacArthur finally waded back onto the Philippines' shores to make good on his pledge and liberate the islands.

AMERICAN HISTORY PARADE

1816   The U.S. Supreme Court affirms its right to review the decisions of state courts.

1922   The USS *Langley*, converted from the collier USS *Jupiter*, is commissioned as the first U.S. Navy aircraft carrier.

1942   In Australia, General Douglas MacArthur pledges to fight his way back to the Japanese-controlled Philippines, declaring "I shall return."

2003   One day after an air attack, a coalition of troops comprised mainly of U.S. and British forces invades Iraq, quickly overwhelming Saddam Hussein's army.

MUCH LEGEND SURROUNDS THE LIFE of Pocahontas, but the known facts are remarkable enough. Born around the year 1595 to Powhatan, chief of a powerful tribe, she was about twelve years old when English colonists founded Jamestown, Virginia. According to Captain John Smith, it was Pocahontas who saved him when the Indians took him prisoner. Just as the executioners were about to bash in his head, Smith wrote, Pocahontas "got his head in her armes, and laid her owne upon his to save him from death."

Some scholars have suggested that what Smith took to be an "execution" was really a ceremony of some kind. At any rate Powhatan set Smith free, and young Pocahontas became a frequent visitor to Jamestown, sometimes bringing food to the hungry settlers. Her friendly nature (her name means "playful one") made her a favorite among the colonists.

A few years later, after Smith left for England, the settlers kidnapped the Indian maiden, intending to hold her until her father returned some prisoners and stolen supplies. During her captivity, Pocahontas converted to Christianity and was baptized as Rebecca. With her father's consent, she married colonist John Rolfe, and the couple had a boy, Thomas. The marriage helped bring peace between the Indians and settlers.

In 1616 the Rolfes sailed to England to help promote the Jamestown colony. There the Indian "princess" was treated as a celebrity and welcomed at royal festivities. But she grew ill and died just before she was to return to Virginia. She was buried on March 21, 1617, in the town of Gravesend.

Pocahontas's story has been told a hundred ways in books, poems, plays, and movies. She was undoubtedly a courageous young woman who tried to bring friendship between two peoples. Captain Smith may have left the best tribute when he said she was "the instrument to [preserve] this colonie from death, famine, and utter confusion."

AMERICAN HISTORY PARADE

1617   Pocahontas, who died just before she was to begin her return voyage to Virginia, is buried in Gravesend, England.

1788   A fire destroys 856 buildings in New Orleans, ruining most of the city.

1790   Thomas Jefferson takes office as America's first secretary of state.

1963   Alcatraz, the federal prison on Alcatraz Island in San Francisco Bay, closes.

1980   President Jimmy Carter announces the United States will boycott the Moscow Olympics in response to the Soviet Union's invasion of Afghanistan.

"YOUR OPINIONS FRETT like a Gangrene and spread like a Leprosie." Such were the criticisms that authorities in the Massachusetts Bay Colony leveled at Anne Hutchinson.

The daughter of an English clergyman, Hutchinson came to Boston with her husband and children in 1634, serving as a midwife in the settlement. She began to invite neighbors into her home to discuss sermons and study the Bible. Anne was well versed in theology, and the meetings attracted a steady following.

Soon Anne's commentaries roused the ire of John Winthrop, longtime Puritan leader. Winthrop considered some of her teachings, such as that people could communicate with God directly without the aid of church officials, a threat to his "city upon a hill." He did not like the idea of an outspoken woman challenging Puritan authorities.

What began as a quarrel over religious doctrine turned into a struggle for influence. Hutchinson was brought to trial and accused of betraying the laws of church and state. She retorted that Winthrop's edicts were "for those who have not the light which makes plain the pathway"—she didn't need colonial officials to tell her how to practice her faith.

Hutchinson refused to yield, and on March 22, 1638, she was banished from the colony. She moved with her family and several followers to Rhode Island, where she helped found Portsmouth. She later moved to New York where, in 1643, she was killed in an Indian attack.

Today Anne Hutchinson is remembered as a pioneer who stood up for some freedoms now embedded in our Constitution. The inscription on her statue in front of Boston's State House reads, in part: "In Memory of Anne Marbury Hutchinson ... Courageous Exponent of Civil Liberty and Religious Toleration."

AMERICAN HISTORY PARADE

1622   Algonquian Indians attack and kill some 350 English colonists near Jamestown, Virginia.

1638   The Massachusetts Bay Colony banishes Anne Hutchinson.

1765   The British Parliament enacts the Stamp Act, a tax that meets with colonial indignation.

1946   The first U.S. rocket to leave the earth's atmosphere, launched from White Sands, New Mexico, reaches an altitude of 50 miles.

1972   Congress sends the Equal Rights Amendment to the states for ratification; it later fails to get enough states' approval to become law.

ON MARCH 23, 1775, with hostilities between Americans and British troops breaking out in New England, Patrick Henry stood in a packed St. John's Church in Richmond, Virginia, and made a fiery argument to the Second Virginia Convention that the time had come for the colonies to gather their strength and commit themselves to action. His ringing words still remind us that freedom must be defended:

Shall we gather strength by irresolution and inaction? Shall we acquire the means of effectual resistance by lying supinely on our backs, and hugging the delusive phantom of Hope, until our enemies shall have bound us hand and foot? . . . The battle, sir, is not to the strong alone; it is to the vigilant, the active, the brave. Besides, sir, we have no election. If we were base enough to desire it, it is now too late to retire from the contest. There is no retreat, but in submission and slavery! Our chains are forged, their clanking may be heard on the plains of Boston! The war is inevitable—and let it come! I repeat it, sir, let it come!

It is in vain, sir, to extenuate the matter. Gentlemen may cry, peace, peace—but there is no peace. The war is actually begun! The next gale that sweeps from the north will bring to our ears the clash of resounding arms! Our brethren are already in the field! Why stand we here idle? What is it that gentlemen wish? What would they have? Is life so dear, or peace so sweet, as to be purchased at the price of chains and slavery? Forbid it, Almighty God! I know not what course others may take; but as for me, give me liberty, or give me death!

AMERICAN HISTORY PARADE

1775   Patrick Henry delivers his "Liberty or Death" speech in Richmond, Virginia.

1806   The Lewis and Clark expedition departs the Pacific coast and begins its return journey east.

1857   Elisha Otis installs the world's first modern passenger elevator in New York City.

1965   America's first two-man space flight begins as *Gemini 3* lifts off from Cape Canaveral with astronauts Gus Grissom and John Young aboard.

ANDREW CARNEGIE EMIGRATED from Scotland to America with his family in 1848, when he was twelve years old. The boy found a job in a Pittsburgh cotton mill, working twelve-hour days for $1.20 a week. He spent his spare time educating himself in a local library and soon managed to get a better job as a messenger, then a telegraph operator.

Eventually his hard work caught the eye of a Pennsylvania Railroad official, who hired the young man as a clerk. After that, Carnegie's rise was rapid. Realizing that the growing United States would need lots of steel, he opened a steel plant in 1875. Over the next quarter century he built a giant business empire. On March 24, 1900, he incorporated his Carnegie Steel Company, and then turned around and sold it a year later for $480 million, a transaction that made him one of the richest men in the world.

The most interesting part was still to come. Carnegie had made up his mind that he would not die rich. He had the idea that a person should spend the first part of life making money, and the second part giving it away. "The man who dies rich, dies disgraced," he said.

He spent the rest of his years giving away his money. Starting public libraries was his special love. Reading books had opened the way for him, and he wanted others to have the same chance. He started more than 2,500 libraries around the world—a gift that has touched millions of lives. By the time he died at age eighty-three, Carnegie had given away the vast majority of his riches to charities.

Carnegie's career had its blemishes. While he earned millions, unskilled laborers in his mills worked for fourteen cents an hour. Yet in the end, he made his mark not by how much he made, but by how much he gave back.

AMERICAN HISTORY PARADE

1765   The British Parliament enacts the hated Quartering Act, requiring American colonists to provide temporary housing for British soldiers.

1900   Andrew Carnegie incorporates his giant Carnegie Steel Company.

1934   Franklin D. Roosevelt signs legislation providing for independence for the Philippine Islands.

1958   Elvis Presley is inducted into the Army for two years.

1989   The tanker *Exxon Valdez* strikes a reef in Alaska's Prince William Sound, spilling an estimated 11 million gallons of oil.

ON MARCH 25, 1634, about two hundred English settlers climbed off of two small ships named the *Ark* and the *Dove* anchored in the Potomac River, rowed ashore to a slice of land they named St. Clement's Island, erected a cross, and held a thanksgiving service. It was the beginning of the colony of Maryland—a good day for religious freedom.

Maryland was founded by Cecilius Calvert, also known as Lord Baltimore, who received a charter from England's King Charles for some 12 million acres at the northern end of the Chesapeake Bay. Calvert was a Roman Catholic at a time when Catholics were persecuted in England, and he founded his colony to be a haven where Catholics could worship freely. He named it Maryland in honor, he said, of Queen Henrietta Maria, King Charles's wife, although Catholics quietly understood the land to be named in honor of Mary, mother of Jesus.

Calvert wanted Maryland to be a place where both Catholics *and* Protestants could worship freely, partly because he knew he would need Protestants to help settle his colony. In 1649 the colonial assembly passed a Toleration Act guaranteeing that no Christian in Maryland would be in "any waies troubled, Molested or discountenanced for or in respect of his or her religion nor in the free exercise thereof." Such toleration led Puritans and Quakers to flee to Maryland from Virginia, where they were persecuted by Anglicans. Maryland became renowned for its religious liberties.

By modern standards, those liberties were restrictive. They applied only to Christians. There were times in the colony's history when Catholics and Protestants fought each other and people were indeed persecuted for their religion.

Nonetheless, Maryland's Toleration Act was a historic step forward for freedom. It laid down a principle now central to our way of life.

AMERICAN HISTORY PARADE

1634   The colony of Maryland is founded by Catholic and Protestant settlers sent by Lord Baltimore.

1865   Robert E. Lee orders his last attack of the Civil War against Fort Steadman, near Petersburg, Virginia.

1911   A fire kills 146 garment workers at the Triangle Shirtwaist Company factory in New York City, leading the public to call for safety reforms.

1965   Civil rights activists led by Martin Luther King Jr. end their historic march from Selma to Montgomery, Alabama, at the steps of the state capitol.

THE WORD *POLIO* TERRIFIED AMERICANS during the first half of the twentieth century. The disease often struck children, killing its victims or leaving them crippled. During the summer, which seemed to bring the worst outbreaks, worried parents kept their children away from swimming pools, movie theaters, and other public places. Newspapers ran regular reports on new cases and deaths.

President Franklin D. Roosevelt, crippled by the virus himself, rallied the country to fight the disease. Scientists worked around the clock to find a vaccine while Americans dug into their pockets and donated change to the March of Dimes to pay for research.

The miracle Americans had been praying for came on March 26, 1953. Dr. Jonas Salk announced on a national radio show that he had successfully tested a polio vaccine. To show that it was safe, he vaccinated himself and his own family.

Salk, the son of Polish immigrants, could have become rich from his discovery. But when asked who held the patent on the vaccine, he answered: "Well, the people, I would say. There is no patent. Could you patent the sun?"

Within months, schoolchildren across the country were receiving the vaccine, and the number of polio cases began to drop. Dr. Albert Sabin developed a second polio vaccine, and the number dropped even further.

Scores of laboratories, thousands of doctors and nurses, and millions of Americans with their dimes and dollars worked together to bring an end to the summers of fear. By the close of the century, polio had been virtually eliminated in much of the world. The United States had taken on a cruel, deadly menace and won.

AMERICAN HISTORY PARADE

1885   The Eastman Dry Plate and Film Company of Rochester, New York, begins commercial production of flexible photographic film.

1953   Dr. Jonas Salk announces that he has successfully tested a vaccine against polio.

1979   At the White House, Israeli prime minister Menachem Begin and Egyptian president Anwar Sadat sign the Camp David peace treaty, brokered by President Carter, ending decades of hostilities between the two countries.

1982   Ground-breaking ceremonies are held for the Vietnam Veterans Memorial in Washington, D.C.

THE WORK OF DR. JONAS SALK, who in March 1953 announced that he had developed a polio vaccine, is one dramatic example of a revolution in medical science that, over the last hundred years, has helped people in the United States live much longer, healthier lives.

Life Expectancy

Year Born	Both Sexes	Men	Women
1900	47.3	46.3	48.3
1910	50.0	48.4	51.8
1920	54.1	53.6	54.6
1930	59.7	58.1	61.6
1940	62.9	60.8	65.2
1950	68.2	65.6	71.1
1960	69.7	66.6	73.1
1970	70.8	67.1	74.7
1980	73.7	70.0	77.4
1990	75.4	71.8	78.8
2000	77.0	74.3	79.7
2004	77.8	75.2	80.4
2006	78.1	75.4	80.7

Source: National Center for Health Statistics. Figures for 2006 are preliminary data.

AMERICAN HISTORY PARADE

1513　Spanish explorer Juan Ponce de León sights Florida.

1794　The government authorizes the creation of a permanent U.S. Navy and the construction of six frigates, including the USS *Constitution*.

1917　The Seattle Metropolitans defeat the Montreal Canadiens to become the first U.S. hockey team to win the Stanley Cup.

1939　Oregon defeats Ohio State 46–33 to win the first NCAA men's basketball tournament.

1964　The Good Friday Earthquake, the strongest known earthquake in American history, measuring 8.4 on the Richter scale, hits Alaska, killing some 130 people.

ON MARCH 28, 1800, the frigate USS *Essex* became the first American warship to round Africa's Cape of Good Hope as it sailed on a mission to escort merchant ships returning from the Dutch East Indies. Since the early days of the republic, American vessels have been venturing across the seven seas.

- In 1819 the SS *Savannah* made the first transatlantic crossing by a steam-powered ship. Rigged with sails, the *Savannah* used an auxiliary steam engine to turn paddle wheels part of the way. As it approached the Irish coast, with smoke billowing from its stack, a rescue ship rushed out to meet it, assuming it was on fire.

- Between 1826 and 1830 the sloop-of-war USS *Vincennes* became the first American warship to circumnavigate the globe, leaving New York City and traveling west by way of Cape Horn and the Cape of Good Hope.

- In 1957 the Coast Guard cutters *Spar*, *Storis*, and *Bramble* became the first American ships to circumnavigate the North American continent, traveling through the elusive Northwest Passage along the way.

- In 1958 the submarine USS *Nautilus* became the first vessel to cross the North Pole. As it sailed beneath the Arctic icepack, it broadcast the famous message "*Nautilus* 90 North."

- In 1960 the USS *Triton* became the first submarine to make a submerged circumnavigation of the globe, traveling 41,500 miles in 84 days. The *Triton* carried a plaque bearing an image reminiscent of Ferdinand Magellan's vessel and the motto *Ave nobilis dux, iterum factum est* ("Hail noble captain, it is done again").

AMERICAN HISTORY PARADE

1776   Spanish explorer Juan Bautista de Anza finds the site where the Presidio of San Francisco is later built.

1797   Nathaniel Briggs of New Hampshire patents an early washing machine.

1920   Some 380 people are killed by 38 storms in the Midwest and South in the Palm Sunday tornado outbreak of 1920.

1979   America gets a scare when the Three Mile Island nuclear power plant in Pennsylvania malfunctions; thousands flee, but no one is injured.

ON MARCH 29, 1943, the U.S. government began requiring Americans to ration fat, meat, and cheese as part of a massive national program to help win World War II. It was just one in a long series of sacrifices made on the home front.

The war could be won, President Franklin D. Roosevelt stressed, only if all Americans shared in the effort. During his second wartime fireside chat, he said that although not everyone could fight overseas, there was "one front and one battle where everyone in the United States—every man, woman, and child—is in action. . . . That front is right here at home, in our daily tasks."

That meant, in part, a rationing program to help save scarce goods for the military and distribute available items fairly. The list of rationed goods included everything from sugar, canned food, and fat (the latter used in the manufacture of explosives) to tires, bicycles, and gasoline. Each item was assigned a price in points, and Americans were given books of Ration Stamps with which to buy things.

"Yes, you can buy rationed shoes from Sears by mail," read a wartime Sears catalog. "Simply detach War Ration Stamp No. 17 from your War Ration Book No. 1 (sugar and coffee book) and pin it to your order." Some things, such as new cars and appliances, were simply not available because factories were busy churning out tanks, planes, and bombs.

People walked instead of driving and used corn syrup in place of sugar. Women went without nylon stockings, men wore "Victory" suits that used less cloth, and children learned to do without new toys. Few complained—they remembered the soldiers who were making the real sacrifice. "Do with less so they'll have enough," a poster from the Office of War Information urged. And Americans did.

AMERICAN HISTORY PARADE

1790 John Tyler, the tenth U.S. president, is born in Charles City County, Virginia.

1848 An ice jam at the source of the Niagara River causes Niagara Falls to stop flowing for the first time in recorded history.

1927 Major Henry O'Neil de Hane Segrave becomes the first man to drive faster than 200 miles per hour, on a course at Daytona Beach, Florida.

1951 Julius and Ethel Rosenberg are convicted of spying for the Soviet Union.

1973 The last U.S. troops depart South Vietnam, ending America's direct military involvement in the Vietnam War.

1974 *Mariner 10* becomes the first space probe to visit the planet Mercury and send back close-up images.

1999 The Dow Jones industrial average closes above 10,000 for the first time.

ON MARCH 30, 1981, President Ronald Reagan became the only president to survive being shot while in office, and in the process taught the nation something about meeting a crisis with grit, grace, and humor.

It happened sixty-nine days into Reagan's presidency, while he was leaving a speaking engagement at the Washington Hilton Hotel in Washington, D.C. As the president walked toward his waiting limousine, a deranged young man fired six shots, grievously wounding White House press secretary Jim Brady and hitting a police officer and Secret Service agent. Another agent shoved Reagan into the limo, and the car sped away.

At first no one realized the president had been shot. Reagan, who felt an excruciating pain, thought he'd broken a rib. He soon began coughing up blood, and the limo headed for the hospital. As he walked into the emergency room, his knees turned rubbery, and he went down.

It would be years before Americans learned how close Reagan came to dying. "He was right on the margin," one of his doctors later recalled. The assassin's bullet had ricocheted off the limo, pierced his side, and lodged close to his heart. But that night a relieved country laughed as it learned Reagan's first words to First Lady Nancy: "Honey, I forgot to duck" (a line borrowed from boxing great Jack Dempsey a half century earlier when he lost the heavyweight championship).

Reagan's sense of humor never lagged. "I hope you're a Republican," he cracked to a doctor as they wheeled him into the operating room.

The 70-year-old president returned to the White House a few days later, temporarily weakened but resolved to rededicate himself to his country. A few words in his diary speak volumes of his determination and faith. "Whatever happens now, I owe my life to God and will try to serve him in every way I can," he wrote.

AMERICAN HISTORY PARADE

1842   Dr. Crawford W. Long of Jefferson, Georgia, becomes the first U.S. physician to perform surgery using anesthesia induced by ether to kill pain.

1858   Hyman Lipman of Philadelphia patents a pencil with an attached eraser.

1867   Secretary of State William H. Seward signs an agreement to purchase Alaska from Russia for $7.2 million, about two cents an acre.

1891   Shoshone National Forest in Wyoming, the country's first national forest, is established.

1981   President Reagan is shot and seriously wounded by John W. Hinckley Jr. outside a Washington, D.C., hotel.

"JOHN FORD PASSIONATELY LOVES FREEDOM," President Nixon said on March 31, 1973. "John Ford, in his works, has depicted freedom in all of its profound depths. . . . John Ford has fought for freedom, and for that reason it is appropriate that tonight, on behalf of all of the American people, he receives the Medal of Freedom."

The son of Irish immigrants (his real name was John Martin Feeney), director John Ford gave generations of moviegoers his vision of America in dozens of beloved Hollywood films—movies such as *Young Mr. Lincoln* (1939), *The Grapes of Wrath* (1940), *The Searchers* (1956), and *The Man Who Shot Liberty Valance* (1962). But some of his work took place far from American shores.

Though already a famous director, Ford joined the Navy during World War II and put together a unit of film crews to document much of the war. In June 1942 he filmed the Battle of Midway from atop the island's powerhouse, a primary target for Japanese bombers. At one point a piece of flying concrete hit him on the head and knocked him out. He came to, grabbed his camera, and kept shooting. When shrapnel tore a hole in his arm, he kept relaying information about the battle's progress to officers on the ground.

Ford went in harm's way from the Pacific to North Africa to the Normandy coast. On D-Day, he oversaw cameramen filming the Allied invasion. After the war, while he continued his legendary Hollywood career, he held the rank of rear admiral in the U.S. Naval Reserve.

Perhaps in part because he knew the cost of freedom, Ford spent a lifetime interpreting his nation's heritage. He accepted the Presidential Medal of Freedom, one of the country's highest civilian honors, with the words, "God bless America."

AMERICAN HISTORY PARADE

1854   In Tokyo, Commodore Matthew Perry signs a treaty opening Japanese ports to American trade.

1880   Wabash, Indiana, becomes the first U.S. town with a totally electric streetlight system (four lights powered by a steam engine).

1896   Chicago inventor Whitcomb Judson patents a "hookless fastener," an early zipper.

1933   Congress establishes the Civilian Conservation Corps to help put men to work during the Depression.

1970   *Explorer I*, the first U.S. satellite, reenters the atmosphere after twelve years in orbit.

1973   President Nixon awards John Ford the Medal of Freedom.

The History of the Stars and Stripes

The early history of the Stars and Stripes is so shrouded by time and legend that facts are difficult if not impossible to pin down. No one is sure exactly what the first official Stars and Stripes looked like, who designed it, where it was first unfurled, or even whether it actually flew during any battles of the Revolutionary War.

The Meteor Flag

The United States was the rebellious child of Great Britain, so it's no surprise that the story of its flag is tied to traditions of the mother country. From **1707** until the Revolution, a British naval flag called the Meteor Flag or Red Ensign was a common sight up and down the Atlantic seaboard in colonial harbors. Flown by ships of the Royal Navy, it was red with a Union Jack (the crosses of St. George and St. Andrew, patron saints of England and Scotland) in the upper left corner.

The Grand Union Flag

As the Revolutionary War got under way, soldiers from various regions showed up to fight carrying all kinds of flags. The Patriots needed a flag that all American forces could use. The Grand Union Flag, also known as the Congress Colors, First Navy Ensign, and Cambridge Flag, emerged as the unofficial national flag during the first part of the Revolution. It was a modified British Meteor Flag with thirteen red and white stripes on its field. The stripes signified the unity of the colonies, while the Union Jack in the upper left corner paid tribute to Americans' British heritage.

The Grand Union Flag was not usually carried by troops in the field but was used more as a naval banner. On December 3, 1775, it was raised aboard the ship *Alfred* by John Paul Jones, then a Navy lieutenant. In early 1776, when the first Continental fleet put to sea with the *Alfred* as its flagship, it sailed under this banner.

The Stars and Stripes

 On June 14, 1777, the Continental Congress passed a resolution directing that "the flag of the thirteen United States be thirteen stripes, alternate red and white; that the union be thirteen stars, white in a blue field representing a new constellation." That resolution marked the birthday of the flag known to us as the Stars and Stripes, which is why we observe Flag Day on June 14 of every year. Congress replaced the Union Jack in the upper left corner of the Grand Union Flag with thirteen white stars on the blue field—a move that reaffirmed America's determination to be free of English rule.

Congress gave no hint as to proportions of the flag, size of the blue field, arrangement of the stars, or even direction of the stripes. (In fact, it wasn't until the early twentieth century that those specifications were formally defined.) Congress also never got around to supplying any official flags to the Continental Army during the Revolutionary War. The upshot was that flagmakers were left to make the national flag to their own liking, and several different designs appeared.

To this day no one is certain who made the very first Stars and Stripes. Tradition gives the honor to Philadelphia upholsterer Betsy Ross. The story goes that one day a committee made of George Washington, George Ross, and Robert Morris visited her shop to ask if she could make a flag. The visitors showed her a rough sketch, which Betsy proceeded to refine. She explained that it would be better to make stars with five points, rather than six. With a few snips of her scissors, she convinced her visitors and went on to sew the first national flag. Unfortunately, historians have not been able to find a convincing record of the incident, and most regard the story as legend.

Francis Hopkinson of New Jersey, a signer of the Declaration of Independence, has the only documented claim to being a designer of the original Stars and Stripes. He served as a congressman, chairman of the Navy board, treasurer of loans for the United States, and judge. In 1780 he submitted a claim to the government stating that he was responsible for designing, among other things, "the Flag of the United States of America," and asking for "a quarter cask of the public wine" as payment. The government never made a payment, though, and historians have never been able to nail down Hopkinson's exact role in designing the flag.

The Stars and Stripes seems to have been intended mainly for naval use, not for battles on land. The first known use on a ship came on July 4, 1777, when Captain John Paul Jones hoisted the flag on the warship *Ranger* while at Portsmouth Harbor, New Hampshire. On February 14, 1778, while at Quiberon Bay, France, Jones's ship received a nine-gun salute from the French, the first formal recognition of the American flag by a foreign power.

The 15-Stripe Flag (The Star-Spangled Banner)

On May 1, 1795, Congress added two stars and two stripes to the flag in recognition of two new states, Vermont and Kentucky. The fifteen-stripe flag was the nation's banner for nearly a quarter of a century. It was the American flag that first flew over the U.S. Capitol when Washington, D.C., became the seat of government in 1800, the flag that replaced the French flag in New Orleans when the United States made the Louisiana Purchase in 1803, and the flag that Lewis and Clark carried when they reached the Pacific Ocean after crossing the continent in 1804 and 1805.

The fifteen-stripe flag was also the one U.S. ships and fortresses flew during the War of 1812. When the British navy attacked Baltimore on September 13, 1814, a giant flag stitched together by seamstress Mary Young Pickersgill was waving over Fort McHenry, which guarded the city's harbor. In the dawn's early light of September 14, 1814, Washington lawyer Francis Scott Key caught sight of the flag still streaming over the fort's ramparts and realized the Americans had withstood the bombardment. Overcome with emotion, Key began scribbling some verses on the back of a letter. An anthem was born, and the fifteen-striped flag was soon known as the Star-Spangled Banner.

Within a few years it was obvious that adding a stripe to the flag for every new state was going to be awkward. In 1818 Congress passed an act creating the third official version of the Stars and Stripes. It directed that the flag revert to thirteen stripes symbolizing the original thirteen colonies, and that a star for each new state be added to the flag on the Fourth of July after each admission. This practice has been followed ever since. No star is specifically identified with any state. The third Stars and Stripes carried thirteen stripes and twenty stars.

THE FORTY-EIGHT-STAR FLAG

The nation added 28 stars over the next 94 years as the United States expanded west. On July 4, 1912, the flag received its 47th and 48th stars after New Mexico and Arizona joined the union. The 48-star flag lasted for the next 47 years, longer than any other version of the Stars and Stripes to that time. It flew through World War I, the Roaring Twenties, the Great Depression, World War II, and the beginning of the Cold War.

THE FIFTY-STAR FLAG

In 1959 the flag received a 49th star for Alaska, and on July 4, 1960, a 50-star flag was hoisted over Fort McHenry near Baltimore to honor the admission of Hawaii. Nine years later, on July 20, 1969, *Apollo* 11 astronauts Neil Armstrong and Buzz Aldrin planted the 50-star flag on the moon. A thin rod ran across its top to make the fabric stand out in the airless atmosphere.

APRIL

THE BEGINNING OF APRIL brings the start of baseball season. Where did the "great American pastime" come from?

Contrary to popular lore, Abner Doubleday did not invent baseball in Cooperstown, New York. Doubleday never claimed to be the inventor, and there is no reliable record connecting him to the game.

Who did invent baseball, then? Lots of people, over many years. It apparently developed from an old English game called *rounders*, which New Englanders played in colonial days. In rounders, players hit the ball with a bat and ran around bases. Fielders threw the ball at runners, and if it hit a runner who was off base, he was out (a custom known as "soaking" or "plugging" the runner).

In the early days of the republic, Americans gradually transformed rounders into a game sometimes called "town ball" (because it was played on town greens in New England), "barn ball," "base ball," and several other names. Exactly how the game was played varied from place to place.

New York City businessman Alexander Cartwright (pictured above) is often called the father of organized baseball. In 1845 he founded the Knickerbocker Base Ball Club of New York and wrote a set of rules for the game. Some of those rules were very different from the ones we know today. Pitchers had to throw underhanded. Catching a ball on the first bounce got the batter out. And a team had to score 21 runs (called "aces") to win a game.

Soldiers in Northern and Southern armies played baseball during the Civil War. Afterward they took the sport home with them, and Americans went crazy for it. Soon baseball clubs were forming all over the country, and the game quickly became the national pastime.

AMERICAN HISTORY PARADE

1789 In New York City, the U.S. House of Representatives holds its first full meeting and elects Frederick Muhlenberg of Pennsylvania as its first Speaker.

1865 Union troops win a victory at the Battle of Five Forks, Virginia, causing Robert E. Lee to tell Jefferson Davis that Petersburg and Richmond must be evacuated.

1945 American troops begin landing on the island of Okinawa in the largest amphibious assault in the Pacific during World War II.

1954 The U.S. Air Force Academy in Colorado Springs, Colorado, is established.

1960 *Tiros I*, the world's first weather satellite, is launched from Cape Canaveral.

1996 Fast-food chain Taco Bell announces it has bought the Liberty Bell and renamed it the Taco Liberty Bell, and thousands believe the April Fool's Day prank.

FLORIDIANS OBSERVE APRIL 2 as Pascua Florida Day, the day in 1513 that Spanish adventurer Juan Ponce de León made the first known landing in Florida by a European explorer.

Ponce de León, born to a noble family in Spain, first came to the New World in 1493 with Christopher Columbus's second expedition. He later conquered Puerto Rico and became its first governor. According to tradition, it was there that the Indians told him of an island to the west blessed with not only gold but a magical spring that restored youth and cured illnesses.

In 1513 the eager conquistador sailed from Puerto Rico with three ships to find the island, its gold, and its miraculous fountain. On April 2 he stepped onto a beach somewhere near present-day St. Augustine (the exact spot is uncertain) and claimed the land for Spain. He named it "Florida" because he arrived at Easter time, which the Spaniards called Pascua Florida, the Feast of the Flowers.

The Spaniards sailed around the southern end of Florida, which they still took to be a giant island, and up the west coast. Finding neither gold nor the mysterious fountain of youth, they returned to Puerto Rico.

Eight years later, Ponce de León made a second trip to Florida, this time determined to found a settlement. He landed on the west coast with some two hundred men, horses, cattle, and supplies, but the Spaniards soon found themselves at war with Calusa Indians who shot poison arrows. One of the arrows struck Ponce de León, and the entire expedition fled for Cuba, where the tough old conquistador soon died. He was buried in Puerto Rico, the words "Here rest the bones of a lion" inscribed on his tomb. So ended the legendary search for the fountain of youth.

AMERICAN HISTORY PARADE

1513   Spanish explorer Juan Ponce de León lands in Florida.

1865   Confederate president Jefferson Davis and most of his cabinet flee Richmond, Virginia, as Union troops draw near the capital.

1902   The Electric Theater, the first American theater devoted to showing motion pictures, opens in Los Angeles.

1917   Woodrow Wilson calls for a declaration of war against Germany, saying, "The world must be made safe for democracy."

1953   The journal *Nature* publishes a paper by British scientist Francis Crick and American scientist James Watson, describing a double helix structure for DNA.

AT THE CLOSE OF WORLD WAR II, Europe lay in shambles. Cities and factories were shattered, businesses had disappeared, and countless people faced hunger. Economies sat on the verge of total collapse. The poverty and desperation that threatened the continent made fertile breeding grounds for would-be dictators.

Americans were weary from war, but they also understood that they had to do something to help. On April 3, 1948, President Truman signed into law a program that provided billions of dollars in aid to help Europe get back on its feet. Dubbed "the Marshall Plan" for Secretary of State George C. Marshall, who first announced it, the program was a massive act of compassion as well as a shrewd strategy to keep Communism at bay, support democratic governments, and build strong trading partners.

The United States offered the aid not just to its former allies but to its former enemies, such as Germany. It also offered to include the Soviet Union, a proposal Joseph Stalin rejected. The Soviet dictator refused to allow Eastern European countries to participate. (Czechoslovakia's foreign minister publicly expressed interest in the plan, and a short time later he was found dead in front of his house.)

But Western European nations welcomed the offer. The British foreign secretary called it "a lifeline to sinking men." Thirteen billion dollars in aid poured into Western Europe to help buy machinery, modernize factories, repair railroads, and rebuild cities. With American help, Western Europe was soon on its way to a remarkable recovery.

If it was not "the most unsordid act in history"—Winston Churchill reserved that title for the United States' earlier Lend-Lease program—the Marshall Plan was surely an act of enormous generosity. Never before had one nation done so much to help mend a war-torn world.

AMERICAN HISTORY PARADE

1860   The Pony Express begins service between St. Joseph, Missouri, and Sacramento, California.

1865   Union forces capture the Confederate capital of Richmond, Virginia.

1882   The outlaw Jesse James is shot and killed in St. Joseph, Missouri, by Robert Ford, a member of his own gang.

1948   President Truman signs legislation establishing the Marshall Plan.

1973   In New York City, Motorola engineer Martin Cooper makes the first call on a portable, handheld cell phone, which he'd just invented.

1974   One of the worst tornado outbreaks in U.S. history strikes, with 148 twisters hitting thirteen states, killing 330 people.

ON THE EVENING OF APRIL 4, 1968, thirty-nine-year-old Rev. Martin Luther King Jr. was struck down by an assassin's bullet while standing on a motel balcony in Memphis, Tennessee.

King had been receiving death threats for more than a decade, but he never shied away from making public appearances. The night before his death, he had spoken at a Memphis church. "We've got some difficult days ahead, but it really doesn't matter with me now, because I've been to the mountaintop," he said. "And I don't mind. Like anybody, I would like to live a long life. Longevity has its place. But I'm not concerned about that now. I just want to do God's will. And he's allowed me to go up to the mountain, and I've looked over, and I've seen the Promised Land. I may not get there with you, but I want you to know tonight that we as a people will get to the Promised Land."

The following evening, Dr. King was leaning over a balcony railing at the Lorraine Motel, where he was staying, when a shot sounded, and he fell dead. James Earl Ray, a drifter and escaped convict, was convicted of the assassination.

As reports of King's murder were broadcast, riots broke out in hundreds of cities and towns. In some places looting and burning continued for days until the National Guard restored order.

Those were times when America felt like a runaway-train ride. But even as millions mourned the loss of an extraordinary leader, they redoubled their efforts to make their country a place of which King would be proud.

A memorial plaque at the site of the assassination quotes Genesis 37:19–20. It reads: "They said one to another, Behold, here cometh the dreamer. Let us slay him and we shall see what becomes of his dreams." The inscription challenges each of us to "see what will become of his dreams."

AMERICAN HISTORY PARADE

1841   President William Henry Harrison dies of pneumonia one month after his inauguration.

1850   The city of Los Angeles is incorporated.

1887   Susanna M. Salter of Argonia, Kansas, becomes the first woman elected mayor of an American town.

1949   The United States and eleven other Western nations sign a treaty creating the North Atlantic Treaty Organization (NATO).

1968   The Reverend Martin Luther King Jr., age 39, is assassinated in Memphis, Tennessee.

ON THIS DAY IN 1860, two "young, skinny, wiry fellows" were galloping on fast horses across the great Western frontier, one headed west and the other east, on the very first run of the Pony Express.

Before the Pony Express, it took weeks if not months for letters to get between eastern and western parts of the country. ("Can somebody tell us what has become of the U. S. mail for this section of the world?" the *Los Angeles Star* asked in 1853, noting that it had been "some four weeks since it has arrived.") The Pony Express promised delivery between St. Joseph, Missouri, the western terminal of the nation's rail system, and Sacramento, California, in ten days or less.

The Pony Express network was a masterpiece of organization covering a 1,966-mile route, with 190 relay stations set 10 to 15 miles apart. A rider carrying up to 20 pounds of mail galloped as fast as he could to the next station, where he leapt onto a fresh horse and headed on. About every eight stations, a new rider took over. The system used 400 horses and 80 riders, who were each paid $25 a week to face empty wilderness, howling blizzards, scorching sun, and occasional Indian attacks. It is said that a Pony Express advertisement read, "Wanted: Young, skinny, wiry fellows not over 18. Must be expert riders willing to risk death daily. Orphans preferred."

The first riders left St. Joseph and Sacramento on April 3, 1860. On April 13 the westbound mail arrived in Sacramento, beating the eastbound delivery by two days.

Ten days to cross the West was like lightning in 1860, but the era of the Pony Express was to be short-lived. On October 24, 1861, the transcontinental telegraph opened. Two days later, the Pony Express went out of business and passed into American legend.

AMERICAN HISTORY PARADE

1614   Indian princess Pocahontas and Jamestown, Virginia, colonist John Rolfe are married.

1621   The *Mayflower* sets sail from Plymouth, Massachusetts, to return to England.

1792   George Washington casts the first presidential veto, rejecting a bill to apportion representatives among the states.

1933   Dr. Evarts A. Graham performs the first operation to remove a lung in St. Louis, Missouri.

1984   Kareem Abdul-Jabbar becomes the highest-scoring NBA player, with 31,421 career points (later retiring with 38,387 points).

"STARS AND STRIPES NAILED TO THE POLE" an exuberant Robert Peary telegraphed from Labrador, Canada, announcing that he had reached a goal long sought by explorers—the North Pole.

Peary, a 52-year-old U.S. Navy commander, had made several arctic expeditions and two failed attempts to reach the Pole. He had spent years learning from the native Inuit the best ways to dress in furs, build igloos, and drive sledges over the ice. On one trip he had lost eight toes to frostbite. But he was determined, he said, "to hurl myself, time after time, against the frigid *No* of the Great North."

On March 1, 1909, Peary set out from his base camp on Ellesmere Island, 413 miles from the Pole. His team counted 24 men, 19 sledges, and 133 dogs. With him was his longtime assistant, Matthew Henson, an expert explorer in his own right.

For weeks the men battled roaring winds and temperatures of -50° F. They hacked trails across rough patches, floundered in snowdrifts, and hauled their sledges across ridges of ice. At times channels of water suddenly opened before them. They waited for the water to refreeze, then scampered over the thin ice.

Peary, Henson, and four Inuit made the final, 133-mile part of the trek. On April 6 Peary calculated that they had reached their goal. "The pole at last!" he wrote in his diary. "The prize of three centuries."

Over the decades, some critics have questioned whether Peary actually made it as far as the North Pole. And for years Henson, who was black, received scant recognition for his role. But today the two men are generally credited as the first to reach the Pole. Both are buried in Arlington National Cemetery. Peary's gravesite is inscribed with his motto: "I shall find a way or make one."

AMERICAN HISTORY PARADE

1841   John Tyler is sworn in as the tenth U.S. president, becoming the first vice president to succeed a president who died in office (William Henry Harrison).

1862   The Battle of Shiloh in Tennessee, one of the bloodiest of the Civil War, begins.

1889   George Eastman begins selling the Kodak camera.

1909   Robert Peary and Matthew Henson reach the North Pole.

1917   The U.S. formally declares war on Germany and enters World War I.

1938   Researcher Roy Plunkett accidentally discovers polytetrafluoroethylene, better known as Teflon.

ON APRIL 7, 1862, two dozen men met near Shelbyville, Tennessee, to hatch one of the most audacious schemes of the Civil War: slip deep behind Confederate lines into Georgia, steal a locomotive, and run it north to Chattanooga, destroying track along the way to cut a vital Southern supply line.

"Boys, we're going into danger," Union spy James Andrews warned, "but for results that can be tremendous."

The raiders, mostly Union soldiers in civilian clothes, made their way to Marietta, Georgia, where they boarded a northbound train pulled by the locomotive the *General*. When it stopped at Big Shanty, where the crew got off for breakfast, the raiders uncoupled the passenger cars and steamed away pulling three empty boxcars. The *General's* astonished conductor and two others sprinted after them. The Great Locomotive Chase was on.

Andrews's raiders chugged north, stopping every once in a while to tear up track and cut telegraph wires. The pursuers kept on their tail, first on foot, then on a handcart, then an engine. When they met torn-up track or obstructions, they ran ahead and jumped onto another engine. Running the locomotive *Texas* backward, they caught up with the *General*. Anderson tried uncoupling boxcars and throwing rail ties onto the tracks to stop the *Texas*, but 87 miles into the chase, the *General* ran out of fuel.

"Every man for himself!" Anderson ordered, and the raiders scattered. Within a week, they'd all been captured. Several, including Anderson, were hanged as spies. The rest eventually escaped or were exchanged for Confederate prisoners.

In March 1863, six of the raiders met with Secretary of War Edwin Stanton, who explained that Congress had created a new medal to honor valor. "Your party shall have the first," he said as he pinned one onto Pvt. Jacob Parrott—the first-ever recipient of the Medal of Honor, the nation's highest military decoration.

AMERICAN HISTORY PARADE

1862   Union forces commanded by General Ulysses S. Grant defeat Confederates at the Battle of Shiloh in Tennessee.

1927   An audience in New York watches Commerce Secretary Herbert Hoover read a speech in Washington, D.C., in the first demonstration of long-distance television transmission.

1959   Scientists at Los Alamos, New Mexico, produce the first atomic-generated electricity.

1970   John Wayne wins his only Oscar for his role in *True Grit*.

"MY MOTTO WAS ALWAYS to keep swinging. Whether I was in a slump or feeling badly or having trouble off the field, the only thing to do was keep swinging."

That was Henry Aaron's approach to baseball and life, especially in the early 1970s, when "Hammerin' Hank" was playing for the Atlanta Braves and getting close to overtaking Babe Ruth as the all-time home-run leader. As he grew closer to the record-breaking 715 mark, the hate mail began to arrive, and what should have been the best time of his life turned into an ordeal.

Some people couldn't stand the thought of a black man taking Ruth's place as the home-run king. There were thousands of malicious letters. "You will be the most hated man in this country." "You're black so you have no business being here." Even death threats. "I'D LIKE TO KILL YOU!! BANG BANG YOUR DEAD. P.S. It mite happen."

He just kept swinging through the ugliness, quietly carrying on the work of Jackie Robinson, who had first broken baseball's color barrier, and taking comfort from the flood of fan mail urging him on.

On April 8, 1974, Henry Aaron stepped up to the plate in Atlanta and hammered number 715 over the left centerfield wall. As he rounded the bases, millions of Americans cheered. Few realized the full extent of the gauntlet he'd run. But his dignity and perseverance were evident. President Nixon may have said it best: "When I think of Hank Aaron, I think of power and poise, of courage and consistency. But most of all, I think of a true gentleman, an outstanding citizen. On the field and off, Hank Aaron represents America at its very best."

AMERICAN HISTORY PARADE

1913   The Seventeenth Amendment, which requires senators to be elected by direct popular vote, is ratified.

1952   President Truman orders the seizure of the nation's steel mills to avert a strike, an act later ruled illegal by the Supreme Court.

1974   Hank Aaron hits his 715th home run, breaking Babe Ruth's record.

1975   Frank Robinson of the Cleveland Indians makes his debut as the first black manager of a major league baseball team.

THE CIVIL WAR CAME TO AN END, for all practical purposes, in April 1865 when Robert E. Lee's starving, exhausted Confederate army found itself hemmed in by Union forces in Virginia. On April 9 Lee met with General Ulysses S. Grant in a farmhouse at Appomattox Court House to offer his surrender. Grant's terms were generous: the Southern soldiers were to be pardoned and could go home with their private property, including their horses, which could be used for a late spring planting. Officers could keep their side arms, and Lee's hungry troops would receive Union rations. "This will have the best possible effect upon the men," Lee observed quietly.

Three days later the formal surrender took place as Confederate troops marched forward to stack their weapons and lay down their flags. The Union officer in charge of the ceremony was Joshua Chamberlain, a hero of Gettysburg. Leading the Southerners was General John B. Gordon, who had been wounded many times in combat.

Chamberlain watched Gordon approaching. As he later described it, "The General was riding in advance of his troops, his chin drooped to his breast, downhearted and dejected in appearance almost beyond description." Something stirred in Chamberlain's breast. He gave an order, a bugle call sounded, and his men came to attention with their rifles on their shoulders. It was a salute of honor.

General Gordon looked up in surprise. Recognizing the gesture, he wheeled his horse, dipped his sword, and ordered his own men to return the salute. Lee's defeated veterans stepped forward with heads high and eyes level—honor saluting honor.

Then it was over. The Union had been tested and had survived. With a salute of soldierly respect, the nation's wounds began to heal. Both sides faced a new beginning as Americans all.

AMERICAN HISTORY PARADE

1682   Sieur de La Salle claims the Mississippi River valley for France.

1865   Robert E. Lee surrenders his Confederate army to Ulysses S. Grant.

1939   Black singer Marian Anderson performs for 75,000 people at the Lincoln Memorial in Washington, D.C., after her concert at Constitution Hall is cancelled because of her race.

1942   Seventy-five thousand starving American and Filipino defenders on the Bataan Peninsula in the Philippines are surrendered to the Japanese.

2003   In Baghdad, Iraqis and U.S. soldiers celebrate the fall of Saddam Hussein by toppling a giant statue of the dictator.

ANDREW JACKSON, the first U.S. president born in a log cabin, was the son of poor Scots-Irish immigrants who scratched a living from the soil of the South Carolina backcountry. His father died about two weeks before he was born, leaving the strong-willed mother, Elizabeth, to raise the Jackson boys. During the Revolutionary War, 13-year-old Andy joined the Patriot militia as an orderly and courier.

On April 10, 1781, the militia had gathered at a Presbyterian church when British troops surprised them. Andy and his brother Robert escaped into the woods, only to be captured the next morning at a nearby cabin. A Tory officer ordered Andy to clean his boots, and the fiery boy shot back: "Sir, I am a prisoner of war and claim to be treated as such!" The furious officer brought his sword down on the young Patriot's head, leaving a scar he carried the rest of his life.

He grew up with the frontier—saddlemaker, schoolteacher, lawyer, planter, land speculator, Indian fighter, U.S. congressman, senator, judge, general, hero of the Battle of New Orleans. "He knew little grammar and many scars, few classics and many fast horses," the writer Carl Sandburg observed.

While a judge in Tennessee, he sent a succession of deputies to apprehend a huge man wanted for a heinous crime. They all returned empty-handed, so Jackson himself arrested the criminal. Asked why he finally surrendered, the man said, "I looked him in the eye, and I saw shoot. And there wasn't shoot in nary other eye in the crowd."

When Old Hickory was elected the seventh U.S. president, frontiersmen rode hundreds of miles to join the inaugural party, overrunning the White House with muddy boots. Refined ladies and gents said it was the beginning of mob rule. Jackson knew better. He knew it was just American democracy on its way to growing up.

AMERICAN HISTORY PARADE

1606   King James I of England charters the London Company to establish settlements in North America.

1781   In South Carolina, young Andrew Jackson is part of a Patriot militia band ambushed by the British.

1849   Walter Hunt of New York City patents the safety pin.

1925   *The Great Gatsby* by F. Scott Fitzgerald is published.

1942   The Japanese begin the Bataan Death March, a brutal 90-mile forced march of Filipino and American soldiers on the Bataan Peninsula to POW camps.

ON APRIL 11, 1970, *Apollo* 13 lifted off from Cape Canaveral carrying astronauts Jim Lovell, Fred Haise, and Jack Swigert on what was supposed to be the third U.S. mission to the moon. Fifty-six hours into the flight, an explosion inside a liquid oxygen tank rocked the ship.

"Houston, we've had a problem," Swigert reported to Mission Control.

At once the spacecraft began to lose power. Lovell looked out a porthole and saw a catastrophe in the making. "We are venting something . . . into space," he radioed.

The ship was losing oxygen used to generate power. The spacecraft was dying—200,000 miles from home.

To save power in the Command Module, the astronauts squeezed into the frigid Lunar Module and used it as a lifeboat. Their best shot at getting home was to loop around the moon and swing back toward Earth. On their current path they'd miss the planet by 4,000 miles. They fired the Lunar Module's engines to put them back on course.

The next three days became a race to solve one problem after another. When carbon dioxide threatened to kill the astronauts, they rigged air scrubbers with tape, plastic, and cardboard. They didn't trust the ship's damaged system to navigate, so they steered by the sun and Earth. To save coolant water, they drank only six ounces a day.

As they approached Earth, they climbed back into the Command Module and separated from the rest of the ship. "There's one whole side of that spacecraft missing!" a stunned Lovell reported, looking out a window.

Mission Control feared the capsule's heat shield had been damaged, but on April 17, *Apollo* 13 splashed down safely in the Pacific just three miles from the carrier *Iwo Jima*. A failed mission had turned into one of NASA's finest hours.

AMERICAN HISTORY PARADE

1945   American troops liberate the Buchenwald concentration camp in Germany.

1947   Jackie Robinson becomes the first black baseball player in the major leagues when he plays an exhibition game as a Brooklyn Dodger.

1951   President Truman relieves General Douglas MacArthur of command for publicly criticizing his Korean War policy.

ON APRIL 12, 1861, at 3:30 a.m., one old friend received a message from another: surrender at once, or be fired upon "in one hour from this time."

The sender of the message was General P. G. T. Beauregard, a Louisianan who had been ordered by the newly formed Confederate government to take Fort Sumter in Charleston harbor, South Carolina. Beauregard had trained at the U.S. Military Academy at West Point and gone on to become superintendent there, but had resigned after his home state seceded from the Union.

Commanding Fort Sumter was Beauregard's old instructor at West Point, Major Robert Anderson, a Kentuckian who felt heartsick at the thought of war between North and South. Beauregard had been one of his finest pupils, and the two had grown fond of each other. Yet Anderson would not surrender, at least not without a fight. His commander in chief, Abraham Lincoln, had pledged to "hold, occupy, and possess" the fort. "If we do not meet again on earth, I hope we may meet in Heaven," Anderson told Beauregard's emissaries.

At 4:30 a.m., the Civil War began as Beauregard's batteries let loose, encircling the fort with a ring of fire, pounding it with more than 4,000 shells. When they shot the American flag off its staff, Sergeant Peter Hart climbed up and nailed it on again. But after thirty-three hours of furious bombardment, Anderson was forced to surrender.

With the victors' permission, Anderson gave the Stars and Stripes a fifty-gun salute before hauling it down. During the salute, an accidental explosion killed a soldier—the only fatality of the seige. Major Anderson carried the shredded flag with him as he boarded a ship and headed north. Beauregard waited until he had gone before entering Fort Sumter, as "it would be an unhonorable thing . . . to be present at the humiliation of his friend."

AMERICAN HISTORY PARADE

1776   North Carolina issues the Halifax Resolves, the first act by a colony authorizing its Continental Congress delegates to vote for independence.

1811   Settlers sponsored by John Jacob Astor establish the first American outpost in the Pacific Northwest near present-day Astoria, Oregon.

1861   The Civil War begins at Fort Sumter in Charleston, South Carolina.

1934   The strongest wind gust on record, 231 miles per hour, hits Mount Washington, New Hampshire.

1945   Franklin D. Roosevelt dies of a cerebral hemorrhage in Warm Springs, Georgia.

1981   The first manned space shuttle flight begins as *Columbia* blasts off from Cape Canaveral, Florida.

THOMAS JEFFERSON, author of the Declaration of Independence and third president of the United States, was born this day in 1743 in Goochland (now Albemarle) County, Virginia. One of the most eloquent tributes to Jefferson came on this same day in 1943, during World War II, when Franklin D. Roosevelt dedicated the Jefferson Memorial in Washington, D.C.:

Today, in the midst of a great war for freedom, we dedicate a shrine to freedom. . . .

[Jefferson] faced the fact that men who will not fight for liberty can lose it. We, too, have faced that fact. . . .

He lived in a world in which freedom of conscience and freedom of mind were battles still to be fought through—not principles already accepted of all men. We, too, have lived in such a world. . . .

He loved peace and loved liberty—yet on more than one occasion he was forced to choose between them. We, too, have been compelled to make that choice. . . .

The Declaration of Independence and the very purposes of the American Revolution itself, while seeking freedoms, called for the abandonment of privileges. . . .

Thomas Jefferson believed, as we believe, in Man. He believed, as we believe, that men are capable of their own government, and that no king, no tyrant, no dictator can govern for them as well as they can govern for themselves.

He believed, as we believe, in certain inalienable rights. He, as we, saw those principles and freedoms challenged. He fought for them, as we fight for them. . . .

The words which we have chosen for this Memorial speak Jefferson's noblest and most urgent meaning, and we are proud indeed to understand it and share it:

"I have sworn, upon the altar of God, eternal hostility against every form of tyranny over the mind of man."

AMERICAN HISTORY PARADE

1743   Thomas Jefferson, the third U.S. president, is born in Albemarle County, Virginia.

1830   In Washington, President Andrew Jackson gives a famous toast during a time of sectional strife: "Our Federal Union: It must be preserved."

1861   After 33 hours of bombardment, Union-held Fort Sumter in Charleston, South Carolina, surrenders to Confederate forces.

1970   The moon-bound *Apollo 13* spacecraft is crippled when an oxygen tank explodes.

1997   Tiger Woods, age twenty-one, becomes the youngest person to win the Masters Tournament in Augusta, Georgia.

APRIL 14 • "I WANT TO MAKE SURE EVERYONE MAKES IT
HOME ALIVE"

ONE DAY, AS MARINE CORPORAL Jason Dunham and his buddies swapped talk in their barracks in Iraq, the conversation turned to the best way to survive a hand grenade attack. The corporal suggested covering a grenade with a Kevlar helmet. "I'll bet a Kevlar would stop it," he said.

Dunham, raised in the small town of Scio, New York, was a 22-year-old with a natural gift for leadership. He'd been a star athlete, setting a Scio Central School baseball record for highest batting average. Now a rifle squad leader, he'd extended his enlistment to stay with his comrades in Iraq.

On April 14, 2004, Dunham was on his way to help a Marine convoy that had been ambushed in western Iraq when an insurgent leaped from a car and attacked him. As two Marines rushed to help wrestle the man to the ground, they heard Dunham yell, "No, no, no—watch his hand!" Before they realized what was happening, Dunham threw his helmet and his own body over a live enemy grenade.

The sacrifice helped contain the blast but left Dunham mortally wounded. He died eight days later at the National Naval Medical Center in Bethesda, Maryland.

In January 2007 President George W. Bush awarded the Medal of Honor posthumously to Jason Dunham. "Corporal Dunham saved the lives of two of his men, and showed the world what it means to be a Marine," the president said. He was the first Marine to earn the Medal of Honor for service in Iraq.

Journalist Michael Phillips, author of *The Gift of Valor*, wrote that shortly before leaving for the Persian Gulf, Dunham told friends of his plans to extend his enlistment.

"You're crazy for extending," a fellow Marine had said. "Why?"

"I want to make sure everyone makes it home alive," Jason Dunham answered.

AMERICAN HISTORY PARADE

1828 The first edition of Noah Webster's *American Dictionary of the English Language* is published.

1865 John Wilkes Booth assassinates Abraham Lincoln at Ford's Theater in Washington, D.C.

1939 *The Grapes of Wrath* by John Steinbeck is published.

1956 The first commercial videotape recorder is demonstrated simultaneously in Redwood City, California, and Chicago.

1981 America's first operational space shuttle, *Columbia*, completes its first flight.

IN APRIL 1910 Theodore Roosevelt gave a speech in Paris in which he reflected on patriotism in a world that was just beginning to resemble what we today might call a "global village." A century later, his words are worth pondering.

> I believe that a man must be a good patriot before he can be, and as the only possible way of being, a good citizen of the world. Experience teaches us that the average man who protests that his international feeling swamps his national feeling, that he does not care for his country because he cares so much for mankind, in actual practice proves himself the foe of mankind; that the man who says that he does not care to be a citizen of any one country, because he is a citizen of the world, is in very fact usually an exceedingly undesirable citizen of whatever corner of the world he happens at the moment to be in. . . . [I]f a man can view his own country and all other countries from the same level with tepid indifference, it is wise to distrust him, just as it is wise to distrust the man who can take the same dispassionate view of his wife and his mother. However broad and deep a man's sympathies, however intense his activities, he need have no fear that they will be cramped by love of his native land.
>
> Now, this does not mean in the least that a man should not wish to do good outside of his native land. On the contrary, just as I think that the man who loves his family is more apt to be a good neighbor than the man who does not, so I think that the most useful member of the family of nations is normally a strongly patriotic nation.

AMERICAN HISTORY PARADE

1850   The city of San Francisco is incorporated by California's legislature.

1865   Andrew Johnson takes the oath as the seventeenth U.S. president a few hours after Abraham Lincoln dies.

1892   The General Electric Company is established.

1912   The British liner *Titanic* sinks en route from Southampton, England, to New York City, killing approximately 1,500 people.

1955   Ray Kroc opens his first McDonald's restaurant in Des Plaines, Illinois.

HARRIET QUIMBY WAS ALREADY A JOURNALIST, theater critic, photographer, and screenwriter when she convinced an aviator to teach her to fly. In 1911, eight years after the Wright brothers' first flight, she became the first woman in the United States to earn a pilot's license. On April 16, 1912, she became the first woman to pilot a plane across the English Channel. Amelia Earhart later described Quimby's fragile craft as "hardly more than a winged skeleton with a motor." Quimby wrote about her flight from Dover to the French coast in *Leslie's Illustrated Weekly*:

> In a moment I was in the air, climbing steadily in a long circle. . . . In an instant I was beyond the cliffs and over the channel. . . . Then the quickening fog obscured my view. Calais was out of sight. I could not see ahead of me or at all below. There was only one thing for me to do and that was to keep my eyes fixed on my compass.
>
> My hands were covered with long Scotch woolen gloves which gave me good protection from the cold and fog; but the machine was wet and my face was so covered with dampness that I had to push my goggles up on my forehead. I could not see through them. I was traveling at over a mile a minute. The distance straight across from Dover to Calais is only twenty-five miles, and I knew that land must be in sight if I could only get below the fog and see it. So I dropped from an altitude of about two thousand feet until I was half that height. The sunlight struck upon my face and my eyes lit upon the white and sandy shores of France.

Quimby's daring flight helped earn her the epithet "America's First Lady of the Air." Tragically, less than three months after her historic flight, she died in a flying accident near Boston.

AMERICAN HISTORY PARADE

1789   President-elect George Washington leaves Mount Vernon for his inauguration in New York City.

1862   Abraham Lincoln signs a bill ending slavery in the District of Columbia.

1912   Harriet Quimby becomes the first woman to fly across the English Channel.

1947   Much of Texas City, Texas, is destroyed when a ship carrying fertilizer blows up in its harbor, killing nearly 600 people.

1963   Martin Luther King Jr. writes his "Letter from Birmingham Jail" while incarcerated for protesting against segregation.

2007   The deadliest school shooting in U.S. history leaves 33 dead at Virginia Tech in Blacksburg, Virginia.

ON APRIL 17, 1942, the aircraft carrier USS *Hornet* steamed west across the Pacific, several hundred miles from Japan. Lashed to its deck were sixteen B-25 bombers—planes never before launched from a carrier on a combat mission. Their secret target: Tokyo.

In the four months after Pearl Harbor, Japan's forces had surged across the Pacific. The Japanese were confident their nation was safe from attack. Lt. Col. James H. "Jimmy" Doolittle and 79 other airmen were determined to prove them wrong with a surprise air attack from the sea. They knew they would not have enough fuel to return to the *Hornet,* so they planned to land in China after dropping their bombs.

Early on April 18, a Japanese patrol boat spotted the task force, and Doolittle realized he must launch earlier than planned. His airmen had spent months training but had never taken off at sea. In the midst of a howling storm, Doolittle got his plane off the pitching deck and into the air, with the other B-25s following.

The bombers roared toward Japan, just twenty feet above the waves to avoid detection. The attack was a complete surprise—many Japanese waved as the bombers flew overhead, not dreaming they could be Allied aircraft. The raiders quickly dropped their bombs on Tokyo and other targets and sped away.

Doolittle and his crews continued toward China, where they crash-landed or parachuted from their planes as they ran out of fuel. One bomber landed in Russia. Most of the men eventually made it home with the help of Chinese who hid them from the Japanese. The Japanese did capture several airmen, executing three and starving one to death.

The audacious raid did little physical damage, but it stunned the Japanese. News of Jimmy Doolittle's "thirty seconds over Tokyo" electrified Americans and helped turn the tide of the war in the Pacific.

AMERICAN HISTORY PARADE

1492   Christopher Columbus signs a contract with Spain, giving him a commission to seek a westward route to the Indies.

1524   Italian navigator Giovanni da Verrazano, exploring for France, becomes the first European to sail into New York Harbor.

1861   Virginia secedes from the Union.

1961   Some 1,200 American-backed Cuban exiles launch the Bay of Pigs invasion, a failed attempt to overthrow Fidel Castro's Communist dictatorship.

1970   The *Apollo 13* astronauts return safely to Earth, four days after an onboard explosion crippled their spacecraft.

APRIL 18, 1775, brought the most famous ride in American history. With the colonies near open rebellion, British general Thomas Gage ordered 700 troops to march from Boston to Concord that night to seize the militia's military supplies and to arrest Patriot leaders Samuel Adams and John Hancock. The British had hoped to move in secret, but Patriot spies were everywhere, and soon silversmith Paul Revere was galloping through the night, spreading the alarm "for the country folk to be up and to arm," as Henry Wadsworth Longfellow put it in his famous poem.

There are several misconceptions about Revere's ride, thanks in part to Longfellow's verse. One is that Revere waited for a signal lantern to be hung in the tower of the Old North Church to know how the redcoats were moving—one if by land, two if "by sea" (across the Charles River). In fact, Revere himself directed the signal be set to warn other Patriots in the area. Another misconception is that Revere galloped along calling, "The British are coming!" He would not have yelled that, since the colonists still thought of themselves as British. More likely, he called something like "The regulars are coming out!"

Revere reached Lexington and warned Hancock and Adams of the danger. With that mission accomplished, he jumped back onto his horse and set out for Concord, though he never got that far. A British patrol captured him, but a companion escaped and rode to Concord to alert the Patriots there.

The British questioned Revere and let him go. By then the warning had flown from village to village. Hundreds of colonists quickly armed themselves. When the redcoats reached Lexington at dawn, the minutemen were waiting.

AMERICAN HISTORY PARADE

1775   Paul Revere makes his famous ride from Boston to Lexington.

1861   As the Civil War approaches, Colonel Robert E. Lee is offered command of the Union armies, an offer he turns down.

1906   The Great San Francisco Earthquake rocks the Bay Area, setting off fires and ultimately destroying most of the city and killing 3,000 people.

1942   Sixteen B-25s led by Lt. Col. James H. Doolittle take off from the aircraft carrier USS *Hornet* and bomb Tokyo.

1978   The U.S. Senate votes to turn the Panama Canal over to Panama by the year 2000.

1983   A suicide bombing by the terrorist group Hezbollah kills 63 people at the U.S. Embassy in Beirut, Lebanon.

ON APRIL 19, 1775, the American Revolution began in the villages of Lexington and Concord near Boston, Massachusetts.

The previous night saw 700 British troops march out of Boston with orders to seize any colonial weapons they might find. By dawn the next morning they had reached Lexington, where they found about 75 American minutemen waiting for them on the village green. "Don't fire unless fired upon," Captain Jonas Parker ordered the Patriots, "but if they mean to have a war, let it begin here!"

The British commander ordered the Americans to lay down their arms.

"You damned rebels, disperse!" he cried, and the outnumbered colonists grudgingly began to drift away. Suddenly someone fired a shot—no one knows who—and the surprised British ranks let loose a volley. A few seconds later, eight dead and ten wounded minutemen lay on Lexington Green.

The redcoats continued up the road to Concord, where hundreds of Americans had gathered. Another small battle ensued before the British decided that it was time to return to Boston.

Then the real fighting began. The road back to Lexington became a nightmarish gauntlet of deadly fire for the redcoats as the Americans lay in ambush behind trees, rocks, and woodpiles. The helpless British columns endured the sniping nearly all the way back to Boston.

When the day was over, about 250 of the king's men had been killed or wounded. The colonists lost about 90. News of the conflict caused militiamen all over New England to shoulder their muskets and tramp toward Boston. The struggle for independence had begun. As Ralph Waldo Emerson wrote in his famous poem "Concord Hymn," the Americans had "fired the shot heard 'round the world."

AMERICAN HISTORY PARADE

1775   The Revolutionary War begins with the Battles of Lexington and Concord.

1865   Funeral services are held for Abraham Lincoln in Washington, D.C.

1897   The first Boston Marathon is run.

1933   Franklin D. Roosevelt announces that the U.S. is going off the gold standard.

1951   General Douglas MacArthur, relieved of command by President Truman, gives a farewell address to Congress, saying, "Old soldiers never die; they just fade away."

1995   A bomb explodes outside the Alfred P. Murrah Federal Building in Oklahoma City, killing 168 people and injuring hundreds more.

AMERICA IS NAMED after the Italian navigator Amerigo Vespucci, one of the early explorers of the New World. Between 1497 and 1504 Vespucci made as many as four voyages across the Atlantic. He took part in expeditions that explored the coast of South America between Venezuela and southern Brazil.

Christopher Columbus had already sailed across the Atlantic in 1492, but he believed that he had made landfall in Asia. Vespucci insisted in a report entitled *Mundus Novus* (New World) that a giant, uncharted land mass lay between Europe and Asia.

In April 1507, a German mapmaker named Martin Waldseemüller published a book called *Cosmographiae Introductio* in which he coined the term *America* to honor Vespucci. He mistakenly believed that Vespucci had been the first to discover the New World. "I do not see why anyone should by right object to name it America . . . after its discoverer, Americus, a man of sagacious mind, since both Europe and Asia took their names from women," Waldseemüller wrote.

Waldseemüller also made maps bearing the name America, and soon other Europeans began using the term. At first the name applied only to South America, which Vespucci had explored, but later mapmakers used *America* for all of the New World.

AMERICAN HISTORY PARADE

1841   Edgar Allen Poe's "The Murders in the Rue Morgue," one of the first detective stories, is published.

1861   Robert E. Lee resigns his command in the U.S. Army.

1912   Fenway Park, home of the Boston Red Sox, opens.

1940   RCA demonstrates the first U.S. electron microscope, capable of magnifying 100,000 times.

1999   At Columbine High School in Littleton, Colorado, two students shoot and kill twelve classmates and a teacher before committing suicide.

ON APRIL 21, 1942, a nervous Lt. Cdr. Edward "Butch" O'Hare stood beside his wife, Rita, at the White House while Franklin Delano Roosevelt awarded him the Congressional Medal of Honor for "one of the most daring, if not the most daring single action in the history of combat aviation."

Butch O'Hare never really wanted a medal—just a chance to do his job. On February 20, 1942, he was on board the aircraft carrier *Lexington* in the South Pacific when radar picked up a formation of Japanese bombers closing in fast. The *Lexington* quickly launched fighters to intercept the oncoming planes. By the time O'Hare got aloft in his Grumman F4F-3 Wildcat, there was no chance to "get in on the brawl," as he later put it, because other fighters had done a magnificent job breaking up the attack.

Then came a frantic message from the *Lexington*: a second wave of Japanese bombers had appeared. Only two Wildcats were in position to head them off—Butch and his wingman "Duff" Dufilho. Dufilho soon discovered that his guns wouldn't fire. That left Butch to fight off the bombers, which were minutes away from his carrier.

Roaring at the bombers, O'Hare began picking them off with deadly aim, one at a time. Sailors on deck watched in awe as he shot down five planes and disabled a sixth, all in a matter of minutes. He stopped only when he ran out of ammunition. When he landed, his first words were, "Just load those ammo belts, and I'll get back up." There was no need—his shooting had broken up the attack and saved the *Lexington*.

Twenty-one months later, Butch O'Hare's plane disappeared over the Pacific during a night attack against some Japanese torpedo bombers. In 1949 Chicago renamed its airport O'Hare International Airport in honor of the Navy's first flying ace.

AMERICAN HISTORY PARADE

1789   John Adams takes the oath to become the first U.S. vice president.

1832   Abraham Lincoln enlists to serve in the Black Hawk War and is elected captain of his militia company.

1836   Texans win independence from Mexico when forces led by Sam Houston defeat General Santa Anna's army at San Jacinto.

1856   A train crosses the Mississippi River for the first time on a new bridge connecting Rock Island, Illinois, and Davenport, Iowa.

1942   Butch O'Hare receives the Medal of Honor.

1956   Elvis Presley hits #1 on the Billboard charts for the first time with "Heartbreak Hotel."

LOOK ON ANY U.S. COIN OR PAPER CURRENCY and you'll find America's national motto, In God We Trust.

The suggestion to recognize God on U.S. money initially came during the Civil War from Pennsylvania minister M. R. Watkinson. "From my heart I have felt our national shame in disowning God as not the least of our present national disasters," Watkinson wrote to Samuel Chase, Abraham Lincoln's secretary of the treasury.

Chase thought the suggestion a good one, and he instructed the U.S. Mint to come up with a motto recognizing that "no nation can be strong except in the strength of God, or safe except in His defense." The resulting phrase, In God We Trust, may have had its inspiration in the fourth stanza of Francis Scott Key's "The Star-Spangled Banner": "Then conquer we must, when our cause is just, and this be our motto: 'In God is our trust.'"

On April 22, 1864, Congress passed legislation authorizing use of the phrase In God We Trust, and it first appeared on two-cent coins issued that same year.

For many years after that, the slogan appeared on some coins and not on others. In 1955 Congress ordered it placed on all U.S. currency, and in 1956 Congress made In God We Trust the official national motto. The phrase continues to remind us that our country has long found strength through faith in God, and that He has bestowed many blessings on America, including our freedom.

AMERICAN HISTORY PARADE

1864   Congress authorizes use of the phrase In God We Trust on U.S. coins.

1876   Baseball's National League begins its first season with the Boston Red Stockings defeating the Philadelphia Athletics 6–5.

1889   The Oklahoma Land Rush begins with thousands of homesteaders hurrying to stake claims on unassigned land.

1898   In the first action of the Spanish-American War, the USS *Nashville* captures the Spanish ship *Buena Vista* off Key West, Florida.

1970   Earth Day is observed across the country for the first time.

ON APRIL 23, 1908, President Theodore Roosevelt created a new component within the U.S. Army—the Medical Reserve Corps. In an age when disease and infection killed more soldiers than battle wounds, the new corps of 360 medical professionals stood ready to become active duty officers with the Army in times of conflict.

That corps was the beginning of the U.S. military's federal reserve force. During the next several years, the Army created additional reserve corps to fight and perform other duties when needed.

Today about 400,000 Americans serve in the federal military reserve for the Army, Navy, Air Force, Marines, and Coast Guard. These ready-to-go civilians put on uniforms once a month or more to train and help maintain day-to-day operations for the military. The president can call them to active service anytime to help meet a national emergency. In recent years thousands of reservists have left behind their families, jobs, and personal lives to fight terrorism overseas.

U.S. military reserve troops and National Guard troops perform very similar duties, and National Guard troops are also frequently referred to as "reserves." The main difference is that the U.S. military reserve is controlled by the federal government. National Guard units answer to state governments, except when called into federal service by the president.

In many ways reservists form the backbone of the U.S. military. Many are highly trained specialists who serve in roles that range from pilots to field doctors to logistics officers. When the nation goes to war, some of the most critical tasks are carried out by reservists. The United States could not engage in a major conflict without these men and women who are ready to go in harm's way for their country. To be a reservist, it is said, is to be twice a citizen.

AMERICAN HISTORY PARADE

1789   President-elect George Washington and his wife, Martha, move into the first presidential mansion, the Franklin House in New York City.

1791   James Buchanan, the fifteenth U.S. president, is born near Mercersburg, Pennsylvania.

1908   President Theodore Roosevelt signs an act creating the Medical Reserve Corps, the beginning of the U.S. military reserve.

1914   Wrigley Field, originally the home of the Chicago Federals and now the Chicago Cubs, opens.

1962   *Ranger 4*, the first U.S. spacecraft to reach the moon's surface, is launched.

THE LIBRARY OF CONGRESS IN WASHINGTON, D.C., is the world's largest library and perhaps the greatest collection of stored knowledge in history. It contains 140 million items, including maps, photographs, films, and recordings, on 650 miles of bookshelves. About 10,000 items are added every workday.

Congress established the library on April 24, 1800, when President John Adams signed a bill appropriating $5,000 for "the purchase of such books as may be necessary for the use of Congress" after it moved to Washington, the new capital city. The first books, ordered from London, arrived in 1801. The original collection consisted of 740 volumes and 3 maps.

The first collection was destroyed during the War of 1812 when the British burned the Capitol. Thomas Jefferson offered to replace it by selling Congress his personal library, one of the finest in the country. In 1815 Congress appropriated $23,950 to buy his 6,487 books. The Jefferson collection became the core of the Library of Congress.

The library serves as the research arm of Congress and the "storehouse of the national memory." Unlike many other national libraries, its collection is not for scholars only. Anyone over high school age may use it. It also makes available, via the Internet, millions of files containing digitized versions of its collections. A library of the people, it has become a symbol of Americans' faith in the power of learning.

AMERICAN HISTORY PARADE

1704   The *Boston News-Letter,* the first continuously published newspaper in British North America, is published.

1800   The Library of Congress is established.

1877   President Rutherford B. Hayes withdraws federal troops from New Orleans, ending post–Civil War military occupation of the South.

1898   Spain declares war on the United States in what becomes known as the Spanish-American War.

1962   The Massachusetts Institute of Technology achieves the first coast-to-coast satellite relay of a TV signal.

1980   An attempt to rescue American hostages in Iran fails; eight soldiers die when a helicopter and transport plane collide in the desert.

ON APRIL 25, 1990, the crew of the space shuttle *Discovery* deployed the Hubble Space Telescope, a space-based observatory that had long been the dream of astronomers. Hubble soon began taking stunning pictures of colliding galaxies, black holes, gas clouds, and space at the edge of the universe.

The telescope, named for American astronomer Edwin P. Hubble, orbits 375 miles above the earth. Since it does not have to look through the atmosphere, it can capture extraordinarily clear images. As big as a large tractor-trailer truck, it was designed so that space-walking astronauts can repair and replace its parts.

Not long after Hubble's launch, engineers realized that a flaw in the telescope's 94-inch light-gathering mirror was affecting the sharpness of images. Engineers quickly came up with a device to fix the problem, which astronauts from the shuttle *Endeavor* installed in 1993.

It has been said that not since Galileo trained his telescope on the night sky has any single instrument changed humankind's understanding of the universe as much as the Hubble Space Telescope. Certainly, it is one of the most important instruments in the history of astronomy, helping scientists gather clues about mysteries such as how stars are formed and the age of the universe.

NASA, which operates Hubble in cooperation with the European Space Agency, controls the telescope with radio commands sent from Goddard Space Flight Center in Greenbelt, Maryland. Every day, the telescope streams data to astronomers all over the world. You can see some of Hubble's breathtaking photos and get news about the project at http://hubble.nasa.gov/ as well as at http://hubblesite.org.

AMERICAN HISTORY PARADE

1898   The United States declares war on Spain in the Spanish-American War.

1945   U.S. and Soviet forces meet at the Elbe River in Central Europe as World War II draws to a close.

1959   The St. Lawrence Seaway, linking the Atlantic Ocean and Great Lakes, opens.

1983   The *Pioneer 10* spacecraft crosses Pluto's orbit, continuing its voyage into space beyond the solar system.

1990   The space shuttle *Discovery* places the Hubble Space Telescope into orbit.

ON APRIL 26, 1607, three small ships from England named the *Susan Constant, Godspeed,* and *Discovery* sailed into the Chesapeake Bay in what is now Virginia. On board were 104 colonists who came ashore, erected a wooden cross, and gave thanks to God for their passage across the Atlantic. In the following days they ventured inland along a wide river they named the James, after their king, and established themselves on a low island sixty miles from the bay's mouth. Jamestown would turn out to be the first permanent English settlement in North America— the very beginning of what would become the United States.

That the colony survived comes close to being a miracle. The land the settlers chose was swampy and mosquito infested. The drinking water was bad. Malaria, typhoid, and dysentery took their toll, as did clashes with the Indians. Some of the colonists were ill prepared for frontier life. At times they spent more energy looking for gold than trying to stay alive. During the first summer, fifty died.

More ships arrived with more colonists and supplies, but still it was tough going. During the winter of 1609–1610, a siege by the Indians brought the "starving time." One settler remembered that "many times three our four [died] in a night; in the morning their bodies trailed out of their cabins like dogs to be buried." Out of about 214 colonists, only 60 survived. They decided to go back to England but had sailed only a few miles downriver when they met a new governor arriving with yet more settlers, so they turned around.

Jamestown endured partly due to the discovery of tobacco—a crop as good as gold—but largely because of dogged perseverance. By 1619 the colony had grown enough to elect its own House of Burgesses—the first representative legislative assembly in the Western Hemisphere.

AMERICAN HISTORY PARADE

1598   An expedition led by Spanish explorer Juan de Onate reaches the Rio Grande.

1607   English colonists come ashore at Cape Henry, Virginia, en route to founding Jamestown.

1865   Federal troops surround and kill John Wilkes Booth, assassin of Abraham Lincoln, near Bowling Green, Virginia.

1961   The integrated circuit is patented by Robert Noyce.

THE END OF APRIL BRINGS NATIONAL ARBOR DAY, a day for planting and caring for trees, observed on the last Friday of this month. The custom originated in Nebraska in 1872 as a way to encourage people to plant trees on the Great Plains. In addition to National Arbor Day, many states observe their own Arbor Day, sometimes on other dates that coincide with their best tree-planting times.

The United States is blessed with some of the most magnificent forests in the world, as well as some of the oldest and grandest trees. For example:

Coast Redwoods are the world's *tallest* trees. They live along the foggy Pacific coast from southern Oregon to central California. Redwoods can grow more than 300 feet high; the tallest grow to more than 360 feet—as tall as a thirty-five-story building. About 95 percent of the old-growth coast redwoods have been logged, but many remaining trees are now protected in California's Redwood National Park. In 2006, researchers found a tree in the park measuring just over 379 feet tall. Nicknamed Hyperion, it currently ranks as the world's tallest tree.

Giant Sequoias are the *largest* trees on earth in terms of volume of wood. They grow on the western slopes of the Sierra Nevada mountains in California. Though not as tall as coast redwoods, giant sequoias have more massive trunks. The world's largest tree, called the General Sherman Tree, stands in Sequoia National Park. Towering 275 feet high, it measures 103 feet around its trunk and is well over 2,000 years old.

Great Basin Bristlecone Pines are among the world's *oldest* living trees. Growing at high altitudes in Utah, Nevada, and California, some were alive when the Egyptians built the pyramids more than 4,000 years ago. The oldest known living bristlecone pine, called Methuselah, lives in the White Mountains of eastern California. It is about 4,800 years old.

AMERICAN HISTORY PARADE

1805   U.S. Marines capture the city of Derna on the shores of Tripoli during the First Barbary War.

1813   American forces capture York (now Toronto) during the War of 1812.

1822   Ulysses S. Grant, the eighteenth U.S. president, is born in Point Pleasant, Ohio.

1865   In the worst maritime disaster in U.S. history, the steamboat *Sultana* explodes near Memphis on the Mississippi, killing 1,700 people, mostly Union veterans.

1887   Philadelphia surgeon George T. Morton performs the first appendectomy.

2001   The oak is chosen as the official National Tree.

ON APRIL 28, 1788, Maryland became the seventh state to ratify the U.S. Constitution. The state took its name from the colony that came before it, chartered in 1632 and named Maryland (*Terra Maria* in Latin) in honor of English King Charles I's wife, Queen Henrietta Maria.

A few more origins of state names:

Idaho — an invented word, once the name of a steamship that traveled the Columbia River

Illinois — from an Algonquin Indian word for "tribe of superior men"

Indiana — coined by Congress in 1800 when it created the Indian Territory out of the Northwest Territory; means "land of the Indians"

Iowa — for the Iowa River and Iowa Indians; the tribal name Iowa (*Ayuxwa*) means "one who puts to sleep"

Kansas — from an Indian word meaning "people of the south wind"

Kentucky — perhaps from an Indian word meaning "meadowland"

Louisiana — in honor of King Louis XIV of France

Maine — unknown; perhaps after the French province of Mayne, or perhaps from the word *main*, a term used by sailors to refer to a mainland

Massachusetts — from Algonquian Indian words meaning "near the great hill"

Michigan — from the Chippewa Indian word *michigama*, meaning "large lake"

AMERICAN HISTORY PARADE

1758   James Monroe, the fifth U.S. president, is born in Westmoreland County, Virginia.

1788   Maryland becomes the seventh state to ratify the U.S. Constitution.

1817   The U.S. and Great Britain agree to limit naval forces in the Great Lakes region, providing for an unfortified U.S.-Canadian border.

1952   The U.S.'s post–World War II occupation of Japan ends.

1965   Fearing that Communists might gain power in the Dominican Republic, Lyndon Johnson sends U.S. forces to the island to help end civil war.

THE EVENTS UNFOLDED HALF A WORLD AWAY, but the last days of April 1975 were dark ones in American history. The United States had withdrawn its forces from Southeast Asia, leaving the Communist North Vietnamese army to overrun South Vietnam. On April 29, as North Vietnamese troops encircled Saigon, American officials began a helicopter evacuation to get thousands of U.S. citizens, South Vietnamese allies, and others out of the capital city. On April 30, South Vietnam surrendered.

Just days earlier, a similar though smaller-scale evacuation had taken place in Phnom Penh, Cambodia, as forces of the Communist Khmer Rouge moved in on that capital. As U.S. officials fled the country, the American ambassador asked Prince Sirik Matak if he would like to leave. Matak's response is difficult for Americans to read:

> I thank you very sincerely for your letter and your offer to transport me towards freedom. I cannot, alas, leave in such a cowardly fashion. As for you, and in particular for your great country, I never believed for a moment that you would have this sentiment of abandoning a people which has chosen liberty. You have refused us your protection, and we can do nothing about it. You leave, and my wish is that you and your country will find happiness under this sky. But, mark it well, that if I shall die here on the spot and in my country that I love, it is no matter, because we are all born and must die. I have only committed this mistake of believing in you.

When the Khmer Rouge seized Phnom Penh, they shot Matak in the stomach. Unattended, it took him three days to die. During the Khmer Rouge's four-year reign of terror, some 1.5 million people died from execution, starvation, and forced labor.

AMERICAN HISTORY PARADE

1854   Ashmun Institute (now Lincoln University), the first college for African American students, is established in Chester County, Pennsylvania.

1898   The first American cancer lab is established at the University of Buffalo.

1913   Gideon Sundback of Hoboken, New Jersey, patents the first modern zipper.

1945   U.S. troops liberate the Dachau concentration camp in Germany.

1975   American officials evacuate Saigon as North Vietnamese troops close in on South Vietnam's capital.

ON APRIL 30, 1789, George Washington took office in New York as the first president of the United States. In his inaugural address, he began his duties by giving thanks to the Almighty for the blessings the new country had received during the Revolution and making of the Constitution:

It would be peculiarly improper to omit in this first official act my fervent supplications to that Almighty Being who rules over the universe, who presides in the councils of nations, and whose providential aids can supply every human defect, that His benediction may consecrate to the liberties and happiness of the people of the United States a Government instituted by themselves for these essential purposes, and may enable every instrument employed in its administration to execute with success the functions allotted to his charge. In tendering this homage to the Great Author of every public and private good, I assure myself that it expresses your sentiments not less than my own. . . . No people can be bound to acknowledge and adore the Invisible Hand which conducts the affairs of men more than those of the United States. Every step by which they have advanced to the character of an independent nation seems to have been distinguished by some token of providential agency. And in the important revolution just accomplished in the system of their united government, the tranquil deliberations and voluntary consent of so many distinct communities from which the event has resulted cannot be compared with the means by which most governments have been established without some return of pious gratitude, along with an humble anticipation of the future blessings which the past seem to presage.

AMERICAN HISTORY PARADE

1789   George Washington takes office as the first U.S. president.

1803   The United States concludes negotiations with France for the Louisiana Purchase, doubling the size of the young republic for $15 million.

1812   Louisiana becomes the eighteenth state.

1939   Lou Gehrig plays his last game with the New York Yankees, ending his streak of 2,130 consecutive games played.

1939   Franklin D. Roosevelt becomes the first president to appear on TV as he opens the World's Fair in New York City.

1975   The last Americans evacuate Saigon as South Vietnam surrenders to the Vietcong.

FIFTY ALL-AMERICAN MOVIES

Here are fifty movies that, one way or another, capture the American spirit. Heroes tall in the saddle, pioneers of land and air, defenders of freedom, men and women who dared to hitch their wagon to a star—they're all here. John Wayne once said that in his work he tried to express a deep and profound love for "a country whose immense beauty and grandeur are matched only by the greatness of her people." That's what these films are about. (Listed in alphabetical order.)

1. *Apollo 13*
2. *The Best Years of Our Lives*
3. *The Big Country*
4. *Boys Town*
5. *Cinderella Man*
6. *Coal Miner's Daughter*
7. *Davy Crockett, King of the Wild Frontier*
8. *Driving Miss Daisy*
9. *Field of Dreams*
10. *Forrest Gump*
11. *Gettysburg*
12. *Giant*
13. *The Glenn Miller Story*
14. *Glory*
15. *Gone with the Wind*
16. *The Grapes of Wrath*
17. *High Noon*
18. *Hoosiers*
19. *How the West Was Won*
20. *Independence Day*
21. *It's a Wonderful Life*
22. *John Adams*
23. *The Last of the Mohicans*
24. *Little Women*
25. *The Man Who Shot Liberty Valance*
26. *Miracle*
27. *Miracle on 34th Street*
28. *The Miracle Worker*
29. *Mr. Smith Goes to Washington*
30. *The Music Man*

31.	*October Sky*	41.	*Saving Private Ryan*
32.	*Oklahoma!*	42.	*Seabiscuit*
33.	*Patton*	43.	*The Searchers*
34.	*The Pride of the Yankees*	44.	*Sergeant York*
35.	*The Pursuit of Happyness*	45.	*Shane*
36.	*Red River*	46.	*Stagecoach*
37.	*Rocky*	47.	*Stand and Deliver*
38.	*Roots*	48.	*To Kill a Mockingbird*
39.	*Rudy*	49.	*Tora! Tora! Tora!*
40.	*Sands of Iwo Jima*	50.	*Yankee Doodle Dandy*

Apollo 13 (1995) Starring Tom Hanks, Kevin Bacon, Bill Paxton, Gary Sinise, Ed Harris. Directed by Ron Howard. A terrific account of the 1970 flight that ran into disaster on the way to the moon. This movie is all about heroism in space and on the ground as NASA struggles to bring its crew home. Rated PG.

The Best Years of Our Lives (1946) Starring Fredric March, Dana Andrews, Harold Russell, Myrna Loy, Teresa Wright, Virginia Mayo, Cathy O'Donnell. Directed by William Wyler. Three soldiers return home after World War II and struggle to pick up the threads of their lives. This film has long been considered one of Hollywood's finest. Not Rated. Contains adult situations.

The Big Country (1958) Starring Gregory Peck, Jean Simmons, Carroll Baker, Charlton Heston. Directed by William Wyler. A sea captain heads west to marry his sweetheart and gets caught up in a fight between two warring ranchers. Stunning photography helps tell this tale of courage in the wide-open spaces. Not Rated. Contains violence.

Boys Town (1938) Starring Spencer Tracy, Mickey Rooney. Directed by Norman Taurog. Tracy gives an unforgettable performance as real-life Father Edward J.

Flanagan, who founded the famous Boys Town in Omaha, Nebraska, for youngsters who had no one to take care of them. Not Rated.

Cinderella Man (2005) Starring Russell Crowe, Renee Zellweger, Paul Giamatti. Directed by Ron Howard. A has-been boxer gets a second chance to fight his way to the top in this Depression-era story about family, hope, and perseverance. Inspired by the life of boxer Jim Braddock. Rated PG-13. Contains boxing violence.

Coal Miner's Daughter (1980) Starring Sissy Spacek, Tommy Lee Jones, Beverly D'Angelo, Levon Helm. Directed by Michael Apted. Based on country singer Loretta Lynn's rags-to-riches journey from the mountains of Kentucky to the Grand Ole Opry and superstardom. Rated PG. Contains adult situations.

Davy Crockett, King of the Wild Frontier (1955) Starring Fess Parker, Buddy Ebsen. Directed by Norman Foster. Follow Davy as he tames the Tennessee wilderness, stands up for justice in Congress, and fights for freedom at the Alamo. This Disney classic inspired a generation of children to don coonskin caps and sing "The Ballad of Davy Crockett." Rated G.

Driving Miss Daisy (1989) Starring Morgan Freeman, Jessica Tandy, Dan Aykroyd. Directed by Bruce Beresford. A rich Jewish widow and her black chauffeur develop a twenty-five-year friendship as social changes sweep the South. Rated PG. Contains adult language.

Field of Dreams (1989) Starring Kevin Costner, Ray Liotta, Amy Madigan, James Earl Jones, Burt Lancaster. Directed by Phil Alden Robinson. An Iowa farmer hears a voice that inspires him to build a baseball diamond in the middle of his cornfield. This celebration of baseball is all about dreams that refuse to die. Rated PG.

Forrest Gump (1994) Starring Tom Hanks, Robin Wright Penn, Gary Sinise, Mykelti Williamson, Sally Field. Directed by Robert Zemeckis. A man with limited intelligence but boundless luck leads a charmed life that includes many brushes with American history—from teaching Elvis Presley to dance to discovering the Watergate break-in. Rated PG-13. Contains adult situations and profanity.

Gettysburg (1993) Starring Tom Berenger, Jeff Daniels, Martin Sheen. Directed by Ronald F. Maxwell. This historical drama recounts the gigantic Civil War battle that determined the fate of the nation. Based on the Pulitzer Prize–winning novel *Killer Angels* by Michael Shaara. Rated PG. Contains battlefield violence.

Giant (1956) Starring Elizabeth Taylor, Rock Hudson, James Dean. Directed by George Stevens. An epic saga about the struggles and triumphs of a cattle baron family and a cowboy who strikes it rich in the Texas oil fields. Not Rated.

The Glenn Miller Story (1953) Starring James Stewart, June Allyson. Directed by Anthony Mann. The big band sound lives again in this film biography about one of America's legendary bandleaders. The score swings with musical greats such as Louis Armstrong, Gene Krupa, Frances Langford, and the Glenn Miller Orchestra. Rated G. Contains lots of great music but also some tragedy.

Glory (1989) Starring Matthew Broderick, Denzel Washington, Cary Elwes, Morgan Freeman. Directed by Edward Zwick. A testament to the courage and determination of the 54th Massachusetts Volunteer Regiment, the first black regular army regiment in the Civil War. Rated R. Contains graphic battle scene violence, adult situations, and profanity.

Gone with the Wind (1939) Starring Vivien Leigh, Clark Gable, Olivia de Havilland, Leslie Howard. Directed by Victor Fleming. Fiery, pampered

Scarlett O'Hara struggles to keep her world together as it crumbles with the Civil War. One of the most beloved films ever made, *Gone with the Wind* is considered a national treasure. Not Rated. Contains adult situations.

The Grapes of Wrath (1940) Starring Henry Fonda, Jane Darwell, John Carradine. Directed by John Ford. The Joad family migrates from the Oklahoma Dust Bowl to California, along with thousands of other Okies, in a struggle to survive the Depression. Based on John Steinbeck's famous novel. Not Rated.

High Noon (1952) Starring Gary Cooper, Grace Kelly, Katy Jurado, Lloyd Bridges. Directed by Fred Zinnemann. A frontier marshal in a cowardly town stands alone against a gang of deadly outlaws in this Western classic about duty, courage, loyalty, and grace under fire. Not Rated.

Hoosiers (1986) Starring Gene Hackman, Barbara Hershey, Dennis Hopper. Directed by David Anspaugh. A washed-up college basketball coach gets a second chance at a small-town high school in Indiana. A straight-from-the-heartland film about pushing hard and aiming high. Rated PG. Contains adult situations and language.

How the West Was Won (1962) Starring Jimmy Stewart, Carroll Baker, Henry Fonda, Gregory Peck, Debbie Reynolds, and many more. Directed by Henry Hathaway, John Ford, and George Marshall. A sweeping tale about a pioneer family and the nation's westward expansion from the Erie Canal to California. Dozens of Hollywood stars, twelve thousand extras, six hundred horses, scores of horse-drawn wagons, and a stampede of two thousand buffalo fill the screen in this western epic. Not Rated. Contains some violence.

Independence Day (1996) Starring Jeff Goldblum, Bill Pullman, Will Smith. Directed by Roland Emmerich. It's hard to resist this often goofy, clichéd science-fiction extravaganza about an invasion of Earth from outer space. The scrappy Americans fall back on good, old-fashioned Yankee ingenuity in a last-ditch effort to save the human race from the evil aliens. Rated PG-13. Contains profanity and scenes of widespread death and destruction.

It's a Wonderful Life (1946) Starring Jimmy Stewart, Donna Reed, Henry Travers, Lionel Barrymore. Directed by Frank Capra. It's Christmas Eve in Bedford Falls, and businessman George Bailey is in so much trouble he wishes he'd never been born. Perhaps America's favorite film, *It's a Wonderful Life* is a Christmas hymn about compassion, self-sacrifice, love, and small-town life. Not Rated.

John Adams (2008) Starring Paul Giamatti, Laura Linney. Directed by Tom Hooper. This fascinating seven-part series depicts the life and times of one of our most extraordinary Founding Fathers. Based on the wonderful biography by David McCullough. Not Rated.

The Last of the Mohicans (1992) Starring Daniel Day-Lewis, Madeleine Stowe, Russell Means. Directed by Michael Mann. The spirit of James Fenimore Cooper comes to life in this adaptation of his novel, set on the New York frontier during the French and Indian War. Rated R. Contains violence.

Little Women (1949) Starring June Allyson, Margaret O'Brien, Elizabeth Taylor, Janet Leigh. Directed by Mervyn LeRoy. Jo, Beth, Amy, and Meg March learn about family strength in this heartfelt adaptation of Louisa May Alcott's beloved novel, set in New England during the Civil War. Not Rated.

The Man Who Shot Liberty Valance (1962) Starring Jimmy Stewart, John Wayne, Vera Miles, Lee Marvin. Directed by John Ford. Civilization meets the Wild West when a greenhorn Eastern lawyer runs afoul of a notorious outlaw, while a gritty, gun-slinging hero stands between. This classic bids a glorious farewell to frontier life as it probes how legend has forged our image of the West. Not rated. Contains violence.

Miracle (2004) Starring Kurt Russell, Patricia Clarkson, Noah Emmerich. Directed by Gavin O'Connor. Follow the U.S. hockey team to the 1980 Winter Olympics for a Cold War showdown and one of the all-time greatest upsets in sports history. Rated PG.

Miracle on 34th Street (1947) Starring Edmund Gwenn, Maureen O'Hara, John Payne, Natalie Wood. Directed by George Seaton. A kind old gent takes a job as Santa in Macy's toy department, and before long a doubting nine-year-old girl begins to wonder if he's not the real thing. A joyous, American Christmas carol about hope, love, and the true meaning of the season. Not Rated.

The Miracle Worker (1962) Starring Anne Bancroft, Patty Duke. Directed by Arthur Penn. The true story of Helen Keller, the Alabama girl struck blind and deaf as a baby, and Annie Sullivan, the remarkable teacher who brought her the gift of language. Based on William Gibson's Broadway play. Not Rated. Contains scenes with intense emotional and physical struggles.

Mr. Smith Goes to Washington (1939) Starring Jimmy Stewart, Claude Rains, Jean Arthur. Directed by Frank Capra. A scoutmaster elected to the U.S. Senate runs into a political machine that tries to chew him up and spit him back to where he came from. "I've got a few things I want to say to this Body," Smith tells the Senate. "I tried to say them once before and I got stopped colder than a mackerel. Well, I'd like to get them said this time, sir. And as a matter of fact, I'm not gonna leave this Body until I do get them said." Not Rated.

The Music Man (1962) Starring Robert Preston, Shirley Jones, Buddy Hackett. Directed by Morton Da Costa. Fast-talking con man Harold Hill organizes a boys' band in an Iowa town just so he can sell instruments and uniforms. Based on Meredith Wilson's Broadway hit, this musical explodes with great tunes and lots of fun. Not Rated.

October Sky (1999) Starring Jake Gyllenhaal, Chris Cooper, Laura Dern. Directed by Joe Johnston. After seeing the Soviet satellite *Sputnik* streak overhead in 1957, four high school students in a West Virginia coal mining town decide to join the space race by designing and launching their own homemade rockets. This inspiring story about aiming for the stars is based on the autobiography of NASA engineer Homer H. Hickam. Rated PG. Contains profanity and adult situations.

Oklahoma! (1955) Starring Shirley Jones and Gordon MacRae. Directed by Fred Zinnemann. Rodgers and Hammerstein's *Oklahoma!* may be the most American of American musicals. This one's got it all: wide-open ranges, barnyard dances, cowboys, farmers, and some of the most beloved tunes in Broadway theater history. "We know we belong to the land, and the land we belong to is grand!" Not Rated.

Patton (1970) Starring George C. Scott, Karl Malden. Directed by Franklin J. Schaffner. Flamboyant George S. Patton, one of the World War II's most brilliant generals, smashes through German lines and battles his own huge ego in this classic film biography. Rated PG. Contains profanity and battlefield violence.

The Pride of the Yankees (1942) Starring Gary Cooper, Teresa Wright, Walter Brennan, Babe Ruth. Directed by Sam Wood. Based on the life of Lou Gehrig, the famous Yankee first baseman who earned the nickname "the Iron Man" because he never missed a game, this movie is regarded by many as one of the greatest sports films of all times. The last line in the movie alone makes it worth watching. Not Rated.

The Pursuit of Happyness (2006) Starring Will Smith, Thandie Newton, Jaden Smith. Directed by Gabriele Muccino. A struggling San Francisco salesman hits rock bottom when he's evicted from his apartment, but he refuses to give up either his responsibility for his young son or his quest for the American dream. Based on the life of self-made millionaire Christopher Gardner. Rated PG-13.

Red River (1948) Starring John Wayne, Montgomery Clift, Walter Brennan. Directed by Howard Hawks. A tough Texas rancher sets out to drive thousands of cattle to Missouri, but his tyrannical behavior causes a rebellion among his hired hands. This beautifully filmed movie reminds us of the courage and determination it took to settle the Old West, as well as the brutality that often marked that era. Not Rated. Contains violence.

Rocky (1976) Starring Sylvester Stallone, Talia Shire, Burt Young, Carl Weathers, Burgess Meredith. Directed by John Avildsen. Rocky Balboa is a small-time, Philadelphia boxer just one step away from becoming an even smaller-time bum. Then he gets his million-to-one shot against champion Apollo Creed. Rated PG. Contains adult situations and plenty of hard hitting in the ring.

Roots (1977) Starring LeVar Burton, John Amos, Ben Vereen. A six-part historical epic based on novelist Alex Haley's story of his own family across several generations in slavery. For a century they struggle for one thing: freedom. Not Rated. Contains adult situations and partial nudity.

Rudy (1993) Starring Sean Astin, Ned Beatty, Charles S. Dutton. Directed by David Anspaugh. Daniel "Rudy" Ruettiger is small for a football player and not much of a scholar, but he's determined to follow his dream: to play football for the Fighting Irish of Notre Dame. This uplifting tale of never-say-die courage is based on a true story. Rated PG. Contains profanity and some gridiron violence.

Sands of Iwo Jima (1949) Starring John Wayne, John Agar, Forrest Tucker. Directed by Allan Dwan. A tough Marine sergeant leads a group of raw recruits on the assault of Iwo Jima in the Pacific. The film uses footage shot during the historic invasion. It culminates with the famous raising of the American flag on Mount Suribachi. Not Rated. Contains battlefield violence.

Saving Private Ryan (1998) Starring Tom Hanks, Tom Sizemore, Matt Damon, Edward Burns. Directed by Steven Spielberg. In this powerful drama about the D-Day operations in World War II, a team of American soldiers sets out on a mission to retrieve a private whose three brothers have all been killed in the war. This film gives viewers a glimpse of the terrible sacrifices made during the Normandy landings. Rated R. Contains extremely graphic violence. Not appropriate for children. For a terrific recounting of the Normandy invasion with less graphic violence, watch *The Longest Day* (1962).

Seabiscuit (2003) Starring Tobey Maguire, Jeff Bridges, Chris Cooper. Directed by Gary Ross. In the depths of the Depression, an almost-discarded racehorse becomes the greatest champion of his time, helping three men—his owner, trainer, and jockey—rebuild their lives. Based on a true, American story of redemption. Rated PG-13. Contains profanity, some sexual situations, and violence.

The Searchers (1956) Starring John Wayne, Jeffrey Hunter, Vera Miles, Natalie Wood. Directed by John Ford. A Confederate veteran spends five years in a relentless search for a niece captured by Comanche Indians, an ordeal that finally leads him to his own humanity. Wayne gives one of the finest performances of his career in this Western masterpiece, which is set against the stunning backdrop of Monument Valley, Utah. Not Rated. Contains violence.

Sergeant York (1941) Starring Gary Cooper, Walter Brennan, Joan Leslie. Directed by Howard Hawks. A backwoods farm boy from Tennessee is a reluctant warrior who decides there are some things worth fighting for. Based on the life of World War I hero Alvin C. York, who captured 132 German soldiers in savage fighting in the Argonne Forest, this war saga is really the story of a good man's quiet determination and faith. Not Rated. Contains battlefield violence.

Shane (1953) Starring Alan Ladd, Jean Arthur, Van Heflin, Brandon De Wilde. Directed by George Stevens. A lone drifter helps a homesteading family fight off the cattle barons who are trying to run them off their land. Along with telling a great story, this film reminds us of the grit and guts it took to settle the West. Not Rated.

Stagecoach (1939) Starring John Wayne, Claire Trevor, George Bancroft. Directed by John Ford. A group of stagecoach passengers sets out on a perilous ride through Apache territory. This is the film that set the standard for Westerns. It also set a little-known B-movie actor named John Wayne on the road to becoming an American movie icon. Not Rated. Contains violence.

Stand and Deliver (1988) Starring Edward James Olmos, Lou Diamond Phillips, Rosana De Soto, Andy Garcia. Directed by Ramon Menendez. A tough, determined math teacher inspires his inner-city students to conquer calculus in this "*Rocky*" of the classroom." Based on the gripping real-life story of teacher extraordinaire Jaime Escalante. Rated PG.

To Kill a Mockingbird (1962) Starring Gregory Peck, Mary Bedham, Brock Peters, Robert Duvall. Directed by Robert Mulligan. One of the greatest American movies ever made, based on one of the greatest American books ever written. A small-town Southern lawyer puts his career on the line when he defends a black man accused of rape. Set in the 1930s, the story is told through the eyes of the attorney's young daughter. Not Rated. Contains adult situations.

Tora! Tora! Tora! (1970) Starring Martin Balsam, Joseph Cotten, E. G. Marshall, Tatsuya Mihashi, Jason Robards, Takahiro Tamura, Soh Yamamura, James Whitmore. Directed by Richard Fleischer, Kinji Fukasaku, Toshio Masuda. American and Japanese directors collaborated to make this riveting drama about the bombing of Pearl Harbor during World War II. Rated PG. Contains violence.

Yankee Doodle Dandy (1942) Starring James Cagney, Joan Leslie, Walter Huston. Directed by Michael Curtiz. This bang-up musical based on the life of Broadway great George M. Cohan features great tunes such as "You're a Grand Old Flag," "Over There," and "I'm a Yankee Doodle Dandy." Released shortly after the Japanese attack on Pearl Harbor, it became an instant American favorite. Not Rated.

MAY

SKYSCRAPERS ARE AN AMERICAN INVENTION—emblems of our country's determination to reach ever higher.

Until the late 1800s, building heights were limited by the number of bricks that could be stacked on top of one another before the walls became too heavy to stand, and by the number of stairs people were willing to climb. In 1857 the installation of the first passenger elevator in a New York City department store made it possible to construct buildings more than a few floors high. Engineers began experimenting with steel frames that could support the weight of several stories.

On May 1, 1884, construction began on the Home Insurance Building in Chicago, considered the father of the skyscraper. Designed by Major William Le Baron Jenney, it was the first tall building to use a steel skeleton for support. Chicagoans were so worried that it would fall down, city officials halted construction until they could investigate the structure's safety. When the building was finished in the fall of 1885, people stood at its base and gaped at its soaring 10 stories.

On May 1, 1931, President Herbert Hoover dedicated the 102-story Empire State Building in Manhattan by pushing a button in the White House that turned on the skyscraper's lights. Measuring 1,250 feet from sidewalk to roof, it was the tallest building in the world when completed and held that record for four decades until construction of the World Trade Center towers in Manhattan. It remains one of the world's most famous buildings and one of the grandest monuments of the twentieth century.

AMERICAN HISTORY PARADE

1884   Construction begins on the Home Insurance Building in Chicago.

1898   A squadron of U.S. ships defeats a Spanish squadron in Manila Bay during the Spanish-American War.

1931   The 102-story Empire State Building is dedicated.

1941   Orson Welles's film *Citizen Kane* debuts at the RKO Palace in New York City.

1963   Jim Whittaker becomes the first American to climb Mount Everest.

1970   The U.S. population tops 200 million, reaching 203,302,031 in the nineteenth census.

ON MAY 2, 1939, loudspeakers at Yankee Stadium stunned the crowd with the announcement that New York first baseman Lou Gehrig would not be in the day's lineup. Gehrig, a fan favorite, had compiled a lifetime batting average of .340. He had slugged 493 home runs during his career, including 23 grand slams, and averaged a staggering 147 RBIs per season. But his most amazing stat was his streak of 2,130 consecutive games played. For thirteen years, he had played through good times and bad—including seventeen fractures and numerous other injuries—without missing a game. The son of working-class German immigrants showed up day after day to give his best in his steady, quiet way. His endurance earned him the nickname "the Iron Horse."

But Gehrig had not played well lately. He could tell something was wrong with his body. He had trouble hitting the ball. In the field, he even had trouble getting to first base in time to take a throw. So he ended his streak. "I'm benching myself," he told his manager. "For the good of the team."

Medical exams brought a bleak diagnosis: amyotrophic lateral sclerosis (ALS), a disease of the nervous system. The chances of long-term survival were slim. Gehrig took the blow with courage and grace, telling friends he was hoping for the best.

On July 4, 1939, Lou Gehrig stood on the field in a packed Yankee Stadium to say good-bye. Surrounded by friends, family, teammates, and fans, the first baseman stepped up to the microphones. "For the past two weeks you have been reading about the bad break I got," he said. "Yet today I consider myself the luckiest man on the face of this earth."

Gehrig died two years later from the disease that now bears his name. Sports fans still remember him as the Iron Horse.

AMERICAN HISTORY PARADE

1497   Explorer John Cabot sets sail from England in search of a westward route to the Indies.

1863   Confederate general Stonewall Jackson is accidentally shot by his own troops at Chancellorsville, Virginia, and he dies eight days later.

1939   New York Yankees first baseman Lou Gehrig's streak of 2,130 consecutive games played comes to an end (his record stands until broken by the Baltimore Orioles' Cal Ripken Jr. in 1995).

1949   Arthur Miller's *Death of a Salesman* wins the Pulitzer Prize.

1965   The *Early Bird* satellite sends TV pictures across the Atlantic for the first time.

IN 1790, a year after George Washington took office as president, Congress authorized him to find a site along the Potomac River for the new nation's capital. It was the first time a country had ever established its permanent capital by legislative action. The president ended up choosing a spot just a few miles upstream from his home at Mount Vernon, Virginia.

Surveyors staked out an area of one hundred square miles straddling the river. The idea was to create a special territory, not part of any state, to contain the capital city. The land came from Maryland and Virginia, and the territory was named the "District of Columbia" ("D.C." for short) in honor of Christopher Columbus.

George Washington hired French engineer Pierre L'Enfant to plan the city that would lie within the new District. In 1791, the District's commissioners decided to name that city "Washington" in honor of the first president. The federal government moved there in 1800.

On May 3, 1802, Washington was incorporated as a city, with a city council elected by local residents, and a mayor appointed by the president. People began to refer to the capital city inside the District of Columbia as "Washington, D.C."—just as they might write "Albany, N.Y." or "Charleston, S.C."

For a long time Washington remained a relatively small town, and much of the land inside the District of Columbia lay undeveloped. In 1846 Congress decided it would never need the District's land on the south side of the Potomac River, so it returned that portion to the state of Virginia. But of course the city did eventually grow, especially after World War II. Today it fills virtually the entire District of Columbia.

AMERICAN HISTORY PARADE

1765 The first U.S. medical school is established at the College of Philadelphia.

1802 Washington, D.C., is incorporated as a city.

1921 West Virginia becomes the first state to impose a sales tax.

1923 Air Service Lts. Oakley Kelly and John Macready land at Coronado Beach, California, completing the first transcontinental nonstop flight in 26 hours, 50 minutes.

1937 Margaret Mitchell wins the Pulitzer Prize for her novel *Gone with the Wind*.

1952 Lt. Cols. William Pershing Benedict and Joseph Otis Fletcher pilot the first plane to land at the North Pole, an Air Force ski-wheeled C-47.

ON MAY 4, 1961, thirteen men and women, black and white, boarded a bus in Washington, D.C., and set out toward New Orleans. Their mission: challenge segregation practices on public transportation. History remembers them as the Freedom Riders.

The U.S. Supreme Court had already ruled that segregation in interstate bus travel was unconstitutional. But in several Southern states where Jim Crow laws still prevailed, it was considered a crime for whites and blacks to sit side by side on a bus. Yet that's exactly what the Freedom Riders did as they headed south. When they stopped at bus stations, they sat together in segregated waiting rooms and at lunch counters.

By the time they reached the Deep South, trouble was waiting. Near Anniston, Alabama, angry whites firebombed the bus. The Freedom Riders barely escaped with their lives. In Birmingham, riders on a second bus were beaten with clubs and lead pipes. In Montgomery a mob surrounded the church where they sought refuge.

Some Civil Rights activists urged the Freedom Riders to halt their journey. Despite the danger, *more* people joined the effort. But the Freedom Ride came to an end in Jackson, Mississippi, where police herded the Riders through the bus station and into paddy wagons. More than 300 went to jail.

The Freedom Riders never made it to New Orleans, but they achieved their objective. Inspired by those brave few, more Americans worked to break segregation and lead the country down a better road. In 2001, when some of the Freedom Riders made a fortieth anniversary bus trip retracing their route, the mayor of Anniston welcomed them with the keys to the city.

AMERICAN HISTORY PARADE

1626   Dutch colonist Peter Minuit arrives in Manhattan; he later buys the island from Indians for $24 worth of trade goods.

1776   Rhode Island declares its freedom from England, two months before the Declaration of Independence.

1942   The Battle of the Coral Sea, the first naval clash fought solely by air power, begins.

1959   Henry Mancini, Perry Como, and Ella Fitzgerald are among the winners of the first Grammy Awards.

1961   The Freedom Riders leave Washington, D.C., to challenge segregation laws.

1970   National Guardsmen kill four Kent State University students protesting the Vietnam War.

THE FIRST THURSDAY IN MAY is the National Day of Prayer, a day that encourages Americans to pray for the United States, its people, and its leaders.

The tradition of a National Day of Prayer dates to 1775, when the Second Continental Congress set aside a day for Americans to pray to "be ever under the care and protection of a kind Providence" as they began the struggle for independence. In the following decades, Congress and the president set aside various days for prayer. In 1863, for example, Lincoln proclaimed "a day of national humiliation, fasting, and prayer" to help the country get through "the awful calamity of civil war" and for "the restoration of our now divided and suffering Country to its former happy condition of unity and peace."

In 1952 Congress and President Truman established a National Day of Prayer as a yearly event. Truman called for a day "on which all of us, in our churches, in our homes, and in our hearts, may beseech God to grant us wisdom to know the course which we should follow, and strength and patience to pursue that course steadfastly."

In 1988, President Reagan designated the first Thursday in May as the National Day of Prayer, urging Americans to ask God for "His blessings, His peace, and the resting of His kind and holy hands on ourselves, our Nation, our friends in the defense of freedom, and all mankind, now and always."

AMERICAN HISTORY PARADE

1749   George Washington receives his surveyor's license from the College of William and Mary.

1809   Mary Kies of Connecticut becomes the first woman to receive a U.S. patent, for a technique for weaving straw with silk and thread.

1864   The Battle of the Wilderness begins in Spotsylvania County, Virginia.

1925   John T. Scopes is arrested in Tennessee for teaching Darwin's theory of evolution.

1961   Astronaut Alan Shepard becomes the first American to travel into space during a fifteen-minute suborbital flight.

1988   The first Thursday in May is designated the National Day of Prayer.

ONE DAY COMEDIAN BOB HOPE got a suggestion from a sponsor: broadcast his popular radio program from March Field, an Army air base at Riverside, California. "Why should we drag the whole show down there?" Hope asked. But he consented, and on May 6, 1941, he performed for hundreds of cheering troops.

That one show changed his life. He couldn't get out of his mind the appreciative response of the young recruits. Seven months later, Japan attacked Pearl Harbor. Throughout the rest of World War II, with only two exceptions, Hope aired his shows from U.S. military installations. He went wherever the soldiers were fighting—Europe, North Africa, the Pacific.

"When the time for recognition of service to the nation in wartime comes to be considered, Bob Hope should be high on the list," John Steinbeck wrote in a newspaper column. "He gets laughter wherever he goes from men who need laughter."

After the war Hope became one of America's most popular entertainers. (And one of its most successful immigrants. His family had emigrated from England when he was a boy, coming through Ellis Island.) He never forgot the troops. For more than half a century, through the Cold War, Korean War, Vietnam War, Persian Gulf War, and times of peace, he led tours around the globe to perform for soldiers. "I wouldn't trade it for my entire career," he said. "Until you've actually seen them in action, you have no conception of their courage." Millions watched his televised Christmas shows for the troops.

Hope received all kinds of awards for service to country, including the Congressional Gold Medal and Presidential Medal of Freedom. In 1997, six years before his death, Congress made him an "Honorary Veteran," the first time it had ever bestowed such a tribute. Hope said it was the greatest honor he had ever received.

AMERICAN HISTORY PARADE

1861   Arkansas secedes from the Union.

1896   On the Potomac River, Samuel Langley demonstrates his "aerodrome," the world's first mechanically propelled, heavier-than-air machine; driven by a small steam engine, the unmanned craft flies about three-quarters of a mile.

1937   The German dirigible *Hindenburg* explodes in Lakehurst, New Jersey, killing 36 of the 97 people on board.

1939   John Steinbeck wins the Pulitzer Prize for *The Grapes of Wrath*.

1941   In Riverside, California, Bob Hope performs his first show for U.S. troops.

ON THIS DAY IN 1775, George Washington was traveling north, having left his home at Mount Vernon, Virginia, to attend the Second Continental Congress in Philadelphia. As he rode along, his thoughts were pulled in opposite directions. Ahead, war loomed—fighting had broken out at Lexington and Concord. Behind him, at his beloved plantation, the fields were full of green wheat and newly planted corn. Herring were running in the river, and the gardens were in bloom. He was not sure when he would be able to return.

Washington inherited Mount Vernon in 1761 from his half brother Lawrence, who had named the estate in honor of Admiral Edward Vernon, Lawrence's commander in the British Navy. The plantation eventually covered about 8,000 acres, and the columned house, atop a bluff overlooking the Potomac River, was one of Virginia's finest. Washington was keenly interested in farming and never tired of trying different crops and breeding livestock.

He could not have known, as he rode north, that he would have to spend years away from his plantation, first as commander of the army, later as president. "It is my full intention to devote my life and fortune in the cause we are engaged in, if need be," he wrote his brother John in 1775. But he always yearned for Mount Vernon.

When the long years of service were finally over, he happily retired to his home. "At the age of sixty-five I am recommencing my agricultural pursuits and rural amusements, which at all times have been the most pleasing occupation of my life, and most congenial with my temper," he wrote in 1797.

Washington was able to live his last years at Mount Vernon, where he died in 1799. He and his wife, Martha, are buried in a simple hillside tomb there.

AMERICAN HISTORY PARADE

1789   The first inaugural ball, honoring George and Martha Washington, is held in New York City.

1915   A German U-boat sinks the British liner *Lusitania* off the Irish coast, killing 1,200, including 128 Americans, hastening U.S. entry into World War I.

1945   Germany surrenders its forces to the Allies in Reims, France, bringing an end to World War II in Europe.

1957   John F. Kennedy is awarded the Pulitzer Prize for *Profiles in Courage*.

1992   The Twenty-seventh Amendment, barring Congress from giving itself a midterm pay raise, is ratified.

CREDIT FOR STARTING MOTHER'S DAY goes to a schoolteacher named Anna Jarvis. Her campaign to organize a holiday began as a way to honor the memory of her own mother, Anna Maria Reeves Jarvis. The elder Jarvis had devoted much of her life to the Andrews Methodist Episcopal Church of Grafton, West Virginia, and in May 1908, at Anna Jarvis's urging, the church held a service honoring mothers. Anna Jarvis, who lived in Philadelphia, also convinced merchant John Wanamaker to join her cause in establishing Mother's Day, and he held an afternoon service in his store. Within just a couple of years, the custom had spread to other states.

At one of the first Mother's Day services, Jarvis distributed white carnations, her mother's favorite flower. Many people still follow the tradition of giving and wearing carnations on Mother's Day—white flowers in memory of deceased mothers, and brightly colored ones for living mothers.

Jarvis and her supporters convinced ministers, politicians, and businessmen to support the goal of starting a national observance. On May 8, 1914, Congress passed a joint resolution designating the second Sunday in May as Mother's Day. The next day, President Woodrow Wilson issued the first Mother's Day presidential proclamation, calling for "a public expression of our love and reverence for the mothers of our country."

AMERICAN HISTORY PARADE

1541   Spanish explorer Hernando de Soto reaches the Mississippi River.

1846   General Zachary Taylor wins the first major battle of the Mexican War at Palo Alto, Texas.

1884   Harry S. Truman, the thirty-third U.S. president, is born in Lamar, Missouri.

1886   Druggist John S. Pemberton sells the first Coca-Cola at Jacob's Pharmacy in Atlanta, Georgia.

1914   Congress establishes the second Sunday in May as Mother's Day.

1945   Americans celebrate victory in Europe over Nazi Germany (VE Day).

ON MAY 9, 1754, the first political cartoon published in America appeared in Benjamin Franklin's *Pennsylvania Gazette*. Franklin himself probably designed the woodcut, which shows a snake severed into pieces representing Britain's American colonies.

The drawing was a reminder that the colonies must unite to defend themselves as they entered the French and Indian War. In an article accompanying the cartoon, Franklin warned of "the present disunited State of the British Colonies, and the extreme Difficulty of bringing so many different Governments and Assemblies to agree in any speedy and effectual Measures for our common Defense and Security." Franklin may have chosen a snake because of a popular superstition that a snake that had been cut into pieces would come back to life if the pieces were joined before sunset.

Dozens of newspapers throughout the colonies reprinted the cartoon. Years later, as the Revolutionary War approached, the snake image became a favorite American symbol for unity and love of liberty.

AMERICAN HISTORY PARADE

1502   Christopher Columbus sails from Cadiz, Spain, on his fourth and final trip to the New World.

1754   Benjamin Franklin's *Pennsylvania Gazette* publishes America's first political cartoon.

1865   Richard Gatling receives a patent for the Gatling gun, an early machine gun.

1926   Explorer Richard Byrd and copilot Floyd Bennett claim to have made the first flight over the North Pole (since disputed by some experts).

1974   The House Judiciary Committee begins impeachment hearings against President Nixon.

IT WAS THE MOST DARING ENGINEERING EFFORT OF ITS TIME. Many said it couldn't be done. The challenge: join East and West by building a railroad across the bulk of the continent and some of the most rugged terrain on earth. One congressman said they might as well try to build a railroad to the moon.

The Union Pacific Railroad started building west from Omaha, Nebraska, in 1863 while the Central Pacific Railroad built east from San Francisco. The plan was to meet somewhere in the middle.

It took six years and two armies totaling 20,000 men. Many of the workers were immigrants from China and Ireland who sweated long hours for one or two dollars a day. They laid tracks across hundreds of miles of prairie and scorching desert. They pushed over heights of 8,000 feet and tunneled their way through hard mountain ridges, sometimes at a rate of only a few inches per day. They bridged stream after stream. The tracks crossed one river alone thirty-one times.

In winter the workers plowed through snowdrifts ten feet high or more. It took thousands of men just to shovel the tracks clear. Sometimes avalanches carried whole crews over the edges of mountains.

On May 10, 1869, the two tracks finally met at Promontory Point, Utah. Officials hammered in the last spike—a golden one bearing the inscription, "May God continue the unity of our Country as this Railroad unites the two great Oceans of the world." A telegrapher sent a signal to the country: "Done!" From New York to San Francisco, the nation cheered.

The transcontinental railroad was the first in the world to cross a continent. It tied America together, helped open the West to settlers, and proved that Americans were a people willing to tackle the impossible.

AMERICAN HISTORY PARADE

1775   Ethan Allen and his Green Mountain Boys capture British-held Fort Ticonderoga in New York.

1865   Union troops capture Confederate president Jefferson Davis at Irwinville, Georgia.

1869   The transcontinental railroad is completed at Promontory Point, Utah.

1872   The Equal Rights Party nominates Victoria Woodhull as the first woman presidential candidate.

1908   The first Mother's Day services take place in Grafton, West Virginia and Philadelphia.

DURING THE REVOLUTIONARY WAR, British forces seized the spacious home of Rebecca Motte on the Congaree River in South Carolina. Motte, a wealthy widow, was forced to take up residence in a smaller nearby house while about 175 British soldiers fortified her home, surrounding it with a trench and parapet.

From May 8 to May 12, 1781, a Patriot force led by Francis Marion and Lighthorse Harry Lee laid siege to Fort Motte, as the British called their compound. Marion and Lee called on Lt. Daniel McPherson, the British commander, to surrender, but he refused. The Patriots soon concluded that to get the British out, they would have to set fire to the house. When Lee broke the news to Mrs. Motte, she responded that she was "gratified with the opportunity of contributing to the good of her country, and should view the approaching scene with delight."

The widow produced a bow and set of arrows and told Lee to put them to use. The Patriots shot flaming arrows at the roof, setting it on fire and forcing a surrender. Then they quickly climbed to the top of the house and managed to put out the flames. That evening, in the tradition of true Southern hospitality, Rebecca Motte served dinner to both the American and British officers in her dining room.

AMERICAN HISTORY PARADE

1647   Peter Stuyvesant arrives in New Amsterdam (later New York) to become governor of the Dutch colony.

1792   Captain Robert Gray becomes the first white explorer to sail into the Columbia River, which he named after his ship.

1858   Minnesota becomes the thirty-second state.

1947   The B. F. Goodrich Company announces the development of a tubeless tire.

1997   IBM's Deep Blue computer beats world chess champ Gary Kasparov, the first time a computer defeats a reigning grand master.

ON MAY 12, 1962, West Point Military Academy awarded General Douglas MacArthur the Thayer Award, given each year to a citizen whose service to the nation has exemplified West Point's motto, Duty, Honor, Country. The following comes from a speech MacArthur delivered to the academy's corps of cadets in acceptance of the award:

Duty. Honor. Country. Those three hallowed words reverently dictate what you ought to be, what you can be, what you will be. They are your rallying points to build courage when courage seems to fail, to regain faith when there seems to be little cause for faith, to create hope when hope becomes forlorn. . . .

The unbelievers will say they are but words. . . . But these are some of the things they do. They build your basic character. They mold you for your future roles as the custodians of the nation's defense. They make you strong enough to know when you are weak, and brave enough to face yourself when you are afraid.

They teach you to be proud and unbending in honest failure, but humble and gentle in success; not to substitute words for action; not to seek the path of comfort, but to face the stress and spur of difficulty and challenge; to learn to stand up in the storm, but to have compassion on those who fall; to master yourself before you seek to master others; to have a heart that is clean, a goal that is high; to learn to laugh, yet never forget how to weep; to reach into the future, yet never neglect the past; to be serious, yet never take yourself too seriously; to be modest so that you will remember the simplicity of true greatness, the open mind of true wisdom, the meekness of true strength.

AMERICAN HISTORY PARADE

1780   Patriot general Benjamin Lincoln surrenders Charleston, South Carolina, and more than 5,000 troops to British general Sir Henry Clinton.

1864   Some of the bloodiest fighting of the Civil War rages at the Battle of Spotsylvania Court House in Virginia.

1943   In World War II, Axis troops in North Africa surrender after advances by Allied forces.

1949   The Soviet Union ends its blockade of West Berlin, which the United States and Britain had overcome with the Berlin Airlift.

ON MAY 13, 1864, Union soldiers buried the remains of 21-year-old Pvt. William Henry Christman of the 67th Pennsylvania Infantry, who had died two days earlier in a Washington, D.C., hospital from complications related to measles. The Civil War was entering its third year, and cemeteries in the capital were full. So Pvt. Christman was laid to rest in a new burial ground on the Virginia side of the Potomac River, on the edge of an estate once belonging to Confederate general Robert E. Lee—thus becoming the first soldier interred in what is now Arlington National Cemetery.

One month later, the War Department officially designated Lee's estate as a military cemetery. The action was instigated by Quartermaster General Montgomery Meigs, who considered the Confederate general a traitor and wanted to make sure his family could never return to their home.

Today Arlington National Cemetery covers 624 acres and contains more than 300,000 graves. It averages about a hundred funerals a week. Veterans of every conflict since the Revolutionary War are buried there. Until 1967 all honorably discharged veterans could be buried at Arlington. Since that time, to conserve space, the Army has restricted burials to those who meet certain requirements, such as members of the armed forces who die on active duty or who serve long enough to officially retire.

Arlington National Cemetery is home to several famous monuments including the Tomb of the Unknown Soldier, President John F. Kennedy's grave, and the Lee mansion, the latter maintained by the National Park Service as a memorial to Robert E. Lee. Most striking, however, are the miles of small, white stones marking the graves of those who served their country. They make the place one of the nation's most revered grounds.

AMERICAN HISTORY PARADE

1607   Colonists found Jamestown, the first permanent English settlement in what is now the United States.

1846   Congress declares that a state of war exists between the United States and Mexico.

1864   The first military burial takes place in Arlington National Cemetery.

1865   The last land battle of the Civil War is fought at Palmito Ranch in south Texas.

1954   President Eisenhower signs the St. Lawrence Seaway Development Act to construct a system of canals between Montreal and Lake Erie.

ON MAY 14, 1805, the Lewis and Clark expedition was pushing up the Missouri River when a sudden squall hit the sail of one of their boats and swamped it. Captains Meriwether Lewis and William Clark, ashore at the time, looked on in horror as "our papers, instruments, books, medicine, a great part of our merchandise, and in short almost every article indispensably necessary to . . . insure the success of the enterprise" threatened to float away.

While the men struggled to get the boat to land, the expedition's only female member quickly and calmly plucked the supplies from the icy river. "The Indian woman, to whom I ascribe equal fortitude and resolution with any person on board at the time of accident, caught and preserved most of the light articles which were washed overboard," Lewis wrote in his journal. Six days later, the grateful captains named "a handsome river of about fifty yards in width" in Montana after Sacagawea, the young Shoshone woman.

Sacagawea (whose name means "bird woman"), the wife of a French trader, was hired by Lewis and Clark as an interpreter. Strapping her baby son on her back, she trekked west with the explorers on their famous "Voyage of Discovery" to the Pacific. Along the way she helped communicate with some of the Indians they encountered. In the Rockies, the Corps of Discovery met a band of Shoshone whose chief turned out to be Sacagawea's brother. She helped persuade them to provide horses needed to cross the mountains.

Sacagawea's fortitude and perseverance have made her a favorite American heroine. In 2000, the U.S. Mint began issuing dollar coins bearing the image of the young explorer carrying her son, Jean Baptiste.

AMERICAN HISTORY PARADE

1787   Delegates begin gathering in Philadelphia for the Constitutional Convention.

1897   In Philadelphia, John Philip Sousa's march "The Stars and Stripes Forever" is performed for the first time.

1904   The first Olympic Games held in the United States open in St. Louis.

1973   *Skylab*, the first U.S. space station, is launched from Cape Canaveral, Florida.

THIS DAY BRINGS AN OCCASION that deserves more notice than it often gets. May 15 is Peace Officers Memorial Day, a time to honor the police officers who keep our neighborhoods and country safe. In 1962 President Kennedy signed a Congressional resolution, which reads, in part:

Whereas the police officers of America have worked devotedly and selflessly in behalf of the people of this Nation, regardless of the peril or hazard to themselves; and

Whereas these officers have safeguarded the lives and property of their fellow Americans; and

Whereas by the enforcement of our laws, these same officers have given our country internal freedom from fear of the violence and civil disorder that is presently affecting other nations;

Whereas these men and women by their patriotic service and their dedicated efforts have earned the gratitude of the Republic:

Now, therefore, be it resolved by the Senate and the House of Representatives of the United States of America in Congress assembled, that the President is authorized and requested to issue proclamations designating May 15 of each year as Peace Officers Memorial Day in honor of the Federal, State, and municipal officers who have been killed or disabled in the line of duty.

Each year, the president calls on Americans to fly flags at half-staff on May 15. By annual proclamation the president also urges Americans to pay tribute to fallen officers and asks them to honor the men and women who work daily in the cause of justice.

AMERICAN HISTORY PARADE

1602   English explorer Bartholomew Gosnold leads the first European exploration of Cape Cod, Massachusetts.

1756   England declares war on France in America, beginning the Seven Years' War.

1911   The Supreme Court upholds an order for the dissolution of the Standard Oil Company, ruling that it is a monopoly.

1940   Crowds of shoppers scramble to buy nylon stockings the first day they go on sale in selected stores.

1951   AT&T announces that it is the first U.S. corporation to have 1 million stockholders.

ON MAY 16, 1842, about 100 pioneers with 18 wagons set out from the Independence, Missouri, area in one of the first wagon trains to the Northwest. Over the next two decades, tens of thousands would follow on the Oregon Trail, the longest of the great overland routes to the western frontier.

"Oregon or the Grave." "Patience and Perseverance." "Never Say Die." Such were the slogans that pioneer families painted on their wagons before striking out on the Oregon Trail, which began at Independence and stretched 2,000 miles across the Great Plains and Rocky Mountains to the valleys of the Oregon Territory. The journey usually took four to six months. The settlers started out in the spring so they could get through the mountains before snow blocked the passes.

They packed as much flour, bacon, salt, dried fruit, and other supplies as they could into the covered wagons, called "prairie schooners" because, from a distance, their white canvas tops looked like ship sails crossing the plains. Once on the trail, the settlers averaged about 15 miles a day. Many *walked* the whole trail beside the wagons.

Along the way, they faced blistering heat, biting cold, pounding rainstorms, and howling blizzards. They crossed flooded rivers and waterless plains. At times they endured hunger and thirst. Indian attacks were a rare but real threat. Cholera, smallpox, and other diseases were more common killers. Thousands died on the trail. The route was lined with broken wheels, smashed wagons, bleached bones of dead oxen, and buried loved ones, making it the nation's longest graveyard.

"We lost everything but our lives," wrote one settler after the trek. Yet thousands kept heading west, determined to make better lives for themselves and their children. The ruts left by their wagon wheels remain in some places—a testament to the iron will of the American pioneer.

AMERICAN HISTORY PARADE

1836   The first steamboat on the Pacific Coast, the *Beaver*, is tested at Vancouver, Washington.

1842   One of the first wagon trains sets out for the Northwest on the Oregon Trail.

1868   The Senate fails by one vote to convict President Andrew Johnson in his impeachment trial; he is later acquitted of all charges.

1888   In Philadelphia, German immigrant Emile Berliner demostrates the first modern phonograph record.

1929   Emil Jannings (Best Actor) and Janet Gaynor (Best Actress) are among the winners of the first Oscars presented at a Hollywood banquet.

1991   Queen Elizabeth II becomes the first British monarch to address Congress.

ON MAY 17, 1952, the *New York Times* ran an article reminding readers of Armed Forces Day, observed that year while American troops were fighting in Korea. "This is the day on which we have the welcome opportunity to pay special tribute to the men and women . . . who are in the service of their country all over the world," the *Times* noted. "Armed Forces Day won't be a matter of parades and receptions for a good many of them. They will all be in the line of duty and some of them may give their lives in that duty."

Armed Forces Day is observed on the third Saturday in May. It's a day to salute soldiers in all branches of the military and remember that we would have no peace, security, or freedom—no United States—without them.

While Memorial Day honors America's war dead, and Veteran's Day honors those who have served in times past, Armed Forces Day recognizes those presently serving. The nation has observed this patriotic holiday since 1950. The military often sponsors parades, air shows, and tours of ships, planes, and bases on Armed Forces Day.

"It is our most earnest hope that those who are in positions of peril, that those who have made exceptional sacrifices, yes, and those who are afflicted with plain drudgery and boredom, may somehow know that we hold them in exceptional esteem," the *Times* noted. "Perhaps if we are a little more conscious of our debt of honored affection they may be a little more aware of how much we think of them."

AMERICAN HISTORY PARADE

1792   The New York Stock Exchange is founded by 24 brokers meeting under a buttonwood tree on what today is Wall Street.

1875   Aristides, ridden by Oliver Lewis, wins the first Kentucky Derby at Churchill Downs in Louisville.

1877   Alexander Graham Bell answers the first interstate phone call, made from New Brunswick, New Jersey, to New York City.

1954   In *Brown v. Board of Education of Topeka*, the Supreme Court rules that racial segregation in public schools is unconstitutional.

1973   The Senate Watergate Committee begins nationally televised hearings.

ON MAY 18, 1896, the U.S. Supreme Court handed down a decision in *Plessy v. Ferguson*, a case that challenged a Louisiana law segregating railroad-car passengers by race. The Court upheld the statute, establishing the policy of "separate but equal" public facilities for blacks and whites. John Marshall Harlan, a former slave owner, was the only justice to dissent from the *Plessy* decision. In the following decades, civil rights advocates often quoted his forceful argument in their quest to end segregation:

> In view of the Constitution, in the eye of the law, there is in this country no superior, dominant, ruling class of citizens. There is no caste here. Our Constitution is color-blind, and neither knows nor tolerates classes among citizens. In respect of civil rights, all citizens are equal before the law. The humblest is the peer of the most powerful. The law regards man as man, and takes no account of his surroundings or of his color when his civil rights as guaranteed by the supreme law of the land are involved. . . .
>
> The arbitrary separation of citizens on the basis of race while they are on a public highway is a badge of servitude wholly inconsistent with the civil freedom and the equality before the law established by the Constitution. It cannot be justified upon any legal grounds. . . .
>
> We boast of the freedom enjoyed by our people above all other peoples. But it is difficult to reconcile that boast with a state of the law which, practically, puts the brand of servitude and degradation upon a large class of our fellow citizens, our equals before the law. The thin disguise of "equal" accommodations for passengers in railroad coaches will not mislead anyone, nor atone for the wrong this day done.

AMERICAN HISTORY PARADE

1860   Republicans nominate Abraham Lincoln for president.

1863   Ulysses S. Grant begins the siege of Vicksburg, Mississippi.

1896   The Supreme Court upholds "separate but equal" racial segregation in *Plessy v. Ferguson*.

1908   Congress requires the motto In God We Trust to appear on certain coins.

1980   Mount St. Helens in Washington erupts, leaving 57 people dead or missing.

IN MAY 1944, Judge Learned Hand, considered one of America's most brilliant legal scholars, addressed a large crowd in New York City's Central Park, on the theme of liberty. Judge Hand's words inspired the nation at a time when the outcome of World War II was still in question, and many wondered what the future held for democratic ideals such as freedom and equality.

What then is the spirit of liberty? I cannot define it; I can only tell you my own faith. The spirit of liberty is the spirit which is not too sure that it is right; the spirit of liberty is the spirit which seeks to understand the mind of other men and women; the spirit of liberty is the spirit which weighs their interests alongside its own without bias; the spirit of liberty remembers that not even a sparrow falls to earth unheeded; the spirit of liberty is the spirit of Him who, near two thousand years ago, taught mankind that lesson it has never learned but never quite forgotten; that there may be a kingdom where the least shall be heard and considered side by side with the greatest. And now in that spirit, that spirit of an America which has never been, and which may never be; nay, which never will be except as the conscience and courage of Americans create it; yet in the spirit of that America which lies hidden in some form in the aspirations of us all; in the spirit of that America for which our young men are at this moment fighting and dying; in that spirit of liberty and of America I ask you to rise and with me pledge our faith in the glorious destiny of our beloved country.

AMERICAN HISTORY PARADE

1749   King George II grants the Ohio Company a large expanse of land to promote settlement of the Ohio River Valley.

1828   President John Quincy Adams signs a protective tariff considered unfair in the South, which labels it the "tariff of abominations."

1864   A Confederate attack against Union forces ends several days of horrific fighting at the Battle of Spotsylvania Court House in Virginia.

1921   Congress places quotas on the number of immigrants entering the United States.

ON THE RAINY MORNING OF MAY 20, 1927, twenty-five-year-old Charles Lindbergh snapped on his helmet and climbed into a tiny one-seat plane at Roosevelt Field in Long Island, New York. Minutes later the aircraft was heading down the unpaved runway. Lindbergh was about to try what no one else had been able to do: fly nonstop from New York to Paris.

He had named his plane *Spirit of St. Louis* because several St. Louis businessmen had helped pay for it. To cut down on weight, he was going without a radio or parachute. Yet the plane was so loaded with fuel it barely cleared the telephone wires at the end of the runway as it headed toward the shifting airs of the northern Atlantic.

For the next 33½ hours, the young pilot bounced through rain squalls and crossed frozen deserts of ice. In the blackness of night, he flew into a cloud that threatened to encrust his wings with ice and drag him into the sea.

As the hours mounted, he battled fatigue. To stay awake, he held his eyelids open with his fingers.

The sun finally rose. A few hours later, Lindbergh saw specks on the water—fishing boats. He had reached the coast of Ireland.

On he flew, over England. Another night fell as he crossed the English Channel to France. "I almost hated to see the lights of Paris," he said, "because the night was clear and I still had gas in my tanks."

Lindbergh's courage and determination thrilled people the world over. Today his *Spirit of St. Louis* hangs in the Smithsonian's Air and Space Museum in Washington, D.C. It is still hard to believe he managed to cross the Atlantic alone in such a fragile craft. It may have been the most daring flight ever.

AMERICAN HISTORY PARADE

1506   Christopher Columbus dies in Spain, still believing that his journeys to the Americas were to the east coast of Asia.

1861   North Carolina secedes from the Union.

1873   Levi Strauss receives a patent for his denim pants with copper rivets.

1899   Taxi driver Jacob German becomes the first driver to be arrested for speeding (going 12 miles per hour on Lexington Avenue in New York City).

1927   Charles Lindbergh takes off on his historic transatlantic flight.

1939   Regular transatlantic airmail service begins with a flight of Pan Am's *Yankee Clipper* from Port Washington, New York, to Lisbon, Portugal.

WHEN THE CIVIL WAR BROKE OUT, former schoolteacher Clara Barton begged Union generals to let her go to the front lines to help the wounded. "A battlefield is no place for a woman," they told her. Barton hounded them until they gave in. Loading a wagon with supplies, she headed to the front and nursed injured men as shells whistled overhead.

At the Battle of Antietam in Maryland, a bullet tore through the sleeve of her dress, killing the wounded soldier she was tending. She kept risking her life at front lines across the South, from Fredericksburg to Charleston. The grateful soldiers began to call her the Angel of the Battlefield.

After the war she directed a search for missing men and helped mark the graves of nearly 13,000 Union soldiers who died at the Andersonville Prison in Georgia. On a trip to Europe, she helped organize the relief efforts of the International Red Cross in the Franco-Prussian War.

A decade later, on May 21, 1881, Barton founded the American Red Cross. For the next two decades, she was on the scene, delivering relief in times of natural disaster and war, including the Johnstown Flood of 1889, the 1898 explosion of the USS *Maine* ("I am with the wounded," she wrote to President McKinley from Cuba), and the Great Galveston Hurricane of 1900. She helped provide relief for victims of famine and war in Russia, the Balkans, Armenia, and Cuba.

Barton served as president of the American Red Cross until age eighty-two. She died in 1912, eight years after her retirement. Her own words sum up her drive to aid others: "The door that nobody else will go in at, seems always to swing open widely for me."

AMERICAN HISTORY PARADE

1542   Spanish explorer Hernando De Soto dies on the banks of the Mississippi River.

1819   The first bicycles in the United States (known then as "velocipedes" and "swift walkers") appear on the streets of New York City.

1832   The first Democratic Party national convention begins in Baltimore.

1881   Clara Barton founds the American Red Cross.

1927   Charles Lindbergh lands his *Spirit of St. Louis* in Paris, completing the first solo nonstop flight across the Atlantic.

1932   Amelia Earhart lands in Ireland to become the first woman to fly nonstop across the Atlantic.

AFTER THE REVOLUTIONARY WAR, some Americans doubted that the newly freed colonies could govern themselves. In May 1782 George Washington received a letter from one of his officers, Colonel Lewis Nicola, proposing that the general use the army to make himself king of the United States.

Washington's response on May 22 was sharp:

> With a mixture of great surprise and astonishment I have read with attention the sentiments you have submitted to my perusal. Be assured sir, no occurrence in the course of the war has given me more painful sensations than your information of there being such ideas existing in the army as you have expressed, [which are] big with the greatest mischiefs that can befall my country. If I am not deceived in the knowledge of myself, you could not have found a person to whom your schemes are more disagreeable. . . . Let me conjure you then, if you have any regard for your country—concern for yourself or posterity—or respect for me, to banish these thoughts from your mind.

Yet there were some who still wondered if General Washington would give up his power. He had the adoration of the people and command of the Continental Army. Washington erased doubts once and for all in late 1783 when he appeared before Congress, meeting in Annapolis, Maryland, to "surrender into their hands the trust committed to me" by resigning his commission.

King George had said that if Washington voluntarily gave up power, then he truly *would* be the greatest man on earth. Oliver Cromwell hadn't done it. Napoleon would not do it. But Washington did. He might have had a kingdom for the asking. He was not interested. He put his country first, not himself.

AMERICAN HISTORY PARADE

1802   Martha Washington dies at Mount Vernon at age seventy.

1843   A wagon train of a thousand pioneers bound for the Northwest leaves Independence, Missouri, on the Oregon Trail.

1849   Abraham Lincoln receives a patent for an invention "for buoying vessels over shoals," which he never puts to use.

1856   In a sign of tensions between North and South, South Carolina congressman Preston Brooks beats Massachusetts senator Charles Sumner with a cane in the Senate chamber.

1972   Richard Nixon becomes the first president to visit Russia.

ON MAY 23, 1788, South Carolina became the eighth state to ratify the U.S. Constitution. The state takes its name from the colony that came before it, which had been named for King Charles I of England in 1629. *Carolina* is a Latin form of Charles.

A few more origins of state names:

Minnesota – from the Dakota words *minne sota*, meaning "sky-tinted water," referring to the Minnesota River or the region's many lakes

Mississippi – after the river, whose Chippewa Indian name means "large river" or "father of waters"

Missouri – after the Missouri River; the word *Missouri* may have come from an Indian word meaning "town of the large canoes"

Montana – from a Latin term for a mountainous region; in Spanish, *montaña* means "mountain"

Nebraska – from the Oto Indian word *nebrathka*, meaning "flat water" and referring to the Platte River

Nevada – from a Spanish word meaning "snow-clad"

New Hampshire – for Hampshire, England

New Jersey – for Jersey, an island in the English Channel

New Mexico – perhaps from an Aztec word meaning "place of Mexitli," an Aztec god; the Spanish called the area *Nuevo Mexico* ("New Mexico")

New York – in honor of the Duke of York, brother of England's King Charles II

AMERICAN HISTORY PARADE

1785   Benjamin Franklin writes in a letter that he has just invented bifocal glasses.

1788   South Carolina becomes the eighth state to ratify the Constitution.

1903   Horatio Nelson Jackson and Sewell Crocker leave San Francisco on the first automobile trip across the United States; they arrive in New York City 63 days later.

1911   The New York Public Library is dedicated.

1934   Police kill bank robbers Bonnie Parker and Clyde Barrow in Bienville Parish, Louisiana.

DURING WORLD WAR II, the U.S. military faced a deadly communications problem in the Pacific: the Japanese often succeeded in intercepting and deciphering Allied messages. It was getting harder and harder to invent codes the enemy couldn't crack.

The solution came from the Navajo "code talkers," men from the Navajo nation who put their native language to work for the Marines. In May 1942, twenty-nine Navajo recruits gathered in San Diego and soon began devising a code that proved to be one of the most foolproof in the history of warfare.

How did the ingenious code work?

The code talkers started by creating strings of seemingly unrelated Navajo words. Once translated into English, the first letter of each word was used to spell out a message. More than one Navajo word could be used to stand for each English letter, making the code even more confusing to the Japanese. For example, for the letter *a*, code talkers could use the words *wol-la-chee* (ant), *be-la-sana*, (apple), or *tse-nill* (ax). One way to send the word *navy* was *tsah* (needle) *wol-la-chee* (ant) *ah-keh-di-glini* (victor) *tsah-ah-dzoh* (yucca). Sometimes the code talkers used Navajo words to stand for military terms. The Navajo word for *hummingbird* stood for a fighter plane. The word for *shark* meant a destroyer.

More than 400 Navajos served as U.S. Marine code talkers in the Pacific, sending radio messages between command posts and front lines. The Japanese never broke the code. Without doubt, these brave men saved countless lives and helped speed the Allied victory. At the battle of Iwo Jima alone, six code talkers sent and received more than 800 messages in the first two days of fighting, all without error. One signal officer later said, "Were it not for the Navajos, the Marines would never have taken Iwo Jima."

AMERICAN HISTORY PARADE

1830   The B&O Railroad, the first passenger railroad in the United States, begins service between Baltimore and Ellicott's Mill, Maryland.

1844   In a long-distance demonstration of his telegraph, Samuel Morse sends the message "What hath God wrought!" from Washington, D.C., to Baltimore.

1856   Antislavery leader John Brown leads an attack against pro-slavery settlers at Pottawatomie Creek, Kansas, killing five.

1883   The Brooklyn Bridge, connecting Brooklyn and Manhattan, opens to traffic.

1962   Astronaut Scott Carpenter, in *Aurora 7*, becomes the second American to orbit the earth.

ON THIS DAY IN 1968, Vice President Hubert Humphrey dedicated the nation's tallest monument, the Gateway Arch in St. Louis, Missouri. The arch, soaring 630 feet above the banks of the Mississippi River, is part of the Jefferson National Expansion Memorial, which honors Thomas Jefferson, the Louisiana Purchase, and the pioneers who settled the West.

The gleaming stainless-steel arch was designed by Finnish-American architect Eero Saarinen and German-American structural engineer Hannskarl Bandel. It stands 75 feet taller than the Washington Monument and more than twice as tall as the Statue of Liberty. Construction began in 1963 and was completed in 1965, though the structure's tram system wasn't fully installed until 1968.

In each leg, visitors can board a tram made of eight five-passenger capsules for a four-minute ride to the top. There, windows give views of the Mississippi River to the east and St. Louis to the west.

St. Louis, which started as a French fur trading post in 1764, became part of the United States in 1803 when President Jefferson bought the Louisiana Territory from France. The next year the Lewis and Clark expedition set out for the Pacific Ocean from the St. Louis area. The town became a "gateway to the West" for settlers, as well as a steamship port and railroad center. The gleaming arch has come to represent the spirit of a nation always ready to take on the next frontier.

AMERICAN HISTORY PARADE

1787   The Constitutional Convention opens in Philadelphia after reaching a quorum of seven states.

1935   Babe Ruth hits the last of his 714 home runs.

1961   President John F. Kennedy asks the nation to commit itself to the goal of landing a man on the moon before the decade is out.

1968   The Gateway Arch in St. Louis is dedicated.

1977   *Star Wars*, one of the most popular movies of all time, opens.

2008   The *Phoenix* spacecraft lands on Mars to search for evidence of microbial life in its soil.

ON MAY 26, 1830, Congress passed the Indian Removal Act, authorizing the removal of American Indians living east of the Mississippi River to western lands. Two days later, President Andrew Jackson signed the act into law. The young French nobleman Alexis de Tocqueville, who toured America writing down everything he observed, described the tragic results of the Indian Removal policy in his classic *Democracy in America*:

> At the end of the year 1831, while I was on the left bank of the Mississippi at a place named Memphis by the Europeans, there arrived a numerous band of Choctaws. . . . These savages had left their country, and were endeavoring to gain the right bank of the Mississippi, where they hoped to find an asylum which had been promised them by the American government. It was then the middle of winter, and the cold was unusually severe; the snow had frozen hard upon the ground, and the river was drifting huge masses of ice. The Indians had their families with them; and they brought in their train the wounded and sick, with children newly born, and old men upon the verge of death. They possessed neither tents nor wagons, but only their arms and some provisions. I saw them embark to pass the mighty river, and never will that solemn spectacle fade from my remembrance. No cry, no sob was heard amongst the assembled crowd; all were silent. Their calamities were of ancient date, and they knew them to be irremediable. The Indians had all stepped into the boat which was to carry them across, but their dogs remained upon the bank. As soon as these animals perceived that their masters were finally leaving the shore, they set up a dismal howl and, plunging all together into the icy waters of the Mississippi, they swam after the boat.

AMERICAN HISTORY PARADE

1637   In the Pequot War a force of Puritans and Mohegans attack a Pequot village at Mystic, Connecticut, killing some 600 men, women, and children.

1830   The Indian Removal Act is passed by Congress.

1865   General Edmund Kirby Smith, commander of the Confederate Trans-Mississippi Department, becomes the last Southern general to surrender in the Civil War.

1868   For the second time the Senate fails by one vote to convict President Andrew Johnson in his impeachment trial.

1896   The *Customer's Afternoon Letter* publishes the Dow Jones Industrial Average for the first time.

ON MAY 27, 1937, at exactly 6:00 a.m., the blare of foghorns announced the opening of San Francisco's Golden Gate Bridge. Boy Scout Walter Kronenberg was first in line to pay the five cents toll to walk onto the ribbon of concrete and steel hanging 220 feet above the water. Before the day was out, nearly 200,000 people—some strolling, others sprinting, roller skating, or dancing—had crossed the 4,200-foot-long central span, at that time the longest suspension bridge span in the world.

The bridge, which crosses the entrance to San Francisco Bay, runs a total of 1.7 miles and connects the peninsula of San Francisco to northern California. It takes its name from the 400-foot deep strait it spans, named *Chrysopylae* ("Golden Gate") in 1846 by Captain John C. Fremont because it reminded him of the Golden Horn, the harbor at Istanbul.

Much credit for the bridge's elegant art deco design belongs to architect Irving Morrow and engineers Alton Ellis and Leon S. Moisseiff. But the driving force behind the project was chief engineer Joseph Strauss, who dreamed of building "the biggest thing of its kind that a man could build." During sixteen years of planning and construction, Strauss overcame a host of obstacles: lawsuits, environmentalists, the Great Depression, tumultuous ocean currents, howling winds, violent storms, and skeptics who called it "the bridge that couldn't be built."

About 83,000 tons of steel and 390,000 cubic yards of concrete make up the Golden Gate Bridge. Its two towers stand 746 feet high, and the two main cables consist of 80,000 miles of wire. The bridge's distinctive color, known as International Orange, helps make it one of the most famous structures in the world, one that represents the hope and promise of America.

AMERICAN HISTORY PARADE

1813   In the War of 1812, Col. Winfield Scott, assisted by American naval forces, captures Fort George, New York.

1890   Louis Glass and William Arnold receive patents for the first jukebox, known as the "Nickel-in-the-Slot."

1919   A Navy seaplane commanded by Albert Read reaches Lisbon, Portugal, on the first transatlantic flight (with a few stops along the way).

1937   San Francisco's Golden Gate Bridge opens.

ON MAY 28, 1937, President Franklin D. Roosevelt pressed a button in Washington, D.C., signaling that the new Golden Gate Bridge in San Francisco was officially open to vehicular traffic. (The bridge had opened to pedestrian traffic the day before.) The Golden Gate Bridge was the longest suspension bridge in the world until the opening of the Verrazano-Narrows Bridge in New York City in 1964.*

The U.S. is home to several great suspension bridges.

Year	Bridge	Location	Length of Main Span (ft.)
1964	**Verrazano-Narrows Bridge**	**New York, NY**	4,260
1937	**Golden Gate Bridge**	**San Francisco Bay**	4,200
1957	**Mackinac Bridge**	**Straits of Mackinac, MI**	3,800
1931	**George Washington Bridge**	**Hudson River, NY-NJ**	3,500
1950	**Tacoma Narrows Bridge**	**Tacoma, WA**	2,800
2007	**Tacoma Narrows Bridge II**	**Tacoma, WA**	2,800
2003	**Al Zampa Memorial Bridge**	**Carquinez Strait, CA**	2,388
1936	**San Francisco-Oakland Bay Bridge**	**San Francisco Bay**	2,310
1939	**Bronx-Whitestone Bridge**	**New York, NY**	2,300
1951	**Delaware Memorial Bridge**	**Wilmington, DE**	2,150
1968	**Delaware Memorial Bridge II**	**Wilmington, DE**	2,150
1957	**Walt Whitman Bridge**	**Philadelphia, PA**	2,000

* The Verrazano-Narrows Bridge is currently the seventh-longest suspension bridge in the world. The longest is the Akashi-Kaiky Bridge in Japan, with a central span of 6,532 feet.

AMERICAN HISTORY PARADE

1754 Virginia militia under Lt. Col. George Washington defeat French troops near Uniontown, Pennsylvania, in an opening skirmish of the French and Indian War.

1902 *The Virginian* by Owen Wister, regarded as the first Western, is published.

1929 *On with the Show*, the first movie with color and sound, debuts in New York.

1957 The National League approves the move of the Brooklyn Dodgers and New York Giants to Los Angeles and San Francisco.

1984 Ronald Reagan leads a funeral in Arlington National Cemetery for an unknown serviceman killed in Vietnam (the remains are later identified as those of Air Force Lt. Michael J. Blassie and moved to St. Louis).

ON MAY 29, 2004, America dedicated the National World War II Memorial in Washington, D.C., which pays tribute to all Americans who served in history's most terrible war. Inscribed near a wall honoring those who gave their lives in World War II is a simple statement from Harry S. Truman: "Our debt to the heroic men and valiant women in the service of our country can never be repaid. They have earned our undying gratitude. America will never forget their sacrifices."

At this time of year, when Americans kick off their summers with holiday weekend vacations and barbecues, it is good to pause and remember our countrymen who have answered the call to serve, especially those who made the ultimate sacrifice.

Conflict	U.S. Military Deaths*
Revolutionary War (1775–1783)	25,000
War of 1812 (1812–1815)	20,000
Mexican War (1846–1848)	13,300
Civil War (1861–1865)	
Union	360,000
Confederate	260,000
Spanish-American War (1898)	2,500
World War I (1917–1918)	116,500
World War II (1941–1945)	405,400
Korean War (1950–1953)	36,600
Vietnam War (1964–1973)	58,200
Persian Gulf War (1990–1991)	380
Afghanistan (2001–)	450**
Iraq War (2003–)	4,100**

*Includes battlefield and other deaths, such as soldiers who died of disease. Because official records may be incomplete, especially prior to World War I, military death figures are estimates.

**Approximate military deaths as of June 2008.

AMERICAN HISTORY PARADE

1765   Patrick Henry attacks the Stamp Act in Virginia's House of Burgesses, saying, "If this be treason, make the most of it!"

1790   Rhode Island becomes the last of the thirteen original states to ratify the Constitution.

1848   Wisconsin becomes the thirtieth state.

1917   John F. Kennedy, the thirty-fifth U.S. president, is born in Brookline, Massachusetts.

MEMORIAL DAY, the last Monday of May, is the day we honor Americans who gave their lives in military service.

This holiday was originally called Decoration Day and honored soldiers who had died during the Civil War. Immediately after the war, various towns in the North and South began to set aside days to decorate soldiers' graves with flowers and flags. Those earliest memorial observances occurred in Waterloo, New York; Columbus, Mississippi; Richmond, Virginia; Carbondale, Illinois; Boalsburg, Pennsylvania, and several other places.

The first widespread observance of Decoration Day came on May 30, 1868, which Maj. Gen. John A. Logan proclaimed as a day to honor the dead. General James Garfield (later the twentieth U.S. president) gave a speech at Arlington National Cemetery in remembrance of fallen soldiers, saying that "for love of country they accepted death, and thus resolved all doubts, and made immortal their patriotism and their virtue." Afterward, 5,000 people helped decorate the graves of more than 20,000 Union and Confederate soldiers.

Over the years the day became an occasion to remember the dead in all American wars, and came to be known as Memorial Day.

On the Thursday before Memorial Day, in a tradition known as "Flags-in," the soldiers of the 3rd U.S. Infantry place small flags before more than a quarter million gravestones at Arlington National Cemetery. They then patrol twenty-four hours a day to make sure each flag remains standing throughout the weekend. On Memorial Day the president or vice president lays a wreath at the Tomb of the Unknown Soldier in the cemetery.

According to the U.S. flag code, American flags should be flown at half-staff until noon on Memorial Day, then raised to the top of the pole. At 3:00 p.m. local time, all Americans are asked to pause for a moment of remembrance.

AMERICAN HISTORY PARADE

1539   Spanish explorer Hernando de Soto lands in Florida.

1806   In Kentucky, Andrew Jackson kills lawyer Charles Dickinson in a duel for allegedly insulting Jackson's wife.

1868   Memorial Day is widely observed for the first time.

1896   In New York City the first recorded car accident occurs when a motor wagon collides with a bicycle.

1911   Ray Harroun wins the first Indianapolis 500 auto race.

1922   The Lincoln Memorial is dedicated in Washington, D.C.

1958   Unidentified soldiers killed in World War II and the Korean War are buried at Arlington National Cemetery.

"THE SIGHT BEFORE US is that of a strong and good nation that stands in silence and remembers those who were loved and who, in return, loved their countrymen enough to die for them," President Ronald Reagan said on May 31, 1982, after laying a wreath at the Tomb of the Unknown Soldier in an annual Memorial Day ceremony.

The Tomb of the Unknown Soldier stands on a hill overlooking Washington, D.C., in Arlington National Cemetery. One of the most solemn monuments in our country, it honors all of the U.S. soldiers whose remains have never been identified.

Beneath the eight-foot-tall, white marble tomb lies the body of an unknown soldier from World War I, placed there in 1921. Inscribed on the tomb are the words:

> HERE RESTS IN
> HONORED GLORY
> AN AMERICAN
> SOLDIER
> KNOWN BUT TO GOD

The tombs of unknown soldiers from World War II, the Korean War, and the Vietnam War lie nearby. The remains of the Vietnam unknown were identified by DNA testing in 1998, so they were removed, and that tomb is now empty. Members of the 3rd U.S. Infantry guard the Tomb of the Unknown Soldier 24 hours a day, 365 days a year.

AMERICAN HISTORY PARADE

1821   The first American cathedral, the Cathedral of the Assumption of the Blessed Virgin Mary, is dedicated in Baltimore.

1889   Some 2,200 people die in Johnstown, Pennsylvania, after a dam breaks and floods the city.

1918   Lt. Douglas Campbell becomes the first ace to fly under American colors when he shoots down his fifth German plane over France.

1927   The Ford Motor Company produces its last Model T.

1977   The trans-Alaska oil pipeline is completed.

1994   The United States announces it will no longer aim nuclear missiles at targets in the former Soviet Union.

FLAG ETIQUETTE:
GUIDELINES FOR
DISPLAYING AND
HANDLING THE U.S. FLAG

The main rule to follow in flying and handling the U.S. flag is *always treat it with honor and respect*. The flag stands for our land and our people. It represents our highest principles, our way of life, and our heritage—including the sacrifice of those who have bled and died for freedom.

The following guidelines are based on the United States Flag Code, which provides recommendations for handling the flag. The Flag Code, adopted by Congress and revised several times, can be found in Title 4, Chapter 1 of the United States Code.

WHEN TO DISPLAY THE FLAG

Citizens may display the flag at any time. When flying the flag outside, it is customary to display it only from sunrise to sunset. If displayed overnight, it should be illuminated.

It is particularly appropriate to fly the flag on the following days:

New Year's Day – January 1

Inauguration Day – January 20

Martin Luther King Day – third Monday in January

Lincoln's Birthday – February 12

Washington's Birthday – February 22

President's Day – third Monday in February

Easter Sunday

Mother's Day – second Sunday in May

Peace Officers Memorial Day (half-staff) – May 15

Armed Forces Day – third Saturday in May

Memorial Day (half-staff until noon) – last Monday in May

Flag Day – June 14

Father's Day – third Sunday in June

Independence Day – July 4

Labor Day – first Monday in September

Patriot Day (half-staff) – September 11

Constitution Day – September 17

POW/MIA Recognition Day – third Friday in September

Gold Star Mother's Day – last Sunday in September

Columbus Day – October 12 (observed second Monday in October)

National Election Day – first Tuesday in November

Veterans Day – November 11

Thanksgiving Day – fourth Thursday in November

Pearl Harbor Remembrance Day (half-staff) – December 7

Christmas Day – December 25

State and local holidays

The date your state was admitted to the Union

The flag should not be flown in rain, sleet, snow, or other bad weather, except when an all-weather flag is used.

The flag should be displayed in or near schools when in session; on or near public buildings when in use; and in or near polling places on election days.

RAISING AND LOWERING THE FLAG

When raising the flag, hoist it briskly. When possible hoist it in the morning, but not earlier than sunrise.

When lowering the flag, lower it slowly. Take it down in the evening before sunset.

FLYING THE FLAG AT HALF-STAFF

Flying the flag at half-staff (halfway up its pole) is a sign of mourning. Hoist it to the top of the staff first for an instant, then lower it to half-staff. When ready to take it down, raise it to the top again, then lower it.

The president may order the flag to be flown at half-staff when prominent leaders die, or at other times when the nation wishes to show its sorrow and respect. Governors may also order the U.S. flag to be flown at half-staff in times of mourning in a particular state.

The flag is flown at half-staff thirty days following the death of a president or former president; ten days following the death of a vice president, chief justice or retired chief justice of the United States, or speaker of the House of Representatives; from the day of death until burial of an associate justice of the Supreme Court, cabinet member, former vice president, or governor; and on the day of death and the following day for a member of Congress.

On Memorial Day the flag should be displayed at half-staff until noon, then raised to the top of the staff.

The flag should also be flown at half-staff on Peace Officers Memorial Day, May 15, unless that day is also Armed Forces Day; Patriot Day, September 11; and Pearl Harbor Remembrance Day, December 7.

Saluting the Flag

Citizens should salute: (1) while saying the Pledge of Allegiance, (2) during the ceremony of hoisting or lowering the flag, and (3) when the flag is passing in a parade or in review. It is also appropriate to salute during the national anthem.

All present should face the flag and stand at attention. Those in uniform should give the military salute. Citizens not in uniform should salute by placing the right hand over the heart. A man wearing a hat should remove it with the right hand and hold it at the left shoulder, so that his hand is over the heart.

During a parade, it is appropriate to salute only the first U.S. flag that passes by.

Displaying the Flag with Other Flags

On Flagpoles – When flown on a flagpole in line with other flags on poles of the same height, the U.S. flag goes on its own right. It should be hoisted first and lowered last.

In a Group on Staffs – The U.S. flag should be at the center and at the highest point of the group when displayed along with state, local, or association flags on staffs.

Crossed Staffs – When displayed with another flag on crossed staffs, the U.S. flag goes on its own right, with its staff in front of the other.

Flags on One Pole – When flown on a pole with other flags (such as state or local flags), the U.S. flag should always be on top.

With Flags of Other Nations – Flags of other sovereign nations should not be flown on the same pole with the U.S. flag, but rather on separate poles of the same height. The flags should be of approximately equal size. International usage forbids the display of one nation's flag above another in time of peace.

In general, in the United States, no other flag should be placed above the U.S. flag, to its right, or in a position of superior honor to the U.S. flag. (The United Nations headquarters in New York City, where the UN flag is given the main position, is an exception to this rule.)

On Walls and in Windows

When hanging the flag on a wall, either horizontally or vertically, the flag's blue union should be at the top, to the flag's own right, and to the observer's left.

The flag should be displayed in a window the same way, so that the observer on the street sees the union on the left.

On Buildings and over Streets

When displayed on a staff that projects from a window, balcony, or building, the flag's blue union goes at the peak of the staff (unless the flag is at half-staff).

When hung across a street on a rope or wire, the flag should hang vertically. The union should hang to the north on an east-west street; it should hang to the east on a north-south street.

When the flag is hung over a sidewalk from a rope extending from a building to a pole at the edge of the sidewalk, it should be displayed vertically with the union furthest from the building.

In Parades and Processions

Always carry the flag aloft and free in a procession—not flat or horizontally. (An exception is when carrying a flag too large to be flown from a staff.)

When carried in a procession with other flags, the U.S. flag should be either on the marching right (that is, the flag's own right), or, if there is a line of other flags, in front of the center of that line.

On floats, cars, and boats in a parade, the flag should be displayed on a staff.

It should not be draped over any part of the float, car, or boat. (Use bunting, not a flag, to drape vehicles.)

Church, Platform, and Auditorium Use

When used on a speaker's platform, if the flag is being displayed flat (hanging on the wall), it should be hung above and behind the speaker.

When displayed from a staff in a church or public auditorium, the U.S. flag should be on the speaker's own right as he or she faces the audience. Other flags, if any, should be on the speaker's left.

The custom of placing the flag on the speaker's right as a position of honor evolved from the fact that the right hand was once regarded as the "weapon hand." Offering the right hand without a weapon was a sign of peace.

When the flag is used to cover a casket, it should be placed so that the blue union is at the head and over the left shoulder. It should not be lowered into the grave or allowed to touch the ground.

Rules of Respect

Keep the flag in good shape and safe. It should be cleaned when soiled and mended when torn. Flags worn or damaged beyond repair should be disposed of in a dignified manner (see "Disposing of a Worn Flag").

The flag should not be dipped to any person or thing. (An exception is that ships at sea sometimes salute one another by dipping their colors.)

The flag should not be displayed with the blue union down, except as a distress signal.

The flag should never touch anything beneath it, such as the ground, the floor, water, or merchandise.

The flag should not be used as drapery, festooned, or drawn up in folds. It should always be allowed to fall free. Bunting of blue, white, and red—rather than the flag itself—should be used for covering a speaker's desk, draping the front of the platform, and for decoration in general.

The flag should not be used as a covering for a ceiling. No words, letters, drawings, pictures, insignia, or any other marks should be placed on it. It should not be used to hold or carry anything, or used to cover a statue or monument.

The flag should not be used as a costume or athletic uniform.

When the flag is worn as a lapel pin, it should be placed on the left lapel, near the heart.

FOLDING THE FLAG

To fold the U.S. flag, two people face each other, each holding an end.

1. Fold it in half lengthwise.
2. Fold it in half lengthwise again, so that the blue union is on the outside.
3. While one person holds the flag by the union, the other makes a triangle fold in the opposite end.
4. Continue to fold the flag in triangles until only the blue union with stars is showing.

RECOMMENDED SIZES OF FLAGS

Flags flown from angled poles on homes and those displayed on standing poles in offices, auditoriums, and other inside locations are usually either 3 x 5 or 4 x 6 feet. Color guards usually carry 4 x 6–foot flags.

The size of a flag flown on a flagpole is determined by the exposed height of the pole. Recommended sizes are as follows:

Flagpole height (ft.)	Flag size (ft.)	Flagpole height (ft.)	Flag size (ft.)
20	4 x 6	70	12 x 18
25	5 x 8	90	15 x 25
40	6 x 10	125	20 x 30
50	8 x 12	200	30 x 40
60	10 x 15	250	40 x 50

Disposing of a Worn Flag

The U.S. Flag Code states that when a flag is in such poor condition that it is unfit for display, it "should be destroyed in a dignified way, preferably by burning."

Some organizations will take worn or faded U.S. flags and see that they receive proper disposal in a fitting ceremony. Check with local Scouts, Veterans of Foreign Wars, or the American Legion to see if they provide such a flag retirement service.

How to Obtain a Flag Flown over the U.S. Capitol

Constituents may arrange to purchase flags that have flown over the U.S. Capitol in Washington, D.C., by getting in touch with their senators or representative. A certificate signed by the Architect of the Capitol accompanies each flag. Flags are available for purchase in sizes of 3 x 5 or 5 x 8 feet.

How to Obtain a Burial Flag for a Veteran

Anyone may have their casket draped with a flag, though the honor is usually reserved for veterans and highly regarded state and national figures.

Any honorably discharged veteran is entitled to a burial flag. Funeral directors, as part of their services, usually can make necessary arrangements for the family on behalf of the veteran. The flag may be used to cover the casket and is later presented to the family as a keepsake. Local offices of the Department of Veterans Affairs can also provide information on the procedure for obtaining a flag for a deceased veteran.

JUNE

DURING THE WAR OF 1812 between the United States and Britain, Captain James Lawrence sailed in command of the 36-gun frigate USS *Chesapeake*. On June 1, 1813, the *Chesapeake* engaged the warship HMS *Shannon* near Boston in a ship-to-ship duel. Lawrence's crew was young and inexperienced, while the *Shannon* had one of the best-trained crews in the Royal Navy. The British guns quickly cut away the *Chesapeake*'s rigging, setting her adrift, and the king's men swarmed onto the American vessel.

Within a few minutes Captain Lawrence was mortally wounded. As he was carried below deck, he gave his last order: "Tell the men to fire faster! Don't give up the ship!"

Despite the captain's exhortation, the *Chesapeake* was soon captured. Lawrence died a few days later, leaving behind a wife and daughter.

When fellow officer Oliver Hazard Perry heard of Lawrence's death, he had his friend's dying words stitched onto a large blue banner, which he flew from his flagship, the USS *Lawrence*—named for Captain Lawrence—when he fought the British on Lake Erie in September 1813.

Perry's flag now hangs in a place of honor in Memorial Hall at the U.S. Naval Academy in Annapolis, Maryland. The words it bears—"Don't Give Up the Ship"—have become a rallying cry of the Navy.

AMERICAN HISTORY PARADE

1774   In response to the Boston Tea Party, Britain closes the port of Boston.

1789   President George Washington signs the first act of Congress, which dealt with oaths of office for public officials.

1792   Kentucky becomes the fifteenth state.

1796   Tennessee becomes the sixteenth state.

1813   Captain James Lawrence gives his last command: "Don't give up the ship!"

1990   President George Bush and Soviet leader Mikhail Gorbachev sign an agreement to end chemical weapon production and begin destroying reserves.

JUNE 2 IS THE BIRTHDAY of Martha Washington, born in 1731 near Williamsburg, Virginia.

By all accounts, America's first First Lady was a dignified, gentle woman. Abigail Adams called her "one of those unassuming characters which create Love and Esteem."

One visitor described meeting Martha: "We dressed ourselves in our most elegant ruffles and silks, and were introduced to her ladyship. And, don't you think, we found her knitting, and with a checked apron on! She received us very graciously and easily, but after the compliments were over, she resumed her knitting."

Like her husband, Mrs. Washington loved home life at Mount Vernon. But during the Revolution, whenever the Continental Army was in winter camp, she left home to join her husband and lift the troops' spirits. "I never in my life knew a woman so busy from early morning until late at night as was Lady Washington, providing comforts for the sick soldiers," recalled one woman who lived at Valley Forge. "Every fair day she might be seen, with basket in hand . . . going among the huts seeking the keenest and most needy sufferers, and giving all the comfort to them in her power."

Martha was a warm, hospitable First Lady, but she wasn't overly fond of the role. "I think I am more like a state prisoner than anything else," she confided to a niece. Yet her willingness to serve equaled her husband's. "I cannot blame him for having acted according to his ideas of duty in obeying the voice of his country," she wrote to a friend. "I am still determined to be cheerful and happy, in whatever situation I may be; for I have also learned from experience that the greater part of our happiness or misery depends upon our dispositions, and not upon our circumstances."

AMERICAN HISTORY PARADE

1731   Martha Washington is born on a plantation near Williamsburg, Virginia.

1835   P. T. Barnum and his circus begin their first U.S. tour.

1886   Grover Cleveland becomes the only president to be married in the White House when he weds Frances Folsom.

1897   The *New York Journal* quotes Mark Twain on rumors he had died: "The report of my death was an exaggeration."

1924   Congress grants U.S. citizenship to American Indians.

1966   *Surveyor* 1 becomes the first U.S. spacecraft to soft land on the moon.

TRADITION SAYS that the first Stars and Stripes flag was the work of Betsy Ross, an upholsterer living in Philadelphia during the Revolutionary War. About June 1776, the 24-year-old widow was working in her shop on Arch Street when three gentlemen called. One was George Washington, commander in chief of the Continental Army. The other two were George Ross, a signer of the Declaration of Independence and uncle of Betsy's deceased husband, and Robert Morris, also a signer of the Declaration.

Washington produced a rough sketch of a flag with thirteen red and white stripes and thirteen six-pointed stars, and asked Betsy if she could make a banner with that design. "I do not know, but I will try," she reportedly answered, and then suggested changing the stars to five points rather than six. She picked up a piece of cloth, folded it a few times, made one snip with her scissors, and out came a perfect five-point star. The men agreed to the change, and patriot Betsy Ross began the work of stitching together the first Stars and Stripes.

Betsy Ross's grandson William Canby first made this story public in 1870. Betsy was clearly an upholsterer living in Philadelphia during the Revolution, and records show that she made flags for the Pennsylvania navy. But historians question the tale of Washington's visit and her making the first American flag since they can find no evidence to back it up. Nevertheless, generations of Americans have loved the legend, and Betsy is fondly regarded as the mother of our flag.

AMERICAN HISTORY PARADE

1770 Gaspar de Portola and Junipera Serra officiate at the founding of a mission at Monterey, California.

1861 Union forces gain a victory at Philippi, West Virginia, in the first land battle of the Civil War.

1864 Seven thousand Union troops are shot down at Cold Harbor, Virginia, on one of the bloodiest days of the Civil War.

1880 In Washington, D.C., Alexander Graham Bell sends the first wireless telephone message on his newly invented photophone.

1916 Louis Brandeis, first Jewish member of the Supreme Court, is sworn in.

1965 Edward White of *Gemini 4* becomes the first American to take a space walk.

THEY CALL HIM THE PAUL REVERE of the South. His ride isn't so well remembered, but it was every bit as daring.

By June 1781, late in the Revolutionary War, the British army had overrun much of Virginia. Patriot-turned-traitor Benedict Arnold had pillaged his way up the James River to Richmond, forcing Governor Thomas Jefferson and the legislature to flee west to Charlottesville. Lord Cornwallis ordered Col. Banastre Tarleton to lead a surprise raid on Charlottesville to capture Jefferson, Patrick Henry, Richard Henry Lee, and other assemblymen. "Bloody Ban" set out with about 250 mounted troops to nab the unsuspecting Virginians.

On the night of June 3, Captain Jack Jouett of the Virginia militia was at the Cuckoo Tavern in Louisa County (asleep on the lawn, according to some accounts) when the passing cavalry awakened him. Guessing what they were up to, 27-year-old Jouett leaped on his horse and galloped off toward Charlottesville, about 40 miles away. The British were on the main road, so the six-foot-four Jouett had to take trails through the hilly backwoods, a near-full moon his only light to guide him through the underbrush.

He arrived at Monticello, Jefferson's home, in the early hours of June 4. After rousing the occupants and accepting a glass of Madeira from the grateful governor, he dashed on to nearby Charlottesville. Jefferson took his time leaving Monticello. He "breakfasted at leisure" with his guests, he later recalled, then collected important papers. When he looked through a telescope and saw British troops swarming the streets of Charlottesville, he jumped on a horse and plunged into the woods.

Jack Jouett, meanwhile, had spread the alarm in town, enabling most of the legislators to get away. Tarleton's raid was foiled, and the Patriots dodged what would have been a serious blow.

AMERICAN HISTORY PARADE

1781   Jack Jouett warns Thomas Jefferson that the British are coming.

1792   Captain George Vancouver claims Puget Sound for Britain.

1896   Henry Ford makes a successful nighttime test drive of his first horseless carriage, called a Quadricycle, in the streets of Detroit.

1927   At Worcester, Massachusetts, the United States beats Britain to win golf's first Ryder Cup.

1942   The Battle of Midway, a turning point in the Pacific in World War II, begins.

IN EARLY JUNE 1944, southern England swarmed with Allied troops preparing for one of the greatest events of World War II—a massive invasion of northern France. The Allies had spent months getting ready for D-Day. The plan: about 2,700 ships carrying landing craft and 176,000 men would cross the English Channel and assault German fortifications across a 60-mile front in Normandy.

General Dwight D. Eisenhower, commander of the invasion, originally chose June 5 as D-Day, but bad weather and rough seas forced a delay. Then Eisenhower received a new weather forecast. The skies would clear and the seas would calm just long enough to launch the invasion the next day. But the window of opportunity would be short.

The general gave the order: "O.K., let's go." Then he went to his portable desk, scribbled the following note, and slipped it into his wallet to use in case things went badly.

Our landings in the Cherbourg-Havre area have failed to gain a satisfactory foothold and I have withdrawn the troops. My decision to attack at this time and place was based on the best information available. The troops, the air and the Navy did all that bravery and devotion to duty could do. If any blame or fault attaches to the attempt it is mine alone.

It was a statement Eisenhower never had to use. His words, however, remind us that democracies need leaders who have the courage to make the tough calls and then take the heat for them, when necessary.

AMERICAN HISTORY PARADE

1851   *Uncle Tom's Cabin* by Harriet Beecher Stowe begins appearing in serial form in the *National Era,* an abolitionist periodical.

1933   The United States goes off the gold standard.

1940   In Akron, Ohio, the B. F. Goodrich Company exhibits synthetic rubber tires.

1947   Secretary of State George C. Marshall outlines a plan to help rebuild post–World War II Europe, a program now known as the Marshall Plan.

1956   A hip-shaking Elvis Presley sings his latest single, "Hound Dog," on *The Milton Berle Show.*

1968   Sen. Robert F. Kennedy is assassinated in Los Angeles by Sirhan Sirhan, an Arab nationalist.

DWIGHT D. EISENHOWER once described the Allied forces assembled in Britain for the D-Day invasion of northern France as "a great human spring, coiled for the moment when its energy would be released and it would vault the English Channel in the greatest amphibious assault ever attempted."

In the early hours of June 6, 1944, that tense, coiled spring was finally released as the Allied fleet reached Normandy. Hundreds of planes dropped paratroopers behind German lines to capture bridges and railroad tracks. At dawn huge battleship guns began blasting away at German coastal fortifications. Amphibious craft landed on five beaches, and thousands of American, British, Canadian, and French troops fought their way ashore.

U.S. forces landing at Omaha Beach struggled with high seas, fog, mines, and enemy fire that poured down from high bluffs. Many soldiers were shot getting off their boats and died in the surf. Those who reached the sand met a wall of bullets. One commander told his men that only two types of people would stay on the beach—those dead and those going to die—so they'd better push forward. In some units on Omaha, 90 percent of the troops were killed or wounded. But the assault force managed to cross the beach and drive the Germans inland.

At Utah Beach, the other U.S. landing zone, the first wave of troops found themselves 2,000 yards south of where they were supposed to be. It was a lucky miss since the area was not as heavily defended as the original target. Quick-thinking commanders ordered troops to follow the first wave ashore to secure a beachhead.

Before D-Day was over, 155,000 Allied troops were ashore. Months of hard fighting lay ahead. But the Allies had at last established a toehold in northern Europe.

AMERICAN HISTORY PARADE

1840   In Columbus, Ohio, William Henry Harrison becomes the first presidential candidate to make a campaign speech (before that time, candidates let others speak on their behalf).

1912   The largest volcanic eruption of the twentieth century begins near Mount Katmai, Alaska.

1933   The first drive-in movie theater opens in Camden, New Jersey.

1944   The Allies assault the beaches of Normandy on D-Day.

ON THIS DAY IN 1769, Daniel Boone made camp among the rolling, forested hills of a hunter's paradise he had long dreamed of exploring. He had spent several weeks trekking over the Appalachian Mountains, having "resigned my domestic happiness for a time, and left my family and peaceable habitation on the Yadkin River in North Carolina, to wander through the wilderness of America, in quest of the country of Kentucke." He later recalled his arrival:

We proceeded successfully, and after a long and fatiguing journey through a mountainous wilderness, in a westward direction, on the seventh day of June following, we found ourselves on Red River . . . and, from the top of an eminence, saw with pleasure the beautiful level of Kentucke. . . . At this place we encamped, and made a shelter to defend us from the inclement season, and began to hunt and reconnoitre the country. We found everywhere abundance of wild beasts of all sorts, through this vast forest. The buffaloes were more frequent than I have seen cattle in the settlements, browzing on the leaves of the cane, or cropping the herbage on those extensive plains, fearless, because ignorant, of the violence of man. Sometimes we saw hundreds in a drove, and the numbers about the salt springs were amazing. In this forest, the habitation of beasts of every kind natural to America, we practised hunting with great success until the twenty-second day of December following.

Boone was already becoming a legendary explorer. ("I can't say as ever I was lost, but I was bewildered once for three days," he said.) In 1775 he blazed the Wilderness Road through Cumberland Gap, establishing a main westward route through the Appalachians. Thousands of tough, resourceful pioneers followed him into the wild, fertile land of Kentucky and beyond.

AMERICAN HISTORY PARADE

1769   Daniel Boone reaches Kentucky.

1776   Richard Henry Lee of Virginia proposes to the Continental Congress that "these united colonies are, and of right ought to be, free and independent states."

1913   Hudson Stuck leads the first successful ascent of Mount McKinley's main summit.

1939   King George VI and his wife, Queen Elizabeth, become the first reigning British monarchs to visit the United States.

1942   During World War II, Japanese troops invade and occupy the American islands of Attu and Kiska in the Aleutians, off Alaska.

ON JUNE 8, 1887, a former Census Bureau employee named Herman Hollerith filed a patent for a "novel sorting device" he had devised as part of an "apparatus for compiling statistics." His name is not as famous as it used to be, but Hollerith was one in a string of American inventors who ushered in the computer age. His machine used punch cards—cards with rows of holes representing information—to quickly tabulate statistics for millions of pieces of data.

Before Hollerith's time it took the Census Bureau eight years to sort through information collected in its once-a-decade census. Hollerith's system allowed workers to tally the 1890 population in just six weeks and publish refined data in a mere two years. "The apparatus works as unerringly as the mills of the gods, but beats them hollow as to speed," one expert marveled. Hollerith's Tabulating Machine Company later merged with two other companies to form the corporation known today as International Business Machines—IBM.

In June 1951 the world's first commerical computer was put into service at the Census Bureau. The UNIVAC I (Universal Automatic Computer I) was built by the Eckert-Mauchly Computer Corporation. The next year, another UNIVAC machine astounded TV viewers when it accurately predicted that Dwight D. Eisenhower would win the 1952 presidential election.

In June 1977, Apple Computer, Inc., began selling the Apple II, the first widely successful personal computer. Apple was the brainchild of Stephen Wozniak and his friend Steve Jobs, who sold his Volkswagen minibus to help fund the company started in his parents' garage. By the early 1980s, microchips in the first generation of personal computers could perform close to 5 million operations per second, compared to the room-size UNIVAC's 1,900.

AMERICAN HISTORY PARADE

1789   In the House of Representatives, James Madison introduces proposed amendments to the Constitution that eventually become the Bill of Rights.

1861   Tennessee secedes from the Union.

1887   Herman Hollerith patents his punch-card calculator.

1948   *Texaco Star Theater*, one of TV's first hit shows, debuts with Milton Berle as host.

1982   In the first address by a president to a joint session of the British Parliament, Ronald Reagan predicts that Communism will end up "on the ash heap of history."

JUNE 9 IS THE BIRTHDAY of an American cartoon favorite—Donald Duck. Donald made his film debut this day in 1934 in *The Wise Little Hen*, a cartoon by Walt Disney.

Today Disney is regarded as one of the geniuses of American popular culture. But throughout his career, he heard people say, "It won't work." As a young man, he tried to get a job with the *Kansas City Star*, but the newspaper said no. He started a little company called Laugh-O-Gram Films to make cartoons, but the money ran out, and he had to declare bankruptcy.

Walt moved to Los Angeles but failed to find a job, so in 1923 he started his own studio in the back of a real estate office. In 1928, when he had an idea for a cartoon rodent, people in Hollywood scoffed. He sold his car to help finance the project. The public fell in love with Mickey Mouse.

A few years later, Walt decided to make a film called *Snow White*. The experts called it "Disney's Folly." Bankers refused to help him. In 1937 it became a huge box office hit.

Several years later, Walt set his heart on building a theme park. Colleagues advised against it. Roy Disney, his brother and business partner, worried that it was too risky. Walt pushed ahead, and in 1955 the world went wild over Disneyland.

"I can't believe that there are any heights that can't be scaled by a man who knows the secrets of making dreams come true," Walt Disney said. "This special secret, it seems to me, can be summarized in four Cs. They are curiosity, confidence, courage, and constancy, and the greatest of all is confidence."

AMERICAN HISTORY PARADE

1732   James Oglethorpe is granted a royal charter for the colony of Georgia.

1790   *The Philadelphia Spelling Book* by John Barry becomes the first book to be copyrighted in the United States.

1863   The Battle of Brandy Station, the largest cavalry battle fought on American soil, takes place in Virginia during the Civil War.

1934   Donald Fauntleroy Duck makes his first film appearance.

1973   Secretariat wins the Belmont Stakes, becoming the first Triple Crown winner in a quarter century.

JUNE 1775 BROUGHT the birth of the U.S. Army. On June 10, 1775, in the aftermath of Lexington and Concord, John Adams urged the Continental Congress to form a Continental Army to take charge of colonial militia facing the British at Boston. On June 14, 1775 (considered the U.S. Army's official birthday), Congress passed a resolution "that six companies of expert riflemen be immediately raised in Pennsylvania, two in Maryland, and two in Virginia," and that they "shall march and join the army near Boston." The next day, June 15, Congress made George Washington commander in chief of the new force. The Army is the oldest of the five major branches of the U.S. Armed Forces (Army, Navy, Air Force, Marines, and Coast Guard).

The U.S. Army flag, adopted in 1956, is a white flag bearing a blue design that dates to the Revolutionary War. A Roman breastplate (symbol of strength and defense) stands at the center. A sword rises out of the neck opening, and on its point rests a Phrygian cap (symbol of liberty). A drum, musket, bayonet, cannon, cannonballs, flags, and other army implements surround the breastplate. Above, a rattlesnake holds a scroll with the motto This We'll Defend. Below, a red scroll reads "United States Army." And at the bottom, the date 1775 signifies the year the Army was created.

AMERICAN HISTORY PARADE

1692   Bridget Bishop, the first colonist to be tried in the Salem witch trials, is hanged.

1809   The *Phoenix*, traveling from New York to Philadelphia, becomes the first steamboat to navigate the open seas.

1854   The U.S. Naval Academy graduates its first class.

1898   U.S. Marines land at Guantánamo Bay in Cuba during the Spanish-American War.

1924   The Republican National Convention, meeting in Cleveland, is the first U.S. political convention to be broadcast on radio.

IN JUNE 1752 Benjamin Franklin sent a kite soaring into a thunderstorm, brought his knuckle near a key he had tied to the string, and watched a spark leap out. He then proceeded to touch the key to a Leyden jar and charge it—thus proving his theory of "the sameness of electrical matter with that of lightning."

That summer, the ever-practical Franklin persuaded the citizens of Philadelphia to erect lightning rods as a "means of securing the habitations and other buildings from mischief from thunder and lightning." In his own house he rigged a lightning rod so that two bells near his bedroom door would ring whenever an approaching storm cloud electrified the rod.

Franklin's theories and experiments made him famous in Europe. He corresponded with members of the Royal Society of London. His papers were widely published and translated into French. King Louis XV took a particular interest in his writings about electricity.

Little did Franklin know that all this would someday help his countrymen win the American Revolution.

In 1776 the colonies desperately needed France's help in their fight against King George, so they sent 70-year-old Benjamin Franklin across the sea to Versailles. The French welcomed the world-famous scientist and philosopher as a hero. Crowds followed him around. Parisians gave balls in his honor. After all, he was the man who had harnessed lightning.

Franklin charmed the French and used his reputation to nudge them into aiding the colonies. In 1781, French forces helped George Washington trap the English at Yorktown, Virginia. Without that support, the Patriots may never have prevailed.

And that is how Ben Franklin's kite helped Americans win their freedom.

AMERICAN HISTORY PARADE

1776   The Continental Congress appoints a committee to draft the Declaration of Independence.

1859   The Comstock silver lode is discovered in Nevada.

1895   Charles Duryea receives the first U.S. patent for a gasoline-powered automobile.

1919   Sir Barton wins the Belmont Stakes after earlier wins at the Kentucky Derby and Preakness Stakes, becoming the first racehorse to claim the Triple Crown.

1963   Alabama governor George Wallace stands in front of an auditorium door at the University of Alabama in an attempt to block the enrollment of two black students.

ON JUNE 12, 1987, President Ronald Reagan stood before the Berlin Wall, symbol of a totalitarian empire that robbed millions of basic human dignity and freedom, and delivered one of the great speeches of the twentieth century. More than a quarter century earlier, Soviet-backed East Germany had built the wall to keep its people from escaping Communist rule. Reagan, who knew his words would be heard on the east side of the wall, spoke directly to Soviet leader Mikhail Gorbachev.

> Behind me stands a wall that encircles the free sectors of this city, part of a vast system of barriers that divides the entire continent of Europe. . . . Standing before the Brandenburg Gate, every man is a German, separated from his fellow men. Every man is a Berliner, forced to look upon a scar. . . .
>
> [I]n the West today, we see a free world that has achieved a level of prosperity and well-being unprecedented in all human history. In the Communist world, we see failure, technological backwardness, declining standards of health. . . . [T]here stands before the entire world one great and inescapable conclusion: Freedom leads to prosperity. Freedom replaces the ancient hatreds among the nations with comity and peace. Freedom is the victor. . . .
>
> General Secretary Gorbachev, if you seek peace, if you seek prosperity for the Soviet Union and Eastern Europe, if you seek liberalization: Come here to this gate! Mr. Gorbachev, open this gate! Mr. Gorbachev, tear down this wall!

Less than three years later, the Berlin Wall came down. The Soviet Union and its puppet states crumbled as the Cold War came to an end. The United States, by standing firm for democracy and human rights, helped free millions from tyranny.

AMERICAN HISTORY PARADE

1665   English colonists establish a municipal government in the old Dutch settlement of New Amsterdam, which they rename New York.

1776   The colony of Virginia adopts a bill of rights asserting that "all men are by nature equally free and independent."

1939   The Baseball Hall of Fame is dedicated in Cooperstown, New York.

1971   President Nixon's daughter Tricia and Edward Cox are married in the White House Rose Garden.

1987   In West Berlin, Ronald Reagan challenges Soviet leader Mikhail Gorbachev to "tear down this wall!"

ONE OF THIS COUNTRY'S GREATEST PATRIOTS was a French nobleman. Born to immense wealth, the Marquis de Lafayette disliked court life and longed to fight for liberty. When he was nineteen years old, he bought a ship and set sail from France to join the American Revolution, arriving in South Carolina on June 13, 1777.

Declaring that "the welfare of America is intimately connected with the happiness of all mankind," Lafayette volunteered to serve in the Patriot army without pay. He fought beside the American troops and suffered with them at Valley Forge. George Washington became like a father to Lafayette, and Lafayette named his son for Washington.

After the Revolution, Lafayette sailed back to France. Twice he returned to America to see his old comrades. The second trip came in 1824, when he was an old, bent man. He traveled from town to town, and everywhere crowds welcomed him as a hero.

At one reception, a story goes, an old soldier in a faded uniform approached the Frenchman. Over his shoulder he carried a tattered blanket. He drew himself up, gave a salute, and asked if Lafayette remembered the snows of Valley Forge.

"I shall never forget them," answered Lafayette.

"One bitter night," continued the soldier, "you came upon a shivering sentry. His clothes were thin, and he was near frozen. You took his musket and said, 'Go to my hut and get my blanket. Bring it to me while I keep guard.'

"The soldier obeyed your directions. When he returned to his post, you took out your sword and cut your blanket in two. One half you kept. The other you gave to the sentry. Here, General Lafayette, is half of the blanket, for I am the soldier whose life you saved."

AMERICAN HISTORY PARADE

1777 The Marquis de Lafayette arrives in the United States to aid the Patriot cause.

1805 The Lewis and Clark expedition reaches the Great Falls of the Missouri River.

1917 The first U.S. troops sent to fight in Europe during World War I depart New York Harbor.

1967 President Lyndon Johnson nominates Thurgood Marshall to become the first black justice on the U.S. Supreme Court.

1983 The probe *Pioneer 10* becomes the first spacecraft to leave the solar system.

BE SURE YOU FLY YOUR FLAG TODAY. June 14 is Flag Day, the day we celebrate the birthday of the Stars and Stripes.

On June 14, 1777, during the Revolutionary War, the Continental Congress in Philadelphia adopted the Stars and Stripes as the official national flag.

Resolved, that the Flag of the thirteen United States be thirteen stripes, alternate red and white; that the Union be thirteen stars, white on a blue field, representing a new constellation.

Congress gave no further instructions as to exactly what the flag should look like, such as its dimensions or how the stars should be arranged. Consequently, early U.S. flags did not all look alike. Some flags had stars with six points, others with eight. Some flag makers sewed the stars in rows on the blue field, others in a circle or scattered without an organized pattern.

The first official, widespread observance of the flag's birthday came on June 14, 1877, when the flag was one hundred years old. Over the next several years, many schools, veterans groups, and patriotic societies turned the day into a yearly celebration. Mayors and governors began to issue proclamations calling for parades and patriotic events on June 14.

In 1916 President Woodrow Wilson established Flag Day as an annual national celebration. In 1949 Congress and President Truman officially made June 14 a permanent yearly observance.

AMERICAN HISTORY PARADE

1775   Congress authorizes the formation of the Continental Army.

1777   Congress adopts the Stars and Stripes as the national flag.

1846   A group of settlers in Sonoma proclaim the California Republic.

1900   Hawaii becomes a U.S. territory.

1922   Warren G. Harding, dedicating the Francis Scott Key Memorial at Fort McHenry, Baltimore, becomes the first president to be heard on radio.

1951   UNIVAC I, the first electronic computer for commercial use, is dedicated at the Census Bureau in Philadelphia.

1954   President Eisenhower signs a bill adding "under God" to the Pledge of Allegiance.

THE CONTINENTAL CONGRESS assigned no specific meanings to the flag's colors in 1777 when resolving that it should be red, white, and blue. Congress may have chosen those colors because they appeared in the British flag that flew over the colonies until the Revolution. But when Congress designed the Great Seal of the United States, it gave some indication of the symbolism. Charles Thompson, secretary of the Continental Congress, stated that the seal's colors "are those used in the flag of the United States of America; White signifies purity and innocence; Red, hardiness and valor; and Blue . . . signifies vigilance, perseverance, and justice."

As every American student learns, the flag's stars represent the states, while the stripes stand for the thirteen original colonies. A book published by Congress adds that "the star is a symbol of the heavens and the divine goal to which man has aspired from time immemorial; the stripe is symbolic of the rays of light emanating from the sun."

In June 1917, as the country entered World War I, Woodrow Wilson said:

This flag, which we honor and under which we serve, is the emblem of our unity, our power, our thought and purpose as a nation. It has no other character than that which we give it from generation to generation. The choices are ours. It floats in majestic silence above the hosts that execute those choices, whether in peace or in war. And yet, though silent, it speaks to us—speaks to us of the past, of the men and women who went before us, and of the records they wrote upon it. . . . From its birth until now it has witnessed a great history, has floated on high the symbol of great events, of a great plan of life worked out by a great people.

AMERICAN HISTORY PARADE

1775   Congress places George Washington in command of the Continental Army.

1804   The Twelfth Amendment, requiring separate electoral votes for president and vice president, is ratified.

1836   Arkansas becomes the twenty-fifth state.

1846   The Oregon Treaty sets the 49th parallel as the U.S.-Canada boundary.

1864   Arlington National Cemetery is established.

1911   The Computing-Tabulating-Recording Company, later renamed International Business Machines (IBM), is incorporated.

ON JUNE 16, 1858, Abraham Lincoln gave an address in Springfield, Illinois, accepting the Illinois Republican Party's nomination to be its candidate for the U.S. Senate. Near the speech's outset, he uttered what has become one of the most famous phrases in American history: "A house divided against itself cannot stand."

Lincoln was drawing on the words of Jesus in the Bible: "Every kingdom divided against itself is brought to desolation; and every city or house divided against itself shall not stand" (Matthew 12:25 KJV). He knew his audience would understand his meaning: slavery and freedom were incompatible. The institution of slavery was a fatal flaw in the American republic. Either the United States must eventually rid itself of slavery and become a truly free nation, or slavery would take hold in every state.

"A house divided against itself cannot stand."

I believe this government cannot endure, permanently half slave and half free.

I do not expect the Union to be dissolved—I do not expect the house to fall—but I do expect it will cease to be divided.

It will become all one thing or all the other.

Either the opponents of slavery will arrest the further spread of it, and place it where the public mind shall rest in the belief that it is in the course of ultimate extinction; or its advocates will push it forward, till it shall become alike lawful in all the States, old as well as new—North as well as South.

Lincoln was unsuccessful in his Senate bid, but the "House Divided" speech helped put him on the national stage. It accurately predicted that the antagonism between North and South over slavery "will not cease until a crisis shall have been reached, and passed."

AMERICAN HISTORY PARADE

1858   Abraham Lincoln gives his "House Divided" speech in Springfield, Illinois.

1884   The first American roller coaster opens at Coney Island, New York.

1922   Henry Berliner makes one of the first helicopter flights, reaching a height of seven feet, at College Park, Maryland.

1933   President Franklin D. Roosevelt launches his New Deal recovery program by signing banking, industry, and public works bills, as well as farm aid legislation.

1967   Thousands of young people flock to the Monterey Pop Festival in Monterey, California, the first widely promoted rock music festival.

JUNE 17, 1775, brought the first major battle of the Revolutionary War, and one of its bloodiest. That morning British general Thomas Gage, occupying Boston, woke up to discover that two hills across the Charles River were covered with Patriot troops and fortifications. New Englanders had spent all night furiously digging earthworks on Breed's Hill. Nearby Bunker Hill was dark with more American troops.

Stung by the surprise, Gage determined to overwhelm the rebels. He ordered General William Howe to take the hills. Howe ferried his men across the river and, vowing never to order them to go where he was unwilling to lead, started them up the slope of Breed's Hill with drums pounding and fifes calling.

On the crest of the hill, the nervous Patriots eyed the advancing bayonets and fought off the impulse to let loose a quick volley before fleeing. "Don't fire until you see the whites of their eyes!" came the order. Some say old Connecticut Indian fighter Israel Putnam barked it out. Others say it came from Colonel William Prescott of Massachusetts. It may well have come from both.

They waited until the redcoats were fewer than fifteen paces away before letting loose a ripping volley that left the hillside covered with bodies. The angry British retreated, attacked a second time, and again fell back.

In bloodstained, white silk breeches, Howe rallied his men and finally gained the crest. By that time the Americans, who had run out of ammunition, were gone.

British casualties were terrible—about half of their 2,000 men. Patriot losses were fewer—about 440 out of 3,200 defenders. Though driven back, the Americans had given the world's best-trained army something to think about. The Battle of Bunker Hill (so-called even though the fighting took place on Breed's Hill) brought the Patriots much-needed confidence.

AMERICAN HISTORY PARADE

1579   Sir Francis Drake anchors in San Francisco Bay and claims the area for Queen Elizabeth I.

1775   Patriot and British troops fight the Battle of Bunker Hill near Boston.

1856   In Philadelphia the Republican Party opens its first presidential nominating convention; John C. Fremont becomes the GOP candidate.

1885   The Statue of Liberty arrives in New York City in sections aboard a French ship.

1972   Five men are arrested for breaking into the Democratic national headquarters in Washington's Watergate complex, setting off the Watergate scandal.

SHORTLY AFTER THE BATTLE OF BUNKER HILL, Abigail Adams wrote one of the many letters she penned to her husband, John, then in Philadelphia serving in the Second Continental Congress. On a hill near her farm with her young son, Johnny, she had watched the smoke of the battle rising above Charlestown. She wrote partly to tell her husband that their friend Dr. Joseph Warren had been killed in the fight.

Dearest Friend,

The Day, perhaps the decisive Day is come on which the fate of America depends. My bursting heart must find vent at my pen. I have just heard that our dear friend Dr. Warren is no more but fell gloriously fighting for his country—saying better to die honorably in the field than ignominiously hang upon the gallows. Great is our loss. He has distinguished himself in every engagement, by his courage and fortitude, by animating the soldiers and leading them on by his own example. . . .

The race is not to the swift, nor the battle to the strong, but the God of Israel is he that giveth strength and power unto his people. Trust in him at all times, ye people pour out your hearts before him. God is a refuge for us—Charleston is laid in ashes. . . .

How [many ha]ve fallen we know not—the constant roar of the cannon is so [distre]ssing that we can not eat, drink, or sleep. May we be supported and sustained in the dreadful conflict. I shall tarry here till tis thought unsafe by my friends, and then I have secured myself a retreat at your brother's, who has kindly offered me part of his house. I cannot compose myself to write any further at present. I will add more as I hear further.

AMERICAN HISTORY PARADE

1812   The United States declares war against Britain in the War of 1812.

1873   Suffragist Susan B. Anthony is fined $100 for trying to vote in the 1872 presidential election (a fine she refuses to pay).

1928   Amelia Earhart becomes the first woman to fly across the Atlantic, as a passenger on a flight piloted by Wilmer Stultz (she later becomes the first woman to make a solo flight across the Atlantic).

1948   Columbia Records unveils the latest in audio technology: a long-playing, 33⅓ rpm phonograph record.

1983   Sally Ride becomes America's first woman in space when she blasts off aboard the space shuttle *Challenger*.

SONORA LOUISE SMART DODD of Spokane, Washington, came up with the idea of a day to honor fathers in 1909. Her own father, William Smart, was a Civil War veteran whose wife had died in childbirth. Dodd thought about the difficulties her father had faced as he struggled to raise his six motherless children on a farm in eastern Washington, and she set her mind to honoring all fathers. She approached local churches, and on Sunday, June 19, 1910, Spokane ministers celebrated the first Father's Day by reminding their congregations of the appreciation fathers deserve and the duties fathers owe to their families.

In 1916 President Woodrow Wilson took part in a Father's Day celebration by pressing a button in the White House that unfurled a flag in Spokane. In 1924 Calvin Coolidge recommended the widespread observance of the holiday to honor dads and "impress upon fathers the full measure of their obligations."

The idea of a national Father's Day was slow to catch on, but communities and states gradually joined the observance. During the Depression, in an effort to boost sales, retailers began encouraging the holiday with "Give Dad Something to Wear" campaigns.

In 1972 President Richard Nixon signed a law officially recognizing the third Sunday in June as Father's Day. Each year, the president issues a proclamation urging Americans to remember all that their fathers have given to family and country.

AMERICAN HISTORY PARADE

1754   The first colonial congress, the Albany Conference, meets in Albany, New York, to discuss better relations with the Iroquois.

1778   George Washington's army leaves its encampment at Valley Forge, Pennsylvania.

1846   The first recorded baseball game between two organized teams takes place in Hoboken, New Jersey (New York Knickerbockers beat the New York Nine, 23–1).

1862   Slavery is outlawed in the U.S. territories.

1905   The world's first Nickelodeon opens in Pittsburgh.

1910   Father's Day is celebrated for the first time in Spokane, Washington.

THE GREAT SEAL of the United States, which you'll find on the back of every one-dollar bill, is our nation's official emblem. Adopted on June 20, 1782, it's full of symbols that have specific meanings about values the Founders wanted to pass on to each generation.

The front of the Great Seal bears the coat of arms of the United States, showing an American bald eagle with a shield on its breast. The shield contains thirteen vertical red and white stripes, representing the thirteen original states. The eagle holds an olive branch with thirteen leaves and thirteen olives in its right talon, symbolizing strength in peace. It holds thirteen arrows in its left talon, meaning strength during war. The eagle faces the olive branch to show that Americans prefer peace.

In its beak the eagle holds a scroll inscribed with the Latin motto *E Pluribus Unum* ("Out of Many, One"). The motto refers to the fact that the U.S. is one nation formed by several states.

Above the eagle's head is a cloud surrounding a constellation of thirteen stars. The constellation breaking through the cloud symbolizes the United States taking its place among the other nations.

The red in the Great Seal symbolizes hardiness and valor. The white stands for purity and innocence; and the blue represents vigilance, perseverance, and justice.

AMERICAN HISTORY PARADE

1782   Congress approves the Great Seal of the United States.

1863   West Virginia becomes the thirty-fifth state.

1898   During the Spanish-American War, the U.S. cruiser *Charleston* captures the island of Guam.

1948   *The Ed Sullivan Show* (originally called *Toast of the Town*) debuts.

1963   The U.S. and U.S.S.R. agree to install a telephone "hotline" between the two superpowers' leaders.

1975   The summer sensation movie *Jaws* is released.

THE BACK OF THE GREAT SEAL is sometimes called its spiritual side. It shows a pyramid built of thirteen levels of stone, representing the thirteen original states in the union. Since ancient times, pyramids have been symbols of strength and duration. As the poet Walt Whitman suggested, the pyramid is shown as unfinished because although the architects of the United States laid its foundations, each generation has the duty of building a strong, good nation.

Above the pyramid is a triangle containing the eye of Providence, which watches over the Union. The Latin motto *Annuit Coeptis* means "He [God] has favored our undertakings."

On the base of the pyramid is the Roman numeral MDCCLXXVI (1776), the date of the Declaration of Independence. Beneath the pyramid a scroll reads *Novus Ordo Seclorum*, meaning "A New Order of the Ages," signifying that 1776 marked the beginning of the American era.

AMERICAN HISTORY PARADE

1788   The U.S. Constitution becomes the law of the land when New Hampshire becomes the ninth and final state needed to ratify it.

1834   Cyrus McCormick of Virginia patents the first successful mechanical grain reaper.

1893   The first Ferris wheel opens at the World Columbian Exposition in Chicago.

2004   *SpaceShipOne*, piloted by Mike Melvill, becomes the first privately built spacecraft to carry a human into space.

"THERE IS NOT A SINGLE INSTANCE IN HISTORY in which civil liberty was lost, and religious liberty preserved entire." So warned Presbyterian minister John Witherspoon, who on June 22, 1776, was elected to represent New Jersey in the Continental Congress in Philadelphia.

Witherspoon had emigrated from Scotland to take the post as president of the College of New Jersey (now Princeton University). Arriving in 1768 with his family and three hundred books for the college library, he threw himself into the task of building up the young school. "He laid the foundation of a course of history in the college, and the principles of taste and the rules of good writing were both happily explained by him, and exemplified in his manner," a colleague said.

As the Revolution approached, Witherspoon's Presbyterian belief that people should choose their own government put him firmly on the Patriot side. He realized the colonies would have to fight Britain. "If your cause is just, if your principles are pure, and if your conduct is prudent, you need not fear the multitude of opposing hosts," he preached.

In the Continental Congress, some delegates worried the country was not yet ripe for independence. "The country is not only ripe for the measure, but in danger of rotting for the want of it!" Witherspoon retorted. He became the only minister to sign the Declaration of Independence.

He lost a son in the Revolution, which also left the college in dire straits. After the war he tackled the job of rebuilding the school. "Do not live useless and die contemptible," he exhorted his students, who included 9 future cabinet officers, 21 senators, 39 congressmen, 3 Supreme Court justices, 12 governors, a vice president, and a president—James Madison, who was also one of 5 Witherspoon students at the Constitutional Convention.

AMERICAN HISTORY PARADE

1793   One of the nation's first important canals, the Middlesex Canal, connecting the Merrimack River and the port of Boston, is chartered.

1944   President Franklin D. Roosevelt signs the G.I. Bill of Rights, offering educational opportunities for World War II vets.

1945   The Battle of Okinawa ends with an Allied victory.

1970   President Richard Nixon signs a bill lowering the voting age to eighteen.

AMERICAN LEGEND SAYS that during one of the first battles of the Revolutionary War, the noise of early morning gunfire woke some sleeping eagles, which flew from their nests and circled overhead. "They are shrieking for freedom," the Patriots said.

The bald eagle has been a national emblem since June 1782, when Congress adopted the Great Seal of the United States, which features a widespread eagle. Congress chose the bald eagle because it is native to only North America, and because eagles have long symbolized strength, courage, freedom, and long life. You can find the eagle, among other places, on quarters, dollar bills, half-dollars, the president's flag, and the mace of the U.S. House of Representatives.

The term *bald* does not mean the eagle lacks feathers. It comes from *piebald*, an old word meaning "spotted with white," and refers to the white feathers on the bird's head and tail.

By the mid-twentieth century, much of the bald eagle population had been wiped out by hunting, trapping, loss of forestland, and pollution from pesticides. In 1963, the Lower 48 states were home to only about 400 nesting pairs.

The bald eagle first gained federal protection in 1940, and in 1967 it was listed as an endangered species. Since that time, it has made a remarkable comeback. By 2007, the Lower 48 were home to some 10,000 nesting pairs. In Alaska, where the bald eagle was never endangered, the population was estimated at between 50,000 and 70,000 birds.

In June 2007 the Interior Department announced that it was taking the bald eagle off the Endangered Species List. Killing or harming these majestic creatures remains a federal crime.

AMERICAN HISTORY PARADE

1683   William Penn signs a treaty of friendship with the Lenni Lenape Indians in Pennsylvania.

1868   Christopher Latham Sholes of Milwaukee patents an invention he calls the "type-writer."

1845   The Congress of the Republic of Texas votes for annexation by the United States.

1964   Jack Kilby of Texas Instruments patents the integrated circuit.

ON HIS FIRST NIGHT on the island of Saipan in June 1944, Marine Private Guy Gabaldon slipped out of camp on his own and returned with two Japanese prisoners. His commanders told him that if left his post again, he'd be court-martialed. But the next night he disappeared again and came back with 50 prisoners. After that, his superiors let him go on his "lone-wolf" missions whenever he wanted.

Gabaldon wasn't simply after prisoners. He was trying to save lives. American troops had stormed Saipan, in the Marianna Islands, to break the Japanese defense line in the Pacific and secure a site for an air base. The Japanese tried to hold the island with desperate suicide charges. Gabaldon figured that more prisoners meant fewer casualties.

Just eighteen years old, Guy Gabaldon had learned street smarts from growing up in East Los Angeles barrios. He also knew some Japanese, thanks to a childhood friendship with a Japanese-American family. His strategy was simple. Working alone, he would creep up to an enemy-held cave or bunker, call out that the Marines were nearby, and assure the Japanese that they would be treated with dignity if they would lay down their arms.

"I must have seen too many John Wayne movies, because what I was doing was suicidal," Gabaldon later said. But his plan kept working.

One day Gabaldon persuaded some 800 Japanese soldiers to surrender and follow him back to the American lines. His astounded comrades nicknamed him the "Pied Piper of Saipan." Before being wounded by machine-gun fire, he captured perhaps 1,500 prisoners.

Gabaldon's bravery earned him the Navy Cross, and Hollywood made a movie, *Hell to Eternity*, about him. But his greatest reward was knowing that, in the midst of a bloody Pacific battle, he had single-handedly saved many American lives.

AMERICAN HISTORY PARADE

1497   John Cabot, exploring for England, becomes the first European since the Vikings to reach the North American mainland, probably in present-day Canada.

1784   In Baltimore 13-year-old Edward Warren makes the first balloon flight in America, going up in a tethered balloon built by Peter Carnes.

1911   John McDermott becomes the first U.S.-born golfer to win the U.S. Open.

1944   U.S. troops are engaged in the monthlong Battle of Saipan in the Pacific.

1949   *Hopalong Cassidy*, the first TV western, begins airing on NBC.

ON THIS DAY IN 1917, transport ships carrying **14,000** U.S. troops in the American Expeditionary Force approached the shores of France, where the soldiers joined the Allied fight against the Central Powers in World War I.

The United States had been reluctant to enter the Great War. Many Americans viewed it as a European fight of which they wanted no part. President Woodrow Wilson had won reelection in 1916 on the slogan "He kept us out of war." But German aggression, including U-boat strikes against American cargo ships, gradually changed public opinion. Wilson realized the country could not avoid a conflict that was engulfing much of the world.

As U.S. troops landed in France, Americans were mindful of an old debt owed that nation. France had been the colonists' most important ally during the Revolutionary War. The Marquis de Lafayette had fought beside Patriot soldiers, equipping some of them at his own expense. He won the affection of George Washington and became a hero to the young nation. Urged on by Lafayette, France had sent ships, troops, and arms that played a key role in the Patriots' victory.

In early July 1917, the newly arrived American Expeditionary Force troops marched under the Arc de Triomphe, cheered by the people of Paris. In a ceremony at Lafayette's tomb, where the Frenchman lies buried under dirt from Bunker Hill, an American officer lay down a wreath of pink and white roses. Another officer stepped forward, snapped a salute, and declared: "Lafayette, we are here!"

U.S. troops went on to help turn the tide of World War I in favor of France and the Allies. The words "Lafayette, we are here" are still a good reminder of the need to stand fast with allies when tyranny threatens.

AMERICAN HISTORY PARADE

1788   Virginia becomes the tenth state to ratify the Constitution.

1868   President Andrew Johnson signs legislation providing for an eight-hour workday for workers employed by the federal government.

1876   At the Battle of Little Bighorn in Montana, Sioux and Cheyenne Indians kill Lt. Col. George Custer and more than 250 soldiers after they attack the Indians' camp.

1917   Ships carrying the first wave of troops of the American Expeditionary Force approach the shores of France.

1950   The Korean War erupts when North Korean troops invade South Korea.

ON JUNE 26, 1963, John F. Kennedy became the first president to stand on the west side of the Berlin Wall and denounce totalitarianism. Kennedy called the wall "the most obvious and vivid demonstration of the failures of the Communist system, for all the world to see." With the words *Ich bin ein Berliner* ("I am a Berliner"), he assured Europeans of U.S. resolve to stand up for freedom.

There are many people in the world who really don't understand, or say they don't, what is the great issue between the free world and the Communist world. Let them come to Berlin. There are some who say that Communism is the wave of the future. Let them come to Berlin. . . .

Freedom has many difficulties and democracy is not perfect, but we have never had to put a wall up to keep our people in, to prevent them from leaving us. . . . [The Berlin Wall is] an offense not only against history but an offense against humanity, separating families, dividing husbands and wives and brothers and sisters, and dividing a people who wish to be joined together. . . .

Freedom is indivisible, and when one man is enslaved, all are not free. When all are free, then we can look forward to that day when this city will be joined as one and this country and this great Continent of Europe in a peaceful and hopeful globe. When that day finally comes, as it will, the people of West Berlin can take sober satisfaction in the fact that they were in the front lines for almost two decades.

All free men, wherever they may live, are citizens of Berlin, and, therefore, as a free man, I take pride in the words *"Ich bin ein Berliner."*

AMERICAN HISTORY PARADE

1844   John Tyler becomes the first U.S. president to get married while in office.

1948   The Berlin Airlift begins delivering supplies to isolated West Berlin.

1959   Queen Elizabeth and President Eisenhower officially open the St. Lawrence Seaway.

1963   At the Berlin Wall, President Kennedy declares *"Ich bin ein Berliner."*

2000   President Bill Clinton and British prime minister Tony Blair announce that scientists have completed the first rough map of the human genetic code.

AS NIGHT FELL ON JUNE 27, 2005, four U.S. Navy Seals dropped from a helicopter onto mountainous, enemy-controlled terrain in Afghanistan to begin a high-risk mission. Lt. Michael Murphy and petty officers Matthew Axelson, Danny Dietz, and Marcus Luttrell had orders to locate a terrorist leader. The team picked its way across rugged terrain and by morning had taken up position on a steep ridge, but three goat herders stumbled across their hiding place and alerted local Taliban forces. About an hour later, dozens of enemy fighters swarmed around the four Americans.

A firefight erupted as the Seals bounded down the mountainside, hoping to reach a place to make a stand. With one man dead and the other two wounded, and realizing that their only chance was to call for help, Murphy made the ultimate sacrifice. He moved into open ground where he could get a phone signal, exposing himself to fire.

"My guys are dying out here . . . we need help," he told headquarters, just before being shot in the back. He pulled himself up, finished relaying their position, and signed off with, "Roger that, sir. Thank you." Then he started firing again.

By the time the fight was over, Murphy, Axelson, and Deitz were dead. A rescue helicopter carrying 16 men was shot down by a Taliban rocket, killing all aboard. Some 35 Taliban fighters died.

In 2007, Michael Murphy was posthumously awarded the Medal of Honor for his courage and loyalty. Marcus Luttrell, the only team member to make it through the operation alive, summed up Murphy's final act in his book *Lone Survivor*: "His objective was clear: to make one last valiant attempt to save his two teammates. . . . Not a gesture. An act of supreme valor."

AMERICAN HISTORY PARADE

1652   New Amsterdam (now New York City) enacts an early traffic law: "No wagons, carts, or sleighs shall be run, rode or driven at a gallop within this city."

1844   A mob kills Mormon leader Joseph Smith and his brother Hyrum in Carthage, Illinois.

1898   Joshua Slocum becomes the first person to circumnavigate the world alone when he lands his boat, the *Spray*, in Rhode Island.

1950   President Truman orders the Air Force and Navy into the Korean War.

1985   Route 66, stretching from Chicago to Los Angeles, ceases to be a U.S. highway, replaced largely by the Interstate Highway System.

IN THE SUMMER OF 1787, the Constitutional Convention met at Independence Hall in Philadelphia to decide how to set up a new government. At times the arguments grew bitter, and tempers flared in the summer heat. Some delegates verged on quitting when they reached an impasse over whether representation was to be based on the population of each state or if each state should be given one vote. Historians have called this period the "critical juncture" in the Convention. The country was brand-new, and already it looked as though it might fall apart.

On June 28, 1787, eighty-one-year-old Benjamin Franklin, the oldest delegate, rose from his seat and made a simple but profound suggestion: they should pray for guidance. He reminded the others that the Continental Congress had asked for divine aid at the start of the Revolutionary War.

"Our prayers, sir, were heard, and they were graciously answered," he said. "And have we now forgotten that powerful Friend? Or do we imagine that we no longer need his assistance? I have lived, sir, a long time, and the longer I live the more convincing proofs I see of this truth: that God governs in the affairs of men. And if a sparrow cannot fall to the ground without his notice, is it probable that an empire can rise without his aid?"

The delegates did not follow Franklin's suggestion to begin each session with prayer—for one thing, they had no funds to hire a clergyman. But his words helped calm the Convention, which soon began to make progress, and that answered Franklin's fervent prayer.

AMERICAN HISTORY PARADE

1776   In Charleston, South Carolina, Patriot troops manning a fort of sand and palmetto logs repulse a British sea attack.

1778   In the Battle of Monmouth, New Jersey, George Washington's Continental Army battles the British to a draw.

1914   A Serb nationalist assassinates Austrian archduke Franz Ferdinand and his wife, Sophie, an event that triggers World War I.

1919   The Treaty of Versailles is signed in France, formally ending World War I.

1939   Regular transatlantic passenger air service begins when Pan Am's *Dixie Clipper* leaves Port Washington, New York, for Lisbon, Portugal, with 22 passengers.

TRADITION SAYS THAT ON THIS DAY IN 1778, the day after the Battle of Monmouth in New Jersey, Mary Ludwig Hays of Pennsylvania—known to her friends as Molly—stood before General Washington and received a warrant as a noncommissioned officer in return for bravery in the battle.

Like many colonial wives, Molly had joined her husband, John, when he marched off to fight the British during the Revolutionary War. She spent her time in the camps, cooking, washing, and taking care of supplies.

June 28, 1778, found John Hays manning a cannon at Monmouth on an afternoon when the temperature soared close to one hundred degrees. Gasping soldiers began to drop from thirst and exhaustion, so Molly grabbed an artillery bucket and carried water from a cool spring to the troops. According to legend, the grateful men cheered "Molly with her pitcher," and afterward she was known as Molly Pitcher.

Molly also nursed the wounded that day. At one point she hoisted an injured soldier to her shoulders and lugged him clear of a British charge. When her husband fell wounded beside his cannon, she seized the rammer staff and worked the rest of the day swabbing and loading the gun under heavy fire. An eyewitness to the battle described how "a cannon shot from the enemy passed directly between her legs without doing any other damage than carrying away all the lower part of her petticoat."

The next day, it is said, George Washington thanked the barefooted, powder-stained Molly. In 1822 the Pennsylvania legislature voted to pay her $40 a year in recognition of her service. Since then, the name Molly Pitcher has come to stand for all the brave women who came to their country's aid during the war for independence.

AMERICAN HISTORY PARADE

1776   Mission San Francisco de Asís is founded on the site of the future city of San Francisco.

1854   Congress ratifies the Gadsden Purchase, agreeing to pay Mexico $10 million for parts of Arizona and New Mexico.

1925   An earthquake levels much of downtown Santa Barbara, California.

1953   President Eisenhower signs legislation creating the Interstate Highway System.

1995   In a post–Cold War show of international cooperation, the shuttle *Atlantis* docks with the Russian space station *Mir*.

ON JUNE 30, 1864, Abraham Lincoln signed legislation granting the Yosemite Valley to California "for public use, resort, and recreation." Twenty-six years later, Yosemite National Park was created, thanks largely to naturalist John Muir, who spent decades studying, promoting, and protecting the area. Muir's descriptions of this grand region still inspire:

Well may the Sierra be called the Range of Light, not the Snowy Range, for only in winter is it white, while all year it is bright.

Of this glorious range the Yosemite National Park is a central section, 36 miles in length and 48 miles in breadth. The famous Yosemite Valley lies in the heart of it, and it includes the head waters of the Tuolumne and Merced rivers, two of the most songful streams in the world; innumerable lakes and waterfalls and smooth silky lawns; the noblest forests, the loftiest granite domes, the deepest ice-sculptured canyons, the brightest crystalline pavements, and snowy mountains soaring into the sky twelve and thirteen thousand feet, arrayed in open ranks and spiry pinnacled groups partially separated by tremendous canyons and amphitheaters; gardens on their sunny brows, avalanches thundering down their long white slopes, cataracts roaring gray and foaming in the crooked rugged gorges, and glaciers in their shadowy recesses working in silence, slowly completing their sculpture; new-born lakes at their feet, blue and green, free or encumbered with drifting icebergs like miniature Arctic Oceans, shining, sparkling, calm as stars.

Nowhere will you see the majestic operations of nature more clearly revealed beside the frailest, most gentle and peaceful things. Nearly all the park is a profound solitude. Yet it is full of charming company, full of God's thoughts, a place of peace and safety amid the most exalted grandeur.

— from *Our National Parks*
(1901) by John Muir

AMERICAN HISTORY PARADE

1859   Frenchman Emile Blondin becomes the first daredevil to cross Niagara Falls on a tightrope.

1864   President Lincoln signs the Yosemite Valley Grant Act.

1950   President Truman orders U.S. ground troops into Korea.

1952   The soap opera *The Guiding Light*, the longest-running drama in television history, moves from radio to TV.

1953   The first Chevrolet Corvette rolls off the assembly line in Flint, Michigan.

How the Declaration of Independence Was Written and Signed

July 4, 1776, marked the formal beginning of the American Revolution, and we celebrate it as our nation's birthday, but the fighting with England was well underway before the events of that famous day. Shots had been fired at Lexington and Concord more than a year earlier. Americans had spilled blood from Quebec to Charleston. George Washington was in the field, commanding the Continental Army, and hopes of reconciling with England had slipped away.

In early June the Second Continental Congress, meeting in Philadelphia, had debated whether to break away from the mother country. It appointed a committee to draft a document that would explain to the world the need for such action. The delegates knew that if they proclaimed independence, the English would view them as traitors. They were putting their lives and their honor on the line. So they wanted a Declaration of Independence that would clearly state to one and all exactly why it was necessary to be free of English rule.

The committee appointed to draw up the Declaration was made up of Benjamin Franklin of Pennsylvania, Philip Livingston of New York, John Adams of Massachusetts, Roger Sherman of Connecticut, and young Thomas Jefferson of Virginia. To Jefferson fell the task of hammering out the first draft. At first he was reluctant—he protested that the older and better-known

Adams was more qualified. Adams told Jefferson exactly why he should take up his pen: "Reason first—you are a Virginian, and a Virginian ought to appear at the head of this business. Reason second—I am obnoxious, suspected and unpopular. You are very much otherwise. Reason third—you can write ten times better than I can."

Jefferson drafted the statement in his rented rooms at Market and Seventh Streets, working away at a portable writing desk of his own design. None of the ideas he set down were original—he borrowed thoughts that had been expressed throughout the ages, from the ancient Greeks and Romans to the philosopher John Locke to recent sermons of the day. But he set down those thoughts in brilliant fashion. It took him about two weeks to forge the draft, with his fellow committee members dropping by from time to time to offer support and suggestions.

On July 1, Congress again took up the resolution to break away from England, entering what John Adams called "the greatest debate of all." The next day, delegates from twelve of the thirteen colonies voted to declare independence. (New York abstained.) At that moment the colonies became the United States. John Adams wrote ecstatically to his wife, Abigail, that "the second day of July 1776 . . . will be celebrated by succeeding generations as the great anniversary festival." He was off by two days.

Congress next turned to reading, discussing, and editing Jefferson's draft. Adams defended and explained the text to his colleagues as Jefferson sat silently, wincing at every change and making notes on his rough draft. Some changes were matters of substance; others, edits in style. Congress deleted 630 words and added 146, leaving a final rext of 1,322 words.

Finally everyone was more or less satisfied. On July 4, twelve of the thirteen state delegations adopted the final draft of the Declaration. (New York adopted it on July 9.)

Many Americans picture all the delegates solemnly signing the famous document on July 4, but that's not the way it happened. Only John Hancock, president of the Second Continental Congress, and Charles Thomson, the Congress's secretary, put their signatures on the Declaration that day. Then it went to a printer to be printed on broadsides. The original handwritten copy the printer used was lost, so later one of his broadsides was attached to a page in the journal of Congress.

By July 5, presses were cranking out copies that were stuffed into saddlebags and hurried to sailing vessels so they could be rushed to other states. On July 8, the Liberty Bell rang out in Philadelphia, summoning citizens to the first public reading of the Declaration. On July 9 George Washington ordered that it be read to his troops in New York City. Up and down the seaboard, Americans pulled down images of George III and other symbols of royal authority after they heard the Declaration's words.

On July 19 Congress ordered that the Declaration be engrossed (written with attractive letters) on parchment and signed by all its members. On August 2 the engrossed copy was ready, and the members of Congress who were in Philadelphia that day gathered around a table to affix their signatures—knowing full well that they could be signing their own death warrants. Delegates who were out of town that day signed during the following weeks. Some new delegates had joined the Congress after July 4, so not all the signers of the Declaration were the same as those who had originally voted for it.

On January 18, 1777, Congress—which by then was in session in Baltimore—ordered that new copies be printed showing the names of all the signers, and sent to each of the states. Today the original engrossed copy of the Declaration of Independence is displayed at the National Archives in Washington, D.C.

The Declaration of Independence

IN CONGRESS, July 4, 1776.

The unanimous Declaration of the thirteen united States of America,

When in the Course of human events, it becomes necessary for one people to dissolve the political bands which have connected them with another, and to assume among the powers of the earth, the separate and equal station to which the Laws of Nature and of Nature's God entitle them, a decent respect to the opinions of mankind requires that they should declare the causes which impel them to the separation.

    We hold these truths to be self-evident, that all men are created equal, that they are endowed by their Creator with certain unalienable Rights, that among these are Life, Liberty and the pursuit of Happiness. —That to secure these rights, Governments are instituted among Men, deriving their just powers from the consent of the governed, —That whenever any Form of Government becomes destructive of these ends, it is the Right of the People to alter or to abolish it, and to institute new Government, laying its foundation on such principles and organizing its powers in such form, as to them shall seem most likely to effect their Safety and Happiness. Prudence, indeed, will dictate that Governments long established should not be changed for light and transient causes; and accordingly all experience hath shewn, that mankind are more disposed to suffer, while evils are sufferable, than to right themselves by abolishing the forms to which they are accustomed. But when a long train of abuses and usurpations, pursuing invariably the same Object, evinces a design to reduce them under absolute Despotism, it is their right, it is their duty, to throw off such Government, and to provide new Guards for their future security. —Such has been the patient sufferance of these Colonies; and such is now the necessity which constrains them to alter their former Systems of Government. The history of the present King of Great Britain is a history of repeated injuries and usurpations, all having in direct object the establishment of an absolute Tyranny over these States. To prove this, let Facts be submitted to a candid world.

He has refused his Assent to Laws, the most wholesome and necessary for the public good.

He has forbidden his Governors to pass Laws of immediate and pressing importance, unless suspended in their operation till his Assent should be obtained; and when so suspended, he has utterly neglected to attend to them.

He has refused to pass other Laws for the accommodation of large districts of people, unless those people would relinquish the right of Representation in the Legislature, a right inestimable to them and formidable to tyrants only.

He has called together legislative bodies at places unusual, uncomfortable, and distant from the depository of their public Records, for the sole purpose of fatiguing them into compliance with his measures.

He has dissolved Representative Houses repeatedly, for opposing with manly firmness his invasions on the rights of the people.

He has refused for a long time, after such dissolutions, to cause others to be elected; whereby the Legislative powers, incapable of Annihilation, have returned to the People at large for their exercise; the State remaining in the mean time exposed to all the dangers of invasion from without, and convulsions within.

He has endeavoured to prevent the population of these States; for that purpose obstructing the Laws for Naturalization of Foreigners; refusing to pass others to encourage their migrations hither, and raising the conditions of new Appropriations of Lands.

He has obstructed the Administration of Justice, by refusing his Assent to Laws for establishing Judiciary powers.

He has made Judges dependent on his Will alone, for the tenure of their offices, and the amount and payment of their salaries.

He has erected a multitude of New Offices, and sent hither swarms of Officers to harrass our people, and eat out their substance.

He has kept among us, in times of peace, Standing Armies without the Consent of our legislatures.

He has affected to render the Military independent of and superior to the Civil power.

He has combined with others to subject us to a jurisdiction foreign to our constitution, and unacknowledged by our laws; giving his Assent to their Acts of pretended Legislation:

For Quartering large bodies of armed troops among us:

For protecting them, by a mock Trial, from punishment for any Murders which they should commit on the Inhabitants of these States:

For cutting off our Trade with all parts of the world:

For imposing Taxes on us without our Consent:

For depriving us in many cases, of the benefits of Trial by Jury:

For transporting us beyond Seas to be tried for pretended offences:

For abolishing the free System of English Laws in a neighbouring Province, establishing therein an Arbitrary government, and enlarging its Boundaries so as to render it at once an example and fit instrument for introducing the same absolute rule into these Colonies:

For taking away our Charters, abolishing our most valuable Laws, and altering fundamentally the Forms of our Governments:

For suspending our own Legislatures, and declaring themselves invested with power to legislate for us in all cases whatsoever.

He has abdicated Government here, by declaring us out of his Protection and waging War against us.

He has plundered our seas, ravaged our Coasts, burnt our towns, and destroyed the lives of our people.

He is at this time transporting large Armies of foreign Mercenaries to compleat the works of death, desolation and tyranny, already begun with circumstances of Cruelty & perfidy scarcely paralleled in the most barbarous ages, and totally unworthy the Head of a civilized nation.

He has constrained our fellow Citizens taken Captive on the high Seas to bear Arms against their Country, to become the executioners of their friends and Brethren, or to fall themselves by their Hands.

He has excited domestic insurrections amongst us, and has endeavoured to bring on the inhabitants of our frontiers, the merciless Indian Savages, whose known rule of warfare, is an undistinguished destruction of all ages, sexes and conditions.

In every stage of these Oppressions We have Petitioned for Redress in the most humble terms: Our repeated Petitions have been answered only by repeated injury. A Prince whose character is thus marked by every act which may define a Tyrant, is unfit to be the ruler of a free people.

Nor have We been wanting in attentions to our Brittish brethren. We have warned them from time to time of attempts by their legislature to extend an unwarrantable jurisdiction over us. We have reminded them of the circumstances of our emigration and settlement here. We have appealed to their native justice and magnanimity, and we have conjured them by the ties of our common kindred to disavow these usurpations, which, would inevitably interrupt our connections and correspondence. They too have been deaf to the voice of justice and of consanguinity. We must, therefore, acquiesce in the necessity, which denounces our Separation, and hold them, as we hold the rest of mankind, Enemies in War, in Peace Friends.

We, therefore, the Representatives of the United States of America, in General Congress, Assembled, appealing to the Supreme Judge of the world for the rectitude of our intentions, do, in the Name, and by Authority of the good People of these Colonies, solemnly publish and declare, That these United Colonies are, and of Right ought to be, Free and Independent States; that they are Absolved from all Allegiance to the British Crown, and that all political connection between them and the State of Great Britain, is and ought to be totally dissolved; and that as Free and Independent States, they have full Power to levy War, conclude Peace, contract Alliances, establish Commerce, and to do all other Acts and Things which Independent States may of right do. And for the support of this Declaration, with a firm reliance on the protection of divine Providence, we mutually pledge to each other our Lives, our Fortunes and our sacred Honor.

The 56 signatures on the Declaration appear in the positions indicated:

Column 1
Georgia - Button Gwinnett; Lyman Hall; George Walton

Column 2
North Carolina: William Hooper; Joseph Hewes; John Penn
South Carolina: Edward Rutledge; Thomas Heyward, Jr.; Thomas Lynch, Jr.;
   Arthur Middleton

Column 3
Massachusetts: John Hancock
Maryland: Samuel Chase; William Paca; Thomas Stone; Charles Carroll of
   Carrollton
Virginia: George Wythe; Richard Henry Lee; Thomas Jefferson; Benjamin
   Harrison; Thomas Nelson, Jr.; Francis Lightfoot Lee; Carter Braxton

Column 4
Pennsylvania: Robert Morris; Benjamin Rush; Benjamin Franklin; John Morton;
   George Clymer; James Smith; George Taylor; James Wilson; George Ross
Delaware: Caesar Rodney; George Read; Thomas McKean

Column 5

New York: William Floyd; Philip Livingston; Francis Lewis; Lewis Morris

New Jersey: Richard Stockton; John Witherspoon; Francis Hopkinson; John Hart; Abraham Clark

Column 6

New Hampshire: Josiah Bartlett; William Whipple

Massachusetts: Samuel Adams; John Adams; Robert Treat Paine; Elbridge Gerry

Rhode Island: Stephen Hopkins; William Ellery

Connecticut: Roger Sherman; Samuel Huntington; William Williams; Oliver Wolcott

New Hampshire: Matthew Thornton

JULY

IN 1999 THE U.S. MINT launched a series of quarters honoring the fifty states. The back of the Delaware quarter, the first in the series, features a man in a tri-corner hat on a galloping horse. The rider is Caesar Rodney, one of Delaware's three signers of the Declaration of Independence.

Rodney was a well-to-do planter who had served in Delaware's legislature, led protests against the Stamp Tax, and organized Patriot militia before being elected to the Continental Congress. Despite such activity, he was a man of poor health. He suffered from asthma as well as skin cancer that had left his face so disfigured, he often hid one side of it behind a green silk scarf. Yet as John Adams noted, there was "fire, spirit, wit, and humor in his countenance."

Rodney was in Delaware on the evening of July 1, 1776, when he received an urgent message from Philadelphia. Congress was ready to vote on the issue of independence. Of the two other Delaware delegates, one favored and one opposed a break with England, so Rodney's vote would decide which way the colony would go—if he could get there in time.

He rode through the night, in thunder and rain, to cover the 80 miles to Philadelphia. The next day, just as Congress prepared to vote, the delegates heard hoofbeats on cobblestones, and a mud-spattered Rodney strode into the hall, still wearing his spurs, exhausted but ready to break the tie in his state's delegation by voting for independence.

On July 2, 1776, the Continental Congress made the momentous decision to break from England: "Resolved, That these United Colonies are, and of right ought to be, free and independent States." Two days later, it adopted the Declaration of Independence.

AMERICAN HISTORY PARADE

1776   Caesar Rodney makes his overnight ride from Dover, Delaware, to Philadelphia.

1863   The three-day Battle of Gettsyburg begins.

1874   The Zoological Society of Philadelphia opens the first U.S. zoo.

1898   In the Spanish-American War, Teddy Roosevelt and his Rough Riders help win a victory for the United States when they charge up San Juan Hill in Cuba.

1941   The Bulova Watch Company sponsors the first TV commercial sanctioned by the Federal Communications Commission.

1971   The Twenty-sixth Amendment, lowering the voting age to eighteen, is ratified.

ON JULY 2, 1937, aviator Amelia Earhart took off from Lae, New Guinea, in her twin engine Lockheed Electra and flew east into overcast skies toward Howland Island, a sliver of land 2,600 miles away in the Pacific Ocean. She was never seen again.

At the time she disappeared, Earhart was a world-renowned aviation pioneer. In 1932 she had become the first woman to make a solo, nonstop flight across the Atlantic, an accomplishment that earned her the Distinguished Flying Cross. The next year she became the first woman to fly nonstop, coast-to-coast across the United States. As she neared her fortieth birthday, she set her sights on a new goal, the "one flight which I most wanted to attempt," a circumnavigation of the globe near the equator.

When she left New Guinea with her navigator, Fred Noonan, Earhart had completed all but 7,000 miles of her 29,000-mile journey. The Coast Guard cutter *Itasca* waited off Howland Island, where the plane was to refuel. As the arrival time approached, the *Itasca* received the message "We must be on you, but we cannot see you. Fuel is running low. Been unable to reach you by radio. We are flying at 1,000 feet." Efforts to make radio contact failed. A massive search followed but turned up no trace of the plane.

Even today, searches for clues about Earhart's fate continue. Some experts believe her plane ran out of fuel and had to ditch in the Pacific. Others theorize that Earhart and Noonan reached another island, where they eventually perished. So far, no solid evidence has turned up. Earhart's sense of adventure and determination to fly farther than before still fascinate Americans. "Courage is the price that life exacts for granting peace," she wrote, words she lived by to the end.

AMERICAN HISTORY PARADE

1776   The Continental Congress votes for independence, passing a resolution that "these United Colonies are, and of right ought to be, free and independent States."

1881   President James Garfield is fatally shot by a deranged man in Washington, D.C.

1890   Congress passes the Sherman Antitrust Act, the first federal antitrust law.

1937   Amelia Earhart and Fred Noonan disappear over the Pacific Ocean.

1964   President Lyndon B. Johnson signs the 1964 Civil Rights Act.

2002   Adventurer Steve Fossett becomes the first person to fly nonstop around the world alone in a balloon.

THE INCIDENT BELOW, related by a Union army veteran in A. L. Long's *Memoirs of Robert E. Lee*, is said to have taken place on July 3, 1863, the last day of the Battle of Gettysburg. It speaks of an American brotherhood that, in the end, transcended that terrible war.

I was at the battle of Gettysburg myself. . . . I had been a most bitter anti-South man, and fought and cursed the Confederates desperately. I could see nothing good in any of them. The last day of the fight I was badly wounded. A ball shattered my left leg. I lay on the ground not far from Cemetery Ridge, and as General Lee ordered his retreat he and his officers rode near me.

As they came along I recognized him, and, though faint from exposure and loss of blood, I raised up my hands, looked Lee in the face, and shouted as loud as I could, "Hurrah for the Union!"

The general heard me, looked, stopped his horse, dismounted, and came toward me. I confess that I at first thought he meant to kill me. But as he came up he looked down at me with such a sad expression upon his face that all fear left me, and I wondered what he was about. He extended his hand to me, and grasping mine firmly and looking right into my eyes, said, "My son, I hope you will soon be well."

If I live to be a thousand years I shall never forget the expression on General Lee's face. There he was, defeated, retiring from a field that had cost him and his cause almost their last hope, yet he stopped to say words like those to a wounded soldier of the opposition who had taunted him as he passed by. As soon as the general had left me I cried myself to sleep there upon the bloody ground.

AMERICAN HISTORY PARADE

1863   The Battle of Gettysburg ends with a Union victory.

1890   Idaho becomes the forty-third state.

1898   The U.S. Navy defeats a Spanish fleet in the harbor of Santiago, Cuba, during the Spanish-American War.

1986   President Reagan presides over the rededication of the 100-year-old, newly renovated Statue of Liberty.

ON JULY 4, 1776, delegates to the Continental Congress in Philadelphia voted to adopt the Declaration of Independence. The men who issued that famous document realized they were signing their own death warrants, since the British would consider them traitors. Many suffered hardship during the Revolutionary War.

William Floyd of New York saw the British use his home for a barracks. His family fled to Connecticut, where they lived as refugees. After the war Floyd found his fields stripped and house damaged.

Richard Stockton of New Jersey was dragged from his bed, thrown into prison, and treated like a common criminal. His home was looted and his fortune badly impaired. He was released in 1777, but his health was broken. He died a few years later.

At age sixty-three, John Hart, another New Jersey signer, hid in the woods during December 1776 while Hessian soldiers hunted him across the countryside. He died before the war's end. The *New Jersey Gazette* reported that he "continued to the day he was seized with his last illness to discharge the duties of a faithful and upright patriot in the service of his country."

Thomas Nelson, a Virginian, commanded militia and served as governor during the Revolution. He reportedly instructed artillerymen to fire at his own house in Yorktown when he heard the British were using it as a headquarters. Nelson used his personal credit to raise money for the Patriot cause. His sacrifices left him in financial distress, and he was unable to repair his Yorktown home after the war.

Thomas Heyward, Arthur Middleton, and Edward Rutledge, three South Carolina signers, served in their state's militia and were captured when the British seized Charleston. They spent a year in a St. Augustine prison and, when released, found their estates plundered.

Such were the prices paid so we may celebrate freedom every Fourth of July.

AMERICAN HISTORY PARADE

1776   The Continental Congress adopts the Declaration of Independence.

1802   The U.S. Military Academy opens at West Point, New York.

1826   John Adams, age ninety, and Thomas Jefferson, age eighty-three, die.

1831   James Monroe, the fifth U.S. president, dies at age seventy-three.

1872   Calvin Coolidge, the thirtieth U.S. president, is born in Plymouth, Vermont.

1959   A forty-ninth star is added to the flag to represent the new state of Alaska.

1960   A fiftieth star is added to the flag to represent the new state of Hawaii.

ON JULY 5, 1926, in a speech in Philadelphia commemorating the 150th anniversary of the Declaration of Independence, President Calvin Coolidge reminded Americans that "in its main features the Declaration of Independence is a great spiritual document."

Our forefathers came to certain conclusions and decided upon certain courses of action which have been a great blessing to the world. . . . They were a people who came under the influence of a great spiritual development and acquired a great moral power.

No other theory is adequate to explain or comprehend the Declaration of Independence. It is the product of the spiritual insight of the people. We live in an age of science and of abounding accumulation of material things. These did not create our Declaration. Our Declaration created them. The things of the spirit come first. Unless we cling to that, all our material prosperity, overwhelming though it may appear, will turn to a barren scepter in our grasp. If we are to maintain the great heritage which has been bequeathed to us, we must be like-minded as the fathers who created it. We must not sink into a pagan materialism. We must cultivate the reverence which they had for the things that are holy. We must follow the spiritual and moral leadership which they showed. We must keep replenished, that they may glow with a more compelling flame, the altar fires before which they worshiped.

AMERICAN HISTORY PARADE

1776   The Continental Congress has the Declaration of Independence printed.

1865   The U.S. Secret Service is established.

1950   Private Kenneth Shadrick of Skin Fork, West Virginia, becomes the first U.S. soldier to be killed in action in the Korean War.

1954   Elvis Presley sings "That's All Right (Mama)" and "Blue Moon of Kentucky" in his first commercial recording session in Memphis, Tennessee.

PEOPLE ALL OVER THE WORLD recognize Uncle Sam—the tall, white-haired gentleman dressed in red, white, and blue—as a symbol of the United States. Where did this old fellow with the top hat come from?

No one knows for sure, but tradition says he first showed up during the War of 1812. Businessman Samuel Wilson of Troy, New York, who was known to friends as Uncle Sam, supplied the Army with beef in barrels. The barrels were labeled "U.S." to show they belonged to the United States government. Somewhere along the way, it is said, folks began to joke that the "U.S." stood for Uncle Sam, and a national symbol was born.

Uncle Sam's stars-and-stripes costume originated in political cartoons of the nineteenth century. The best-known image first appeared on July 6, 1916, during World War I, on the cover of *Leslie's Weekly* magazine with the title "What Are You Doing for Preparedness?" The artist, James Montgomery Flagg, based his portrait of Uncle Sam on his own likeness to save the cost of hiring a model. The picture was so popular, the U.S. government eventually turned it into the famous recruiting poster of Uncle Sam declaring, "I Want You."

AMERICAN HISTORY PARADE

1699   Captain William Kidd, the pirate, is captured in Boston and later sent to England, where he is hanged.

1785   Congress adopts a currency system with a basic unit called the dollar.

1854   The first official meeting of the Republican Party takes place in Jackson, Michigan.

1892   A strike at the Carnegie Steel plant in Homestead, Pennsylvania, erupts in violence, resulting in 18 deaths and dozens more wounded.

1916   The most famous image of Uncle Sam appears on the cover of *Leslie's Weekly*.

1928   *The Lights of New York*, the first all-talking feature film, premieres in New York.

1976   The U.S. Naval Academy admits women for first time.

ON THE NIGHT OF JULY 7, 1954, Memphis disc jockey Dewey Phillips played a brand-new recording of the song "That's All Right" sung by 19-year-old Elvis Presley, who lived there in Memphis. Right away, listeners starting calling, demanding that he play it again, asking exactly what kind of music it was—blues? rock 'n' roll?—and wanting to know more about the singer.

Dewey played the song fourteen times that night. During one break, he called the Presley home, wanting to get Elvis down to the studio for an interview. Elvis, who'd been told that his record might be on the radio, had been too nervous to listen. "I thought people would laugh at me," he later explained. So he'd gone to the movies.

Dewey asked his mother to find him, saying, "I played that record of his, and them bird-brain phones haven't stopped ringing since." Mr. and Mrs. Presley hurried to the theater, searched the dark rows, found their son, and hustled the boy off to WHBQ for the interview.

As a child, Elvis Presley soaked up gospel music at church. He listened to country music on *The Grand Ole Opry* radio show, blues singers on the streets of Memphis, spirituals at tent revivals, symphony orchestra concerts in the park, opera on the family's wind-up Victrola.

"What kind of singer are you?" the manager of a Memphis recording studio asked him when he made his very first record. "Aw, I sing all kinds," he answered. "Who do you sound like?" she pressed. "I don't sound like nobody," he insisted.

His answer was more than youthful boasting. Presley's unabashedly original style embraced all kinds of American music and crossed all borders of race, class, and region. As biographers have noted, that democratic principle of his music helped win legions of fans.

AMERICAN HISTORY PARADE

1846   Naval forces raise the American flag at Monterey, proclaiming California part of the United States.

1865   Four people are hanged in Washington, D.C., for conspiring with John Wilkes Booth to assassinate Abraham Lincoln.

1898   The United States annexes Hawaii.

1946   Italian-born Mother Frances Xavier Cabrini is canonized as the first American saint.

1954   Elvis Presley makes his radio debut on WHBQ in Memphis.

1976   West Point enrolls its first women cadets.

TRADITION SAYS THAT ON JULY 8, 1776, the Liberty Bell rang from the tower of the Pennsylvania State House (now known as Independence Hall) as it summoned Philadelphians to hear Col. John Nixon give the first public reading of the Declaration of Independence.

The Pennsylvania Assembly ordered the 2,000-pound bell from London in 1751, specifying that it bear an inscription from the Bible: "Proclaim LIBERTY throughout all the Land unto all the inhabitants thereof" (Lev. 25:10 KJV). It arrived in Philadelphia the next year but cracked on its very first test, probably due to a flaw in its casting, so it was melted down and recast twice to make a new bell.

Over the years the bell rang often to call people for announcements and special events. It pealed in 1765 for Philadelphians to discuss the Stamp Act, in 1774 for the First Continental Congress, and in 1775 after the Battles of Lexington and Concord.

At some point—no one is certain when—the bell cracked again. On February 22, 1846, during a ringing for Washington's birthday, the crack grew so much that the bell became unusable. It no longer rings, though on special occasions, such as the Fourth of July, it is gently tapped. On June 6, 1944, when the Allies landed on the beaches of Normandy, officials struck the bell and broadcast its tone across the nation.

Today the Liberty Bell sits near Independence Hall in a pavilion known as the Liberty Bell Center. Lines from an old poem capture Americans' attachment to the venerable icon:

> The old bell now is silent,
> And hushed its iron tongue,
> But the spirit it awakened
> Still lives—forever young.

AMERICAN HISTORY PARADE

1776   The Liberty Bell rings for the first public reading of the Declaration of Independence.

1853   Commodore Matthew Perry sails into Tokyo Bay seeking diplomatic and trade relations between the United States and Japan.

1889   The first issue of the *Wall Street Journal* is published.

1932   The Dow Jones Industrial Average falls to 41.22, its lowest closing of the Great Depression.

1950   General Douglas MacArthur is named commander of United Nations forces fighting in Korea.

ON JULY 9, 1955, "Rock Around the Clock," recorded by Bill Haley and His Comets, hit #1 on the *Billboard* music charts, a spot it would hold for eight weeks. Written by Max Freedman and James E. Myers (a.k.a. Jimmy DeKnight), the song was the first rock 'n' roll recording to top the charts. It had attracted little attention when Haley's band first released it in 1954, but after it appeared in the soundtrack of the movie *The Blackboard Jungle*, millions of young people adopted it as their anthem. "Rock Around the Clock" became a worldwide hit, an event that helped launch the rock 'n' roll revolution.

American music has become the most popular in the world, perhaps because, like America, it reflects traditions and cultures from all over the world. Here are a few styles that have won hearts in every corner of the globe:

Blues emerged in the South after the Civil War, growing out of African American field songs, ballads, and spirituals.

Country music developed in the South in the 1800s, blending British and Irish folk music, blues, Southern religious music, and popular American songs.

Jazz originated in New Orleans around 1900, spreading to Chicago, Kansas City, Memphis, and cities across the country. Its many roots include African American field songs, hymns, blues, New Orleans brass band music, and European harmonies.

Broadway musicals developed in the years following World War I, evolving out of vaudeville, burlesque, and minstrel shows. Early musicals blended popular entertainment with elements of European musical stage traditions.

Rock 'n' Roll emerged in the United States in the 1950s, mixing elements of rhythm and blues, country, dance-band jazz, and pop music.

AMERICAN HISTORY PARADE

1755   During the French and Indian War, General Edward Braddock is mortally wounded in the Battle of the Monongahela, near what is now Pittsburgh.

1846   During the Mexican-American War, American troops under Commodore John Montgomery raise an American flag in Yerba Buena, later renamed San Francisco.

1850   Zachary Taylor, the twelfth U.S. president, dies after serving only sixteen months in office.

1868   The Fourteenth Amendment, designed to grant citizenship to and protect the civil liberties of recently freed slaves, is ratified.

1922   In Alameda, California, Johnny Weissmuller becomes the first person to swim the 100-meter freestyle in less than a minute.

1955   "Rock Around the Clock" reaches #1 on the *Billboard* music charts.

ON JULY 10, 1858, during his campaign for the U.S. Senate, Abraham Lincoln gave a speech in Chicago, in which he reflected on the Declaration of Independence:

> It happens that we meet together once every year, sometime about the 4th of July. . . . We run our memory back over the pages of history [to 1776]. We find a race of men living in that day whom we claim as our fathers and grandfathers. They were iron men. They fought for the principle that they were contending for; and we understand that by what they then did, it has followed that the degree of prosperity that we now enjoy has come to us. We hold this annual celebration to remind ourselves of all the good done, of how it was done and who did it, and how we are historically connected with it. . . .
>
> We have [among us immigrants] who are not descendants at all of these men. . . . If they look back through this history to trace their connection with those days by blood, they find they have none. . . . But when they look through that old Declaration of Independence, they find that those old men say that "We hold these truths to be self-evident, that all men are created equal." And then they feel that that moral sentiment taught in that day evidences their relation to those men, that it is the father of all moral principle in them, and that they have a right to claim it as though they were blood of the blood, and flesh of the flesh of the men who wrote that Declaration. And so they are. That is the electric cord in that Declaration that links the hearts of patriotic and liberty-loving men together, that will link those patriotic hearts as long as the love of freedom exists in the minds of men throughout the world.

AMERICAN HISTORY PARADE

1778   France declares war on Britain in support of the American Revolution.

1850   Vice President Millard Fillmore is sworn in as the thirteenth U.S. president following the death of Zachary Taylor.

1890   Wyoming becomes the forty-fourth state.

1913   Death Valley, California, hits 134° F, the highest temperature ever recorded in the United States.

1962   *Telstar I*, the first commercial communications satellite, is launched from Cape Canaveral.

JULY 11, 1804, brought the most famous duel in American history and the fatal shooting of one of the nation's founders.

The duel between Vice President Aaron Burr and former treasury secretary Alexander Hamilton was the result of longstanding enmity. Politics and personal insults had driven the two men to detest each other. In 1804, when Burr ran for governor of New York, Hamilton attacked his character, denouncing him as an unprincipled adventurer. Burr lost the election and demanded satisfaction of Hamilton. In those times, that meant a duel.

Hamilton felt he could not refuse Burr's challenge without appearing cowardly. It could not have been an easy decision; Hamilton's eldest son, Phillip, had been killed in a duel. Hamilton apparently made up his mind to throw away his first shot at Burr, even if it meant death. He was resolved to "live innocent" rather than "die guilty" of shedding another man's blood.

Early on July 11, the two men faced each other on a dueling ground at Weehawken, New Jersey. Hamilton fired into the air, missing Burr on purpose. Burr leveled his pistol and shot Hamilton in the abdomen, the bullet passing through his enemy's liver and diaphragm.

Hamilton knew the wound was mortal. His friends ferried him over the Hudson River to New York City, where he died after thirty hours of pain. His death was widely mourned, even by political opponents. He was the only one of the Founding Fathers to die a violent death.

Burr was indicted for murder but not arrested. He fled New York, eventually returning to Washington, D.C., where he finished his term as vice president. The duel brought an end to his political career, and the shooting is still regarded as one of the saddest episodes in American political history.

AMERICAN HISTORY PARADE

1767   John Quincy Adams, the sixth U.S. president, is born in Braintree, Massachusetts.

1804   Aaron Burr fatally wounds Alexander Hamilton in a duel at Weehawken, New Jersey.

1955   The Air Force Academy inducts its first class of cadets at a temporary site at Lowry Air Force Base in Colorado.

1960   *To Kill a Mockingbird* by Harper Lee is published.

1979   The abandoned space station *Skylab* makes a fiery return to Earth, burning up in the atmosphere over the Indian Ocean and Australia.

IN THE SUMMER OF 1775, as the Revolutionary War got underway, Patriots in the foothills of western South Carolina organized to fight for independence. The frontiersmen called themselves the Spartan Regiment after the ancient Greek city-state famous for its warriors, and they chose as their leader Col. John Thomas, a sturdy Welch pioneer. Even after the British captured Charleston, overran much of the state, and threw Colonel Thomas in prison, the Spartan Regiment refused to give in.

In July 1780, John Thomas's wife, Jane, was visiting her husband at the settlement of Ninety-Six, where he was confined, when a conversation between several Loyalist women caught her ear. One of them mentioned that Loyalist forces were planning a surprise raid for the next night against a Patriot camp at Cedar Springs. The information startled Jane. It was the place where her son, John Thomas Jr., now in command of the Spartan Regiment, was organizing his men.

Realizing there was no time to lose, she started out early the next morning, July 12. It was 60 miles to Cedar Springs, but Jane Thomas, who was about 60 years old, pushed her horse through the enemy-infested backcountry. By evening she had reached her son's camp.

John Thomas Jr. wasted no time. The Patriots built up their campfires and slipped into the woods. The Loyalists soon arrived and rushed into the camp, expecting to find the hapless rebels asleep in their blankets. Instead, they met a sharp volley of musket balls. In the light of the campfires, they made easy targets for the Patriot backwoodsmen. The Loyalists retreated, leaving behind several dead. Thanks to Jane Thomas, the Battle of Cedar Springs helped launch a resurgence of Patriot fortunes in South Carolina, and brought a much-needed boost in morale.

AMERICAN HISTORY PARADE

1780   A fast-riding Jane Thomas warns Patriot militia of an impending Loyalist attack at the Battle of Cedar Springs in South Carolina.

1804   Alexander Hamilton dies a day after being shot by Vice President Aaron Burr in a duel.

1862   Congress creates the U.S. Army Medal of Honor to be awarded to soldiers for "gallantry in action."

2003   The USS *Ronald Reagan*, the first aircraft carrier named for a living president, is commissioned in Norfolk, Virginia.

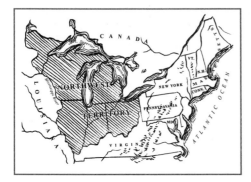

ON JULY 13, 1787, Congress enacted the Northwest Ordinance, one of the greatest achievements of the young American republic. The legislation provided for the government of a huge region then called the Northwest Territory—the modern states of Ohio, Indiana, Michigan, Illinois, Wisconsin, and part of Minnesota.

Under that wise, far-seeing measure, slavery was forever banned in those lands. Further, the lands were divided into townships 6 miles square and subdivided into 36 sections of 640 acres each. One of these sections was donated for the purposes of public education. "Religion, morality, and knowledge being necessary to government and the happiness of mankind, schools and the means of education shall be forever encouraged," Congress said. Thus, even from the beginning of the republic, the focus of education was on the moral as well as the intellectual development of youth.

The Northwest Ordinance treated each new territory as a state-in-embryo. Settlers in the territories could establish free governments and write constitutions, and once they had achieved 60,000 inhabitants, they could apply for admission to the Union as new states. Each state would be admitted on an equal basis with all previous states.

This was the first time in the history of the world that the principle of equality was so recognized. American territories would not be colonies, held in perpetual subordination to the "mother" country.

A crucial feature of the Northwest Ordinance was its treatment of religion. The first article stated: "No person, demeaning himself in a peaceable and orderly manner, shall ever be molested on account of his mode of worship or religious sentiments, in the said territory." This enlightened doctrine was little short of revolutionary for its time. No other government had ever laid out such a principle for administering newly acquired territories.

AMERICAN HISTORY PARADE

1787 Congress adopts the Northwest Ordinance, providing for the government of the region north of the Ohio River and west of Pennsylvania.

1863 Rioting against a Civil War military draft erupts in New York City, leaving more than 100 people dead.

1865 In a *New York Tribune* editorial, Horace Greeley advises, "Go west, young man, and grow up with the country."

1923 The famous Hollywood Sign (originally reading "Hollywoodland" to advertise a real estate development) is dedicated on the hills above Hollywood.

WHICH PRESIDENT WAS BORN with the name Leslie Lynch King Jr.? Hint: He was born July 14, 1913, in Omaha, Nebraska.

Still don't know? You'll find the answer below.

Who was the first president to be born a U.S. citizen? *Martin Van Buren, December 5, 1782*

Who was the only president to have a child born in the White House? *Grover Cleveland, September 9, 1893*

Who was the first president born in a log cabin? *Andrew Jackson, March 15, 1767*

Who was the last president born in a log cabin? *James Garfield, November 19, 1831*

Who was the first president born in a hospital? *Jimmy Carter, October 1, 1924*

Who was the only president to undergo a complete name change? *Gerald Ford, born as Leslie Lynch King Jr. His mother's second husband, Gerald R. Ford, later adopted and renamed him.*

Who was the only former president to become a member of the U.S. House of Representatives? *John Quincy Adams, 1831*

Who was the only former president to become a U.S. senator? *Andrew Johnson, 1875*

Who was the only former president to become chief justice of the U.S. Supreme Court? *William Howard Taft, 1921*

Which former president joined the Confederate government? *John Tyler, 1861*

Who was the first president to reside in Washington, D.C.? *John Adams, 1800*

Who was the first president to visit the West Coast while in office? *Rutherford B. Hayes, 1880*

Who was the first president to visit a foreign country while in office? *Theodore Roosevelt, Panama, 1906*

AMERICAN HISTORY PARADE

1798   Congress passes the Sedition Act, making it a crime to publish false, scandalous, or malicious writings about the United States government.

1853   The first World's Fair to be held in the United States opens in New York City.

1881   Outlaw William H. Bonney ("Billy the Kid") is shot and killed by former friend Pat Garrett in Fort Sumner, New Mexico.

1913   Gerald Ford, the thirty-eighth U.S. president, is born in Omaha, Nebraska.

1965   The space probe *Mariner 4* flies by Mars, sending back the first close-up photos of that planet.

IN JULY 1865 *New York Tribune* editor Horace Greeley popularized an enduring American slogan when he advised in his newspaper, "Go west, young man, and grow up with the country." Thousands of men and women were already doing just that, striking out for western frontiers in search of cheap land and wide-open opportunities.

Each decade, the Census Bureau calculates the mean center of population—the place where an imaginary map of the U.S. would balance if all residents were the same weight. In other words, it's the "middle point" of where we all live. As the nation has grown, the center of population has moved west. In 1790 it lay near Chestertown, Maryland. By 2000 it lay more than 1,000 miles away near Edgar Springs, Missouri.

Census Year	Approximate Location
1790	23 miles east of Baltimore, Maryland
1800	18 miles west of Baltimore, Maryland
1820	16 miles east of Moorefield, West Virginia
1840	16 miles south of Clarksburg, West Virginia
1860	20 miles south by east of Chillicothe, Ohio
1880	8 miles west by south of Cincinnati, Ohio (in Boone County, Kentucky)
1900	6 miles southeast of Columbus, Indiana
1920	8 miles south-southeast of Spencer, Indiana
1940	2 miles southeast by east of Carlisle, Indiana
1960	6.5 miles northwest of Centralia, Illinois
1980	A quarter mile west of DeSoto, Missouri
2000	2.8 miles east of Edgar Springs, Missouri

AMERICAN HISTORY PARADE

1862   The Confederate ironclad *Arkansas* pounds its way through a fleet of Union warships blockading Vicksburg on the Mississippi River.

1912   Jim Thorpe, one of the greatest athletes in U.S. history, shatters the world record in the decathlon at the Olympics in Stockholm, Sweden.

1913   Augustus Bacon of Georgia becomes the first senator elected by popular vote (before the Seventeenth Amendment, senators were elected by state legislators).

1916   Pacific Aero Products, later renamed The Boeing Company, is founded in Seattle by William Boeing.

"DAY BY DAY this country seems to grow bigger and bigger with great walls and fortress-like bastions rising up to defend the west coast. They force us to make many detours, thus more than doubling the length of our march."

So wrote Franciscan friar Junipero Serra in the summer of 1769 as he limped north through the desert with a Spanish expedition headed from Mexico to San Diego Bay. The 56-year-old Serra, a native of the Spanish island of Majorca, had been given the task of starting the first mission in what is now California.

He was not in the best condition for trail blazing. An infection caused by an insect bite had left one of his legs permanently injured. "When I saw him with his swollen foot and leg with its ulcer, I could not keep back the tears," recalled another padre who saw him begin the trek. The soldiers in the expedition urged Serra to return to Mexico. The friar, who had adopted the motto "Always go forward and never turn back," refused.

At one point, his foot grew so inflamed, he could not walk. He asked the young man who took care of the mules to make a poultice. "But father, I only know how to treat sores on mules," the man protested. "Then pretend I am a mule," Serra replied, and the muleteer applied an ointment.

On July 1, 1769, the expedition rendezvoused with two ships at San Diego Bay and began building a settlement at what is now the city of San Diego. On July 16, Serra founded Mission San Diego de Alcalá when he raised a wooden cross and sang a mass. The tireless friar spent the remaining fifteen years of his life limping hundreds of miles up and down the coast, founding a string of missions that became the first major European effort to settle California.

AMERICAN HISTORY PARADE

1769   Junipero Serra founds the first Catholic mission in California at San Diego.

1790   George Washington signs an act stipulating that the president select a site on the Potomac River for the nation's permanent capital.

1862   David Farragut becomes the first rear admiral in the United States Navy.

1945   The United States explodes its first experimental atomic bomb at Alamogordo Air Base, New Mexico.

1969   *Apollo 11* lifts off from Cape Canaveral on the first manned mission to the moon.

ON JULY 17, 1945, the final "Big Three" World War II conference between the United States, Great Britain, and the Soviet Union opened in Potsdam, Germany. There, Harry S. Truman, who had become president only three months earlier when Franklin D. Roosevelt died, met Winston Churchill and Joseph Stalin for the first time.

Truman entered the conference knowing they had giant issues to resolve: the political future of Eastern Europe, the fate of recently defeated Germany, the still ongoing conflict with Japan. And then there was a question he alone must decide—whether to use the atomic bomb. At Potsdam, Truman received a secret telegram informing him that scientists had set off the world's first nuclear explosion in the New Mexico desert. "Operated on this morning," the telegram said. "Diagnosis not yet complete but results seem satisfactory and already exceed expectation."

When he became president, many political observers held low expectations for Truman, the unassuming son of a Missouri livestock dealer. He quickly proved he was willing to make hard choices and stick by them, a characteristic summed up by a small sign he kept on his desk that read, "The Buck Stops Here."

The saying comes from the slang expression "pass the buck," which means passing responsibility to someone else. "Pass the buck" is said to have come from the game of poker. In frontier days, a knife with a buckhorn handle (made from the antler of a male deer) was often placed on the table to designate the dealer. Players could pass the buck, as the marker was called, to the next player if they did not want to deal the cards.

"The President—whoever he is—has to decide," Truman once said. "He can't pass the buck to anybody. No one else can do the deciding for him. That's his job."

AMERICAN HISTORY PARADE

1897   The Klondike Gold Rush begins in Seattle when news of gold in Alaska arrives.

1945   President Harry S. Truman meets with Winston Churchill and Joseph Stalin at the Potsdam Conference in Germany.

1955   Disneyland opens in Anaheim, California.

1975   An Apollo spaceship rendezvouses with a Soviet Soyuz spaceship in the first superpower docking in space.

1997   After nearly 120 years in business, the F. W. Woolworth Company closes its last 400 five-and-dime stores.

As dusk fell on the evening of July 18, 1863, about 600 men of the 54th Massachusetts Volunteer Infantry assembled on a beach near Charleston, South Carolina. At the shout "Forward, Fifty-fourth!" they began to move across a narrow spit of sand toward Fort Wagner, a massive sand-and-wood Confederate stronghold with walls that rose thirty feet high. As they neared the fort, a storm of cannonballs and bullets tore into the blue-coated line.

The 54th Massachusetts was a Northern black regiment organized shortly after Abraham Lincoln issued the Emancipation Proclamation. Its ranks were full of young men who volunteered to fight because they knew that if blacks helped win the Civil War, no one could ever think of them as slaves again.

Twenty-three-year-old Sergeant William Carney helped lead the assault on Fort Wagner. At his side ran Sergeant John Wall, carrying the American flag. When enemy fire struck Wall down, Carney threw his rifle aside and grasped the colors before they hit the ground.

As he pressed forward, a bullet hit him in the thigh. He fell to his knees but managed to get up and struggle onto a parapet, where he planted the flag. There he knelt, bearing the colors as the battle raged around him.

When the overwhelmed Union troops fell back, Carney struggled back down the earthworks, determined not to let the flag fall into enemy hands. He was shot twice more as he staggered across the sand to his own lines, still clutching the Stars and Stripes. "Boys, the old flag never touched the ground," he exclaimed as he collapsed.

The 54th Massachusetts lost nearly half of its men during the assault, but its courage won respect for black soldiers in the North. William Carney recovered from his wounds. For his bravery in protecting the flag that night, he received the Medal of Honor, the nation's highest military award.

AMERICAN HISTORY PARADE

1853   Trains begin running between Maine and Quebec over North America's first international railroad route.

1863   The 54th Massachusetts leads a bloody assault against Fort Wagner on Morris Island near Charleston, South Carolina.

1918   Some 85,000 U.S. troops join a successful Allied counterattack in the Second Battle of the Marne, a turning point of World War I.

1968   Intel Corporation, a leader in the development of the microchip, is incorporated.

1986   Researchers at the Woods Hole Oceanographic Institution in Massachusetts release deep-sea videos of the remains of the RMS *Titanic*.

IN 1840, when American abolitionists Elizabeth Cady Stanton and Lucretia Mott traveled to the World Anti-Slavery Convention in London, they were discouraged to find that women could not participate. Female delegates had to sit quietly and watch the proceedings in an area curtained off from the main hall. The irony that women lacked the freedom to speak at a meeting about freedom for slaves was not lost on Stanton and Mott. They told each other that someday they would hold a convention to discuss their own rights.

Eight years later, on July 19, 1848, Stanton stood on a platform inside the Wesleyan Chapel in Seneca Falls, New York, and opened the nation's first conference on women's rights. Unaccustomed to speaking in public, she was nervous about addressing the roomful of women and men. She later said that she felt like "abandoning all her principles and running away." Instead, she slowly read a draft Declaration of Rights and Sentiments modeled on the Declaration of Independence. "We hold these truths to be self-evident: that all men and women are created equal," it ran.

That afternoon, the convention discussed resolutions calling for women to have rights and responsibilities equal to men's. The most radical resolution demanded suffrage for women. Even Lucretia Mott, a devout Quaker, wondered if that step was too bold. "Why Lizzie, thee will make us look ridiculous," she told Stanton. But abolitionist Frederick Douglass, in attendance, convinced the crowd that women's suffrage was necessary and right.

Reactions to the two-day meeting were mixed. Some newspapers praised it, while others mocked the efforts of "women out of their latitude." It would take decades for women to achieve many of the conference's goals. But the Seneca Falls Convention helped launch a struggle that ultimately changed the place of women in much of the world.

AMERICAN HISTORY PARADE

1848   The first women's rights convention in the United States convenes at Seneca Falls, New York.

1946   Twentieth Century Fox gives Marilyn Monroe her first screen test.

1984   The Democratic National Convention in San Francisco nominates Congresswoman Geraldine Farraro for vice president, making her the first woman on a major political party's presidential ticket.

ON JULY 20, 1969, *Apollo* 11 astronauts Neil Armstrong and Buzz Aldrin floated high above the lifeless surface of the moon in a boxy, four-legged landing vehicle named the *Eagle*. The radio hissed, and a voice called across space from Mission Control in Houston, a quarter of a million miles away: "You are go for powered descent." An engine fired, and the fragile craft began its downward journey.

It would not go exactly as planned.

Alarm signals flashed inside the tiny cabin, warning that *Eagle*'s computer was overloaded. As the spacecraft hurtled toward the surface, engineers in Houston had seconds to decide whether to abort the mission.

"*Eagle*, you are a go for landing," they directed.

The astronauts continued their descent, but when Armstrong looked out the window to study the moon's surface, he realized they were not where they should be. The computer was supposed to guide the *Eagle* to a smooth landing area. It had overshot the mark by four miles and was heading toward a crater of jagged boulders.

Another warning light blinked. They were running out of landing fuel.

Armstrong took command from the computer. The *Eagle* scooted over ridges and craters as he searched for a place to set down. The low-fuel signal flashed. There was no turning back now.

A cloud of dust rose toward the *Eagle*. Silence . . . and then Neil Armstrong's voice crackled to Earth across the gulf of space: "The *Eagle* has landed."

A few hours later, Armstrong and then Aldrin stepped onto the moon's surface. Together they planted a U.S. flag. When they departed, they left behind a plaque bearing this message:

HERE MEN FROM THE PLANET EARTH
FIRST SET FOOT UPON THE MOON
JULY 1969, A.D.
WE CAME IN PEACE FOR ALL MANKIND

AMERICAN HISTORY PARADE

1801   Farmers in Cheshire, Massachusetts, begin pressing a 1,235-pound cheese ball, which they later present to President Thomas Jefferson at the White House.

1881   Sioux leader Sitting Bull, a fugitive since the Battle of the Little Bighorn, surrenders to the U.S. Army at Fort Buford, North Dakota.

1940   *Billboard* publishes its first pop charts with "I'll Never Smile Again," played by Tommy Dorsey's band and sung by Frank Sinatra, at the #1 spot.

1969   Astronaut Neil Armstrong becomes the first man to walk on the moon.

1976   The unmanned *Viking I* becomes the first spacecraft to land successfully on Mars.

IN THE SUMMER OF 1862, Civil War casualties poured into Washington, D.C. Day after day, steamers carrying injured soldiers arrived at the city's Sixth Street Wharf. Makeshift hospitals sprang up throughout the capital in churches, government buildings, hotels, and private homes.

The First Lady, Mary Todd Lincoln, formed the almost daily habit of visiting the wounded. Arriving with a carriage full of fruit and fresh flowers, she would spend hours sitting at their bedsides, talking and reading to them, trying to make them more comfortable amid the stench and groans of the suffering.

Often she helped them write letters home. "I am sitting by the side of your soldier boy," she wrote in one. "He has been quite sick and is getting well. He tells me to say that he is all right." She signed the letter, "With respect [for] the mother of a young soldier."

Mary Lincoln was not popular with the Washington newspapers. They often criticized her for her receptions and decorating projects at the White House. One of the president's assistants believed she should publicize her hospital visits. "If she were worldly wise she would carry newspaper correspondents . . . every time she went," he observed.

But the First Lady kept her hospital visits discreet and let the newspapers lavish praise on society women more press-savvy in their charity work. Her attempts to comfort the wounded were too profound to be a public relations tool. "She found something more gratifying than public acknowledgment," notes historian Doris Kearns Goodwin. "For in the hours she spent with these soldiers she must have sensed their unwavering belief in her husband and in the Union for which they fought. Such a faith was not readily found elsewhere—not in the cabinet, the Congress, the press, or the social circles of the city."

AMERICAN HISTORY PARADE

1861   Confederates win the first major land battle of the Civil War at Manassas, Virginia.

1925   In Dayton, Tennessee, the Scopes "Monkey Trial," testing a law which forbade teaching evolution, ends with the conviction of teacher John Scopes.

1944   During World War II, U.S. troops land on Guam to retake it from the Japanese.

1969   *Apollo 11* astronauts Neil Armstrong and Buzz Aldrin blast off from the moon.

1997   A restored USS *Constitution* ("Old Ironsides") sets sail from Boston under its own power for the first time in more than one hundred years.

IN 1893 a young English professor from Massachusetts named Katharine Lee Bates traveled to Colorado Springs to spend a few weeks teaching a summer session at Colorado College. On July 22—the "supreme day of our Colorado sojourn," as she put it—Bates and other visiting teachers piled into a wagon for a bumpy ride to the top of Pikes Peak, which towered over the town. From the snow-capped summit she "gazed in wordless rapture over the far expanse of mountain ranges and the sea-like sweep of plain" before her.

That night, back in her room, Bates scratched out the opening lines of a poem that had floated into her mind on the mountaintop, words that originally ran: "O beautiful for halcyon skies, / For amber waves of grain, / For purple mountain majesties, / Above the enameled plain!"

Two years later, on July 4, 1895, her poem was printed in the *Congregationalist*, a popular church magazine. It quickly found an appreciative audience. Several years after that, it was set to the hymn tune "Materna," composed by Samuel A. Ward. By that time Bates had made some revisions to her verses, including changing "halcyon skies" to "spacious skies" and "enameled plain" to "fruited plain." Today the song—which reminds us that America can be great only as long as the beauty of the land is matched by the goodness of its citizens—is one of the nation's favorite patriotic hymns.

AMERICAN HISTORY PARADE

1587   Englishman John White establishes the "Lost Colony" of Roanoke Island, North Carolina, which eventually disappears under mysterious circumstances.

1620   Thirty-five English Pilgrims who had taken refuge in Holland leave that country for England to emigrate to America.

1796   Surveyor Moses Cleaveland chooses a site that becomes the city of Cleveland.

1862   President Abraham Lincoln informs his cabinet that he intends to emancipate the slaves.

1893   Katharine Lee Bates writes "America the Beautiful."

1933   Aviator Wiley Post completes the first solo flight around the world.

1934   Federal agents shoot and kill bank robber John Dillinger in Chicago.

IN 1884 Ulysses S. Grant, former general of the Union armies and president of the United States, suddenly found himself penniless and humiliated. His brokerage firm, Grant and Ward, had collapsed with the discovery that his partner, Ferdinand Ward, was a crook who had stolen investors' money. Sixty-two-year-old Grant, an honorable and beloved man, was devastated.

And it got worse. That fall he consulted a doctor about a nagging soreness in his throat. The expression on the specialist's face told Grant the news was bad. "Is it cancer?" he asked. It was, and there was little hope of survival.

Grant quickly made a decision. He had never wanted to write his memoirs, but he realized that would be the best way to provide for his wife, Julia, and his family. If the book sold well, they would have some financial security when he was gone. His friend Mark Twain agreed to publish the work.

So Grant started writing, in a race against death. "My family is American, and has been for generations, in all its branches, direct and collateral," he began. The Grants moved to the Adirondack Mountains, hoping the mountain air would make him more comfortable. Every day he sat on the porch, propped in a chair, barely able even to swallow, suffering from intense pain in his throat, but writing steadily.

He wrote mainly of his military career, but also of his confidence that Northerners and Southerners would once again be fast friends. "I cannot stay to be a living witness to the correctness of this prophecy," he wrote, "but I feel it within me that it is to be so."

Grant finished the manuscript on July 18, 1885. Five days later, on July 23, he died. *The Personal Memoirs of Ulysses S. Grant* was a huge best seller, providing large royalties for the general's widow. Written in clear, unadorned prose, it remains a classic of American literature.

AMERICAN HISTORY PARADE

1715   Massachusetts authorizes the building of the Boston Light, the first lighthouse constructed in America.

1885   Ulysses S. Grant, the eighteenth U.S. president, dies in Mount McGregor, New York.

2000   Tiger Woods wins the British Open at age twenty-four, becoming the youngest golfer to win a career Grand Slam (the Masters, PGA Championship, U.S. Open, and British Open).

ON THIS DAY IN 1775, during the Revolutionary War, the newly appointed commander in chief of the Continental Army was busy organizing his troops. As he rode through the camps on the hills outside Boston, George Washington surely heard his men singing a ditty they had taken a liking to, with words that started, "Yankee Doodle went to town, / a'riding on a pony . . ."

The origins of the song are obscure, but British soldiers reportedly sang it during the French and Indian War to mock shabby American troops. "Yankee" was a nickname for New Englanders. The term may have come from *Yengee*, an Indian pronunciation for the word "English." A "doodle" was a nitwit. According to the song, Yankee Doodle stuck a feather in his cap and called it macaroni. "Macaroni" was slang for a dandy young man who liked to dress in style.

Once the Revolutionary War began, Patriot soldiers proudly appropriated the song. At Bunker Hill they sang the verse:

> Father and I went down to camp,
> along with Captain Good'in,
> And there we saw the men and boys
> as thick as hasty puddin'.

After George Washington took command of the army, a new verse appeared:

> And there was Captain Washington
> upon a slapping stallion,
> A'giving orders to his men;
> I guess there was a million.

The song became a favorite of fife and drum bands, and it is said the Patriots played "Yankee Doodle" when the British surrendered at Yorktown.

AMERICAN HISTORY PARADE

1701   Detroit is founded as a French fur-trading post.

1847   Brigham Young leads Mormon pioneers into the valley of the Great Salt Lake.

1911   American explorer Hiram Bingham discovers Machu Picchu, the "lost city" of the Incas in the Andes Mountains of Peru.

1969   The *Apollo 11* astronauts splash down in the Pacific.

ON JULY 25, 1952, Puerto Rico became a self-governing commonwealth with a constitution written by Puerto Ricans and modeled after the U.S. Constitution. The island had been a U.S. possession since 1898, when Spain surrendered it at the end of the Spanish-American War.

Puerto Rico is the largest of a handful of island territories under the jurisdiction of the federal government.

	Location	Area	Approx. Pop.
Puerto Rico	**Caribbean**	3,515 sq. mi.	4,000,000
Guam	**Pacific**	212 sq. mi.	175,000
U.S. Virgin Islands	**Caribbean**	136 sq. mi.	108,000
Northern Mariana Islands	**Pacific**	184 sq. mi.	85,000
American Samoa	**Pacific**	77 sq. mi.	58,000
Johnston Atoll	**Pacific**	1 sq. mi.	0*
Midway Islands	**Pacific**	2 sq. mi.	0
Wake Island	**Pacific**	3 sq. mi.	0
Baker, Howland, and Jarvis Islands	**Pacific**	3 sq. mi.	0
Kingman Reef	**Pacific**	1 sq. mi.	0
Navassa Island	**Caribbean**	2 sq. mi.	0
Palmyra Atoll	**Pacific**	5 sq. mi.	0

* No indigenous inhabitants. Some smaller U.S. territories are inhabited by a few U.S. government personnel.

AMERICAN HISTORY PARADE

1866 Following the Civil War, President Andrew Johnson elevates *Lieutenant General* Ulysses S. Grant to the rank of general of the U.S. Army, making him the first American officer to hold that rank.

1898 During the Spanish-American War, U.S. troops begin to land in Puerto Rico.

1952 Puerto Rico becomes a self-governing commonwealth of the United States.

1956 The Italian ocean liner *Andrea Doria* sinks off Nantucket, Massachusetts, after colliding with the Swedish liner *Stockholm*; some 50 people die, but 1,660 are rescued.

ON JULY 26, 1788, New York became the eleventh state to ratify the U.S. Constitution. The state takes its name from the colony that came before it, which had been named for James, Duke of York and brother of England's King Charles II. In 1685 James became King James II of England.

A few more origins of state names:

North Carolina and South Carolina – for King Charles I of England (*Carolina* is a Latin form of Charles)

North Dakota and South Dakota – for the Dakota tribe, *Dakota* being a Sioux word meaning "friend" or "ally"

Ohio – from the Ohio River, *Ohio* being an Iroquoian word meaning "great river"

Oklahoma – from the Choctaw words *okla* (people), and *humma* (red), meaning "red people"

Oregon – uncertain; perhaps from the Algonquian word *wauregan*, meaning "beautiful"

Pennsylvania – in honor of Admiral William Penn, father of William Penn, founder of the colony (*Pennsylvania* means "Penn's woods")

Rhode Island – perhaps from the Dutch words *roodt eylandt* (red island), referring to red earth along the coast

AMERICAN HISTORY PARADE

1775   Benjamin Franklin becomes the first postmaster general.

1788   New York becomes the eleventh state to ratify the Constitution.

1835   The first large-scale sugar plantation in Hawaii is started at Koloa, Kauai.

1908   The Federal Bureau of Investigation (FBI) is founded.

1947   President Truman signs legislation creating the Department of Defense, National Security Council, and Central Intelligence Agency.

1948   President Truman signs an executive order ending racial segregation in the U.S. military.

CYRUS WEST FIELD made so much money in the wholesale paper business, by age thirty-three he had retired to a mansion in New York City. He was feeling restless in 1853 when he had the wild idea of laying an underwater telegraph line across the Atlantic Ocean. At that time messages between the U.S. and Europe still went aboard sailing ships. A transatlantic cable would connect America with the rest of the world.

With little knowledge of oceans or telegraphy, Field threw himself at the task. He queried scientists, rounded up investors, and hired engineers. He convinced the U.S. and British navies to lend him two ships.

In 1857 the steamship *Niagara* began laying cable from Ireland's coast. The line snapped after 350 miles had been laid, and the attempt was abandoned.

A depression reduced Field's personal fortune, but he continued to work without pay. In June 1858 two ships met in the middle of the Atlantic, spliced together two halves of a cable, and proceeded toward opposite shores, laying cable as they went. Again the line broke.

A month later, Field tried again. This time he got the cable laid. President Buchanan and Queen Victoria exchanged messages. New York City celebrated with parades and fireworks. Then the line went dead. Somewhere on the ocean floor, the cable had failed. Field went from being a hero to being called a fraud.

Public disillusionment and the Civil War forced a wait of seven more years. In 1865 Field bought the *Great Eastern*, the world's largest steamship, and tried again with an improved cable. The ship had paid out more than 1,000 miles when the line snapped.

On July 27, 1866, on the fifth attempt, the *Great Eastern* arrived at Newfoundland trailing 2,000 miles of line. "Thank God, the cable is laid," an exhausted Field telegraphed. Since that day, the Old and New Worlds have been wired together.

AMERICAN HISTORY PARADE

1866   Cyrus W. Field succeeds in laying the first successful transatlantic cable.

1909   Orville Wright makes a record flight of 1 hour, 12 minutes, and 40 seconds while demonstrating the *Military Flyer*, the first military plane, at Fort Myer, Virginia.

1940   Bugs Bunny makes his debut in the cartoon *A Wild Hare*.

1953   The Korean War armistice is signed at Panmunjom, a village on the border between North and South Korea.

1995   The Korean War Veterans Memorial is dedicated in Washington, D.C.

ON JULY 28, 1896, the hamlet of Miami was incorporated with a population of just a few hundred people. By 1900 it had more than 1,600 residents. By 1910 the town's population had reached nearly 5,500, and by 1925, as new subdivisions and resorts were built, it had soared to more than 100,000. The city changed so fast, people said it was "growing like magic," and Miami came to be known as the "Magic City."

Americans love to give nicknames to their hometowns. A few more examples:

City	Nickname
Boston	Bean Town
Chicago	The Windy City
Dallas	Big D
Denver	Mile High City
Detroit	Motor City (Motown)
Los Angeles	City of Angels
Milwaukee	Brew City
Nashville	Music City
New Orleans	The Big Easy
New York	The Big Apple
Philadelphia	City of Brotherly Love
Pittsburgh	Steel City
St. Louis	Gateway to the West
San Francisco	City by the Bay
Seattle	Emerald City

AMERICAN HISTORY PARADE

1896   The city of Miami is incorporated.

1932   President Herbert Hoover orders the U.S. Army to evict the "Bonus Army" of World War I veterans who had gathered in Washington, D.C., seeking cash payments for bonus certificates the government had issued.

1945   A U.S. Army bomber crashes into the seventy-ninth floor of the fog-shrouded Empire State Building, killing more than a dozen people.

MARTIN TREPTOW, a native of Chippewa Falls, Wisconsin, was working as a barber in Cherokee, Iowa, in 1917 when he enlisted in the Army to fight in World War I. His regiment arrived in France in December of that year, and he wrote a pledge in his diary as a New Year's resolution for 1918. Ronald Reagan, in his first inaugural address, spoke of Treptow's fate:

Under [a] marker lies a young man, Martin Treptow, who left his job in a small town barbershop in 1917 to go to France with the famed Rainbow Division. There, on the western front, he was killed trying to carry a message between battalions under heavy artillery fire.

We're told that on his body was found a diary. On the flyleaf under the heading "My Pledge," he had written these words: "America must win this war. Therefore I will work, I will save, I will sacrifice, I will endure, I will fight cheerfully and do my utmost, as if the issue of the whole struggle depended on me alone."

The crisis we are facing today . . . [requires] our best effort, and our willingness to believe in ourselves and to believe in our capacity to perform great deeds; to believe that together, with God's help, we can and will resolve the problems which now confront us.

And, after all, why shouldn't we believe that? We are Americans.

Note: Treptow was killed in the Chateau-Thierry area of France. Official records give July 29, 1918, as the date of his death, although it is possible that he was killed on July 28.

AMERICAN HISTORY PARADE

1773   Moravian missionaries in Schoenbrunn, Ohio, build the first schoolhouse west of the Allegheny Mountains.

1786   The *Pittsburgh Gazette*, the first newspaper west of the Alleghenies, begins publication.

1958   President Eisenhower signs legislation creating the National Aeronautics and Space Administration (NASA).

2005   Astronomers announce that images taken at the Palomar Observatory in California have revealed evidence of a distant object larger than Pluto orbiting the sun.

THE STORY OF MARY DRAPER INGLES is a good reminder of the harsh and sometimes brutal conditions that early settlers faced.

On July 30 or 31, 1755 (the exact date is uncertain), a band of Shawnee Indians swooped down on a frontier settlement called Draper's Meadow in what is now Blacksburg, Virginia, killing four people and capturing several more. Among the hostages were 23-year-old Mary Draper Ingles and her two sons, 4-year-old Thomas and 2-year-old George. Mary's husband, William, who had been in a field, harvesting wheat, avoided capture.

The Shawnee headed northwest, forcing their captives over the Appalachian Mountains. According to one account, Mary was pregnant and soon gave birth to a daughter, who may have died on the trail. Other reports make no mention of a baby. At any rate, the Shawnee led their captives to a village on the Ohio River. There Mary was separated from her sons. She and another captive described as "the Old Dutch Woman" were taken farther north to Big Bone Lick, near present-day Cincinnati, where they were put to work making salt.

One October afternoon, the two white women slipped into the forest and set off on an 800-mile-long escape. Avoiding trails for fear of recapture, they backtracked over the mountains, scaling cliffs in places, living on walnuts and wild grapes as they fled. Winter arrived. They trudged through snow and slept in hollow logs. Half mad from exhaustion and hunger, the Old Dutch Woman tried to kill Mary, who managed to get away.

Six weeks after escaping the Indians, a skeletal, ragged Mary Draper Ingles staggered into a cornfield near her old home. She soon reunited with her husband, who had gone to Tennessee and Georgia looking for her. They resumed their pioneer lives and went on to have four more children. Mary lived until 1815, dying at age eighty-three.

AMERICAN HISTORY PARADE

1619   The first representative assembly in America convenes in Jamestown, Virginia.

1729   The city of Baltimore is founded.

1775   Mary Draper Ingles is kidnapped by Shawnee Indians at Draper's Meadow, Virginia.

1946   The first rocket to attain a 100-mile altitude, a captured German V-2 rocket, is launched from the White Sands Proving Ground, New Mexico.

1956   The phrase "In God We Trust" becomes the official national motto.

ON JULY 31, 1846, the band of settlers known as the Donner Party left Fort Bridger, Wyoming, on their journey to California, electing to take a new, untried route recommended by a promoter named Lansford Hastings. "Hastings Cutoff . . . is said to be a saving of 350 or 400 miles," wrote party member James Reed in a letter that day. It turned out to be a road to disaster.

The nucleus of the emigrant party consisted of the families of George Donner, his brother Jacob, and their friend James Reed. They had set out in April from Springfield, Illinois, with dreams of new lives in California. Others joined them, and eventually the hopeful party numbered 87 people and 23 wagons.

Within a few days of leaving Fort Bridger, they were in trouble. Hastings Cutoff proved a tortuous route. The men had to chop a trail across the Wasatch Mountains in Utah. They ran out of water crossing the deserts. Oxen began to die, and some wagons were abandoned. The emigrants were way behind schedule when they reached the Sierra Nevada. Then came snow—eventually 22 feet of it—trapping them in a mountain pass in northern California.

They set up camp, hoping to ride out the winter, but provisions were dangerously low. Fifteen of them, calling themselves the "Forlorn Hope," set off across the mountains for help. Only seven survived the trek.

Four relief parties went after the stranded settlers. When the first rescuers reached their camp and called out, a few bony figures crawled out of holes in the snow. "Are you men from California, or do you come from heaven?" one emaciated woman asked. Some of the starving settlers had been forced to eat their comrades' dead bodies to survive.

Only 46 of the 87 Donner Party members lived through the cold and hunger. Their ordeal is a somber reminder of the fortitude of thousands who crossed the mountains and plains.

AMERICAN HISTORY PARADE

1790   The government grants the first U.S. patent to Samuel Hopkins of Vermont for a process of making potash and pearlash, ingredients used to produce soap.

1846   The Donner Party leaves Fort Bridger, Wyoming.

1914   The New York Stock exchange closes for four months due to World War I.

1964   *Ranger 7* becomes the first U.S. probe to transmit close-up pictures of the moon.

1971   *Apollo 15* astronauts become the first to ride a lunar rover on the moon.

1991   President George H. W. Bush and Soviet president Mikhail Gorbachev sign the Strategic Arms Reduction Treaty to reduce long-range nuclear weapon stockpiles.

How the Constitution
Was Written and
Ratified

The men who gathered in **1787** at the Constitutional Convention in Philadelphia had trouble on their hands. Times were bad for the new nation. The Revolutionary War had left debts the states were unwilling or unable to pay. The Articles of Confederation had set up a weak national government. Congress had few real powers. There was no executive branch to enforce laws, no Supreme Court to interpret them. Quarrels between the states were spreading. The so-called union was a mess. "Something must be done, or the fabric must fall, for it is certainly tottering," George Washington observed.

Writing a whole new constitution wasn't the original aim of the leaders who traveled to Philadelphia to meet in the same building where independence had been declared eleven years earlier. They intended to strengthen the Articles of Confederation, but it didn't take them long to realize that starting from scratch made more sense. So the fifty-five delegates set about coming up with a new scheme for American government. James Wilson of Pennsylvania observed that for the first time in history, a nation's people were going "to weigh deliberately and calmly, and to decide leisurely and peacefully, upon the form of government by which they will bind themselves and their posterity."

The convention formally opened on May **25**, with George Washington presiding as its president. It turned out to be a long, stormy session. The states were used to going their own ways. Each delegation had a different set of interests to protect. Many feared that a strong national government would end up squelching liberty. So sharp were some disagreements that at times, the convention seemed on the point of dissolving. Day after day through the hot summer they argued while George Washington looked on in despair, holding things together by the force of his character even as he wondered if the infant union was about to fall apart.

But somehow they managed to pull it off. The scheme of government that came out of that long summer of debate may well be the greatest political document in history. To a large degree, it followed a plan set forth by James Madison of Virginia, who has come to be known as the Father of the Constitution. On September 17, 1787, thirty-eight of the delegates signed the Constitution, some with reservations. (One other, John Dickinson of Delaware, had left the convention but asked another delegate to sign for him.)

At the beginning of the Constitutional Convention, Benjamin Franklin, at age eighty-one the oldest delegate, had noticed that the back of George Washington's chair was decorated with the image of a sun. At the convention's end Franklin commented, "I have often and often in the course of the session, and the vicissitudes of my hopes and fears as to its issue, looked at that behind the president without being able to tell whether it was rising or setting. But now at length I have the happiness to know that it is a rising and not a setting sun."

Congress then sent the new plan to the states for ratification—which was by no means a certainty. Many Americans did not trust the idea of a central governing power. Others thought something stronger was needed. There was even talk of putting a king on an American throne to run things—perhaps a son of George III, or even George Washington himself. The debate started all over again, this time in state houses, taverns, and newspaper pages. Alexander Hamilton, James Madison, and John Jay laid out the arguments for the Constitution in a brilliant series of published essays that came to be known as *The Federalist Papers*. Written in the white heat of the struggle over ratification, *The Federalist Papers* stand as the best exposition of our nation's founding principles.

Nine states were needed to ratify the Constitution in order for it to take effect. On December 7, 1787, Delaware became the first. Pennsylvania followed five days later, then New Jersey, Georgia, Connecticut, Massachusetts, Maryland, and South Carolina. On June 21, 1788, New Hampshire became the crucial ninth state to give its consent.

Still, no one was sure the Constitution would really be accepted until the important states of Virginia and New York ratified it. Virginia ratified on June 25, 1788, and New York on July 26. North Carolina and Rhode Island followed. Congress convened in New York City on March 4, 1789, officially putting the U.S. Constitution into operation. It is the oldest written federal constitution in effect in the world today.

The Constitution
of the United States

Note: The following text is a transcription of the Constitution in its original form.

Items in italics have since been amended or superseded.

We the People of the United States, in Order to form a more perfect Union, establish Justice, insure domestic Tranquility, provide for the common defence, promote the general Welfare, and secure the Blessings of Liberty to ourselves and our Posterity, do ordain and establish this Constitution for the United States of America.

Article I.

Section 1.

All legislative Powers herein granted shall be vested in a Congress of the United States, which shall consist of a Senate and House of Representatives.

Section 2.

The House of Representatives shall be composed of Members chosen every second Year by the People of the several States, and the Electors in each State shall have the Qualifications requisite for Electors of the most numerous Branch of the State Legislature.

No Person shall be a Representative who shall not have attained to the Age of twenty five Years, and been seven Years a Citizen of the United States, and who shall not, when elected, be an Inhabitant of that State in which he shall be chosen.

Representatives and direct Taxes shall be apportioned among the several States which may be included within this Union, according to their respective Numbers, which shall be determined by adding to the whole Number of free Persons, including those bound to Service for a Term of Years, and excluding Indians not taxed, three fifths of all other Persons. The actual Enumeration shall be made within three Years after the first Meeting of the Congress of the United States, and within every subsequent Term of ten Years, in such Manner as they shall by Law direct. The Number of Representatives shall not exceed one for every thirty Thousand, but each State shall have at Least one Representative; and until such enumeration shall be made, the State of New Hampshire shall be entitled to chuse three, Massachusetts eight, Rhode-Island and Providence Plantations one, Connecticut five, New-York six, New Jersey four, Pennsylvania eight, Delaware one, Maryland six, Virginia ten, North Carolina five, South Carolina five, and Georgia three.

When vacancies happen in the Representation from any State, the Executive Authority thereof shall issue Writs of Election to fill such Vacancies.

The House of Representatives shall chuse their Speaker and other Officers; and shall have the sole Power of Impeachment.

Section 3.

The Senate of the United States shall be composed of two Senators from each State, *chosen by the Legislature* thereof for six Years; and each Senator shall have one Vote.

Immediately after they shall be assembled in Consequence of the first Election, they shall be divided as equally as may be into three Classes. The Seats of the Senators of the first Class shall be vacated at the Expiration of the second Year, of the second Class at the Expiration of the fourth Year, and of the third Class at the Expiration of the sixth Year, so that one third may be chosen every second Year; *and if Vacancies happen by Resignation, or otherwise, during the Recess of the Legislature of any State, the Executive thereof may make temporary Appointments until the next Meeting of the Legislature, which shall then fill such Vacancies.*

No Person shall be a Senator who shall not have attained to the Age of thirty Years, and been nine Years a Citizen of the United States, and who shall not, when elected, be an Inhabitant of that State for which he shall be chosen.

The Vice President of the United States shall be President of the Senate, but shall have no Vote, unless they be equally divided.

The Senate shall chuse their other Officers, and also a President pro tempore, in the Absence of the Vice President, or when he shall exercise the Office of President of the United States.

The Senate shall have the sole Power to try all Impeachments. When sitting for that Purpose, they shall be on Oath or Affirmation. When the President of the United States is tried, the Chief Justice shall preside: And no Person shall be convicted without the Concurrence of two thirds of the Members present.

Judgment in Cases of Impeachment shall not extend further than to removal from Office, and disqualification to hold and enjoy any Office of honor, Trust or Profit under the United States: but the Party convicted shall nevertheless be liable and subject to Indictment, Trial, Judgment and Punishment, according to Law.

Section 4.

The Times, Places and Manner of holding Elections for Senators and Representatives, shall be prescribed in each State by the Legislature thereof; but the Congress may at any time by Law make or alter such Regulations, except as to the Places of chusing Senators.

The Congress shall assemble at least once in every Year, and such Meeting shall *be on the first Monday in December,* unless they shall by Law appoint a different Day.

Section 5.

Each House shall be the Judge of the Elections, Returns and Qualifications of its own Members, and a Majority of each shall constitute a Quorum to do Business; but a smaller Number may adjourn from day to day, and may be authorized to compel the Attendance of absent Members, in such Manner, and under such Penalties as each House may provide.

Each House may determine the Rules of its Proceedings, punish its Members for disorderly Behaviour, and, with the Concurrence of two thirds, expel a Member.

Each House shall keep a Journal of its Proceedings, and from time to time publish the same, excepting such Parts as may in their Judgment require Secrecy; and the Yeas and Nays of the Members of either House on any question shall, at the Desire of one fifth of those Present, be entered on the Journal.

Neither House, during the Session of Congress, shall, without the Consent of the other, adjourn for more than three days, nor to any other Place than that in which the two Houses shall be sitting.

Section 6.

The Senators and Representatives shall receive a Compensation for their Services, to be ascertained by Law, and paid out of the Treasury of the United States. They shall in all Cases, except Treason, Felony and Breach of the Peace, be privileged from Arrest during their Attendance at the Session of their respective Houses, and in going to and returning from the same; and for any Speech or Debate in either House, they shall not be questioned in any other Place.

No Senator or Representative shall, during the Time for which he was elected, be appointed to any civil Office under the Authority of the United States, which shall have been created, or the Emoluments whereof shall have been encreased during such time; and no Person holding any Office under the United States, shall be a Member of either House during his Continuance in Office.

Section 7.

All Bills for raising Revenue shall originate in the House of Representatives; but the Senate may propose or concur with Amendments as on other Bills.

Every Bill which shall have passed the House of Representatives and the Senate, shall, before it become a Law, be presented to the President of the United States: If he approve he shall sign it, but if not he shall return it, with his Objections to that House in which it shall have originated, who shall enter the Objections at large on their Journal, and proceed to reconsider it. If after such Reconsideration two thirds of that House shall agree to pass the Bill, it shall be sent, together with the Objections, to the other House, by which it shall likewise be reconsidered, and if approved by two thirds of that House, it shall become a Law. But in all such Cases the Votes of both Houses shall be determined by yeas and Nays, and the Names of the Persons voting for and against the Bill shall be entered on the Journal of each House respectively. If any Bill shall not be returned by the President within ten Days (Sundays excepted) after it shall have been presented to him, the Same shall be a Law, in like Manner as if he had signed it, unless the Congress by their Adjournment prevent its Return, in which Case it shall not be a Law.

Every Order, Resolution, or Vote to which the Concurrence of the Senate and House of Representatives may be necessary (except on a question of Adjournment) shall be presented to the President of the United States; and before the Same shall take Effect, shall be approved by him, or being disapproved by him, shall be repassed by two thirds of the Senate and House of Representatives, according to the Rules and Limitations prescribed in the Case of a Bill.

Section 8.

The Congress shall have Power To lay and collect Taxes, Duties, Imposts and Excises, to pay the Debts and provide for the common Defence and general Welfare of the United States; but all Duties, Imposts and Excises shall be uniform throughout the United States;

To borrow Money on the credit of the United States;

To regulate Commerce with foreign Nations, and among the several States, and with the Indian Tribes;

To establish an uniform Rule of Naturalization, and uniform Laws on the subject of Bankruptcies throughout the United States;

To coin Money, regulate the Value thereof, and of foreign Coin, and fix the Standard of Weights and Measures;

To provide for the Punishment of counterfeiting the Securities and current Coin of the United States;

To establish Post Offices and post Roads;

To promote the Progress of Science and useful Arts, by securing for limited Times to Authors and Inventors the exclusive Right to their respective Writings and Discoveries;

To constitute Tribunals inferior to the supreme Court;

To define and punish Piracies and Felonies committed on the high Seas, and Offences against the Law of Nations;

To declare War, grant Letters of Marque and Reprisal, and make Rules concerning Captures on Land and Water;

To raise and support Armies, but no Appropriation of Money to that Use shall be for a longer Term than two Years;

To provide and maintain a Navy;

To make Rules for the Government and Regulation of the land and naval Forces;

To provide for calling forth the Militia to execute the Laws of the Union, suppress Insurrections and repel Invasions;

To provide for organizing, arming, and disciplining, the Militia, and for governing such Part of them as may be employed in the Service of the United States, reserving to the States respectively, the Appointment of the Officers, and the Authority of training the Militia according to the discipline prescribed by Congress;

To exercise exclusive Legislation in all Cases whatsoever, over such District (not exceeding ten Miles square) as may, by Cession of particular States, and the Acceptance of Congress, become the Seat of the Government of the United States, and to exercise like Authority over all Places purchased by the Consent of the Legislature of the State in which the Same shall be, for the Erection of Forts, Magazines, Arsenals, dock-Yards, and other needful Buildings;—And

To make all Laws which shall be necessary and proper for carrying into Execution the foregoing Powers, and all other Powers vested by this Constitution in the Government of the United States, or in any Department or Officer thereof.

Section 9.

The Migration or Importation of such Persons as any of the States now existing shall think proper to admit, shall not be prohibited by the Congress prior to the Year one thousand eight hundred and eight, but a Tax or duty may be imposed on such Importation, not exceeding ten dollars for each Person.

The Privilege of the Writ of Habeas Corpus shall not be suspended, unless when in Cases of Rebellion or Invasion the public Safety may require it.

No Bill of Attainder or ex post facto Law shall be passed.

No Capitation, or other direct, Tax shall be laid, *unless in Proportion to the Census or enumeration herein before directed to be taken.*

No Tax or Duty shall be laid on Articles exported from any State.

No Preference shall be given by any Regulation of Commerce or Revenue to the Ports of one State over those of another; nor shall Vessels bound to, or from, one State, be obliged to enter, clear, or pay Duties in another.

No Money shall be drawn from the Treasury, but in Consequence of Appropriations made by Law; and a regular Statement and Account of the Receipts and Expenditures of all public Money shall be published from time to time.

No Title of Nobility shall be granted by the United States: And no Person holding any Office of Profit or Trust under them, shall, without the Consent of the Congress, accept of any present, Emolument, Office, or Title, of any kind whatever, from any King, Prince, or foreign State.

Section 10.

No State shall enter into any Treaty, Alliance, or Confederation; grant Letters of Marque and Reprisal; coin Money; emit Bills of Credit; make any Thing but gold and silver Coin a Tender in Payment of Debts; pass any Bill of Attainder, ex post facto Law, or Law impairing the Obligation of Contracts, or grant any Title of Nobility.

No State shall, without the Consent of the Congress, lay any Imposts or Duties on Imports or Exports, except what may be absolutely necessary for executing it's inspection Laws: and the net Produce of all Duties and Imposts, laid by any State on Imports or Exports, shall be for the Use of the Treasury of the United States; and all such Laws shall be subject to the Revision and Controul of the Congress.

No State shall, without the Consent of Congress, lay any Duty of Tonnage, keep Troops, or Ships of War in time of Peace, enter into any Agreement or Compact with another State, or with a foreign Power, or engage in War, unless actually invaded, or in such imminent Danger as will not admit of delay.

ARTICLE II.

Section 1.

The executive Power shall be vested in a President of the United States of America. He shall hold his Office during the Term of four Years, and, together with the Vice President, chosen for the same Term, be elected, as follows:

Each State shall appoint, in such Manner as the Legislature thereof may direct, a Number of Electors, equal to the whole Number of Senators and

Representatives to which the State may be entitled in the Congress: but no Senator or Representative, or Person holding an Office of Trust or Profit under the United States, shall be appointed an Elector.

The Electors shall meet in their respective States, and vote by Ballot for two Persons, of whom one at least shall not be an Inhabitant of the same State with themselves. And they shall make a List of all the Persons voted for, and of the Number of Votes for each; which List they shall sign and certify, and transmit sealed to the Seat of the Government of the United States, directed to the President of the Senate. The President of the Senate shall, in the Presence of the Senate and House of Representatives, open all the Certificates, and the Votes shall then be counted. The Person having the greatest Number of Votes shall be the President, if such Number be a Majority of the whole Number of Electors appointed; and if there be more than one who have such Majority, and have an equal Number of Votes, then the House of Representatives shall immediately chuse by Ballot one of them for President; and if no Person have a Majority, then from the five highest on the List the said House shall in like Manner chuse the President. But in chusing the President, the Votes shall be taken by States, the Representation from each State having one Vote; A quorum for this purpose shall consist of a Member or Members from two thirds of the States, and a Majority of all the States shall be necessary to a Choice. In every Case, after the Choice of the President, the Person having the greatest Number of Votes of the Electors shall be the Vice President. But if there should remain two or more who have equal Votes, the Senate shall chuse from them by Ballot the Vice President.

The Congress may determine the Time of chusing the Electors, and the Day on which they shall give their Votes; which Day shall be the same throughout the United States.

No Person except a natural born Citizen, or a Citizen of the United States, at the time of the Adoption of this Constitution, shall be eligible to the Office of President; neither shall any Person be eligible to that Office who shall not have attained to the Age of thirty five Years, and been fourteen Years a Resident within the United States.

In Case of the Removal of the President from Office, or of his Death, Resignation, or Inability to discharge the Powers and Duties of the said Office, the Same shall devolve on the Vice President, and the Congress may by Law provide for the Case of Removal, Death, Resignation or Inability, both of the President and Vice President, declaring what Officer shall then act as President, and such Officer shall act accordingly, until the Disability be removed, or a President shall be elected.

The President shall, at stated Times, receive for his Services, a Compensation, which shall neither be increased nor diminished during the Period for which he shall have been elected, and he shall not receive within that Period any other Emolument from the United States, or any of them.

Before he enter on the Execution of his Office, he shall take the following Oath or Affirmation:—"I do solemnly swear (or affirm) that I will faithfully execute the Office of President of the United States, and will to the best of my Ability, preserve, protect and defend the Constitution of the United States."

Section 2.

The President shall be Commander in Chief of the Army and Navy of the United States, and of the Militia of the several States, when called into the actual Service of the United States; he may require the Opinion, in writing, of the principal Officer in each of the executive Departments, upon any Subject relating to the Duties of their respective Offices, and he shall have Power to grant Reprieves and Pardons for Offences against the United States, except in Cases of Impeachment.

He shall have Power, by and with the Advice and Consent of the Senate, to make Treaties, provided two thirds of the Senators present concur; and he shall nominate, and by and with the Advice and Consent of the Senate, shall appoint Ambassadors, other public Ministers and Consuls, Judges of the supreme Court, and all other Officers of the United States, whose Appointments are not herein otherwise provided for, and which shall be established by Law: but the Congress may by Law vest the Appointment of such inferior Officers, as they think proper, in the President alone, in the Courts of Law, or in the Heads of Departments.

The President shall have Power to fill up all Vacancies that may happen during the Recess of the Senate, by granting Commissions which shall expire at the End of their next Session.

Section 3.

He shall from time to time give to the Congress Information of the State of the Union, and recommend to their Consideration such Measures as he shall judge necessary and expedient; he may, on extraordinary Occasions, convene both Houses, or either of them, and in Case of Disagreement between them, with Respect to the Time of Adjournment, he may adjourn them to such Time as he shall think proper; he shall receive Ambassadors and other public Ministers; he shall take Care that the Laws be faithfully executed, and shall Commission all the Officers of the United States.

Section 4.

The President, Vice President and all civil Officers of the United States, shall be removed from Office on Impeachment for, and Conviction of, Treason, Bribery, or other high Crimes and Misdemeanors.

ARTICLE III.

Section 1.

The judicial Power of the United States shall be vested in one supreme Court, and in such inferior Courts as the Congress may from time to time ordain and establish. The Judges, both of the supreme and inferior Courts, shall hold their Offices during good Behaviour, and shall, at stated Times, receive for their Services a Compensation, which shall not be diminished during their Continuance in Office.

Section 2.

The judicial Power shall extend to all Cases, in Law and Equity, arising under this Constitution, the Laws of the United States, and Treaties made, or which shall be made, under their Authority;—to all Cases affecting Ambassadors, other public Ministers and Consuls;—to all Cases of admiralty and maritime Jurisdiction;—to Controversies to which the United States shall be a Party;—to Controversies between two or more States;—*between a State and Citizens of another State*;—between Citizens of different States;—between Citizens of the same State claiming Lands under Grants of different States, and between a State, or the Citizens thereof, and foreign States, Citizens or Subjects.

In all Cases affecting Ambassadors, other public Ministers and Consuls, and those in which a State shall be Party, the supreme Court shall have original Jurisdiction. In all the other Cases before mentioned, the supreme Court shall have appellate Jurisdiction, both as to Law and Fact, with such Exceptions, and under such Regulations as the Congress shall make.

The Trial of all Crimes, except in Cases of Impeachment, shall be by Jury; and such Trial shall be held in the State where the said Crimes shall have been committed; but when not committed within any State, the Trial shall be at such Place or Places as the Congress may by Law have directed.

Section 3.

Treason against the United States, shall consist only in levying War against them, or in adhering to their Enemies, giving them Aid and Comfort. No Person shall be convicted of Treason unless on the Testimony of two Witnesses to the same overt Act, or on Confession in open Court.

The Congress shall have Power to declare the Punishment of Treason, but no Attainder of Treason shall work Corruption of Blood, or Forfeiture except during the Life of the Person attainted.

ARTICLE IV.

Section 1.

Full Faith and Credit shall be given in each State to the public Acts, Records, and judicial Proceedings of every other State. And the Congress may by general

Laws prescribe the Manner in which such Acts, Records and Proceedings shall be proved, and the Effect thereof.

Section 2.

The Citizens of each State shall be entitled to all Privileges and Immunities of Citizens in the several States.

A Person charged in any State with Treason, Felony, or other Crime, who shall flee from Justice, and be found in another State, shall on Demand of the executive Authority of the State from which he fled, be delivered up, to be removed to the State having Jurisdiction of the Crime.

No Person held to Service or Labour in one State, under the Laws thereof, escaping into another, shall, in Consequence of any Law or Regulation therein, be discharged from such Service or Labour, but shall be delivered up on Claim of the Party to whom such Service or Labour may be due.

Section 3.

New States may be admitted by the Congress into this Union; but no new State shall be formed or erected within the Jurisdiction of any other State; nor any State be formed by the Junction of two or more States, or Parts of States, without the Consent of the Legislatures of the States concerned as well as of the Congress.

The Congress shall have Power to dispose of and make all needful Rules and Regulations respecting the Territory or other Property belonging to the United States; and nothing in this Constitution shall be so construed as to Prejudice any Claims of the United States, or of any particular State.

Section 4.

The United States shall guarantee to every State in this Union a Republican Form of Government, and shall protect each of them against Invasion; and on

Application of the Legislature, or of the Executive (when the Legislature cannot be convened), against domestic Violence.

ARTICLE V.

The Congress, whenever two thirds of both Houses shall deem it necessary, shall propose Amendments to this Constitution, or, on the Application of the Legislatures of two thirds of the several States, shall call a Convention for proposing Amendments, which, in either Case, shall be valid to all Intents and Purposes, as Part of this Constitution, when ratified by the Legislatures of three fourths of the several States, or by Conventions in three fourths thereof, as the one or the other Mode of Ratification may be proposed by the Congress; Provided that no Amendment which may be made prior to the Year One thousand eight hundred and eight shall in any Manner affect the first and fourth Clauses in the Ninth Section of the first Article; and that no State, without its Consent, shall be deprived of its equal Suffrage in the Senate.

ARTICLE VI.

All Debts contracted and Engagements entered into, before the Adoption of this Constitution, shall be as valid against the United States under this Constitution, as under the Confederation.

This Constitution, and the Laws of the United States which shall be made in Pursuance thereof; and all Treaties made, or which shall be made, under the Authority of the United States, shall be the supreme Law of the Land; and the Judges in every State shall be bound thereby, any Thing in the Constitution or Laws of any State to the Contrary notwithstanding.

The Senators and Representatives before mentioned, and the Members of the several State Legislatures, and all executive and judicial Officers, both of the United States and of the several States, shall be bound by Oath or Affirmation, to support this Constitution; but no religious Test shall ever be required as a Qualification to any Office or public Trust under the United States.

ARTICLE VII.

The Ratification of the Conventions of nine States, shall be sufficient for the Establishment of this Constitution between the States so ratifying the Same.

The Word, "the," being interlined between the seventh and eighth Lines of the first Page, the Word "Thirty" being partly written on an Erazure in the fifteenth Line of the first Page, The Words "is tried" being interlined between the thirty second and thirty third Lines of the first Page and the Word "the" being interlined between the forty third and forty fourth Lines of the second Page.

Done in Convention by the Unanimous Consent of the States present the Seventeenth Day of September in the Year of our Lord one thousand seven hundred and Eighty seven and of the Independence of the United States of America the Twelfth In witness whereof We have hereunto subscribed our Names,

G. Washington
Presidt and deputy from Virginia

New Hampshire – John Langdon, Nicholas Gilman

Massachusetts – Nathaniel Gorham, Rufus King

Connecticut – Wm. Saml. Johnson, Roger Sherman

New York – Alexander Hamilton

New Jersey – Wil: Livingston, David Brearley, Wm. Paterson, Jona: Dayton

Pennsylvania – B Franklin, Thomas Mifflin, Robt. Morris, Geo. Clymer, Thos. FitzSimons, Jared Ingersoll, James Wilson, Gouv Morris

Delaware – Geo: Read, Gunning Bedford jun, John Dickinson, Richard Bassett, Jaco: Broom

Maryland – James McHenry, Dan of St Thos. Jenifer, Danl. Carroll

Virginia – John Blair, James Madison Jr.

North Carolina – Wm. Blount, Richd. Dobbs Spaight, Hu Williamson

South Carolina – J. Rutledge, Charles Cotesworth Pinckney, Charles Pinckney, Pierce Butler

Georgia – William Few, Abr Baldwin

Attest: William Jackson, Secretary

The Bill of Rights

At the end of the Constitutional Convention of 1787, some delegates refused to sign the Constitution because they believed it did not fully protect fundamental rights and liberties. When Congress sent the document to the states to be ratified, several states had the same reaction. They had adopted their own state constitutions during the Revolution, and most included clear statements describing inviolable rights. Many prominent voices called for the national Constitution to include the same sort of guarantees to safeguard individual freedoms. Otherwise, they signaled, they wanted no part of the new federal government.

James Madison originally considered a list of protected rights unnecessary. He believed the Constitution gave the government no power to violate citizens' liberties. He also worried that listing specific rights ran the risk of inviting the government to limit rights left off the list. Nevertheless, he was persuaded that a statement of inviolable rights would help win acceptance of the new federal government.

When the First Congress met in New York City in 1789, Madison led the effort to write amendments spelling out basic rights. These additions were based in part on the Virginia Declaration of Rights, written by George Mason in 1776. (Mason had been one of those delegates to the Constitutional Convention who refused to sign the Constitution precisely because it lacked a statement of rights.)

Congress sent twelve amendments to the states. Ten were eventually ratified, and these first ten amendments to the Constitution have come to be known as the Bill of Rights. They went into effect on December 15, 1791.

Amendment I

Congress shall make no law respecting an establishment of religion, or prohibiting the free exercise thereof; or abridging the freedom of speech, or of the press; or the right of the people peaceably to assemble, and to petition the Government for a redress of grievances.

Amendment II

A well regulated Militia, being necessary to the security of a free State, the right of the people to keep and bear Arms, shall not be infringed.

Amendment III

No Soldier shall, in time of peace be quartered in any house, without the consent of the Owner, nor in time of war, but in a manner to be prescribed by law.

Amendment IV

The right of the people to be secure in their persons, houses, papers, and effects, against unreasonable searches and seizures, shall not be violated, and no Warrants shall issue, but upon probable cause, supported by Oath or affirmation, and particularly describing the place to be searched, and the persons or things to be seized.

Amendment V

No person shall be held to answer for a capital, or otherwise infamous crime, unless on a presentment or indictment of a Grand Jury, except in cases arising in the land or naval forces, or in the Militia, when in actual service in time of War or public danger; nor shall any person be subject for the same offence to be twice put in jeopardy of life or limb; nor shall be compelled in any criminal case to be a witness against himself, nor be deprived of life, liberty, or property, without due process of law; nor shall private property be taken for public use, without just compensation.

Amendment VI

In all criminal prosecutions, the accused shall enjoy the right to a speedy and public trial, by an impartial jury of the State and district wherein the crime shall have been committed, which district shall have been previously ascertained by law, and to be informed of the nature and cause of the accusation; to be confronted with the witnesses against him; to have compulsory process for obtaining witnesses in his favor, and to have the Assistance of Counsel for his defence.

Amendment VII

In Suits at common law, where the value in controversy shall exceed twenty dollars, the right of trial by jury shall be preserved, and no fact tried by a jury, shall be otherwise re-examined in any Court of the United States, than according to the rules of the common law.

Amendment VIII

Excessive bail shall not be required, nor excessive fines imposed, nor cruel and unusual punishments inflicted.

Amendment IX

The enumeration in the Constitution, of certain rights, shall not be construed to deny or disparage others retained by the people.

Amendment X

The powers not delegated to the United States by the Constitution, nor prohibited by it to the States, are reserved to the States respectively, or to the people.

Amendments to the U.S. Constitution Since the Bill of Rights

Amendment XI

Passed by Congress March 4, 1794. Ratified February 7, 1795.

Note: Article III, section 2, of the Constitution was modified by the Eleventh Amendment.

The Judicial power of the United States shall not be construed to extend to any suit in law or equity, commenced or prosecuted against one of the United States by Citizens of another State, or by Citizens or Subjects of any Foreign State.

Amendment XII

Passed by Congress December 9, 1803. Ratified June 15, 1804.

Note: A portion of Article II, section 1 of the Constitution was superseded by the Twelfth Amendment.

The Electors shall meet in their respective states and vote by ballot for President and Vice-President, one of whom, at least, shall not be an inhabitant of the same state with themselves; they shall name in their ballots the person voted for as President, and in distinct ballots the person voted for as Vice-President, and they shall make distinct lists of all persons voted for as President, and of all persons voted for as Vice-President, and of the number of votes for each, which lists they shall sign and certify, and transmit sealed to the seat of the government of the United States, directed to the President of the Senate; — the President of the Senate shall, in the presence of the Senate and House of Representatives, open all the certificates and the votes shall then be counted; — The person having the greatest number of votes for President, shall be the President, if such number be a majority of the whole number of Electors appointed; and if no person have such majority, then from the persons having the highest numbers not exceeding three on the list of those voted for as President, the House of Representatives shall choose immediately, by ballot, the President. But in choosing the President, the votes shall be taken by states, the representation from each state having one vote; a quorum for this purpose shall consist of a member or members from two-thirds of the states, and a majority of all the states shall be necessary to a choice. [*And if the House of Representatives shall not choose a President whenever the right of choice shall devolve upon them, before the fourth day of March next following, then the Vice-President shall act as President, as in case of the death or other constitutional disability of the President.* —]* The person having the greatest number of votes as Vice-President, shall be the Vice-President, if such number be a majority of the whole number of Electors appointed, and if no person have a majority, then from the two highest numbers on the list, the Senate shall choose the Vice-President; a quorum for the purpose shall consist of two-thirds of the whole number of Senators, and a majority of the whole number shall be necessary to a choice. But no person constitutionally ineligible to the office of President shall be eligible to that of Vice-President of the United States.

Superseded by section 3 of the Twentieth Amendment.

AMENDMENT XIII

Passed by Congress January 31, 1865. Ratified December 6, 1865.

Note: A portion of Article IV, section 2, of the Constitution was superseded by the Thirteenth Amendment.

Section 1.

Neither slavery nor involuntary servitude, except as a punishment for crime whereof the party shall have been duly convicted, shall exist within the United States, or any place subject to their jurisdiction.

Section 2.

Congress shall have power to enforce this article by appropriate legislation.

Amendment XIV

Passed by Congress June 13, 1866. Ratified July 9, 1868.

   Note: Article I, section 2, of the Constitution was modified by section 2 of the Fourteenth Amendment.

Section 1.

All persons born or naturalized in the United States, and subject to the jurisdiction thereof, are citizens of the United States and of the State wherein they reside. No State shall make or enforce any law which shall abridge the privileges or immunities of citizens of the United States; nor shall any State deprive any person of life, liberty, or property, without due process of law; nor deny to any person within its jurisdiction the equal protection of the laws.

Section 2.

Representatives shall be apportioned among the several States according to their respective numbers, counting the whole number of persons in each State, excluding Indians not taxed. But when the right to vote at any election for the choice of electors for President and Vice-President of the United States, Representatives in Congress, the Executive and Judicial officers of a State, or the members of the Legislature thereof, is denied to any of the male inhabitants of such State, being twenty-one years of age,* and citizens of the United States, or in any way abridged, except for participation in rebellion, or other crime, the basis of representation therein shall be reduced in the proportion which the number of such male citizens shall bear to the whole number of male citizens twenty-one years of age in such State.

Changed by section 1 of the Twenty-sixth Amendment.

Section 3.

No person shall be a Senator or Representative in Congress, or elector of President and Vice-President, or hold any office, civil or military, under the United States, or under any State, who, having previously taken an oath, as a member of Congress, or as an officer of the United States, or as a member of any State legislature, or as an executive or judicial officer of any State, to support the Constitution of the United States, shall have engaged in insurrection or rebellion against the same, or given aid or comfort to the enemies thereof. But Congress may by a vote of two-thirds of each House, remove such disability.

Section 4.

The validity of the public debt of the United States, authorized by law, including debts incurred for payment of pensions and bounties for services in suppressing insurrection or rebellion, shall not be questioned. But neither the United States nor any State shall assume or pay any debt or obligation incurred in aid of insurrection or rebellion against the United States, or any claim for the loss or emancipation of any slave; but all such debts, obligations and claims shall be held illegal and void.

Section 5.

The Congress shall have the power to enforce, by appropriate legislation, the provisions of this article.

AMENDMENT XV

Passed by Congress February 26, 1869. Ratified February 3, 1870.

Section 1.

The right of citizens of the United States to vote shall not be denied or abridged by the United States or by any State on account of race, color, or previous condition of servitude.

Section 2.

The Congress shall have the power to enforce this article by appropriate legislation.

Amendment XVI

Passed by Congress July 2, 1909. Ratified February 3, 1913.

Note: Article I, section 9, of the Constitution was modified by the Sixteenth Amendment.

The Congress shall have power to lay and collect taxes on incomes, from whatever source derived, without apportionment among the several States, and without regard to any census or enumeration.

Amendment XVII

Passed by Congress May 13, 1912. Ratified April 8, 1913.

Note: Article I, section 3, of the Constitution was modified by the Seventeenth Amendment.

The Senate of the United States shall be composed of two Senators from each State, elected by the people thereof, for six years; and each Senator shall have one vote. The electors in each State shall have the qualifications requisite for electors of the most numerous branch of the State legislatures.

When vacancies happen in the representation of any State in the Senate, the executive authority of such State shall issue writs of election to fill such vacancies: *Provided,* That the legislature of any State may empower the executive thereof to make temporary appointments until the people fill the vacancies by election as the legislature may direct.

This amendment shall not be so construed as to affect the election or term of any Senator chosen before it becomes valid as part of the Constitution.

AMENDMENT XVIII

Passed by Congress December 18, 1917. Ratified January 16, 1919. Repealed by the Twenty-first Amendment.

Section 1.
After one year from the ratification of this article the manufacture, sale, or transportation of intoxicating liquors within, the importation thereof into, or the exportation thereof from the United States and all territory subject to the jurisdiction thereof for beverage purposes is hereby prohibited.

Section 2.
The Congress and the several States shall have concurrent power to enforce this article by appropriate legislation.

Section 3.
This article shall be inoperative unless it shall have been ratified as an amendment to the Constitution by the legislatures of the several States, as provided in the Constitution, within seven years from the date of the submission hereof to the States by the Congress.

AMENDMENT XIX

Passed by Congress June 4, 1919. Ratified August 18, 1920.

The right of citizens of the United States to vote shall not be denied or abridged by the United States or by any State on account of sex.

Congress shall have power to enforce this article by appropriate legislation.

Amendment XX

Passed by Congress March 2, 1932. Ratified January 23, 1933.

Note: Article I, section 4, of the Constitution was modified by section 2 of this amendment. In addition, a portion of the Twelfth Amendment was superseded by section 3.

Section 1.

The terms of the President and the Vice President shall end at noon on the 20th day of January, and the terms of Senators and Representatives at noon on the 3d day of January, of the years in which such terms would have ended if this article had not been ratified; and the terms of their successors shall then begin.

Section 2.

The Congress shall assemble at least once in every year, and such meeting shall begin at noon on the 3d day of January, unless they shall by law appoint a different day.

Section 3.

If, at the time fixed for the beginning of the term of the President, the President elect shall have died, the Vice President elect shall become President. If a President shall not have been chosen before the time fixed for the beginning of his term, or if the President elect shall have failed to qualify, then the Vice President elect shall act as President until a President shall have qualified; and the Congress may by law provide for the case wherein neither a President elect nor a Vice President shall have qualified, declaring who shall then act as President, or the manner in which one who is to act shall be selected, and such person shall act accordingly until a President or Vice President shall have qualified.

Section 4.

The Congress may by law provide for the case of the death of any of the persons from whom the House of Representatives may choose a President whenever the right of choice shall have devolved upon them, and for the case of the death of any of the persons from whom the Senate may choose a Vice President whenever the right of choice shall have devolved upon them.

Section 5.

Sections 1 and 2 shall take effect on the 15th day of October following the ratification of this article.

Section 6.

This article shall be inoperative unless it shall have been ratified as an amendment to the Constitution by the legislatures of three-fourths of the several States within seven years from the date of its submission.

AMENDMENT XXI

Passed by Congress February 20, 1933. Ratified December 5, 1933.

Section 1.

The eighteenth article of amendment to the Constitution of the United States is hereby repealed.

Section 2.

The transportation or importation into any State, Territory, or Possession of the United States for delivery or use therein of intoxicating liquors, in violation of the laws thereof, is hereby prohibited.

Section 3.

This article shall be inoperative unless it shall have been ratified as an amendment to the Constitution by conventions in the several States, as provided in the Constitution, within seven years from the date of the submission hereof to the States by the Congress.

Amendment XXII

Passed by Congress March 21, 1947. Ratified February 27, 1951.

Section 1.

No person shall be elected to the office of the President more than twice, and no person who has held the office of President, or acted as President, for more than two years of a term to which some other person was elected President shall be elected to the office of President more than once. But this Article shall not apply to any person holding the office of President when this Article was proposed by Congress, and shall not prevent any person who may be holding the office of President, or acting as President, during the term within which this Article becomes operative from holding the office of President or acting as President during the remainder of such term.

Section 2.

This article shall be inoperative unless it shall have been ratified as an amendment to the Constitution by the legislatures of three-fourths of the several States within seven years from the date of its submission to the States by the Congress.

Amendment XXIII

Passed by Congress June 16, 1960. Ratified March 29, 1961.

Section 1.

The District constituting the seat of Government of the United States shall appoint in such manner as Congress may direct:

A number of electors of President and Vice President equal to the whole number of Senators and Representatives in Congress to which the District would be entitled if it were a State, but in no event more than the least populous State; they shall be in addition to those appointed by the States, but they shall be considered, for the purposes of the election of President and Vice President, to be electors appointed by a State; and they shall meet in the District and perform such duties as provided by the twelfth article of amendment.

Section 2.

The Congress shall have power to enforce this article by appropriate legislation.

Amendment XXIV

Passed by Congress August 27, 1962. Ratified January 23, 1964.

Section 1.

The right of citizens of the United States to vote in any primary or other election for President or Vice President, for electors for President or Vice President, or for Senator or Representative in Congress, shall not be denied or abridged by the United States or any State by reason of failure to pay poll tax or other tax.

Section 2.

The Congress shall have power to enforce this article by appropriate legislation.

Amendment XXV

Passed by Congress July 6, 1965. Ratified February 10, 1967.

Note: Article II, section 1, of the Constitution was affected by the Twenty-fifth Amendment.

Section 1.

In case of the removal of the President from office or of his death or resignation, the Vice President shall become President.

Section 2.

Whenever there is a vacancy in the office of the Vice President, the President shall nominate a Vice President who shall take office upon confirmation by a majority vote of both Houses of Congress.

Section 3.

Whenever the President transmits to the President pro tempore of the Senate and the Speaker of the House of Representatives his written declaration that he is unable to discharge the powers and duties of his office, and until he transmits to them a written declaration to the contrary, such powers and duties shall be discharged by the Vice President as Acting President.

Section 4.

Whenever the Vice President and a majority of either the principal officers of the executive departments or of such other body as Congress may by law provide, transmit to the President pro tempore of the Senate and the Speaker of the House of Representatives their written declaration that the President is unable to discharge the powers and duties of his office, the Vice President shall immediately assume the powers and duties of the office as Acting President.

Thereafter, when the President transmits to the President pro tempore of the Senate and the Speaker of the House of Representatives his written declaration that no inability exists, he shall resume the powers and duties of his office unless the Vice President and a majority of either the principal officers of the executive department or of such other body as Congress may by law provide, transmit within four days to the President pro tempore of the Senate and the Speaker of the House of Representatives their written declaration that the President is unable to discharge the powers and duties of his office. Thereupon Congress shall decide the issue, assembling within forty-eight hours for that purpose if not in session. If the Congress, within twenty-one days after receipt of the latter written declaration, or, if Congress is not in session, within twenty-one days after Congress is required to assemble, determines by two-thirds vote of both Houses that the President is unable to discharge the powers and duties of his office, the Vice President shall continue to discharge the same as Acting President; otherwise, the President shall resume the powers and duties of his office.

Amendment XXVI

Passed by Congress March 23, 1971. Ratified July 1, 1971.

Note: Amendment 14, section 2, of the Constitution was modified by section 1 of the Twenty-sixth Amendment.

Section 1.

The right of citizens of the United States, who are eighteen years of age or older, to vote shall not be denied or abridged by the United States or by any State on account of age.

Section 2.

The Congress shall have power to enforce this article by appropriate legislation.

Amendment XXVII

Originally proposed Sept. 25, 1789. Ratified May 7, 1992.

No law, varying the compensation for the services of the Senators and Representatives, shall take effect, until an election of representatives shall have intervened.

AUGUST

THE CONSTITUTION requires that the government conduct a census once every ten years. The results are used to allocate Congressional seats, electoral votes, and government funding. The first U.S. census reported that as of August 1, 1790, the country contained nearly 4 million people. According to Census Bureau estimates, by 2008 the population had surpassed 300 million.

Year	Population	Land Area, sq. mi.	People per sq. mi.
1790	3,929,214	864,746	4.5
1800	5,308,483	864,746	6.1
1810	7,239,881	1,681,828	4.3
1820	9,638,453	1,749,462	5.5
1830	12,866,020	1,749,462	7.4
1840	17,069,453	1,749,462	9.8
1850	23,191,876	2,940,042	7.9
1860	31,443,321	2,969,640	10.6
1870	38,558,371	3,540,705	10.9
1880	50,189,209	3,540,705	14.2
1890	62,979,766	3,540,705	17.8
1900	76,212,168	3,547,314	21.5
1910	92,228,496	3,547,045	26.0
1920	106,021,537	3,546,931	29.9
1930	123,202,624	3,551,608	34.7
1940	132,164,569	3,551,608	37.2
1950	151,325,798	3,552,206	42.6
1960	179,323,175	3,540,911	50.6
1970	203,302,031	3,536,855	57.5
1980	226,542,199	3,539,289	64.0
1990	248,709,873	3,536,278	70.3
2000	281,424,603	3,537,438	79.6

AMERICAN HISTORY PARADE

1790 The first U.S. census shows a population of 3,929,214.

1873 San Francisco's first cable car begins operation on Clay Street Hill.

1876 Colorado becomes the thirty-eighth state.

1907 The Army establishes an aeronautical division that eventually becomes the U.S. Air Force.

1941 During World War II, the first Jeep rolls off an assembly line in Toledo, Ohio.

IN THE EARLY MORNING HOURS of August 2, 1943, torpedo boat PT-109 was patrolling the Blackett Strait in the Solomon Islands when suddenly a black shape loomed in the darkness off the starboard bow. A crewman yelled, "Ship at two o'clock!" but it was too late. The Japanese destroyer *Amagiri* plowed into the little boat, slicing it in half. The collision threw the PT's commander, Lt. John F. Kennedy Jr., hard against the side of the cockpit, and as gasoline ignited on the water around him, he thought, *So this is how it feels to die.*

Two crew members were killed in the crash. The eleven who survived, including Kennedy, clung to wreckage. When the remains of the hull began to sink, they made a four-hour swim to a tiny deserted island three miles away. Most of the crew clung to a large piece of timber as they swam, but one man was badly burned, so Kennedy clenched the straps of the man's life jacket in his teeth and towed him, swimming the breaststroke.

Leaving his crew on the island, Kennedy swam out again, hoping to flag down another PT boat, but none appeared. Exhausted, he barely made it back to the island. The next day he led his men to another islet. Several times he ventured out into the shark-infested waters, looking for help but found none.

On August 6, two Solomon Islanders in a dugout canoe found the stranded sailors. Kennedy carved a message onto a coconut, which they took to Allied troops: NAURO ISL NATIVE KNOWS POSIT HE CAN PILOT 11 ALIVE NEED SMALL BOAT KENNEDY. Within two more days, the PT crew had been rescued. When he became president of the United States, Kennedy kept the coconut with its scratched message on his desk in the Oval Office to remind himself of the awful ordeal and his two lost comrades.

AMERICAN HISTORY PARADE

1776   Members of the Continental Congress begin signing an engrossed copy of the Declaration of Independence.

1876   Western frontiersman Wild Bill Hickok is shot dead while playing poker in a Deadwood, South Dakota, saloon.

1923   Warren G. Harding, the twenty-ninth U.S. president, dies in office while in San Francisco.

1939   Albert Einstein signs a letter to President Roosevelt, urging him to develop an atomic bomb before the Nazis do.

1943   John F. Kennedy's PT-109 is ripped in two by a Japanese destroyer off the Solomon Islands.

AUGUST 3 • "IF THERE IS NO STRUGGLE, THERE IS NO PROGRESS."

ON AUGUST 3, 1857, in a speech at Canandaigua, New York, abolitionist Frederick Douglass reminded his fellow Americans of the costs of freedom. His words, which foreshadowed the coming Civil War, are among the most famous of his many orations:

> The general sentiment of mankind is that a man who will not fight for himself, when he has the means of doing so, is not worth being fought for by others, and this sentiment is just. For a man who does not value freedom for himself will never value it for others, or put himself to any inconvenience to gain it for others. . . .
>
> The whole history of the progress of human liberty shows that all concessions yet made to her august claims have been born of earnest struggle. The conflict has been exciting, agitating, all-absorbing, and for the time being, putting all other tumults to silence. It must do this or it does nothing. If there is no struggle there is no progress. Those who profess to favor freedom and yet deprecate agitation are men who want crops without plowing up the ground; they want rain without thunder and lightning. They want the ocean without the awful roar of its many waters.
>
> This struggle may be a moral one, or it may be a physical one, and it may be both moral and physical, but it must be a struggle. Power concedes nothing without a demand. It never did and it never will. Find out just what any people will quietly submit to and you have found out the exact measure of injustice and wrong which will be imposed upon them, and these will continue till they are resisted with either words or blows, or with both. The limits of tyrants are prescribed by the endurance of those whom they oppress.

AMERICAN HISTORY PARADE

1492   Christopher Columbus sails from Palos, Spain, with the *Nina*, *Pinta*, and *Santa Maria* on his famous journey to find a western route to the Indies.

1846   Abraham Lincoln is elected to the U.S. House.

1852   In America's first intercollegiate athletic event, crews from Yale and Harvard race on Lake Winnipesaukee in Center Harbor, New Hampshire.

1923   Calvin Coolidge is sworn in as the thirtieth U.S. president, following the death of Warren G. Harding.

1958   The submarine *Nautilus* becomes the first vessel to reach the North Pole.

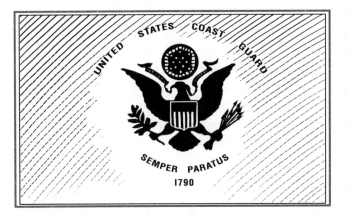

THE COAST GUARD FLAG is a white flag bearing the national coat of arms, which also appears on the Great Seal of the United States. Above the arms are the words "United States Coast Guard," and below is the Coast Guard's motto, *Semper Paratus*, which means "always prepared."

The flag carries the date 1790 because on August 4 of that year, Congress established the Revenue Cutter Service with a fleet of ten cutters to enforce tariff laws. From 1790 to 1798, the Revenue Cutter Service was the nation's only armed force on the sea. In the early days of the republic, its cutters chased smugglers, battled pirates, captured slave ships, and fought in the War of 1812.

In 1915 the Revenue Cutter Service merged with the U.S. Life-Saving Service to form the U.S. Coast Guard, whose mission included the duty for which the Coast Guard is now renowned: coming to the aid of stricken ships. Over the following decades, Coast Guard cutter activities ranged from rescuing hurricane victims to chasing rumrunners during Prohibition and patrolling for enemy subs during World War II.

The Coast Guard is part of the Department of Homeland Security during peacetime. In times of war, it becomes part of the Navy. Its many missions include search and rescue operations, enforcing maritime laws, keeping ports secure, intercepting illegal immigrants, catching drug smugglers, and defending the nation from terrorism.

AMERICAN HISTORY PARADE

1735   In an important case for freedom of the press, John Peter Zenger, publisher of the *New York Weekly Journal*, is acquitted of charges of libel against Gov. William Cosby.

1790   Congress establishes the Revenue Cutter Service, later to become the U.S. Coast Guard.

1914   Hoping to avoid conflict, President Woodrow Wilson declares U.S. neutrality as World War I begins.

1916   The U.S. purchases the Danish West Indies (now U.S. Virgin Islands) for $25 million.

AUGUST 5, 1864, saw the last major naval battle of the Civil War when Admiral David Glasgow Farragut led a fleet of Union ships against Mobile Bay, Alabama, one of the most heavily defended ports in the South. The entrance to the bay was protected by Fort Morgan and Fort Gaines, four Confederate ships, including the giant ironclad *Tennessee*, and dozens of mines, which in those days were called "torpedoes." The Confederates had arranged the mines, which lurked just beneath the water's surface, to create a narrow channel running into the bay.

As the attack began, Farragut climbed into the rigging of his flagship, the *Hartford*, to get a good view. There he watched in dismay as one of his ships, the ironclad *Tecumseh*, steered into the minefield and hit a torpedo. An explosion erupted beneath its waterline. The *Tecumseh* lurched to one side, stopped dead in the water, and a few minutes later went straight to the bottom, taking more than 90 men to their deaths.

At once the rest of the fleet faltered and began to drift toward Fort Morgan. The Confederate gunners raked the Union vessels with deadly fire. Farragut knew that to hesitate would mean disaster, and he shouted his famous order: "Damn the torpedoes! Full speed ahead!"

Farragut's ship steamed forward, straight through the minefield. The horrified sailors heard the mine cases thudding against the hull, but none exploded. The other ships followed, and soon Mobile Bay was in Union hands. Farragut's exclamation has become a rallying cry for Americans in times that call for meeting danger head-on.

AMERICAN HISTORY PARADE

1774   George Washington is elected a delegate to the Continental Congress.

1861   The federal government levies its first income tax to help pay for the Civil War.

1864   Admiral David G. Farragut leads a Union fleet against Mobile Bay, Alabama.

1884   The cornerstone for the Statue of Liberty is laid.

1914   The first electric traffic lights are installed in Cleveland, Ohio.

1957   *American Bandstand*, hosted by Dick Clark, debuts on national TV.

BY THE SUMMER OF 1945, it was becoming clear that the Allies would win World War II in the Pacific. But it was also clear that Japan intended to make it a long, ghastly fight.

Some U.S. war planners feared that as many as 300,000 Americans could die in an invasion of the Japanese home islands, where Japan had some 2.5 million regular troops. Japanese civilians, ready to fight with everything from bamboo spears to suicide bombs, prepared themselves with the slogan "A hundred million will die together for the emperor and the nation!" Thousands of planes stood ready for kamikaze missions. Japanese ground troops had already begun mass suicide attacks. Devastating American losses at Iwo Jima and Okinawa, the continuing unwillingness of the Japanese military to consider surrender, and the death each month of thousands of Allied prisoners held by Japan convinced President Harry Truman of the need to use the newly developed atomic bomb to end the war quickly.

On August 6, 1945, a B-29 named the *Enola Gay* dropped a single atomic bomb on the city of Hiroshima. An intense flash gave way to a huge mushroom cloud that rose over the city, followed by a fireball that destroyed five square miles and resulted in 140,000 deaths. When the Japanese did not surrender, the U.S. dropped a second bomb on Nagasaki on August 9. More than 70,000 people were killed instantly. An additional 75,000 were horribly injured, alerting the world to the nightmare of radiation poisoning.

On August 15, Emperor Hirohito called upon his people to "endure the unendurable" and surrender. In all the Allied countries, people burst forth in an outpouring of unrestrained joy. But with the celebrations came the sobering realization that the world would never be the same again.

AMERICAN HISTORY PARADE

1787   The Constitutional Convention in Philadelphia begins to debate a draft of the proposed U.S. Constitution.

1945   The United States drops an atomic bomb on Hiroshima, Japan.

1965   President Lyndon B. Johnson signs the Voting Rights Act, which outlaws literacy tests for would-be voters.

1996   NASA announces that American scientists have found possible evidence of a "primitive form of microscopic life" on Mars; the evidence came from fossils on a meteorite believed to have originated on Mars.

ON AUGUST 7, 1782, George Washington created the Purple Heart, America's oldest military decoration. Washington called the award the Badge of Military Merit. His order of that day read in part:

> The General, ever desirous to cherish virtuous ambition in his soldiers as well as foster and encourage every species of military merit, directs that whenever any singularly meritorious action is performed, the author of it shall be permitted to wear on his facings, over his left breast, the figure of a heart in purple cloth or silk edged with narrow lace or binding. Not only instances of unusual gallantry but also of extraordinary fidelity and essential service in any way shall meet with due reward.

The badge permitted the wearer to pass sentinels without challenge. Only three soldiers—Elijah Churchill, William Brown, and Daniel Bissell Jr.—are known to have received the award during the Revolutionary War.

After the Revolution the badge fell out of use. In 1932 the military revived the decoration to help celebrate the two hundredth anniversary of George Washington's birth. The Order of the Purple Heart is now awarded to members of the armed services who have been wounded or killed in action. The modern medal has a bronze heart bearing Washington's silhouette in its purple center and the Washington coat-of-arms at the top.

Why did George Washington choose purple? No one is sure, but for ages purple had been the color of royalty. In Washington's eyes the common soldier who sacrificed for his country deserved as much respect as a king. As he wrote in his order creating the decoration, "The road to glory in a patriot army and a free country is thus open to all."

AMERICAN HISTORY PARADE

1782   George Washington creates the Purple Heart.

1789   Congress establishes the War Department (now the Department of Defense).

1942   U.S. troops land at Guadalcanal, marking a shift by Allied forces from defensive operations to an offensive campaign in the Pacific in World War II.

1959   The United States launches *Explorer 6*, the first satellite to photograph Earth from orbit.

1998   Al-Qaeda explodes bombs at U.S. embassies in Nairobi, Kenya, and Dar es Salaam, Tanzania, killing 224 people, including 12 Americans.

ON THIS DAY IN 1787, delegates to the Constitutional Convention in Philadelphia were in the midst of the eleventh week of a long, hot summer spent hammering out a new government for the United States. One young delegate from Virginia never missed a session. He sat up front so he could hear every word and take notes on every speech. At the end of each day, he went back to his boardinghouse to read over what had been said and write out new arguments.

The young Virginian was James Madison. A graduate of the College of New Jersey (now Princeton University), he was a short, slight man with a soft voice. Someone once observed that he seemed "no bigger than half a piece of soap." But his influence on this country was profound.

Madison had come to Philadelphia with a plan for a central government with three branches. He envisioned a nation where citizens would vote for their representatives. He had spent months studying ancient democracies and republics, and he knew that the strength of the government must come not from harsh laws or armies, but from the people.

That summer, Madison made more than 150 speeches in his soft voice. His fellow delegates sometimes had to shout "Louder!" but when he spoke, they knew he would bring sound reason to the debate. Madison answered questions and proposed solutions. He worked on every detail. At the end of the convention, the new Constitution that the delegates signed largely followed his plan.

Madison spent the rest of his life making sure the Constitution worked. His labors included cowriting *the Federalist Papers*, authoring the Bill of Rights, and serving as congressman, secretary of state, and the fourth U.S. president. For his ideas and hard work, history remembers him as the Father of the Constitution.

AMERICAN HISTORY PARADE

1866   Queen Emma of the Sandwich Islands (Hawaii) becomes the first queen to visit the U.S.

1876   Thomas Edison receives a patent for the mimeograph, used for a century to make multiple paper copies until the electronic copier took its place.

1974   President Nixon announces he will resign the next day due to the Watergate scandal.

2007   Barbara Morgan becomes the first teacher to safely reach space, aboard the shuttle *Endeavor* (Christa McAuliffe had died in the 1986 *Challenger* explosion).

JESSE OWENS came from humble beginnings—he was the son of a sharecropper and grandson of a slave. When he was a boy in Cleveland, a coach saw him running in gym class and invited him to join the track team. Jesse couldn't go to the team's after-school practices because he had a job to help support his family, so the coach trained him in the mornings. By the time he was in college, Owens was a star. At one track meet, in a span of forty-five minutes, he broke three world records and tied a fourth.

In 1936 he traveled to Berlin to compete in the Summer Olympics, in which Adolf Hitler planned to show the world the "Aryan superiority" of German youth.

In three days Owens won three gold medals in the 100-meter dash, 200-meter dash, and long jump. A few days later, American athletes Marty Glickman and Sam Stroller—both Jewish—were yanked from the 400-meter relay team to appease Hitler. The American coach told Owens that he and Frank Metcalfe would run in their place. "I've won the races I set out to win," Owens protested. "Let Marty and Sam run." The coach insisted, and on August 9, 1936, Owens won his fourth gold medal.

Hitler, who had stopped shaking each winner's hand, was asked if he wanted to make an exception for Jesse. The Führer shouted: "Do you really think I would allow myself to be photographed shaking hands with a Negro?" But German crowds cheered the American champion with the cry of "*Oh-vens! Oh-vens!*" African American athletes won almost one-quarter of all U.S. medals in the 1936 Olympics, a firm rebuke of Hitler's venomous theories about the so-called superiority of the Aryan race.

AMERICAN HISTORY PARADE

1854   Henry David Thoreau publishes his classic, *Walden.*

1936   Jesse Owens wins his fourth gold medal at the Berlin Olympics.

1945   The United States drops an atomic bomb on Nagasaki, prompting Japan to surrender in World War II.

1974   Gerald Ford is sworn in as the thirty-eighth U.S. president, following Richard Nixon's resignation.

1988   President Reagan nominates Lauro Cavazos to be secretary of education and the first Hispanic to serve in a president's Cabinet.

THE SMITHSONIAN INSTITUTION, headquartered in Washington, D.C., is the world's largest museum complex and research organization. Composed of 19 museums and 9 research centers, its collection encompasses more than 136 million items.

A somewhat obscure British scientist by the name of James Smithson planted the seed for the institution when he died in 1829 and left behind a will containing a curious provision. It stipulated that if Smithson's nephew were to die without heirs, the estate would go "to the United States of America, to found at Washington, under the name of the Smithsonian Institution, an establishment for the increase and diffusion of knowledge among men." American officials were surprised by the provision since Smithson had never set foot in the United States, and apparently he had never corresponded with anyone here. Nevertheless, after the nephew died without heirs in 1835, the bequest fell into Congress's lap. Then came several years of heated debate over exactly what to do with the legacy, which amounted to more than $500,000. On August 10, 1846, President James Polk signed into law an act creating the Smithsonian Institution.

The institution's mission is exactly what James Smithson specified: "the increase and diffusion of knowledge." That largely means connecting Americans to their history and heritage. The Smithsonian's holdings range from the original Star-Spangled Banner to the ruby slippers worn by Dorothy in *The Wizard of Oz* to the space capsule that carried the *Apollo* 11 astronauts to the moon and back. The astounding assortment has earned the Smithsonian the nickname "the nation's attic." Since most Smithsonian museums charge no entrance fee, one of the world's greatest collections of artwork, artifacts, and scientific specimens is free for all to see.

AMERICAN HISTORY PARADE

1821   Missouri becomes the twenty-fourth state and the first state west of the Mississippi.

1846   President Polk signs legislation establishing the Smithsonian Institution.

1869   O. B. Brown of Malden, Massachusetts, receives the first patent for a movie projector.

1874   Herbert Clark Hoover, the thirty-first U.S. president, is born in West Branch, Iowa.

1990   The spacecraft *Magellan* lands on Venus on the anniversary of the day that Ferdinand Magellan's ships set sail in 1519 on the first circumnavigation of the globe.

IN AUGUST 1909, Americans went wild for the brand-new Lincoln penny, the first U.S. coin to bear the likeness of a president. Teddy Roosevelt was behind the change from the old "Indian Head" penny to the Lincoln cent. Roosevelt, a great admirer of Lincoln, wanted to honor the sixteenth president to commemorate the centennial of his birth. Since that time, the U.S. Mint has placed images of presidents and other famous Americans on coins and bills.

Currency	Obverse	Reverse
Penny	Abraham Lincoln	Lincoln Memorial; Lincoln's Life designs
Nickel	Thomas Jefferson	Monticello; Westward Journey designs
Dime	Franklin D. Roosevelt	Torch, Olive & Oak Branches
Quarter	George Washington	Bald Eagle; Fifty States designs
Half-dollar	John F. Kennedy	Presidential Coat of Arms
$1 Coin	Sacagawea	Bald Eagle; Native American commemorations
$1 Bill	George Washington	Great Seal of the U.S.
$2 Bill	Thomas Jefferson	Signing of the Declaration
$5 Bill	Abraham Lincoln	Lincoln Memorial
$10 Bill	Alexander Hamilton	U.S. Treasury Building
$20 Bill	Andrew Jackson	White House
$50 Bill	Ulysses S. Grant	U.S. Capitol
$100 Bill	Benjamin Franklin	Independence Hall

AMERICAN HISTORY PARADE

1860   The first successful American silver mill begins operations near Virginia City, Nevada.

1877   Astronomer Asaph Hall discovers the two moons of Mars.

1924   The first newsreel of U.S. presidential candidates, showing Calvin Coolidge and Robert M. La Follette, is filmed in Washington, D.C.

1965   Racial tensions trigger several days of rioting in the Watts neighborhood of Los Angeles.

1992   The Mall of America, the largest shopping mall in the United States, opens in Bloomington, Minnesota.

ON AUGUST 12, 1805, Captain Meriwether Lewis of the famed Lewis and Clark expedition climbed a ridge near the Continental Divide and "the most distant fountain of the waters of the Mighty Missouri, in search of which we have spent so many toilsome days and restless nights." The expedition had spent weeks trekking to the headwaters of the Missouri, one of the world's great rivers.

The United States is blessed with more than 250,000 rivers and streams—3.5 million miles of rivers in all—including a dozen exceeding 1,000 miles in length.

	Length	Origin	Mouth
Missouri River	2,540 miles	**Montana**	**Mississippi River (near St. Louis)**
Mississippi River	2,340 miles	**Minnesota**	**Gulf of Mexico**
Yukon River	1,980 miles	**British Columbia**	**Bering Sea**
Rio Grande	1,900 miles	**Colorado**	**Gulf of Mexico**
St. Lawrence River	1,900 miles	**Lake Ontario**	**Gulf of St. Lawrence**
Arkansas River	1,460 miles	**Colorado**	**Mississippi River (in Arkansas)**
Colorado River	1,450 miles	**Colorado**	**Gulf of California**
Ohio River	1,310 miles	**Pennsylvania**	**Mississippi River (at Cairo, Illinois)**
Red River	1,290 miles	**Texas**	**Atchafalaya River (in Louisiana)**
Brazos River	1,280 miles	**Texas**	**Gulf of Mexico**
Columbia River	1,240 miles	**British Columbia**	**Pacific Ocean (at Astoria, Oregon)**
Snake River	1,040 miles	**Yellowstone Nat. Park**	**Columbia River (in Washington)**

AMERICAN HISTORY PARADE

1658   The first police force in the United States is established in New Amsterdam (now New York).

1833   Chicago is incorporated with a population of 350.

1877   Thomas Edison invents the phonograph (he patents it six months later).

1898   The peace protocol ending the Spanish-American War is signed.

1918   The post office establishes the first U.S. regular airmail service, between New York City and Washington, D.C.

1960   The first experimental communications satellite, *Echo 1*, is launched from Cape Canaveral, Florida.

TODAY IS THE BIRTHDAY of sharpshooter Annie Oakley, born Phoebe Ann Moses in 1860 in a cabin in Darke County, Ohio. She took her first shot at age eight ("one of the best shots I ever made," she later said) and soon began shooting rabbits to help feed her destitute family. Around age fifteen she started shooting game for a nearby grocer, who sold it to hotels. She earned enough to pay off the mortgage on her widowed mother's house.

When expert marksman Frank Butler passed through the area, Annie entered a shooting match against him. "I almost dropped dead when a little slim girl in short dresses stepped out to the mark with me," Butler recalled. They each shot at 25 pigeons. Butler hit 24; Annie hit all 25. "Right then and there I decided if I could get that girl I would do it," Butler said. They courted and married. She adopted the stage name Annie Oakley, and they performed together in shooting exhibitions.

Buffalo Bill hired them for his Wild West show. Crowds lined up to see her shoot the flame off a distant candle, or the heart in the ace of hearts. She shot apples from her husband's head and the ashes off cigarettes in his mouth. Sometimes she shot backward looking into a mirror.

The Sioux chief Sitting Bull called her "Little Sure Shot" and admired her so much that he adopted her. When touring in Europe, Germany's crown prince (the future Kaiser Wilhelm) invited her to shoot a cigarette out of his mouth. She demurred but did shoot a cigarette out of his hand.

The Broadway musical *Annie Get Your Gun*, with songs by Irving Berlin, is based on Annie Oakley's life. Will Rogers called her the "greatest rifle shot the world has ever produced. Nobody took her place. There was only one."

AMERICAN HISTORY PARADE

1784   The U.S. Congress meets for the final time in Annapolis, Maryland, temporary capital after the Revolutionary War.

1860   Annie Oakley is born in Darke County, Ohio.

1918   Opha Mae Johnson becomes the first woman to enlist in the Marine Corps Reserve.

1960   The first two-way telephone conversation by satellite takes place, via the balloon satellite *Echo I*.

1981   President Reagan signs a package of tax and budget reductions that mark a historic change in direction for the federal government.

ON AUGUST 14, 1765, a group of Bostonians calling themselves the Sons of Liberty gathered under a large elm tree to protest the Stamp Act imposed by England. From a branch they hung an effigy of the Boston official in charge of administering the hated Stamp Act tax. The elm became known as the Liberty Tree.

By the time of the Revolution, just about every American town had its own Liberty Tree, a living symbol of freedom and resistance to tyranny. Patriots met under the trees to swap information and plot rebellion. In some towns, folks erected a tall Liberty Pole to symbolize a tree.

Thomas Paine wrote a popular song called "The Liberty Tree" to rouse Patriots' spirits. "From the east to the west, blow the trumpet to arms; through the land let the sound of it flee," the song ran. "Let the far and the near, all unite with a cheer, in defense of our Liberty Tree."

During the Revolutionary War, Patriot soldiers sometimes carried into battle flags emblazoned with a Liberty Tree. Some banners carried the words "An Appeal to Heaven" to show that the colonists sought guidance from God for their cause.

A 1999 hurricane dealt a deathblow to the last of the Revolutionary War–era Liberty Trees, a 400-year-old giant tulip poplar in Annapolis, Maryland. The conservation group American Forests grew fourteen seedlings from the tree's seeds to plant in Washington, D.C., and the thirteen original states.

AMERICAN HISTORY PARADE

1755　During the French and Indian War, George Washington is appointed commander in chief of Virginia forces protecting the frontier.

1765　In Boston the Sons of Liberty protest the Stamp Act under the Liberty Tree.

1784　On Kodiak Island, Russian fur traders found the first permanent Russian settlement in Alaska.

1848　Congress creates the Oregon Territory, an area encompassing today's Oregon, Idaho, Washington, and western Montana.

1945　Japan surrenders unconditionally, ending World War II.

FROM THE DAY THE U.S. STARTED DIGGING the Panama Canal in 1904, doubters scoffed. To link the Atlantic and Pacific would mean digging across 50 miles of rugged hills and hot, suffocating jungle. In the late nineteenth century, the French had tried and failed. Teddy Roosevelt didn't care. He sent engineers to the isthmus with instructions to "make dirt fly."

Thousands of men went to work digging, blasting, and dredging. They fought floods, mudslides, and yellow fever. Red tape and logistical problems threatened to stymie the project. Then the chief engineer quit, probably out of sheer exhaustion, and Roosevelt had to find someone else to see the canal through. He resolved to get "men who will stay on the job until I get tired of having them there, or till I say they may abandon it. I shall turn it over to the Army."

In 1907 he appointed Col. George Washington Goethals as the canal's new chief engineer. A master at organizing, Goethals set to work an army of civilians and soldiers numbering as many as 57,000 men. They dug out more than 200 million cubic yards of earth, constructed a dam to create a lake, and designed huge locks operated by giant electric motors (manufactured by a new company called General Electric).

Every week, it seemed, brought a setback. One explosion killed 23 men. One mudslide lasted 10 days. With every adversity, the naysayers predicted failure. Goethals said nothing in return. He kept working, year after year.

"Aren't you going to answer your critics?" one staff member asked. "In time," said the chief engineer. "How?" the man asked. "With the canal," Goethals answered.

The Panama Canal, one of history's great engineering triumphs, opened to traffic on August 15, 1914.

AMERICAN HISTORY PARADE

1814   Andrew Jackson assumes command of American troops at New Orleans during the War of 1812.

1846   The first newspaper in California, the *Californian*, is launched in Monterey.

1914   The Panama Canal officially opens to traffic.

1939   MGM's *The Wizard of Oz* premieres at Grauman's Chinese Theater in Hollywood.

1945   The Allies proclaim the day after Japan agrees to unconditional surrender in World War II as V-J Day (Victory over Japan Day).

1969   The Woodstock Music and Art Fair opens in upstate New York.

ON THIS DAY IN 1790, President George Washington was beginning a goodwill tour of New England. His first stop would be Newport, Rhode Island, where citizens met him with booming cannons and a public dinner where dignitaries gave "thirteen toasts abounding with patriotic sentiment." Moses Seixas, warden of the Hebrew Congregation of Newport, penned a letter welcoming the president to the city. Washington's response, written the next day, has become a famous pronouncement on religious freedom:

> The citizens of the United States of America have a right to applaud themselves for having given to mankind examples of an enlarged and liberal policy, a policy worthy of imitation. All possess alike liberty of conscience and immunities of citizenship. It is now no more that toleration is spoken of as if it was by the indulgence of one class of people that another enjoyed the exercise of their inherent natural rights. For, happily, the government of the United States, which gives to bigotry no sanction, to persecution no assistance, requires only that they who live under its protection should demean themselves as good citizens in giving it on all occasions their effectual support.

As Claremont professor Harry Jaffa has pointed out, this was the first time in history that any ruler addressed the Jews as *equals*. President Washington closed his letter with these gentle words, taken from Scripture: "May the Children of the Stock of Abraham, who dwell in this land, continue to merit and enjoy the good will of the other inhabitants; while every one shall sit in safety under his own vine and fig tree, and there shall be none to make him afraid. May the father of all mercies scatter light and not darkness in our paths, and make us all in our several vocations useful here, and in his own due time and way everlastingly happy."

AMERICAN HISTORY PARADE

1777   A Patriot force routs British troops near Bennington, Vermont.

1780   British troops inflict heavy losses on a Patriot army at Camden, South Carolina.

1790   George Washington sails to New England on a goodwill tour.

1812   An American force surrenders Fort Detroit to a British and Indian force during the War of 1812.

1898   Edwin Prescott patents a roller coaster with a loop-the-loop, which he installs in 1900 at Coney Island, New York.

1977   Elvis Presley, age forty-two, dies at Graceland in Memphis, Tennessee.

IN 1787 young Robert Fulton of Pennsylvania traveled to London to study painting. The Industrial Revolution was beginning in Britain, as well as a revolution in transportation, so the American heard much excited talk of steam engines and canals. Fulton had an inventive mind—as a boy, he had made skyrockets and designed a hand-turned paddle wheel for a rowboat. In England he decided to put aside painting and try his hand at scientific pursuits.

He invented a machine for making rope, and another for dredging canal channels. Then he built a submarine called the *Nautilus*, which could dive 25 feet underwater, and tried to sell it to Napoleon. The conqueror said no, but Fulton met Robert Livingston, the American ambassador to France, and the two men built a steamboat that chugged up and down the Seine River in Paris.

Returning to the United States, Fulton determined to build a 130-foot steam-powered paddleboat on the Hudson River. On August 17, 1807, a crowd gathered on the riverbank to watch him launch the "boat driven by a tea kettle" on its maiden voyage from New York City to Albany. Most called it "Fulton's folly" and predicted it would explode. "There were not, perhaps, thirty persons in the city who believed that the boat would ever move one mile per hour," Fulton wrote.

He lit the boiler, and the vessel went puffing up the river at the astounding speed of four miles per hour while people lined the banks to cheer. The famous boat came to be known as the *Clermont* after the Hudson River estate of Fulton's partner, Robert Livingston.

Robert Fulton did not invent the steamboat. But his *Clermont*, the first commercially successful paddle steamer, ushered in a new age in transportation. Soon steamers were carrying passengers and freight on rivers throughout the growing country.

AMERICAN HISTORY PARADE

1943   In World War II, U.S. and British troops complete the Allied conquest of Sicily.

1969   Hurricane Camille slams the Gulf Coast, killing approximately 250 people.

1978   Ben Abruzzo, Maxie Anderson, and Larry Newman of Albuquerque, New Mexico, become the first to successfully cross the Atlantic in a balloon when they land the *Double Eagle II* near Paris, 137 hours after leaving Maine.

THE FATE OF THE LOST COLONY of Roanoke remains one of the great unsolved mysteries of American history. There were actually two attempts to establish a settlement at Roanoke Island just off the North Carolina mainland, both organized by Sir Walter Raleigh. The first, in 1585, was England's earliest attempt to colonize America. It lasted a year before the weary, half-starved settlers returned home.

In 1587 Raleigh sent a second expedition, 117 men, women, and children under the leadership of John White. On August 18, 1587, shortly after they reached Roanoke, Governor White's daughter, Eleanor White Dare, gave birth to the first child of English parents born in America. The baby girl was christened Virginia Dare.

A few days later, John White departed for England to procure much-needed provisions. He arrived home at a bad time. Britain and Spain were at war, and no ships or supplies could be spared for the tiny colony. Three years passed before the anxious governor could return to Roanoke.

He arrived on his granddaughter's third birthday. But the colonists were gone. Carved on a post, White found the word CROATOAN. Reasoning that the colonists had moved to the nearby island of the friendly Croatoan Indians, White sailed in that direction, but a storm arose, damaging his ships and forcing him back to England. He was never able to return to the New World.

What happened to little Virginia Dare and her companions? Some believe that hostile Indians or Spaniards destroyed the colony. Others suggest that, giving up hope of relief, they sailed for England in boats White had left them, but were lost at sea. Still others believe that the Lost Colonists of Roanoke made their way inland, where they lived with the Indians, and that their blood still runs in twenty-first-century Carolinian veins.

AMERICAN HISTORY PARADE

1587   Virginia Dare becomes the first child of English parents to be born on American soil, on Roanoke Island, North Carolina.

1590   John White, governor of the Roanoke colony, returns from England to find the settlement deserted.

1872   Aaron Montgomery Ward of Chicago issues the first mail-order catalog, a single-sheet price list.

1913   The Veterans of Foreign Wars organizes in Denver.

1920   The Nineteenth Amendment, guaranteeing women suffrage, is ratified.

THE WORLD'S OLDEST COMMISSIONED WARSHIP AFLOAT is the USS *Constitution*, a sailing frigate launched in Boston in **1797**. She was built from **2,000** trees with sturdy oak planks that measured up to seven inches thick. Paul Revere forged the copper bolts that held the timbers in place and the copper sheathing that helped protect the hull.

The *Constitution* first put to sea in July **1798** to cruise the West Indies, protecting U.S. merchant ships from French privateers. In **1803** President Jefferson sent her to the Mediterranean to fight the Barbary pirates. The *Constitution* led an American squadron that chased the pirates and bombarded fortifications until the Barbary States agreed to stop preying on American merchant vessels.

On August 19, **1812**, during the War of 1812, the *Constitution* met the British frigate *Guerriere* and within twenty minutes had turned it into a dismasted hulk. The British seamen watched in amazement as their cannonballs seemed to bounce harmlessly off the *Constitution*'s tough hull. "Her sides are made of iron!" one sailor cried—and the nickname "Old Ironsides" was born. With every battle won, the ship's reputation spread.

In **1830** a Boston newspaper reported (inaccurately) that the Navy had plans to scrap the aging ship. When poet Oliver Wendell Holmes learned of the report, he dashed off a verse titled "Old Ironsides" to warn his countrymen that the "eagle of the sea" was in peril. The public outcry helped convince the Navy to refurbish the vessel, and the poem cemented the public's affection for the ship.

In **1941** the Navy placed the *Constitution* in permanent commission. Now open to the public at the Charlestown Navy Yard in Boston, millions have visited this proud old symbol of America's strength, courage, and liberty.

AMERICAN HISTORY PARADE

1812   During the War of 1812, the USS *Constitution* defeats the British frigate *Guerriere* some 600 miles east of Nova Scotia.

1814   British troops land at Benedict, Maryland, en route to capturing Washington, D.C.

1856   Gail Borden of Brooklyn, New York, receives a patent for his process for condensed milk, the beginning of a variety of instant foods.

1946   Bill Clinton, the forty-second U.S. president, is born in Hope, Arkansas.

E PLURIBUS UNUM is the Latin motto on the Great Seal of the United States. It means "out of many, one" and refers to the creation of this country out of many states. It also reminds us that America consists of people from just about every country and culture on earth, and that all of these people together make one great nation.

Benjamin Franklin, John Adams, and Thomas Jefferson suggested the motto in 1776. The three sat on a committee appointed by Congress to design a seal for the new nation, and they turned to artist Pierre Eugène du Simitière for help in coming up with ideas. The design they submitted to Congress on August 20, 1776, included the words *E Pluribus Unum*.

The committee probably borrowed the phrase from *Gentleman's Magazine*, a popular journal published in England and read in the colonies. Once a year, the *Gentleman's Magazine* published an anthology volume that contained the best articles, essays, and poetry selected from the previous twelve months' issues—and the motto of that annual collection was *E Pluribus Unum*. The magazine did not coin the phrase. It appears in sources dating back to ancient Roman days.

Congress did not like the original design that Franklin, Adams, and Jefferson submitted. But it did like the phrase *E Pluribus Unum* and later included it in the design adopted for the Great Seal of the United States. Since 1873 Congress has required that the motto *E Pluribus Unum* appear on every U.S. coin.

AMERICAN HISTORY PARADE

1776   Adams, Franklin, and Jefferson recommend the motto *E Pluribus Unum* to Congress.

1833   Benjamin Harrison, the twenty-third U.S. president, is born in North Bend, Ohio.

1911   The *New York Times* sends the first around-the-world telegram via commercial service; it takes about 16 minutes to circle the globe.

1920   The first commercial radio station to broadcast regularly scheduled programs, 8MK (later WWJ), begins operations in Detroit.

1971   Texas Instruments introduces the first electronic pocket calculator.

1977   NASA launches *Voyager 2*, the first spacecraft to travel to Uranus and Neptune.

AUGUST 21, 1858, brought the first of the famous Lincoln-Douglas debates in Illinois between Abraham Lincoln and Stephen Douglas, both running for the U.S. Senate. There were seven debates in all, the first in the town of Ottawa, and they set the prairies ablaze as people flocked by the thousands to see the tall, lanky Lincoln match wits with the short, square-shouldered, broad-chested Douglas.

The debates centered on the question of whether slavery should be allowed to expand into U.S. territories. Douglas, a famous sitting senator, argued that the people of each territory should decide whether to allow slavery in their land. Lincoln opposed any expansion of slavery, which he regarded as a "moral, social, and political wrong." In the final debate Lincoln argued:

> That is the issue that will continue in this country when these poor tongues of Judge Douglas and myself shall be silent. It is the eternal struggle between two principles. The one is the common right of humanity, and the other the divine right of kings. It is the same spirit that says, "You toil and work and earn bread, and I'll eat it." No matter in what shape it comes, whether from the mouth of a king who seeks to bestride the people of his own nation and live by the fruit of their labor, or from one race of men as an apology for enslaving another race, it is the same tyrannical principle.

Newspapers across the country followed the debates, and although Lincoln lost the Senate race to Douglas, his careful arguments helped turn him from a relatively obscure prairie lawyer into a national figure. The Lincoln-Douglas debates were the most important since the ratification of the Constitution. Lincoln showed a mastery of law, philosophy, and history that raised him above not only Douglas but ultimately every other statesman of the age.

AMERICAN HISTORY PARADE

1831   Nat Turner leads a violent slave revolt in Southampton County, Virginia.

1858   The first of the seven Lincoln-Douglas debates takes place in Ottawa, Illinois.

1888   William Burroughs of St. Louis patents the first successful adding machine in the United States.

1912   Arthur Eldred of Oceanside, New York, becomes the first Eagle Scout in the Boy Scouts of America.

1944   The Dumbarton Oaks Conference in Washington, D.C., lays the groundwork for the United Nations.

1959   President Eisenhower signs an executive order making Hawaii the fiftieth state.

ON AUGUST 22, 1902, Theodore Roosevelt became the first U.S. president to ride in a car in public when he rolled through the streets of Hartford, Connecticut, in a purple-lined Columbia Electric Victoria, followed by a twenty-carriage procession. The *New York Times* reported that "two expert New York chauffeurs" had charge of the automobile. "The President expressed his satisfaction at the substitution of drives for conventional handshaking," the paper said. "This method of entertainment seems to have given the people the opportunity desired of seeing him." A few more presidential firsts:

Who was the first president to ride a train while in office? *Andrew Jackson*, June 6, 1833

Who was the first president to be photographed in office? *James Polk*, February 14, 1849

Who was the first president to have a White House telephone? *Rutherford B. Hayes*, 1879

Who was the first president to have electricity in the White House? *Benjamin Harrison*, 1891

Who was the first president to make a radio broadcast? *Warren G. Harding*, June 14, 1922

Who was the first president to appear on TV? *Franklin D. Roosevelt*, at the New York World's Fair, New York City, April 30, 1939

Who was the first president to fly in an airplane while in office? *Franklin D. Roosevelt*, January 1943, to the Casablanca Conference with Winston Churchill

Who was the first president to hold a press conference filmed for TV? *Dwight D. Eisenhower*, January 19, 1955

Who was the first president to fly in a helicopter? *Dwight D. Eisenhower*, July 12, 1957

Who was the first president to hold a live televised press conference? *John F. Kennedy*, January 25, 1961

AMERICAN HISTORY PARADE

1787   Inventor James Fitch tests a steamboat on the Delaware River as delegates to the Constitutional Convention look on.

1851   The schooner *America* defeats several other yachts off the English coast to win the trophy that becomes known as the America's Cup.

1902   In Hartford, Connecticut, Theodore Roosevelt becomes the first president to ride in an automobile in public.

1906   The Victor Talking Machine Company of Camden, New Jersey, manufactures the first Victrola.

1996   President Clinton signs legislation ending federal guarantees of lifetime welfare benefits.

THE VETERANS OF FOREIGN WARS of the United States is the nation's oldest major veterans organization and one of the country's great patriotic institutions. It traces its roots to 1899, when veterans of the Spanish-American War (1898) and the Philippine Insurrection (1899–1902) began founding organizations to help sick and wounded comrades. In August 1913, at a meeting in Denver, the groups combined to become the VFW.

VFW membership is open to men and women, either on active duty or honorably discharged, who have fought in a foreign military campaign. The VFW and its Auxiliaries (organizations made up of spouses and relatives of veterans) include 2.3 million members in 8,400 posts worldwide. The headquarters are in Kansas City, Missouri.

The VFW's mission is to "honor the dead by helping the living." Its work includes providing a voice for veterans, assisting needy veterans and their families, developing friendships among members, honoring deceased veterans, and supporting troops overseas.

VFW and Auxiliary members donate millions of volunteer hours in community service, from working in blood drives to funding college scholarships. They also promote citizenship, patriotism, and interest in American history with school programs, essay contests, and education about the American flag. The character of the VFW is set forth in its charter, granted by Congress, which states that the organization's purpose is to "extend the institutions of American freedom and to preserve and defend the United States from all her enemies, whomsoever."

AMERICAN HISTORY PARADE

1775   King George III proclaims the American colonies to be in a state of rebellion.

1784   Part of North Carolina declares itself the State of Franklin, which is denied admission to the Union (the area is now part of eastern Tennessee).

1859   The six-story Fifth Avenue Hotel in New York City becomes the first American hotel with an elevator.

1889   A lightship off San Francisco sends the first ship-to-shore wireless message received in the United States, signaling the arrival of an Army troopship.

1966   *Lunar Orbiter 1* takes the first photo of Earth from the moon.

ON AUGUST 24, 1814, during the War of 1812, British troops marched on Washington, D.C. Outside the city waited a ragtag American army along with President James Madison and his advisors, who had raced to the battlefield to witness the capital's defense. The crack British forces quickly overran the American lines.

Panic reigned in Washington as fleeing soldiers and statesmen began straggling through the city's streets. Many public records, including the Declaration of Independence, had already been packed into linen bags and carted off to Virginia, where they were piled in an empty house. Now the roads leading out of town began to fill with wagons carrying families and their valuables. In nearby Georgetown and Alexandria, citizens made plans to surrender at the first sight of a British officer.

First Lady Dolley Madison calmly directed last-minute details at the White House. A large portrait of George Washington hung in the dining room. It would be a disgrace if it fell into British hands. Dolley ordered two servants to bring it along, but the huge frame was screwed so tightly to the wall that no one could get it down. Minutes ticked by as they tugged and tugged, to no avail. The First Lady refused to leave without the portrait. At last someone produced a penknife and carefully cut the canvas from the frame. With the precious painting in hand, Dolley and her comrades headed toward Virginia.

Later that evening, the British entered a dark and empty Washington. The Capitol building and White House went up in flames, and the night sky glowed red as the city burned. It was the only time our nation's capital has fallen into enemy hands. The determined Americans would rebuild. In the meantime Dolley Madison had saved a piece of the national pride.

AMERICAN HISTORY PARADE

1814 British troops invade Washington, D.C., setting fire to the U.S. Capitol and White House.

1932 Amelia Earhart becomes the first woman to fly nonstop across the United States, traveling from Los Angeles to Newark, New Jersey, in 19 hours.

1959 Three days after Hawaii becomes the fiftieth state, Hiram L. Fong is sworn in as the first Chinese-American U.S. senator, and Daniel K. Inouye is sworn in as the first Japanese-American U.S. House member.

1992 Hurricane Andrew smashes into southern Florida, causing record damage.

AUGUST 25, 1830, brought one of the oddest races in American history—between a steam engine and a horse. The race took place on the Baltimore and Ohio Railroad, one of the nation's first railroads, which ran thirteen miles from Baltimore west to Ellicott's Mills, Maryland. The engine was the *Tom Thumb*, the first American-built steam locomotive. The horse, "a gallant gray of great beauty and power" belonging to the Stockton & Stokes stagecoach line, pulled a car on a parallel track. The stagecoach company, worried about competition, wanted to demonstrate that clumsy steam engines were no match for its horses. John Latrobe, a lawyer for the B&O, described the scene.

> The start being even, away went horse and engine, the snort of the one and the puff of the other keeping time and tune. At first the gray had the best of it . . . [but] the engine gained on the horse . . . the race was neck and neck, nose and nose—then the engine passed the horse, and a great hurrah hailed the victory. But it was not repeated; for just at this time, when the gray's master was about giving up, the band which drove the pulley, which drove the blower, slipped from the drum, the safety valve ceased to scream, and the engine for want of breath began to wheeze and pant. . . . The horse gained on the machine, and passed it; and although the band was presently replaced, and steam again did its best, the horse was too far ahead to be overtaken, and came in the winner of the race.

It was a short-lived victory for a mode of transportation doomed by the iron horse. Within a mere ten years, American railroads had laid more than **3,000** miles of track.

AMERICAN HISTORY PARADE

1718   French colonists found New Orleans, named for Philippe II, duke of Orleans.

1830   The *Tom Thumb* of the B&O Railroad loses a race to a horse.

1840   The first practical seeding machine is patented by Joseph Gibbons of Michigan.

1944   The Allies liberate Paris after four years of Nazi occupation.

1981   Photos sent by the *Voyager 2* spacecraft reveal the complex structure of the rings surrounding Saturn.

ON AUGUST 26, 1873, the St. Louis, Missouri, board of education established the first public school kindergarten in the U.S. Directed by Susan E. Blow, the kindergarten opened the following September in the Des Peres School with 42 students.

Here are a few other firsts in the U.S.A.

First	City	Date
Library	Charleston, SC	established 1698
Successful newspaper	Boston, MA	published 1704 (*Boston News-Letter*)
Theater building	Williamsburg, VA	built 1718
Public museum	Charleston, SC	organized 1773
Cathedral	Baltimore, MD	built 1806–51
Railroad station	Baltimore, MD	built 1830 by B&O Railroad
Department store	Vincennes, IN	opened 1842 by Adam Gimbel
Passenger elevator	New York City, NY	installed 1857 by Elisha Otis
Cable car	San Francisco, CA	began operating 1873
Zoo	Philadelphia, PA	opened 1874
Electric streetlights	Wabash, IN	installed 1880
Skyscraper	Chicago, IL	built 1885 (10 stories)

AMERICAN HISTORY PARADE

1791   John Fitch and James Rumsey, rival inventors, both receive patents for steamboats.

1839   The slave ship *Amistad* is captured off Long Island, leading to a trial over the legal status of the Africans on board, who had taken control of the ship.

1873   The St. Louis board of education establishes the nation's first public school kindergarten.

1968   As the Democratic National Convention begins in Chicago, thousands of anti-Vietnam War demonstrators take to the streets and clash with police.

AUGUST 27, 1776, brought one of the largest battles of the Revolutionary War, the Battle of Long Island, involving more than 40,000 men. It was not a good outcome for the Patriots. Marching through the night, the British took the Americans by surprise and overwhelmed most of their lines. George Washington, watching the enemy cut down his men, cried out, "Good God, what brave fellows I must this day lose!"

Only grim resistance by Maryland and Delaware troops avoided a complete rout. "If a good bleeding can bring those Bible-faced Yankees to their senses, the fever of independency should soon abate," one British officer predicted.

The Americans retreated to Brooklyn Heights, where they sat on the verge of disaster. Washington realized that he must somehow get his men off Long Island.

British warships were prepared to sail up the East River, which lay between Long Island and Manhattan, to cut off any retreat. Fortunately for the Patriots, winds kept the ships out of the river, but Washington realized that it was only a matter of time before he was trapped.

The general ordered a search for all available boats. On the night of August 29, under cover of rain, oarsmen began ferrying the army across the East River. One Connecticut officer remembered making eleven trips across the river that night, carrying men to safety. The troops hurried in strict silence—if discovered in retreat, the Patriot force would be annihilated.

Only a portion of the army had crossed by daybreak. As historian David McCullough notes, "Incredibly, yet again, circumstances—fate, luck, Providence, the hand of God, as would be said so often—intervened." A heavy fog settled over Brooklyn, concealing the American movement. When it lifted, the stunned British realized that more than 9,000 men had slipped out of their grasp. The bruised Patriot army would live to fight another day.

AMERICAN HISTORY PARADE

1665   The first theatrical performance in the colonies, a play called *The Bare and the Cubb*, is given at Accomack, Virginia.

1776   British forces defeat the Patriots at the Battle of Long Island.

1859   Edwin Drake drills the first successful commercial oil well at Titusville, Pennsylvania.

1908   Lyndon B. Johnson, the thirty-sixth U.S. president, is born near Stonewall, Texas.

1962   NASA launches *Mariner 2*, the first probe to fly by and gather data on another planet (Venus).

ON AUGUST 28, 1963, more than 200,000 people, black and white, gathered in the nation's capital to urge Congress to pass President John F. Kennedy's civil rights bill, which prohibited racial discrimination in public places, employment, and education.

The daylong celebration of speeches, songs, and prayers climaxed with an address by the Reverend Martin Luther King Jr., who spoke from the steps of the Lincoln Memorial:

I have a dream that one day on the red hills of Georgia the sons of former slaves and the sons of former slave owners will be able to sit down together at the table of brotherhood. . . . I have a dream that my four little children will one day live in a nation where they will not be judged by the color of their skin but by the content of their character. I have a dream today! . . . And so let freedom ring . . . from Stone Mountain of Georgia. Let freedom ring from Lookout Mountain of Tennessee. Let freedom ring from every hill and molehill of Mississippi—from every mountainside. Let freedom ring. And when this happens—when we allow freedom to ring from every village and every hamlet, from every state and every city, we will be able to speed up that day when all of God's children—black men and white men, Jews and Gentiles, Protestants and Catholics—will be able to join hands and sing in the words of the old Negro spiritual: "Free at last! Free at last! Thank God Almighty, we are free at last!"

Rarely can it be said that speeches change things. But King's "I have a dream" speech, one of the greatest in the nation's history, helped secure passage of the 1964 Civil Rights Act. The speech helped change millions of hearts and minds. It changes things still.

AMERICAN HISTORY PARADE

1609   English explorer Henry Hudson discovers Delaware Bay.

1845   *Scientific American* magazine publishes its first issue.

1922   The first radio commercial airs on WEAF in New York City with a ten-minute ad by the Queensboro Realty Co., for which it paid $100.

IN THE MID-NINETEENTH CENTURY, much of the Southwest was unknown territory—a blank space on U.S. maps labeled "Unexplored." Reports from a few hunters and Native Americans told of an enormous canyon carved by the Colorado River. In 1869 geologist John Wesley Powell set out to find the canyon and ride the river between its walls.

Powell started on the Green River with four boats and a handful of companions. They got a hint of what was to come when foaming torrents tossed one of the boats against a boulder and dashed it to pieces.

Several days later, Powell—who had lost an arm in the Civil War—decided to climb a cliff to get a view of the water's current. Eighty feet up, he found himself clinging to a rock with no good foothold, and nowhere to go. His climbing partner took off his pants and lowered them to Powell, who made a life-or-death lunge for the waving cloth, grabbed hold, and scrambled to safety.

The explorers floated into the Colorado River and its huge canyon. Three-thousand-foot walls loomed overhead. Traveling west, they passed carved arches and spires. At times they battled whirlpools and craggy falls. They ran short on food and supplies. Then they came upon a stretch of monstrous rapids.

Three of the men decided to climb out of the canyon and walk back to civilization. They were never seen again.

The rest decided to take two boats and run the terrifying rapids. They dashed into the boiling tide, disappeared in the foam—and then reappeared, the men still clinging on.

On August 29, 1869, three months and a thousand miles after they started, the boats floated into open country. Powell had accomplished one of the most storied journeys in American exploration: the first expedition through the Grand Canyon.

AMERICAN HISTORY PARADE

1776   Having lost the Battle of Long Island, Patriot troops escape over the East River to Manhattan.

1869   John Wesley Powell's expedition floats out of the Grand Canyon.

1944   American troops march down the Champs-Élysées in Paris in celebration of the city's liberation from the Nazis.

1957   Senator Strom Thurmond of South Carolina ends the longest filibuster by one person in Senate history (24 hours 18 minutes), against a civil rights bill.

2005   Hurricane Katrina hits the Gulf Coast, causing massive damage in Louisiana and Mississippi, destroying much of New Orleans, and killing 1,800 people.

WILLIAM PENN was a constant source of frustration for his father, a wealthy English admiral. The rebellious younger Penn got kicked out of Oxford University for refusing to attend Anglican (Church of England) services. Then he joined the Society of Friends, a religious sect known as the Quakers because their leader had once told an English judge to "tremble at the Word of the Lord." Quakers' religious beliefs and refusal to swear allegiance to any king but God led to their persecution. William Penn found himself imprisoned more than once.

Admiral Penn was an old friend of King Charles II and loaned the monarch a good deal of money. When the admiral died, William asked that the debt be paid with land in America. The king liked William, despite his religious beliefs, and granted him a huge tract of wilderness, which Charles named Pennsylvania, meaning "Penn's woods."

On August 30, 1682, William Penn sailed for America to begin his "Holy Experiment"—a colony that would be a refuge for not only Quakers but settlers of various faiths. Penn's guarantee of religious freedom was then one of the most comprehensive in the world. Indeed, his plan to include diverse populations while extending a broad measure of religious and political equality was nothing less than revolutionary for its time.

Catholics, Lutherans, Baptists, Presbyterians, French Huguenots, and even Anglicans rushed to settle the rich lands. By 1700, Pennsylvania had as many as 21,000 settlers. The capital, Philadelphia ("City of Brotherly Love"), became a thriving metropolis, soon the largest of North America's colonial cities. As settlers arrived—English, Scots-Irish, Welch, German, Dutch, Swedish, and more—Penn's woods began to resemble the famous American "melting pot."

AMERICAN HISTORY PARADE

1682   William Penn sets sail from Deal in Kent, England, for Pennsylvania.

1781   A French fleet arrives at Yorktown, Virginia, with 3,000 troops to help trap the British army there.

1836   Brothers Augustus Chapman Allen and John Kirby Allen found Houston, Texas.

1862   Confederate forces defeat Union troops at the Second Battle of Manassas, Virginia.

1967   The Senate confirms Thurgood Marshall as the first black justice on the Supreme Court.

1983   Guion S. Bluford Jr. becomes the first black American astronaut to travel in space when the shuttle *Challenger* lifts off.

AUGUST 31 • THE CODE OF CONDUCT FOR AMERICAN SOLDIERS

IN AUGUST 1955, President Eisenhower authorized the Code of Conduct for members of the U.S. armed forces. The code is an ethical guide that instructs armed forces members when they are prisoners of war or are in danger of capture. It's a good reminder of the solemn duty shouldered by American soldiers.

1. I am an American fighting in the forces which guard my country and our way of life. I am prepared to give my life in their defense.

2. I will never surrender of my own free will. If in command, I will never surrender the members of my command while they still have the means to resist.

3. If I am captured I will continue to resist by all means available. I will make every effort to escape and aid others to escape. I will accept neither parole nor special favors from the enemy.

4. If I become a prisoner of war, I will keep faith with my fellow prisoners. I will give no information or take part in any action which might be harmful to my comrades. If I am senior, I will take command. If not, I will obey the lawful orders of those appointed over me and will back them up in every way.

5. When questioned, should I become a prisoner of war, I am required to give name, rank, service number, and date of birth. I will evade answering further questions to the utmost of my ability. I will make no oral or written statements disloyal to my country and its allies or harmful to their cause.

6. I will never forget that I am an American, fighting for freedom, responsible for my actions, and dedicated to the principles which made my country free. I will trust in my God and in the United States of America.

AMERICAN HISTORY PARADE

1842   Congress establishes the U.S. Naval Observatory, one of the nation's oldest scientific agencies.

1886   An earthquake centered near Charleston, South Carolina, destroys much of the city, kills scores of people, and is felt in distant places such as Boston and Chicago.

1920   Station 8MK (later WWJ) in Detroit broadcasts the first news program on a U.S. radio station, an announcement of local election returns.

1955   General Motors Corporation demonstrates the world's first solar-powered car in Chicago.

THE GETTYSBURG ADDRESS

Abraham Lincoln gave the Gettysburg Address on November 19, 1863, at Gettysburg, Pennsylvania, as part of a ceremony to dedicate a military cemetery. Just a few months earlier, armies from the North and South had fought one of the bloodiest battles of the Civil War there. The main speaker of the day, Edward Everett, spoke for two hours. When he was through, Lincoln took to the podium and spoke fewer than three hundred words. His remarks have gone down in history as one of the greatest American speeches ever. Everett later wrote to Lincoln, "I should be glad if I could flatter myself that I came as near to the central idea of the occasion in two hours as you did in two minutes."

The speech came at a time when many in the North would have settled for peace at any price. President Lincoln's words explained the need to continue the war. They asserted that the real purpose of fighting on was to salvage the ideal on which the country was founded: the dream that *all* people are created equal, that *all* people have inalienable rights. The Gettysburg Address was, at bottom, a promise that the United States would not be what it had been—a country that mixed slavery with claims of equality and democracy. By continuing the fight, Lincoln said, the nation would live up to its founding principles. There would be a new birth of freedom.

Four score and seven years ago our fathers brought forth on this continent, a new nation, conceived in Liberty, and dedicated to the proposition that all men are created equal.

Now we are engaged in a great civil war, testing whether that nation, or any nation so conceived and so dedicated, can long endure. We are met on a great battlefield of that war. We have come to dedicate a portion of that field, as a final resting place for those who here gave their lives that that nation might live. It is altogether fitting and proper that we should do this.

But, in a larger sense, we can not dedicate—we can not consecrate—we can not hallow—this ground. The brave men, living and dead, who struggled here, have consecrated it, far above our poor power to add or detract. The world will little note, nor long remember what we say here, but it can never forget what they did here. It is for us the living, rather, to be dedicated here to the unfinished work which they who fought here have thus far so nobly advanced. It is rather for us to be here dedicated to the great task remaining before us—that from these honored dead we take increased devotion to that cause for which they gave the last full measure of devotion—that we here highly resolve that these dead shall not have died in vain—that this nation, under God, shall have a new birth of freedom—and that government of the people, by the people, for the people, shall not perish from the earth.

THE EMANCIPATION PROCLAMATION

Abraham Lincoln came to the presidency regarding slavery as a moral evil, but like many Americans, he hoped that if the practice could be limited to the South and allowed to die a gradual death, the Union might be preserved. The Civil War changed his mind. Lincoln realized that slavery would have to be stamped out to save American democracy. In September 1862 he issued a preliminary decree stating that all slaves in areas still rebelling on January 1, 1863, would be "forever free."

In reality, Lincoln's Emancipation Proclamation of January 1, 1863, did not free any slaves, at least not right away. It applied only to Confederate territory, where Lincoln had no control. It did not affect slavery in border states that were loyal to the Union. But it did strengthen the North's war efforts. Some half a million slaves fled north to freedom by the war's end. About 200,000 blacks, many former slaves, fought in the Union army and navy. Most important, the Emancipation Proclamation changed the moral character of the war. It turned the struggle from a fight to save the Union into a battle for human freedom. It paved the way for the Thirteenth Amendment to the Constitution, ratified in December 1865, which ended slavery in the United States once and for all.

By the President of the United States of America:

A Proclamation.

Whereas, on the twenty-second day of September, in the year of our Lord one thousand eight hundred and sixty-two, a proclamation was issued by the

President of the United States, containing, among other things, the following, to wit:

"That on the first day of January, in the year of our Lord one thousand eight hundred and sixty-three, all persons held as slaves within any State or designated part of a State, the people whereof shall then be in rebellion against the United States, shall be then, thenceforward, and forever free; and the Executive Government of the United States, including the military and naval authority thereof, will recognize and maintain the freedom of such persons, and will do no act or acts to repress such persons, or any of them, in any efforts they may make for their actual freedom.

"That the Executive will, on the first day of January aforesaid, by proclamation, designate the States and parts of States, if any, in which the people thereof, respectively, shall then be in rebellion against the United States; and the fact that any State, or the people thereof, shall on that day be, in good faith, represented in the Congress of the United States by members chosen thereto at elections wherein a majority of the qualified voters of such State shall have participated, shall, in the absence of strong countervailing testimony, be deemed conclusive evidence that such State, and the people thereof, are not then in rebellion against the United States."

Now, therefore I, Abraham Lincoln, President of the United States, by virtue of the power in me vested as Commander-in-Chief, of the Army and Navy of the United States in time of actual armed rebellion against the authority and government of the United States, and as a fit and necessary war measure for suppressing said rebellion, do, on this first day of January, in the year of our Lord one thousand eight hundred and sixty-three, and in accordance with my purpose so to do publicly proclaimed for the full period of one hundred days, from the day first above mentioned, order and designate as the States and parts of States wherein the people thereof respectively, are this day in rebellion against the United States, the following, to wit:

Arkansas, Texas, Louisiana, (except the Parishes of St. Bernard, Plaquemines,

Jefferson, St. John, St. Charles, St. James Ascension, Assumption, Terrebonne, Lafourche, St. Mary, St. Martin, and Orleans, including the City of New Orleans) Mississippi, Alabama, Florida, Georgia, South Carolina, North Carolina, and Virginia, (except the forty-eight counties designated as West Virginia, and also the counties of Berkley, Accomac, Northampton, Elizabeth City, York, Princess Ann, and Norfolk, including the cities of Norfolk and Portsmouth), and which excepted parts, are for the present, left precisely as if this proclamation were not issued.

And by virtue of the power, and for the purpose aforesaid, I do order and declare that all persons held as slaves within said designated States, and parts of States, are, and henceforward shall be free; and that the Executive government of the United States, including the military and naval authorities thereof, will recognize and maintain the freedom of said persons.

And I hereby enjoin upon the people so declared to be free to abstain from all violence, unless in necessary self-defence; and I recommend to them that, in all cases when allowed, they labor faithfully for reasonable wages.

And I further declare and make known, that such persons of suitable condition, will be received into the armed service of the United States to garrison forts, positions, stations, and other places, and to man vessels of all sorts in said service.

And upon this act, sincerely believed to be an act of justice, warranted by the Constitution, upon military necessity, I invoke the considerate judgment of mankind, and the gracious favor of Almighty God.

In witness whereof, I have hereunto set my hand and caused the seal of the United States to be affixed.

Done at the City of Washington, this first day of January, in the year of our Lord one thousand eight hundred and sixty three, and of the Independence of the United States of America the eighty-seventh.

By the President: ABRAHAM LINCOLN
WILLIAM H. SEWARD, Secretary of State.

THE PLEDGE
OF ALLEGIANCE

I pledge allegiance to the flag of the United States of America and to the Republic for which it stands, one Nation under God, indivisible, with liberty and justice for all.

For more than a century, Americans have recited the Pledge of Allegiance as a promise of loyalty to the United States. When saying the Pledge, all should stand at attention and face the flag. The U.S. Flag Code advises that those not in uniform should place the right hand over the heart. Those not in uniform who are wearing a nonreligious hat should remove it with the right hand and hold it at the left shoulder, so that the hand is over the heart. Soldiers and others in uniform (such as scouts) should remain silent, face the flag, and give the appropriate salute.

The Pledge of Allegiance was first published in September 1892 in a magazine called the *Youth's Companion*. The magazine printed it to help celebrate the four hundredth anniversary of Columbus reaching America. Schoolchildren first recited the pledge on Columbus Day, October 12, 1892. The original words read: "I pledge allegiance to my Flag and to the Republic for which it stands, one Nation indivisible, with liberty and justice for all."

The words were altered in the early 1920s to change "my flag" to "the flag of the United States of America." In 1942 the Pledge received official recognition by Congress when it was included in the U.S. Flag Code. Congress added the phrase "under God" in 1954.

Francis Bellamy, a clergyman and editor at the *Youth's Companion*, is believed to have written the Pledge of Allegiance. In the 1930s some people suggested that James B. Upham, who also worked at the magazine, was the author. By the time the question arose, both men were deceased. In 1939 a panel of scholars gave credit to Bellamy.

THE AMERICAN'S CREED

I believe in the United States of America as a government of the people, by the people, for the people; whose just powers are derived from the consent of the governed; a democracy in a Republic; a sovereign Nation of many sovereign States; a perfect Union, one and inseparable; established upon those principles of freedom, equality, justice, and humanity for which American patriots sacrificed their lives and fortunes.

I therefore believe it is my duty to my country to love it; to support its Constitution; to obey its laws; to respect its flag; and to defend it against all enemies.

The American's Creed came out of a nationwide contest during World War I for the best summary of American political faith. The winner was William Tyler Page of Maryland, a longtime employee of the U.S. House of Representatives and Clerk of the House from 1919 to 1931. The Creed's two short paragraphs remind us of the principles that make America great and the duties required to preserve those principles.

Page was coming home from church one Sunday in 1917 when he got the idea of fashioning a creed along the lines of the Apostles' Creed. A student of history, he composed the creed by drawing on great American writings such as the Declaration of Independence, Preamble to the Constitution, and Gettysburg Address. His submission won the contest, and in 1918 the U.S. House of Representatives accepted it on behalf of the American people as the American's Creed. A few days later, Page used his $1,000 prize money to buy Liberty Bonds and gave them to his church.

SEPTEMBER

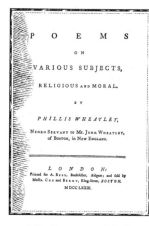

SEPTEMBER 1, 1773, saw the publication of Phillis Wheatley's *Poems on Various Subjects, Religious and Moral*, the first volume of poetry by an African American poet.

Born in Senegal, West Africa, Phillis Wheatley was sold into slavery around age seven, taken to Boston, and purchased off a slave ship by John Wheatley, a wealthy merchant. The Wheatley family taught her to read and write, and by age fourteen she began composing poetry. Most Bostonians found it hard to believe that a young slave girl could produce such lyrics, but a group of the city's most notable citizens, including John Hancock, gave her an oral examination and signed a letter "To the Publick" attesting to her authorship.

No Boston publisher would print her work, so admirers arranged for publication in London. Freed by the Wheatleys, Phillis sailed for a visit to England, where the Lord Mayor of London welcomed her. Her reputation spread both in Europe and at home.

In 1776, her poem "To His Excellency George Washington," honoring Washington's appointment as commander in chief of the Continental Army, earned her more praise and the thanks of Washington himself. Throughout her verses, Wheatley celebrated the ideals for which the young republic stood.

> Auspicious Heaven shall fill with fav'ring Gales,
> Where e'er *Columbia* spreads her swelling sails:
> To every Realm shall *Peace* her Charms display,
> And Heavenly *Freedom* spread her golden Ray.

Wheatley was mindful that millions of African-Americans remained enslaved. "In every human breast, God has implanted a principle, which we call love of freedom," she wrote. "It is impatient of oppression, and pants for deliverance." Decades later, abolitionists revived her poems as a reminder of that universal love of liberty. Phillis Wheatley thus left a legacy that struck a blow for freedom.

AMERICAN HISTORY PARADE

1821   William Becknell begins his journey from Arrow Rock, Missouri, to Santa Fe, New Mexico, in a wagon train, opening the Santa Fe Trail.

1916   Congress passes the first federal child labor law.

1972   Bobby Fisher defeats Boris Spassky of the U.S.S.R. to become the first American to win a world chess championship.

ON SEPTEMBER 2, 1944, George Herbert Walker Bush, the youngest pilot then serving in the U.S. Navy, climbed into a TBM Avenger torpedo bomber, catapulted off the deck of the carrier *San Jacinto*, and headed toward Chichi Jima, a Japanese island 600 miles south of Tokyo. With him rode two crewmen, radioman Jack Delaney and gunnery officer Ted White. Their target: a Japanese radio installation.

As Bush dove toward the station, black splotches of antiaircraft fire exploded around the Avenger. "Suddenly there was a jolt, as if a massive fist had crunched into the belly of the plane," he later wrote. "Smoke poured into the cockpit, and I could see flames rippling across the crease of the wing, edging toward the fuel tanks." He managed to unload his bombs on the target and head the Avenger to sea, yelling for his crewmates to bail out. As the aircraft lost altitude, Bush jumped as well, colliding with the plane's tail on the way. He landed bleeding but alive in the water. Delaney and White did not survive—one's parachute failed to open, and the other never made it out of the plane.

Bush climbed into a life raft as Japanese boats sped toward him. U.S. fighter planes drove them back, but currents pushed the raft toward Chichi Jima, where (unbeknownst to Bush) the Japanese had executed and cannibalized American POWs. Using his hands, Bush paddled furiously against the tide.

A few hours later, he saw a periscope break the water's surface, followed by the hull of the sub USS *Finback*. Within minutes, the downed pilot was safely aboard.

The Navy sent Bush to Hawaii for rest and recovery. But he couldn't sit still while the war raged, especially when he thought of his lost comrades. So the future president cut short his leave and headed back to the *San Jacinto* to finish his tour of duty.

AMERICAN HISTORY PARADE

1789   The U.S. Treasury Department is established.

1864   Union general William T. Sherman's forces occupy Atlanta.

1935   The Labor Day Hurricane slams the Florida Keys, killing more than 400 people.

1944   Navy pilot George H. W. Bush, later the forty-first U.S. president, is shot down and rescued in the Pacific.

1945   Japan formally surrenders aboard the USS *Missouri* in Tokyo Bay, ending World War II.

ACCORDING TO TRADITION, American troops carried the Stars and Stripes into battle for the first time on September 3, 1777, at Cooch's Bridge, Delaware, during the Revolutionary War. A small Patriot force under General William Maxwell laid an ambush for advancing British and Hessian troops, but was soon outgunned and forced to retreat. Here are a few more firsts for the Stars and Stripes.

June 14, 1777 – Congress adopts the Stars and Stripes as the national standard.

July 4, 1777 – Captain John Paul Jones raises the Stars and Stripes for the first time on an American warship, the *Ranger*, in Portsmouth Harbor, New Hampshire. The flag was given to him by a group of young ladies who made it out of gowns.

February 14, 1778 – The flag receives the first salute from a foreign nation, fired by the French at Quiberon Bay, France, to the *Ranger*, commanded by John Paul Jones. The nine-gun salute was an acknowledgment of American independence.

August 9, 1790 – The *Columbia*, which had sailed from Boston in 1787 on a fur-trading voyage, returns to port, becoming the first ship to carry the flag around the world.

April 27, 1805 – The flag flies over a fortress of the old world for the first time when the Marines raise the Stars and Stripes at Derna, on the "shores of Tripoli" in North Africa during the First Barbary War.

May 1812 – The flag flies for the first time over a log schoolhouse, in Colrain, Massachusetts.

July 4, 1960 – The fifty-star flag, reflecting Hawaii's statehood, becomes official.

August 10, 1960 – The flag first orbits the earth aboard the satellite *Discoverer* 8.

July 20, 1969 – *Apollo* 11 astronauts plant the flag on the moon.

AMERICAN HISTORY PARADE

1777   The Stars and Stripes is reportedly flown in battle for first time at Cooch's Bridge, Delaware.

1783   The Treaty of Paris officially ends the Revolutionary War.

1954   The last of 2,956 radio episodes of *The Lone Ranger* is broadcast.

1976   The *Viking* 2 spacecraft lands on Mars to take photos of the planet's surface.

September 4, 1609 This day the people of the country came aboard, seeming very glad of our coming, and brought green tobacco and gave us of it for knives and beads. They go in deer skins loose, well dressed. . . . They have great store of maize or Indian wheat.

So reads the log of the *Half Moon*, Henry Hudson's ship, as it probed waters near the mouth of the broad river that now bears the explorer's name. Hudson himself called the stream the Great River of the Mountains. The Dutch East India Company had hired him to find a new route to the Indies, and for several days the 80-ton *Half Moon* sailed upstream hoping to locate the fabled Northwest Passage.

Along the way the crew both traded and fought with Indians, and marveled at the scenery. "The land is the finest for cultivation that I ever in my life set foot upon," Hudson wrote. The explorers saw "very goodly oaks" and "a great many salmon in the river." They noted mountains that looked "as if some metal or mineral were in them," and cliffs that seemed to promise copper or silver mines.

The *Half Moon* pushed up the Hudson River to the vicinity of present-day Albany, New York. By then it was clear that was not the way to China, so the ship made its way back downstream and sailed past Manhattan Island into the Atlantic. Its captain perished less than two years later on another voyage in search of the Northwest Passage. Far to the north, in the vast inland sea of Canada now known as Hudson Bay, a mutinous crew set Henry Hudson, his son John, and seven others adrift in a small boat. Its occupants disappeared forever into the ice and fog.

AMERICAN HISTORY PARADE

1609   Henry Hudson explores New York Harbor before sailing up the Hudson River.

1781   Spanish settlers found Los Angeles.

1886   After years of fighting white settlement, the Apache leader Geronimo surrenders to U.S. troops in Arizona.

1888   George Eastman patents the Kodak camera, the first to use film rolls.

1951   In the first coast-to-coast telecast, President Truman speaks at the Japanese peace treaty conference in San Francisco.

1957   Arkansas governor Orval Faubus calls out the National Guard to keep nine black students from entering an all-white high school in Little Rock.

FOR MILLIONS OF AMERICANS, Labor Day is a holiday for backyard cookouts, long-weekend getaways, and saying good-bye to summer. But on September 5, 1882, when the first Labor Day parade was held in New York City, it was a time for workers to call attention to problems brought on by the Industrial Revolution—factories where owners demanded 14-hour workdays, sweatshops where exhausted immigrants worked for pennies an hour, dirty mills where children tended grinding, clanking machines.

Samuel Gompers, the first president of the American Federation of Labor, was one who insisted that a laborer was more than "a mere producing machine." A Jewish immigrant from England, he had no wish to destroy capitalism or see workers take over government—often the goals of labor movements in other countries. He simply wanted a better life for the American worker. As he saw it, that was the whole point of America.

"The fact of the matter is that we live in the United States of America, the richest country on the face of the globe," Gompers said in 1904. "And the millions of honest toilers of America are willing to work to produce the great wealth and place it at the feet of the people of our country, but in return the toiling masses, the great producers of wealth . . . insist that there should be a better life and better home and better surroundings for the great producers of wealth."

It took some struggle, and at times bloodshed, but the forces of collective bargaining, capitalism, and democratic government managed to make better lives for millions. For decades American workers have enjoyed one of the world's highest standards of living. Today's Labor Day barbecues are a restful testament to the work of reformers like Samuel Gompers.

AMERICAN HISTORY PARADE

1774   The First Continental Congress assembles in Philadelphia to draw up a declaration of rights and grievances against Britain.

1781   A French fleet defeats a British fleet at the entrance to the Chesapeake Bay, stranding Lord Cornwallis's British army at Yorktown, Virginia.

1836   Sam Houston is elected president of the Republic of Texas.

1882   In New York City, 10,000 workers march in the first Labor Day parade.

1975   In Sacramento, California, President Gerald Ford escapes an assassination attempt by Lynette "Squeaky" Fromme when Secret Service agents grab her pistol.

"DEMOCRATIC GOVERNMENT, associated as it is with all the mistakes and shortcomings of the common people, still remains the most valuable contribution America has made to the moral life of the world," wrote Jane Addams, born this day in 1860 in Cedarville, Illinois. She heightened that contribution with Hull House, a "settlement house" in Chicago where Addams and other reformers helped the poor, including immigrant families.

As Addams recounted in her book *Twenty Years at Hull House*, the seeds of her passion were planted at about age seven on a day when she passed through the poorest part of a neighboring town with her father, a prosperous miller.

> On that day I had my first sight of the poverty which implies squalor, and felt the curious distinction between the ruddy poverty of the country and that which even a small city presents in its shabbiest streets. I remember launching at my father the pertinent inquiry why people lived in such horrid little houses so close together, and that after receiving his explanation I declared with much firmness when I grew up I should, of course, have a large house, but it would not be built among the other large houses, but right in the midst of horrid little houses like these.

More than two decades later, Addams moved into a dilapidated Chicago mansion once owned by businessman Charles J. Hull. There in the crowded immigrant slums, she and her fellow reformers provided shelter, education, and affection for thousands—everything from maternal care and concerts to language classes and lessons in citizenship. Addams served as head resident of Hull House for 46 years—the rest of her life—practicing a democracy that welcomed "the common people" from around the world.

AMERICAN HISTORY PARADE

1781   British troops under Benedict Arnold burn New London, Connecticut.

1860   Jane Addams, founder of Hull House, is born in Cedarville, Illinois.

1901   President William McKinley is shot and mortally wounded by an anarchist at the Pan-American Exposition in Buffalo, New York.

1995   Baltimore Orioles shortstop Cal Ripken Jr. plays in his 2,131st consecutive game, breaking Lou Gehrig's record.

2002   Congress convenes in New York City to pay homage to the victims and heroes of the September 11, 2001, terrorist attacks.

SEPTEMBER 7 • PHILO FARNSWORTH, THE FORGOTTEN INVENTOR

ON SEPTEMBER 7, 1927, in a San Francisco laboratory, inventor Philo Farnsworth and a small team of assistants placed a slide containing an image of a triangle in front of a machine Farnsworth called an Image Dissector, and then gathered around a receiving tube on the other side of a partition. As they watched, one line of the triangle appeared in a small bluish square of light on the receiver. At Farnsworth's instructions, someone rotated the slide. As if by magic, the image of the line on the receiver turned as well.

"That's it, folks!" Farnsworth exclaimed. "We've done it! There you have electronic television!"

As Farnsworth refined his device, he surely thought that fame and fortune awaited him. It wasn't to be. Russian immigrant Vladimir Zworykin, who had also been trying to develop a television system, claimed that *he* was the true inventor of TV. Zworykin worked for the Radio Corporation of America (RCA), which began to sell television sets and broadcast programs.

Years of legal battles followed, and though the U.S. Patent Office sided with Farnsworth, he lost other lawsuits, and years passed before RCA paid him for his work.

Farnsworth never received much public recognition for his world-changing invention. Ironically, he appeared on national television only once. In 1957, he was a mystery guest on the TV game show *I've Got a Secret*. A panel of celebrities peppered him with questions about his secret, but failed to guess what it was: "I invented electronic television." His prize for stumping the panel was $80 and a carton of cigarettes.

Nearly two decades after Farnsworth's death, his home state of Utah placed a statue of him in Statuary Hall in the U.S. Capitol. On the statue's base are inscribed the words *Father of Television*.

AMERICAN HISTORY PARADE

1896   At the Rhode Island State Fair in Cranston, A. H. Whiting wins the first car race ever held on a racetrack in the United States.

1899   In Newport, Rhode Island, 19 cars decorated with flowers and flags participate in the first automobile parade in the United States.

1927   Philo T. Farnsworth transmits the first image sent by electronic television.

1963   The Pro Football Hall of Fame is dedicated in Canton, Ohio.

The oldest Catholic parish in the United States is the parish of St. Augustine, Florida. It traces its roots to September 8, 1565, when a Spanish landing party led by Pedro Menéndez de Avilés came ashore and conducted a mass. The parish register dates to 1594.

The first Protestant church in a permanent settlement was erected at Jamestown, Virginia, in 1607. At first the settlers used a tent to worship, then a series of wooden structures. In 1617 they built a church of timber construction on a foundation of brick and cobble. In 1619 the first representative legislative assembly in the Western Hemisphere met in this church.

The oldest standing Protestant church building is Historic St. Luke's Church in Smithfield, Virginia. Built around 1632 and once known as the Old Brick Church, it was founded as an Anglican church. It is the nation's only original Gothic church building. It also houses the nation's oldest intact organ.

The first synagogue was a one-room house in New York City, rented in 1682 by Congregation Shearith Israel (the nation's oldest Jewish congregation, established in 1654). In 1730 the congregation constructed a small stone building on Mill Street (now South William Street).

The oldest standing synagogue is the Touro Synagogue in Newport, Rhode Island, completed in 1763. In a famous letter to the congregation about religious liberty, George Washington avowed that the United States "gives to bigotry no sanction," and that when anyone wishes to worship God in his own way, "there shall be none to make him afraid."

The first cathedral was the Baltimore Cathedral, now officially known as the Basilica of the National Shrine of the Assumption of the Blessed Virgin Mary. Its cornerstone was laid July 7, 1806, and the building was dedicated on May 31, 1821.

AMERICAN HISTORY PARADE

1565   A Spanish expedition founds the first permanent European settlement and first Roman Catholic parish in the United States at St. Augustine, Florida.

1636   The General Court of Massachusetts appropriates £400 to start Harvard College.

1892   The Pledge of Allegiance is first published in the *Youth's Companion* magazine.

1900   The Galveston Hurricane strikes Galveston, Texas, killing 6,000 people.

1921   In Atlantic City, New Jersey, Margaret Gorman of Washington, D.C., becomes the first winner of the contest that comes to be known as the Miss America Pageant.

ON SEPTEMBER 9, 1836, Abraham Lincoln earned his license to practice law in Illinois—a sweet victory for a prairie lad with less than a year of formal education. Like all others, Lincoln's life was bumpy with both successes and setbacks. "I do the very best I know how, the very best I can, and I mean to keep doing so until the end," he said.

1832 – Elected captain of an Illinois militia company

1832 – Defeated for state legislature

1833 – Failed in business

1833 – Appointed postmaster of New Salem, Illinois

1834 – Elected to state legislature

1835 – Sweetheart died

1836 – Received license to practice law in Illinois

1838 – Defeated for Speaker of the Illinois House

1841 – Suffered deep depression

1842 – Married Mary Todd

1844 – Established his own law practice

1846 – Elected to U.S. Congress

1849 – Failed to get appointment to U.S. Land Office

1850 – Four-year-old son died

1855 – Defeated for U.S. Senate

1857 – Earned large attorney fee in a successful case

1858 – Again defeated for Senate

1860 – ELECTED PRESIDENT OF THE UNITED STATES

AMERICAN HISTORY PARADE

1776   The Second Continental Congress makes official the term "United States."

1850   California becomes the thirty-first state.

1893   Frances Cleveland, wife of President Grover Cleveland, gives birth to a daughter, Esther, in the White House.

1956   Elvis Presley makes his first appearance on *The Ed Sullivan Show*.

1957   President Eisenhower signs the first civil rights law since Reconstruction.

WHEN OLIVER HAZARD PERRY ventured onto Lake Erie to battle the British on September 10, 1813, during the War of 1812, he sailed on a flagship he had named the *Lawrence* in honor of his friend Captain James Lawrence, killed in battle three months earlier. The flagship flew a banner emblazoned with Captain Lawrence's final order: Don't Give Up the Ship. The motto signaled Perry's resolution to fight to the end.

The British squadron numbered six ships with 63 cannons. The American fleet counted nine vessels, but their 54 guns had only half the range of the British cannon, so Perry knew he must draw close to have a chance.

The battle began just before noon, and at once things went wrong. A 24-pound cannonball smashed into the *Lawrence*, killing and wounding sailors. The British ships concentrated their fire on the stricken ship. The *Lawrence*'s guns roared back, but the American vessel was overwhelmed by the hailstorm of balls ripping into her sides. By midafternoon, the flagship was a crippled hulk.

Calmly taking his banner, Perry climbed into a longboat and rowed through a gauntlet of cannon fire to the *Lawrence*'s sister ship, the *Niagara*. Two British ships bore down on the *Niagara*, but the enemy vessels collided and became entangled. Quickly taking advantage of the blunder, Perry charged through the confused British line, pounding away with broadsides. One by one, the British ships struck their colors until the entire fleet surrendered.

With Lake Erie now under American control, Perry scrawled on an old envelope his now-famous message to headquarters: "We have met the enemy and they are ours. Two ships, two brigs, one schooner and one sloop. Yours with great respect and esteem, O. H. Perry."

AMERICAN HISTORY PARADE

1608   In Virginia, John Smith is elected president of the Jamestown council.

1794   The U.S.'s first nondenominational college, Blount College in Knoxville (now the University of Tennessee) is chartered.

1813   Following the Battle of Lake Erie, Oliver Hazard Perry sends the message "We have met the enemy and they are ours."

1846   Elias Howe of Spencer, Massachusetts, patents a hand-cranked sewing machine.

1913   The Lincoln Highway, the first coast-to-coast paved U.S. highway, stretching from New York City to San Francisco, opens (now replaced by I-80).

1955   The TV show *Gunsmoke* premieres on CBS, beginning a 20-year run.

ON TUESDAY, SEPTEMBER 11, 2001, nineteen al-Qaeda terrorists, mostly from Saudi Arabia, hijacked four commercial jetliners and turned them into flying bombs. Two of the hijacked planes slammed into the 110-story twin towers of the World Trade Center in New York City. Americans watched their TV screens in horror as the two skyscrapers, among the tallest in the world, collapsed. Another plane hit the Pentagon, and the fourth jet crashed in rural Pennsylvania.

Nearly 3,000 people died in the attacks, including more than 400 firefighters, police officers, and emergency medical services workers who had rushed to the World Trade Center to help survivors before the buildings fell.

Among the day's heroes were passengers on board United Flight 93, which had left Newark International Airport for San Francisco but changed course toward Washington, D.C., after four terrorists seized control. Passengers who began making frantic calls on their cell phones learned that other airliners had been hijacked and crashed in suicide missions. Realizing their captors must be headed toward a high-profile target, a group of Flight 93 passengers resolved to stop them.

Passenger Todd Beamer told an operator that he and a few others were going to jump the hijackers. "Are you guys ready?" the operator heard him say to someone. "Let's roll!"

Moments later, Flight 93 went down in rural southwestern Pennsylvania. All aboard were killed. The hijackers' target was probably the U.S. Capitol building or the White House.

Congress and the president have designated September 11 as Patriot Day. The flag should be flown at half-staff, and Americans are asked to observe a moment of silence to honor the innocent victims who perished during the worst acts of terrorism ever carried out against the United States.

AMERICAN HISTORY PARADE

1777   The British defeat the Patriots at Brandywine Creek in Pennsylvania.

1789   Alexander Hamilton is appointed the first secretary of the treasury.

1814   During the War of 1812, an American fleet destroys a British fleet in the Battle of Lake Champlain.

1936   President Franklin D. Roosevelt dedicates Boulder Dam (now Hoover Dam) in Nevada.

1941   A groundbreaking ceremony takes place for construction of the Pentagon in Arlington, Virginia.

2001   Terrorists hijack four airliners for suicide attacks against the United States.

ON SEPTEMBER 12, 1782, some 250 Indians and 40 British soldiers watched in surprise as the gate of a fort they had surrounded creaked open and a teenage girl darted out. Some of the Indians laughed and called "Squaw!" while the girl ran quickly but coolly across a field toward a cabin sixty yards away and disappeared inside.

Fort Henry, built in 1774 on the Ohio River, protected families settling what is now northern West Virginia. During the Revolutionary War, the British encouraged Indian assaults such as the 1782 attack.

By the second day of the siege, the desperate pioneers inside Fort Henry were running out of gunpowder. Sixteen-year-old Betty Zane volunteered to fetch more from the cabin of her brother, Colonel Ebenezer Zane, where other settlers were holding out.

Betty realized that, since she was a girl, the attackers wouldn't give her trouble on the run to the cabin. The return trip would be something else. When she emerged from the cabin with a tablecloth slung over her shoulder, the besiegers immediately guessed that it was full of gunpowder, and they opened fire.

Bullets "hissed close to her ears and cut the grass in front of her," wrote Western writer Zane Grey, a descendent of Colonel Zane. "They pattered like hail on the stockade-fence, but still untouched, unharmed, the slender brown figure sped toward the gate." Betty reached the fort safely, enabling the defenders to win one of the last battles of the Revolution. The city of Wheeling has taken Fort Henry's place, but the closing lines of an old poem recall the girl's courage.

> Upon those half-cleared, rolling lands,
> A crowded city proudly stands;
> But of the many who reside
> By green Ohio's rushing tide,
> Not one has lineage prouder than
> (Be he poor or rich) the man
> Who boasts that in his spotless strain
> Mingles the blood of Betty Zane.

AMERICAN HISTORY PARADE

1782   Betty Zane runs for more gunpowder during the siege of Fort Henry.

1857   The SS *Central America* sinks in a hurricane off Cape Hatteras, North Carolina, with a loss of about 400 lives and a fortune in gold from California.

1918   In France, U.S. forces launch their first major offensive of World War I.

1954   The TV series *Lassie* premieres.

IN SEPTEMBER 1814, during the War of 1812, a British fleet sailed up the Chesapeake Bay and closed in on Baltimore, Maryland. The bustling port was one of the largest cities in the young United States and a rich prize. To capture it, the British had to get past Fort McHenry, which guarded the harbor. As the ships crept upstream, their crews could see a gigantic American flag fluttering over the fort's walls.

On September 13 the big British guns took aim at the flag and let loose a horrifying fire, including huge bombshells that often blew up in midair. When dark fell, gunpowder-filled Congreve rockets traced fiery arcs across the night sky. It was a spectacular sight.

Francis Scott Key had an agonizing view of the battle. The young American lawyer had sailed out to a British warship before the fighting began to gain the release of a friend being held prisoner. He succeeded, but the British grew concerned he might have picked up information about their plans, so they detained him as the attack got underway. Key had no choice but to wait out the night, pacing the deck and hoping the fort could hold out. When dawn's light finally came on September 14, he spotted the Stars and Stripes still proudly waving through the smoke. Fort McHenry stood, and the British were giving up.

Overcome with emotion, Key scribbled a few lines that began, "O say, can you see by the dawn's early light . . ." A few days later the poem was printed and distributed in Baltimore. People began singing the words to a popular tune, and soon "The Star-Spangled Banner" was a hit. More than a century later, in 1931, Congress designated the song as our national anthem.

AMERICAN HISTORY PARADE

1788   Congress establishes New York City as the temporary national capital and authorizes the first presidential election for the following February 4.

1814   A British fleet bombards Fort McHenry at Baltimore, Maryland, as Francis Scott Key looks on.

1847   During the Mexican War, U.S. troops storm Chapultepec, the fortress guarding Mexico City.

1948   Republican Margaret Chase Smith of Maine is elected to the U.S. Senate, becoming the first woman elected to both houses of Congress.

AT 2:15 AM ON SEPTEMBER 14, 1901, President William McKinley died in Buffalo, New York, from wounds left by an assassin's bullet. A few minutes after 3:30 p.m. on the same day, Theodore Roosevelt stood in the library of a friend's house in Buffalo and took the oath of office to become the twenty-sixth president of the United States. At age forty-two, he was the youngest man ever to assume the office.

"It is a dreadful thing to come into the presidency in this way," Roosevelt observed. Yet he woke the next morning ready to stride into the arena of history, exclaiming "I feel bully!" A friend once said that Roosevelt was a many-sided man and "every side was like an electric battery." Cowboy, explorer, naturalist, Rough Rider, author, politician—he was just the dynamo the young United States needed for a new century. Several years later, in a speech on "Citizenship in a Republic," Teddy Roosevelt described his approach to governing and to life:

It is not the critic who counts: not the man who points out how the strong man stumbles or where the doer of deeds could have done better. The credit belongs to the man who is actually in the arena, whose face is marred by dust and sweat and blood, who strives valiantly, who errs and comes up short again and again, because there is no effort without error or shortcoming, but who knows the great enthusiasms, the great devotions, who spends himself for a worthy cause; who, at the best, knows, in the end, the triumph of high achievement, and who, at the worst, if he fails, at least he fails while daring greatly, so that his place shall never be with those cold and timid souls who knew neither victory nor defeat.

AMERICAN HISTORY PARADE

1716   Boston Light, the first lighthouse in America, is kindled for the first time.

1814   Francis Scott Key writes "The Star-Spangled Banner" after watching the British bombard Fort McHenry in Baltimore during the War of 1812.

1847   U.S. forces, including Marines, capture Mexico City and raise the flag over the "halls of Montezuma."

1975   Elizabeth Ann Seton is canonized as the first American-born Catholic saint.

IN JUNE 1950, when North Korean troops poured over the 38th Parallel and swept across South Korea, Harry Truman realized that the United States had to stop the naked aggression "no matter what." If left unchecked, he argued, the Communists would soon challenge Western defenses elsewhere in Asia, Europe, and Latin America. Truman turned to General Douglas MacArthur, who just five years earlier had stood on the deck of the USS *Missouri* in Tokyo Bay to receive the Japanese surrender that ended World War II.

The 70-year-old MacArthur came up with a plan that was audacity itself. He proposed a seaborne invasion behind the Red lines at Inchon, a port on the northwest coast of South Korea just 25 miles from its capital, Seoul. "We drew up every conceivable natural and geographic handicap, and Inchon had them all," said one of MacArthur's military aids. Those hazards included deadly 30-foot tides, dangerous currents, and a harbor surrounded by sea walls. MacArthur's naval chief could muster no better endorsement of the plan than it was "not impossible." MacArthur kept his own counsel, puffing constantly on his trademark corncob pipe.

The general gathered 261 ships, and on September 15, 1950, the Marines stormed ashore at Inchon. For breathtaking boldness, the assault ranked alongside Washington's crossing of the Delaware and Grant's descent on Shiloh. The invasion caught the North Koreans off guard— they had considered Inchon invulnerable to attack. American troops pushed inland and within eleven days entered Seoul. South Korea's aged president, Syngman Rhee, accepted the return of his liberated capital with tearful gratitude: "We love you," he told MacArthur, "as the savior of our race." The war would last nearly three more years, but the daring landing at Inchon ultimately saved millions of Koreans from a totalitarian regime.

AMERICAN HISTORY PARADE

1776   British forces under General William Howe occupy New York City.

1857   William Howard Taft, the twenty-seventh U.S. president and only president to also serve as chief justice of the Supreme Court, is born in Cincinnati, Ohio.

1858   The Butterfield Overland Mail Company begins the first mail delivery to the Pacific Coast, with stagecoaches running between Tipton, Missouri, and San Francisco.

1950   During the Korean War, U.N. forces led by U.S. Marines land at Inchon.

2001   President George W. Bush names Osama bin Laden as the prime suspect in the September 11 terrorist attacks and warns Americans that a long, hard war against terrorism lies ahead.

ON SEPTEMBER 16, 1620 (September 6, by the Old Style calendar), the Pilgrims boarded the *Mayflower* and set sail from Plymouth, England, for the New World. One hundred and two passengers plus crew crowded onto the tiny ship, which probably measured about 100 feet long and 25 feet wide. William Bradford, longtime governor of the Plymouth Colony, left us a flavor of the perilous two-month voyage across the Atlantic in his book *Of Plymouth Plantation.*

After they had enjoyed fair winds and weather for a season, they were encountered many times with cross winds and met with many fierce storms with which the ship was shroudly [wickedly] shaken, and her upper works made very leaky; and one of the main beams in the midships was bowed and cracked, which put them in some fear that the ship could not be able to perform the voyage. . . . But in examining of all opinions, the master and others affirmed they knew the ship to be strong and firm under water; and for the buckling of the main beam, there was a great iron screw the passengers brought out of Holland, which would raise the beam into his place; the which being done, the carpenter and master affirmed that with a post put under it, set firm in the lower deck and otherwise bound, he would make it sufficient. And as for the decks and upper works, they would caulk them as well as they could, and though with the working of the ship they would not long keep staunch, yet there would otherwise be no great danger, if they did not over-press her with sails. So they committed themselves to the will of God and resolved to proceed.

AMERICAN HISTORY PARADE

1620   The *Mayflower* departs Plymouth, England, for the New World.

1893   In one of the wildest land runs in history, about 100,000 settlers pour into a section of Oklahoma called the Cherokee Strip, to claim homesteads.

1908   William Crapo "Billy" Durant founds General Motors in Flint, Michigan.

1919   Congress grants a national charter to the American Legion.

1940   President Franklin D. Roosevelt signs the Selective Training and Service Act, the first peacetime military draft in the United States.

SEPTEMBER 17, 1787, brought a world-changing event: the signing of the United States Constitution.

The day dawned clear and chilly in Philadelphia, where delegates from the thirteen states had spent a long, hot summer writing and debating the new Constitution for their young country. They assembled in Independence Hall and listened as their work was read aloud one last time. Then they heard an address from old Benjamin Franklin, who urged them all to sign the document. Franklin was too frail to make his speech, so another delegate read it for him.

Thirty-eight delegates filed forward to put their names at the bottom of the Constitution. George Washington signed first as president of the convention. The other delegates signed in geographical order from north to south, starting with New Hampshire and ending with Georgia. Franklin was helped forward from his seat, and it was reported that he wept as he signed. Their work done, the delegates closed the Constitutional Convention, and the document was sent to the states to be ratified.

In writing the Constitution, the Founding Fathers launched a daring experiment. The idea that a free people could begin a new country by designing their own government and writing down the laws and principles they would follow had never been tried before.

The Constitution has guaranteed freedom, equality, opportunity, and justice to hundreds of millions of people. It is the oldest written constitution still in effect and has become a model for nations around the world. It is, as Great Britain's prime minister William Gladstone called it, "the most wonderful work ever struck off at a given time by the brain and purpose of man."

AMERICAN HISTORY PARADE

1630   English Puritans led by John Winthrop found Boston, Massachusetts.

1776   Spanish explorers found the Presidio, around which San Francisco will grow.

1787   The Constitutional Convention approves the final draft of the U.S. Constitution.

1862   Union troops stop a Confederate invasion of Maryland at the Battle of Antietam, the bloodiest day of fighting in the Civil War.

1920   The American Professional Football Association—later renamed the National Football League—is formed in Canton, Ohio.

1978   At the White House, Egyptian president Anwar el-Sadat and Israeli prime minister Menachem Begin sign the Camp David Accords.

THE UNITED STATES AIR FORCE was established on September 18, 1947, when the National Security Act, which made the Air Force an independent branch of the military, went into effect. Fittingly, President Harry Truman signed the law aboard *The Sacred Cow*, the C-54 transport plane used for presidential flights in those days.

The beginnings of an American air-going force stretch back to 1907, less than four years after the Wright Brothers' first powered flight, when the U.S. Army Signal Corps formed an Aeronautical Division. In 1909 the Army bought its first plane, the Wright *Military Flyer*.

When World War I started in Europe, the Army owned only five planes. By the end of the war, military strategists realized that to win battles, they must control the skies. During World War II, the U.S. Army Air Forces reached a peak strength of 80,000 planes. The critical role of air power led Truman to make the Air Force a full partner with the Army and Navy. Today the Air Force maintains more than 5,700 active aircraft.

The U.S. Air Force flag is blue and bears the Air Force coat of arms. The shield carries an image of a pair of wings, a vertical thunderbolt, and lightning flashes—all symbolizing the power to strike from the air. Above the shield, a bald eagle perches in front of a cloud. Thirteen stars surround the coat of arms, representing the thirteen original states. The top three stars also symbolize the Departments of the Army, Navy, and Air Force.

AMERICAN HISTORY PARADE

1793   George Washington lays the cornerstone of the U.S. Capitol.

1850   Congress passes the Fugitive Slave Act, which mandates the return of slaves who escaped into free states or free territories.

1889   In Chicago, reformer Jane Addams establishes Hull House to help working-class people.

1947   The United States Air Force is established.

1984   Retired Air Force colonel Joe Kittinger becomes the first person to complete a solo balloon flight across the Atlantic.

IN A WORLD STILL RULED BY KINGS, President George Washington's decision to not seek a third term clearly signaled that the United States would be governed by the *people*, not any ruler-for-life. Washington's Farewell Address—really an open letter to the American people—appeared in newspapers on September 19, 1796. The president reminded his fellow citizens that national strength rests on the pillars of private morality, especially religion. The word he used to describe those pillars of American democracy is not "optional" or "desirable" or "helpful"; it is "indispensable."

Of all the dispositions and habits which lead to political prosperity, religion and morality are indispensable supports. In vain would that man claim the tribute of patriotism who should labor to subvert these great pillars of human happiness, these firmest props of the duties of men and citizens. The mere politician, equally with the pious man, ought to respect and to cherish them. A volume could not trace all their connections with private and public felicity. Let it simply be asked: Where is security for property, for reputation, for life, if the sense of religious obligation desert the oaths which are the instruments of investigation in courts of justice? And let us with caution indulge the supposition that morality can be maintained without religion. Whatever may be conceded to the influence of refined education on minds of peculiar structure, reason and experience both forbid us to expect that national morality can prevail in exclusion of religious principle.

'Tis substantially true that virtue or morality is a necessary spring of popular government. The rule indeed extends with more or less force to every species of free government. Who that is a sincere friend to it can look with indifference upon attempts to shake the foundation of the fabric?

AMERICAN HISTORY PARADE

1676   In an uprising by some Virginia colonists, Nathaniel Bacon burns Jamestown.

1777   Patriot forces withstand a British attack in the First Battle of Saratoga, New York.

1796   George Washington's Farewell Address is published.

1881   President James Garfield dies of wounds suffered during a July 2 shooting.

1960   Chubby Checker's recording of "The Twist," which gave birth to a popular dance, hits the top of the music charts.

SEPTEMBER 20, 1863, brought the end of the Battle of Chickamauga in northwest Georgia, some of the hardest fighting of the Civil War. As Union casualties streamed into Chattanooga, Tennessee, many soldiers were surprised to find that the doctor tending their wounds was a woman dressed in gold-striped trousers, a green surgeon's sash, and a straw hat with an ostrich feather.

Mary Edwards Walker had graduated from Syracuse Medical College eight years earlier, becoming one of America's first female doctors. That was unusual enough, but Walker set herself even further apart by refusing to wear long, heavy dresses, opting instead for pants. She was born to break molds. When the Civil War began, she volunteered to serve as a doctor. The Army wasn't sure what to make of her, but doctors were in short supply, and she was soon working near Union lines as a volunteer field surgeon. She requested a commission as an officer but was turned down since she was a woman. She went on volunteering, treating both soldiers and civilians. In April 1864 she was captured and spent four months in a Richmond prison until exchanged for a Confederate officer.

After the war the Army awarded Dr. Walker the Medal of Honor in recognition of her service. To Walker, the medal represented the recognition she had so long wanted. She was outraged when, in 1916, the Army decided to rescind more than 900 medals as undeserved—including hers, because she had never officially been in the Army. Walker refused to return her award. On the contrary, she proudly wore it every day for the rest of her life.

In 1977 the Army restored Mary Edwards Walker's medal on the grounds that, had she been a man, she would have been commissioned as an officer. She remains the sole female recipient of the Medal of Honor.

AMERICAN HISTORY PARADE

1863   Confederates win the Battle of Chickamauga in northwest Georgia.

1881   Chester A. Arthur becomes the twenty-first U.S. president after James Garfield's death.

1984   A truck bomb explodes outside the U.S. Embassy near Beirut, Lebanon, killing two dozen people.

1998   Cal Ripken Jr. of the Baltimore Orioles ends his record-breaking streak of playing 2,632 consecutive baseball games spanning sixteen seasons.

2001   In an address to a joint session of Congress, President George W. Bush declares "war on terror."

ON SEPTEMBER 21, 1780, General Benedict Arnold betrayed his country when he gave the British information that could allow them to capture the American fort at West Point on the Hudson River in New York.

At the time, Americans regarded Arnold as a hero for his bravery in the Revolutionary War. He had fought with daring skill at Fort Ticonderoga, Quebec, Valcour Island, and Saratoga. But he grew resentful at promotions other officers received, and he hungered for money to support the lifestyle he enjoyed with his young wife, the beautiful young Peggy Shippen. Arnold began exchanging secret messages with the enemy, offering betrayal in exchange for money and high rank in the British army.

On the night of September 21, he sealed the traitorous deal when he met with Major John André, aide to the commander of all British forces in North America, and handed him detailed information on West Point, which Arnold commanded. Arnold returned to the fort while André, disguised in civilian's clothes, made his way toward the British lines.

Two days later, Patriot militiamen stopped André and were shocked to discover who he was—and that he carried details about West Point in his boots, including some papers in Arnold's handwriting. Arnold was at breakfast when he received word of André's capture. He quickly excused himself, boarded his barge, and escaped to a British warship anchored in the Hudson—aptly named HMS *Vulture*.

Arnold fought for the British for the rest of the Revolution, leading troops that burned Richmond, Virginia, and New London, Connecticut. After the war he went to England, where he died in 1801, scorned by many even there. Like almost all traitors, Arnold acted not for any ideals, but for personal gain, and he earned himself the most infamous name in American history.

AMERICAN HISTORY PARADE

1780   Benedict Arnold gives detailed plans of West Point to Major John André.

1784   The *Pennsylvania Packet and Daily Advertiser*, the first successful American daily newspaper, begins publication in Philadelphia.

1893   In Springfield, Massachusetts, Charles and Frank Duryea take what is believed to be the first gasoline-powered automobile built in the United States for a maiden drive.

1897   The *New York Sun* runs an editorial answering eight-year-old Virginia O'Hanlon's question: "Yes, Virginia, there is a Santa Claus."

1970   *Monday Night Football* debuts on ABC (Browns defeat Jets, 31–21).

NATHAN HALE was teaching school in New London, Connecticut, when the American Revolution began. In July 1775 he closed his schoolhouse doors and joined the Patriot army. He was a captain by late 1776, when the British captured New York City. George Washington desperately needed to know the strength and position of the king's forces, so he asked for a volunteer to go behind enemy lines to gather information. Nathan Hale stepped forward.

Changing his uniform for a plain suit of brown clothes and taking his Yale diploma in hand, Hale disguised himself as a schoolteacher. He slipped through the British lines and gathered the needed information, which he carefully recorded in Latin and hid under the soles of his shoes. His mission accomplished, he began to make his way back. He got past all the British guards except the last ones. They stopped him, searched, and found the secret papers. Nathan Hale was arrested and carried before the British commander, General William Howe.

Howe took one look at the young American in civilian clothes, realized he was a spy, and ordered that he be hung the next morning.

The next several hours were cruel, lonely ones for Nathan Hale. He asked for a minister. His jailor refused. He asked for a Bible. That, too, was denied.

On the morning of September 22, 1776, Hale was led to a spot not far from what is now Central Park in New York City. The British officers who saw him marveled at his calmness and dignity. In the end he stood straight and unflinching. No American can ever forget the words he uttered before they slipped the noose around his neck: "I only regret that I have but one life to lose for my country."

AMERICAN HISTORY PARADE

1776   Nathan Hale is hanged by the British in New York City.

1862   Abraham Lincoln issues the preliminary Emancipation Proclamation, declaring the freedom of all slaves in Confederate-controlled regions as of January 1, 1863.

1975   In San Francisco, President Ford survives a second assassination attempt in three weeks.

1989   Hurricane Hugo, one of the most destructive storms of the twentieth century, comes ashore at Charleston, South Carolina.

SEPTEMBER 23, 1779, brought one of the most storied battles in the history of the U.S. Navy. It happened during the Revolutionary War. Captain John Paul Jones, in command of an aging vessel named the *Bonhomme Richard*, was cruising off England's coast when he encountered the *Serapis*, a British ship of war.

Jones engaged the enemy as night was falling. With the opening broadsides, however, two of the *Richard*'s old cannons exploded, killing crew members and ripping away a chunk of the ship's side. The *Serapis* fired broadside after broadside into the stricken *Richard*. With his ship hit below the water line and leaking badly, Jones knew his only chance was to run into the British vessel and board her decks. He managed to lock the two ships together, but the *Serapis* kept blasting away into the *Richard*'s side, setting its old timbers on fire.

It seemed only a question of time before the American ship would go down. The British commander asked if the *Richard* was ready to surrender. It was then that Jones flung out his famous reply: "I have not yet begun to fight!"

The British shook their heads in disbelief. The Americans fought on. One of them managed to toss a grenade down an open hatch on the *Serapis*'s deck. The grenade hit some gunpowder, and explosions ripped through the British ship. Both vessels were now drifting wrecks. Still Jones refused to give in. After more than three and a half hours of savage battle by moonlight, the British commander surrendered. The victorious Americans boarded the *Serapis* and watched as the *Richard* disappeared beneath the waves.

Today, when the going gets tough, Americans remember the words of Captain John Paul Jones: "I have not yet begun to fight!"

AMERICAN HISTORY PARADE

1642   Harvard College confers upon nine graduates the first bachelor of arts degrees given in America.

1779   John Paul Jones declares, "I have not yet begun to fight!"

1780   John André, a British spy, is captured with papers revealing that Benedict Arnold was planning to surrender West Point to the British.

1806   The Lewis and Clark expedition returns to St. Louis from the Pacific Coast.

1845   The Knickerbocker Base Ball Club of New York, the first baseball team, is organized.

THE SERVICE FLAG (also known as the Blue Star Flag or the Service Star Flag) is a banner authorized by the Department of Defense for display during wartime by families with members serving in the armed forces. The rectangular flag, which has a white field with a red border, holds one blue star (symbolizing hope and pride) for each immediate family member in the armed forces. A blue star is covered with a gold star (symbolizing sacrifice to the cause of freedom) when a family member is killed or dies while serving in the armed forces.

The tradition of the Service Flag dates to World War I, when Captain Robert L. Queissner of the 5th Ohio Infantry designed the banner to honor two sons serving on the front lines. On September 24, 1917, Ohio congressman Ivory Emerson introduced the flag to Congress, explaining that it was a tribute to those families "who gave to this great cause of liberty . . . the dearest thing in all the world to a father and mother—their children." Banners began to appear in the windows of homes across the country, to symbolize loved ones in service.

The Service Flag saw widespread use during World War II but was less popular by the time of the Vietnam War. The tradition began to revive during the 1990 Persian Gulf War and the War on Terror. Organizations such as businesses, churches, and schools may also honor members fighting in the armed forces by displaying Service Flags.

AMERICAN HISTORY PARADE

1789   Congress passes the Judiciary Act, establishing the U.S. Supreme Court and federal judicial system.

1869   Gold prices plummet, causing a financial panic, after financiers Jay Gould and James Fisk try to corner the gold market.

1906   President Theodore Roosevelt signs a bill establishing Devils Tower in Wyoming as the first national monument.

1957   The Brooklyn Dodgers play their final game at Ebbets Field before moving to Los Angeles.

TO BECOME A PILOT, Eddie Rickenbacker had to fib about his age—the second time he'd had to do so to get a job. The first time came in 1904, when he was thirteen. His father had died, and Rickenbacker quit school to help support his family. Child labor laws required workers to be fourteen, so he claimed that age to get a job in a glass factory for $3.50 a week. But he soon developed an interest in the new "horseless carriages" and turned himself into one of the nation's best race car drivers, competing in the Indianapolis 500 and setting a world speed record of 134 miles per hour at Daytona.

When the United States entered World War I, Rickenbacker enlisted and went to France, hoping to become a pilot. "War flying is for youngsters just out of school," he was told. So now he had to claim he was *younger* than his twenty-seven years. He talked his way into the Army Air Service, took pilot's training, and wound up in the 94th Aero Pursuit Squadron, the famous "Hat-in-the-Ring Squadron." In less than three months, he shot down five enemy planes, becoming the second American ace of the war.

On September 25, 1918, while flying alone near Verdun, Rickenbacker spotted seven German aircraft—two reconnaissance planes escorted by five fighter planes. Climbing as high as he could, he switched off his engine, glided toward the rear fighter, and shot it down. Instead of scrambling to safety, he roared into the enemy formation. "I saw tracer bullets go whizzing and streaking past my face," he later recalled. He managed to shoot down one of the reconnaissance planes before turning for home.

For his courage that day, Rickenbacker was awarded the Medal of Honor. Before the war's end, he shot down 26 enemy craft, an American record that earned him the title "Ace of Aces."

AMERICAN HISTORY PARADE

1690   *Publick Occurences Both Foreign and Domestic*, the first American newspaper, is published in Boston (unhappy authorities quickly close it down).

1775   Patriot Ethan Allen is captured by the British during an attack on Montreal.

1789   Congress sends twelve amendments to the Constitution to the states for ratification; ten are later ratified and become the Bill of Rights.

1918   Eddie Rickenbacker earns the Medal of Honor in the skies near Verdun, France.

1957   Army troops escort nine black students into Central High School in Little Rock, Arkansas, to enforce desegregation laws.

1981   Sandra Day O'Connor is sworn in as the first female U.S. Supreme Court justice.

TODAY IS THE BIRTHDAY of John Chapman, better known as Johnny Appleseed, born in 1774 in Leominster, Massachusetts. So much lore surrounds his life, it is difficult to separate fact from fiction, but Chapman was a real man and a folk hero during his own lifetime.

According to one story, he got the idea to plant apple trees after a horse kicked him in the head, which gave him a vision of heaven filled with apple orchards in bloom. Be that as it may, by around 1800 he had headed west and was seen drifting down the Ohio River past Steubenville, Ohio, with two canoes lashed together and loaded with apples from cider presses in western Pennsylvania. He used the cargo to plant trees.

Chapman was a wanderer and an eccentric. He reportedly wore a coffee sack for a shirt and a tin pot for a hat. But he was also a smart businessman in his own way. His strategy was to travel the frontier and plant nurseries where he thought pioneers would settle. By the time they showed up, his young trees were ready to be sold or bartered. He walked thousands of miles, always shoeless, planting and tending orchards scattered through Ohio, Indiana, and Illinois.

It didn't take long for folks to give him the nickname Johnny Appleseed. Stories of his strange kindness are legion. It is said he once put out his campfire because the blaze burned a mosquito. Pioneer families welcomed him on his travels, and he was likely to pull out his Bible and preach news "right fresh from Heaven."

When Chapman died in 1845, he owned about 1,200 acres of nurseries, much of it prime real estate. Far more valuable are the legends he left behind of humble, barefoot Johnny Appleseed.

AMERICAN HISTORY PARADE

1774   John Chapman, a.k.a. Johnny Appleseed, is born in Leominster, Massachusetts.

1777   British troops occupy Philadelphia during the Revolutionary War.

1789   George Washington names Thomas Jefferson as the first secretary of state.

1950   During the Korean War, American-led UN troops recapture Seoul, South Korea, from the North Koreans.

1960   In Chicago, John F. Kennedy and Richard Nixon square off in the first televised presidential election debate.

American Gold Star Mothers is an organization of mothers who have lost a son or daughter in the armed forces. Founded shortly after World War I, the group takes its name from the gold star on the Service Flag that represents a family member lost in the line of duty.

Gold Star Mothers dedicate themselves to honoring their deceased children, performing community service, helping veterans, and healing one another. Congress has designated the last Sunday in September as Gold Star Mothers Day, a time to pay respects to these women who show perseverance and grace despite their own loss.

Gold Star Wives, founded in 1945, is an organization of military widows dedicated to honoring the memory of those who died for their country. Gold Star Wives help one another face the future with courage, and aid the widows and children of soldiers who made the supreme sacrifice. They also promote principles such as justice, freedom, and democracy.

Blue Star Mothers, founded in 1942, is an organization of women who have or have had children serving in the military. The group takes its name from the blue star on the Service Flag that represents a family member serving in the armed forces. Blue Star Mothers support one another and their children, as well as promote patriotism.

AMERICAN HISTORY PARADE

1722   Samuel Adams, a leader in the call for independence from Britain, is born in Boston.

1777   Lancaster, Pennsylvania, becomes the national capital for one day as Congress flees from British-held Philadelphia to York, Pennsylvania.

1936   The first national Gold Star Mothers Day is observed.

1941   In Baltimore, Maryland, the United States launches the SS *Patrick Henry*, the first of more than 2,700 Liberty Ships built to carry cargo during World War II.

1964   The Warren Commission releases a report concluding that Lee Harvey Oswald acted alone in assassinating President John F. Kennedy.

FOOTBALL SEASON is a good time to remember Pat Tillman. As an Arizona State University linebacker he weighed barely 200 pounds, but he gained a reputation for bone-rattling hits and helped lead his team to the Rose Bowl in 1997. His teammates nicknamed him Braveheart.

After college he turned pro, even though critics said he was too small and slow for the NFL. The Arizona Cardinals took him as their next-to-last draft pick. In 2000 he set a team record with 224 tackles in a single season.

Then came the terrorist attacks of September 11, 2001, and Tillman started thinking about things larger than football. He spoke of family members who had fought for their country, such as his great-grandfather at Pearl Harbor. "I haven't done a damn thing as far as laying myself on the line like that," he said. Eight months later, Tillman shocked the sports world by turning down a $3.6 million football contract and joining the Army with his brother.

He enlisted without fanfare, refusing to talk to the press about his decision. "He truly felt committed and felt a sense of honor and duty," his Cardinals coach said. He joined the Army Rangers, an elite outfit that routinely goes in harm's way. On April 22, 2004, he was on patrol near an isolated mud-brick village in southeast Afghanistan, a region rife with terrorist operatives, when gunfire erupted. Pat Tillman was killed by friendly fire. He was twenty-seven.

Controversy later erupted with revelations that Army officers initially hid the fact that U.S. troops accidentally shot Tillman. That does not diminish his own sacrifice.

Very few walk away from riches and fame to serve as Tillman did. But there are many who quietly and humbly protect American ideals with everything they have to offer— including their lives. As one of his coaches said, "The spirit of Pat Tillman is the heart of this country."

AMERICAN HISTORY PARADE

1542   Portuguese navigator Juan Rodriguez Cabrillo sails into San Diego Bay, becoming the first known European to explore the Californian coast.

1781   American and French troops begin a siege of the British at Yorktown, Virginia.

1787   Congress votes to transmit the new Constitution to the states for ratification.

1924   Two Army planes land in Seattle to complete the first aerial circumnavigation of the world, which lasted 175 days and took 57 stops.

2001   President George W. Bush reiterates the U.S. demand that Afghanistan's Taliban government turn over all terrorists it has been harboring.

ON THE NIGHT OF SEPTEMBER 29, 1780, militia loyal to King George III were camped on Black Mingo Creek in coastal South Carolina when suddenly a Patriot force materialized out of the steamy darkness with guns blazing. The surprised Tories put up a sharp defense but soon fled across the Santee River, leaving behind their supplies and ammunition.

Francis Marion had struck again.

One of the heroes of the American Revolution, Marion was a short, quiet man who wore a sword so seldom drawn it rusted in its scabbard. His men knew the secret paths of the low-country swamps, and like phantoms they could appear out of cypress mazes for quick surprise attacks against much larger forces before melting away to the dark recesses of their forest retreats. Most were farmers, fighting without pay. Few had uniforms of any kind. They were always short on guns, ammunition, and food, but they fought with the zeal of true Patriots.

Marion's guerrilla warfare kept the British in a constant state of confusion and alarm. With grudging respect, the redcoats began to refer to him as the Swamp Fox.

It is said that one day Marion invited a British officer to dinner in his camp under a flag of truce and served a meal of fire-baked potatoes on a slab of bark, with vinegar and water to wash it down. His guest was surprised at how little the Patriots had to eat. "But surely, General," he inquired, "this can't be your usual fare?"

"Indeed, sir, it is," Marion replied, "and we are fortunate on this occasion, entertaining company, to have more than our usual allowance."

The story goes that the British officer was so overcome by the Americans' determination and sacrifice that he resigned his commission and sailed back to England.

AMERICAN HISTORY PARADE

1780   Patriots under General Francis Marion surprise loyalist forces on Black Mingo Creek, South Carolina.

1892   At Mansfield, Pennsylvania, the first nighttime football game is played when Mansfield Teachers College faces Wyoming Seminary beneath twenty electric lights.

1915   In the first transcontinental demonstration of radiotelephone, speech is transmitted from New York City to Honolulu.

1957   Baseball's New York Giants play their final game at the Polo Grounds, losing to the Pittsburgh Pirates 9–1, before moving to San Francisco the next season.

1988   The space shuttle *Discovery* lifts off on the first shuttle flight since the 1986 *Challenger* disaster.

THE END OF WORLD WAR II left Germany divided into two rival systems. Western Germany, occupied by the United States, Britain, and France, was a free zone with a rebounding economy. Eastern Germany, controlled by Soviet Communists, was a grim, totalitarian police state. The city of Berlin, Hitler's old capital, was divided the same way, but it lay deep inside Communist East Germany.

In 1948 Soviet dictator Joseph Stalin moved to take all of Berlin by closing roads and train tracks leading into the city's free, western portion. Sealed off from the rest of the world, more than 2 million West Berliners faced starvation. Harry Truman realized he could not get supplies to the city by ground without starting World War III. So he decided to do it by *air*.

Thus began the Berlin Airlift, one of history's greatest humanitarian efforts. Beginning in June 1948, American and British planes made more than 277,000 flights delivering food, coal, medicine, and other supplies. At times, planes landed in West Berlin as often as every four minutes. Just a few years earlier, Allied bombers had been pounding Berlin to rubble. Now U.S. cargo planes dropped candy by parachute to German children, who scrambled to retrieve it.

Nearly one hundred U.S. and British servicemen lost their lives during the operation. But after eleven months, Stalin gave in and lifted the blockade. The planes kept flying through September 30, 1949, to build emergency stockpiles. In all, they delivered some 2.3 million tons of supplies, more than a ton for every man, woman, and child. As a result of the Berlin Airlift and the heroic struggle of the West Berliners, freedom survived in its most exposed outpost.

AMERICAN HISTORY PARADE

1777   Forced to flee Philadelphia, the Continental Congress meets in York, Pennsylvania.

1868   Louisa May Alcott publishes *Little Women*.

1882   The world's first hydroelectric power plant to furnish incandescent lighting begins operation in Appleton, Wisconsin.

1889   Wyoming legislators write the first state constitution granting women suffrage.

1935   President Franklin D. Roosevelt dedicates Hoover Dam on the Colorado River.

1949   The fifteen-month-long Berlin Airlift comes to an end.

Songs of American Patriotism

The Star-spangled Banner

Francis Scott Key

Francis Scott Key wrote this poem during the War of 1812 after witnessing the British bombardment of Fort McHenry in Baltimore's harbor on September 13–14, 1814. It was printed on broadsides and sung to a tune called "To Anacreon in Heaven." Congress designated it the National Anthem in 1931.

Oh say, can you see by the dawn's early light
What so proudly we hailed at the twilight's last gleaming?
Whose broad stripes and bright stars, through the perilous fight,
O'er the ramparts we watched, were so gallantly streaming?
And the rockets' red glare, the bombs bursting in air,
Gave proof through the night that our flag was still there.
Oh say, does that Star-Spangled Banner yet wave
O'er the land of the free and the home of the brave?

On the shore dimly seen, through the mists of the deep,
Where the foe's haughty host in dread silence reposes,
What is that which the breeze, o'er the towering steep,
As it fitfully blows, half conceals, half discloses?

Now it catches the gleam of the morning's first beam,
In full glory reflected, now shines on the stream:
'Tis the Star-Spangled Banner! Oh long may it wave
O'er the land of the free and the home of the brave!

And where is that band who so vauntingly swore
That the havoc of war and the battle's confusion,
A home and a country should leave us no more?
Their blood has washed out their foul footsteps' pollution.
No refuge could save the hireling and slave
From the terror of flight or the gloom of the grave.
And the Star-Spangled Banner in triumph doth wave
O'er the land of the free and the home of the brave!

Oh, thus be it ever when free men shall stand
Between their loved homes and the war's desolation!
Blest with victory and peace, may the heav'n-rescued land
Praise the Power that hath made and preserved us a nation.
Then conquer we must, when our cause it is just,
And this be our motto: "In God is our trust."
And the Star-Spangled Banner in triumph shall wave
O'er the land of the free and the home of the brave!

AMERICA

Samuel Francis Smith

Samuel Francis Smith wrote the words to this hymn in 1831 in Andover, Massachusetts, where he was studying to become a Baptist minister. He penned it to fit a melody he found in a German songbook. The British anthem "God Save the King" uses the same melody. Smith's patriotic hymn was first sung in public later that year at a Boston church school's Fourth of July celebration.

My country, 'tis of Thee,
Sweet Land of Liberty
Of thee I sing.
Land where my fathers died,
Land of the Pilgrims' pride,
From every mountain side
Let freedom ring.

My native country, thee,
Land of the noble free
Thy name I love.
I love thy rocks and rills
Thy woods and templed hills
My heart with rapture thrills
Like that above.

Let music swell the breeze
And ring from all the trees
Sweet freedom's song.
Let mortal tongues awake
Let all that breathe partake
Let rocks their silence break
The sound prolong.

Our fathers' God, to Thee,
Author of Liberty
To Thee we sing.
Long may our land be bright
With freedom's holy light,
Protect us by Thy might
Great God, our King.

AMERICA THE BEAUTIFUL

Katharine Lee Bates

Educator Katharine Lee Bates was inspired to write this hymn in 1893 after seeing her country from atop snow-capped Pikes Peak in Colorado. The words are set to the music of Samuel A. Ward's "Materna."

O beautiful for spacious skies,
For amber waves of grain,
For purple mountain majesties
Above the fruited plain!
America! America!
God shed His grace on thee,
And crown thy good with brotherhood
From sea to shining sea!

O beautiful for pilgrim feet,
Whose stern, impassioned stress
A thoroughfare for freedom beat
Across the wilderness!
America! America!
God mend thine every flaw,
Confirm thy soul in self-control,
Thy liberty in law!

O beautiful for heroes proved
In liberating strife,
Who more than self their country loved,
And mercy more than life!
America! America!
May God thy gold refine,

Till all success be nobleness,
And every gain divine!

O beautiful for patriot dream
That sees beyond the years
Thine alabaster cities gleam
Undimmed by human tears!
America! America!
God shed His grace on thee,
And crown thy good with brotherhood
From sea to shining sea!

YANKEE DOODLE

British soldiers reportedly sang "Yankee Doodle" during the French and Indian War to make fun of ragged Colonial troops, but instead of being offended, Americans adopted the song. "Yankee," originally a nickname for New Englanders, may have come from *Yengee*, an Indian pronunciation for the word *English*. A "doodle" was a nitwit. "Macaroni" was slang for a dandy young man who liked to dress in style.

Yankee Doodle went to town
A-riding on a pony
Stuck a feather in his hat
And called it macaroni.

Chorus:
Yankee Doodle, keep it up
Yankee Doodle dandy
Mind the music and the step
And with the girls be handy.

Father and I went down to camp
Along with Captain Gooding
And there we saw the men and boys
As thick as hasty pudding.

There was Captain Washington
Upon a slapping stallion
A-giving orders to his men
I guess there was a million.

And there I saw a wooden drum
With heads made out of leather,
They knocked upon it with some sticks
To call the folks together.

And then they'd fife away like fun
And play on cornstalk fiddles,
And some had ribbons red as blood
All bound around their middles.

But I can't tell you half I saw,
They kept up such a smother,
So I took my hat off, made a bow,
And scampered home to mother.

COLUMBIA, THE GEM OF THE OCEAN

First published in 1843, "Columbia, the Gem of the Ocean" was a favorite patriotic song through the early twentieth century. It remains a popular concert band tune. "Columbia" is a poetic name for the United States. In Great Britain, the same tune is known as "Britannia, the Pride of the Ocean."

O, Columbia! the gem of the ocean,
The home of the brave and the free,
The shrine of each patriot's devotion,
A world offers homage to thee.
Thy mandates make heroes assemble
When Liberty's form stands in view.
Thy banners make tyranny tremble
When borne by the red, white and blue!
When borne by the red, white and blue!
When borne by the red, white and blue!
Thy banners make tyranny tremble
When borne by the red, white and blue!

When war wing'd its wide desolation,
And threaten'd the land to deform,
The ark then of freedom's foundation,
Columbia rode safe thro' the storm;
With her garlands of vict'ry around her,
When so proudly she bore her brave crew,
With her flag proudly floating before her,
The boast of the red, white and blue!
The boast of the red, white and blue!
The boast of the red, white, and blue!
With her flag proudly floating before her,
The boast of the red, white and blue!

The Star-Spangled Banner bring hither,
O'er Columbia's true sons let it wave!
May the wreaths they have won never wither,
Nor its stars cease to shine on the brave.

May thy service, united ne'er sever,
But hold to their colors so true.
The Army and Navy forever,
Three cheers for the red, white and blue!
Three cheers for the red, white and blue!
Three cheers for the red, white and blue!
The Army and Navy forever,
Three cheers for the red, white and blue!

BATTLE HYMN OF THE REPUBLIC

Julia Ward Howe

Abolitionist Julia Ward Howe wrote "Battle Hymn of the Republic" during the Civil War after hearing Union soldiers singing "John Brown's Body," the words of which were set to the tune of a hymn. A clergyman suggested she compose new words for the tune. Union troops quickly adopted her lyrics after their publication in the *Atlantic Monthly* in 1862.

Mine eyes have seen the glory of the coming of the Lord.
He is trampling out the vintage where the grapes of wrath are stored.
He hath loosed the fateful lightning of His terrible swift sword.
His truth is marching on.

Chorus:
Glory, glory hallelujah!
Glory, glory hallelujah!
Glory, glory hallelujah!
His truth is marching on.

I have seen Him in the watch fires of a hundred circling camps.
They have builded Him an altar in the evening dews and damps.

I can read His righteous sentence by the dim and flaring lamps.
His day is marching on.

I have read a fiery gospel writ in burnished rows of steel:
"As ye deal with My contemners, so with you My grace shall deal."
Let the Hero born of woman crush the serpent with His heel
Since God is marching on.

He has sounded forth the trumpet that shall never call retreat.
He is sifting out the hearts of men before His judgment seat.
Oh be swift, my soul, to answer Him! Be jubilant, my feet!
Our God is marching on.

In the beauty of the lilies Christ was born across the sea
With a glory in His bosom that transfigures you and me.
As He died to make men holy, let us die to make men free,
While God is marching on.

In times of peace, the line "As He died to make men holy, let us die to make men free" is often changed to, "As He died to make men holy, let us live to make men free."

When Johnny Comes Marching Home

Patrick S. Gilmore

Irish immigrant Patrick Sarsfield Gilmore, a famous bandleader of the nineteenth century, wrote this song during the Civil War to honor returning soldiers. Military bands still play it as American troops arrive home from overseas.

When Johnny comes marching home again
Hurrah! hurrah!

We'll give him a hearty welcome then
Hurrah! hurrah!
The men will cheer and the boys will shout
The ladies, they will all turn out
And we'll all feel gay
When Johnny comes marching home.

The old church-bell will peal with joy
Hurrah! hurrah!
To welcome home our darling boy
Hurrah! hurrah!
The village lads and lasses say
With roses they will strew the way
And we'll all feel gay
When Johnny comes marching home.

Get ready for the jubilee
Hurrah! hurrah!
We'll give the hero three times three
Hurrah! hurrah!
The laurel wreath is ready now
To place upon his loyal brow
And we'll all feel gay
When Johnny comes marching home.

Let love and friendship on that day
Hurrah! hurrah!
Their choicest treasures then display
Hurrah! hurrah!
And let each one perform some part

To fill with joy the warrior's heart.
And we'll all feel gay
When Johnny comes marching home.

STARS AND STRIPES FOREVER

John Philip Sousa

John Philip Sousa wrote "Stars and Stripes Forever" in 1896, and his band played it at almost every concert until his death more than thirty-five years later. In 1987 Congress designated it the national march.

Hurrah for the flag of the free!
May it wave as our standard forever,
The gem of the land and the sea,
The banner of the right.
Let despots remember the day
When our fathers with mighty endeavor
Proclaimed as they marched to the fray
That by their might and by their right
It waves forever.

I'M A YANKEE DOODLE DANDY

George M. Cohan

This song, from George Cohan's 1904 musical *Little Johnny Jones*, was an immediate hit with Americans. *Yankee Doodle Dandy* became the title of the 1942 Hollywood musical celebrating Cohan's life and career.

I'm a Yankee Doodle Dandy,
A Yankee Doodle, do or die,

A real live nephew of my Uncle Sam
Born on the Fourth of July.

I've got a Yankee Doodle sweetheart.
She's my Yankee Doodle joy.
Yankee Doodle came to London
Just to ride the ponies.
I am a Yankee Doodle Boy.

YOU'RE A GRAND OLD FLAG

George M. Cohan

Broadway great George M. Cohan wrote this tune for his 1906 musical *George Washington, Jr.* The idea for the song came when he heard a Civil War veteran affectionately say of his battalion's tattered banner, "She's a grand old rag." The song's original title was "You're a Grand Old Rag," but when some objected to referring to the Stars and Stripes that way, Cohan changed "Rag" to "Flag."

You're a grand old flag,
You're a high flying flag
And forever in peace may you wave.
You're the emblem of
The land I love.
The home of the free and the brave.

Every heart beats true
'Neath the Red, White and Blue,
Where there's never a boast or brag.
Should auld acquaintance be forgot,
Keep your eye on the grand old flag.

OVER THERE

George M. Cohan

George Cohan wrote "Over There" in 1917 shortly after the United States entered World War I. In 1936 Congress awarded him the Congressional Gold Medal for this song and other works. It is still a favorite band tune.

> Over there, over there,
> Send the word, send the word over there—
> That the Yanks are coming,
> The Yanks are coming,
> The drums rum-tumming
> Everywhere.
> So prepare, say a prayer,
> Send the word, send the word to beware.
> We'll be over, we're coming over,
> And we won't come back till it's over,
> Over there.

GOD BLESS AMERICA

Irving Berlin

When Russian immigrant Irving Berlin wrote his original version of "God Bless America" during World War I, he wasn't quite satisfied with the song, so he laid it aside for twenty years. In 1938, when singer Kate Smith asked Berlin for a patriotic song she could perform on the radio in honor of Armistice Day (now Veterans Day), he dug up his old composition, made some changes, and gave it to her. The immensely popular song has been called America's unofficial national anthem.

God bless America,
Land that I love,
Stand beside her and guide her
Through the night with a light from above.
From the mountains, to the prairies,
To the oceans white with foam,
God bless America,
My home sweet home.[1]

THE ARMY GOES ROLLING ALONG

"The Army Goes Rolling Along" is based on the famous field artillery song
"The Caissons Go Rolling Along," written by Edmund Louis Gruber when he
was a lieutenant in the Philippines in 1908. During World War I, bandleader
John Philip Sousa popularized the tune by performing it as a spirited march.
The Army updated the lyrics in the 1950s.

First to fight, for the right,
And to build the nation's might,
And the Army goes rolling along.
Proud of all we have done,
Fighting till the battle's won
And the Army goes rolling along.

Chorus:
Then it's Hi! Hi! Hey!
The Army's on its way.
Count off the cadence loud and strong
(Two! Three!)
For where e'er we go, you will always know,
That the Army goes rolling along.

Valley Forge, Custer's ranks,
San Juan Hill and Patton's tanks,
And the Army went rolling along.
Minute men, from the start,
Always fighting from the heart,
And the Army keeps rolling along.

Men in rags, men who froze,
Still that Army met its foes,
And the Army went rolling along.
Faith in God, then we're right,
And we'll fight with all our might,
As the Army keeps rolling along.

Older Lyrics:
Over hill, over dale
As we hit the dusty trail,
And the caissons go rolling along.
In and out, hear them shout,
Counter march and right about,
And the caissons go rolling along.

Then it's Hi! Hi! Hee!
In the field artillery,
Shout out your numbers loud and strong,
For where e'er you go,
You will always know
That the caissons go rolling along.

ANCHORS AWEIGH

"Anchors Aweigh" is the song of the U.S. Navy. The tune was composed by Lt. Charles A. Zimmermann in 1906. The original lyrics were written by Midshipmen Alfred Hart Miles and Royal Lovell as a football fight song for the U.S. Naval Academy in Annapolis. The revised lyrics are by George D. Lottman.

Stand, Navy, out to sea, Fight our battle cry.
We'll never change our course, so vicious foe steer shy-y-y-y.
Roll out the TNT, Anchors aweigh. Sail on to victory
And sink their bones to Davy Jones, hooray!

Anchors aweigh, my boys, Anchors aweigh.
Farewell to foreign shores, we sail at break of day-ay-ay-ay.
Through our last night on shore, drink to the foam,
Until we meet once more. Here's wishing you a happy voyage home.

Original Lyrics
Stand Navy down the field, sails set to the sky.
We'll never change our course, so Army you steer shy-y-y-y.
Roll up the score, Navy, Anchors Aweigh.
Sail Navy down the field and sink the Army, sink the Army Grey.

Get underway, Navy, Decks cleared for the fray,
We'll hoist true Navy Blue So Army down your Grey-y-y-y.
Full speed ahead, Navy; Army heave to,
Furl Black and Grey and Gold and hoist the Navy, hoist the Navy Blue.

Blue of the Seven Seas; Gold of God's great sun
Let these our colors be Till all of time be done-n-n-ne,
By Severn shore we learn Navy's stern call:
Faith, courage, service true With honor over, honor over all.

THE MARINES' HYMN

The opening lines of this song were inspired by some early exploits of the Marine Corps. In 1805, in the war against the Barbary States of North Africa, a small force of Marines led the storming of a stronghold at Derna, Tripoli (now Libya). It was the first time an American flag was hoisted over a fortress of the Old World. In 1847, during the Mexican War, Marines helped capture Mexico City and raise the flag over Chapultee Castle, otherwise known as the "Halls of Montezuma."

From the Halls of Montezuma
To the shores of Tripoli,
We fight our country's battles
In the air, on land, and sea.
First to fight for right and freedom
And to keep our honor clean,
We are proud to claim the title
Of United States Marine.

Our flag's unfurled to every breeze
From dawn to setting sun.
We have fought in every clime and place
Where we could take a gun.
In the snow of far off northern lands
And in sunny tropic scenes,
You will find us always on the job—
The United States Marines.

Here's health to you and to our Corps
Which we are proud to serve.
In many a strife we've fought for life

And never lost our nerve.
If the Army and the Navy
Ever look on Heaven's scenes,
They will find the streets are guarded
By United States Marines.

SEMPER PARATUS

Francis Saltus Van Boskerck

In **1922** Captain Francis Saltus Van Boskerck wrote the original words to the Coast Guard song in the cabin of a cutter in Savannah, Georgia. Five years later, while stationed in the remote Aleutian Islands, Alaska, he used an old piano owned by a fur trader to compose the music. *Semper Paratus* ("Always Ready") had long been a Revenue Cutter and Coast Guard slogan. Van Boskerck's lyrics have been revised several times over the years.

From Aztec Shore to Arctic Zone
To Europe and Far East.
The Flag is carried by our ships,
In times of war and peace.
And never have we struck it yet
In spite of foe-men's might,
Who cheered our crews and cheered again,
For showing how to fight.

Chorus:
We're always ready for the call,
We place our trust in Thee.
Through surf and storm and howling gale,
High shall our purpose be.

"Semper Paratus" is our guide,
Our fame, our glory, too.
To fight to save or fight and die,
Aye! Coast Guard we are for you!

Hail to the Chief

English composer James Sanderson wrote the music known as "Hail to the Chief" around 1810 for a play based on Sir Walter Scott's poem *The Lady of the Lake*. The melody may have been adapted from an old Scottish air. The tune reached the United States by 1812. It is said that in the 1840s, First Lady Julia Tyler started the custom of having the song played to announce the arrival of the president. The tradition continued over the years, and gradually the piece came to be America's official presidential anthem. There are words to the music, but they are almost never sung—which is probably for the best.

Hail to the Chief we have chosen for the nation,
Hail to the Chief! We salute him, one and all.
Hail to the Chief, as we pledge co-operation
In proud fulfillment of a great, noble call.

Yours is the aim to make this grand country grander,
This you will do, that's our strong, firm belief.
Hail to the one we selected as commander,
Hail to the President! Hail to the Chief!

Taps

Daniel Butterfield

This famous bugle call was composed by Union general Daniel Butterfield in July 1862, during the Civil War. Butterfield (who most likely revised an older call) wanted a somber tune to signal the day's end. Today "Taps" is sounded at funerals, memorial services, and to signal "lights out." There are no official words to the music, but popular verses include:

Fading light dims the sight
And a star gems the sky, gleaming bright
From afar drawing nigh,
Falls the night.

Day is done, gone the sun
From the hills, from the lake, from the sky
All is well, safely rest;
God is nigh.

Then goodnight, peaceful night;
Till the light of the dawn shineth bright.
God is near, do not fear,
Friend, goodnight.

OCTOBER

ON OCTOBER 1, 1996, Congress declared Agnes Gonxha Bojaxhiu, better known as Mother Teresa, an honorary citizen of the United States. A native of what is now the Republic of Macedonia, the Roman Catholic nun spent a lifetime helping orphaned and abandoned children, the poor, the sick, and the dying in regions throughout the world, including the United States.

Only a handful of non-citizens have been declared honorary U.S. citizens. According to Congress, it is "an extraordinary honor not lightly conferred nor frequently granted." The other honorary citizens are:

- 🏛 **Winston Churchill** (1963), the great British statesmen whose "bravery, charity and valor, both in war and in peace, have been a flame of inspiration in freedom's darkest hour," as President Kennedy put it.

- 🏛 **Raoul Wallenberg** (1981), the Swedish businessman who risked his life to save tens of thousands of Hungarian Jews from the Nazis, and who died after being imprisoned by Soviet authorities.

- 🏛 **William Penn** (1984), the English Quaker who in 1681 founded Pennsylvania to carry out an experiment based upon representative government, and his wife, **Hannah Penn**, who administered the Province of Pennsylvania for six years.

- 🏛 **The Marquis de Lafayette** (2002), the French soldier and statesman who fought alongside American Patriots during the Revolutionary War. An American flag flies over his grave in Paris.

In 2007 the U.S. Senate passed a resolution to make Casimir Pulaski, the Polish-born hero of the American Revolution, an honorary citizen. If the House follows suit and the president signs the legislation, Pulaski would become the seventh person to be so recognized.

AMERICAN HISTORY PARADE

1811   The first steamboat to travel down the Mississippi River, the *New Orleans*, reaches its namesake city after a monthlong trip from Pittsburgh.

1890   Yosemite National Park is established.

1908   Henry Ford introduces the Model T automobile, priced at $850.

1924   Jimmy Carter, the thirty-ninth U.S. president, is born in Plains, Georgia.

1942   The first U.S. jet, the Bell XP-59A, makes its maiden flight at Muroc Dry Lake, California.

1971   Disney World, the number-one tourist destination in the world, opens in Orlando, Florida.

THE U.S. SUPREME COURT begins its work year on the first Monday in October. The term opens with the traditional chant of the court crier: "Oyez! Oyez! Oyez! All persons having business before the Honorable, the Supreme Court of the United States, are admonished to draw near and give their attention, for the Court is now sitting. God save the United States and this Honorable Court!" *Oyez* is an old Anglo-French term meaning "Hear ye."

The nine black-robed justices meet in Washington, D.C., in a courthouse resembling a Roman temple, one of the largest marble buildings in the world. Carved above the main entrance are the words EQUAL JUSTICE UNDER LAW.

One of the Court's many traditions, the "Conference handshake," dates to the late nineteenth century. When the justices gather to sit on the bench, and when they meet in private to discuss decisions, each shakes hands with the other eight. According to the Supreme Court, Chief Justice Melville W. Fuller began the practice "as a reminder that differences of opinion on the Court did not preclude overall harmony of purpose."

The justices and their clerks stay busy, with more than **10,000** cases on the docket each term. The Supreme Court hears oral arguments in about **100** cases and produces thousands of pages of written opinions each year.

The Court's main job is to interpret and protect the Constitution. Few other courts in the world have such power, and none has exercised it as long. As Chief Justice Charles Evans Hughes observed, the U.S. Supreme Court is "distinctly American in concept and function."

AMERICAN HISTORY PARADE

1780   In Tappan, New York, British major John André is hanged as a spy after he is captured carrying papers for traitor Benedict Arnold.

1835   The Texas Revolution against Mexico begins as American settlers resist Mexican troops at Gonzales.

1919   President Woodrow Wilson suffers a stroke that leaves him an invalid.

1950   The comic strip *Peanuts* by Charles M. Schulz is first published.

1967   Thurgood Marshall, the first black justice on the U.S. Supreme Court, is sworn in.

AS A GIRL, Mary McLeod Bethune dreamed of becoming a missionary in Africa. Born in 1875 to parents who had been slaves, she grew up near Maysville, South Carolina, working in cotton fields. Her burning desire to learn made her the star student in Maysville's one-room school for black children. Scholarships led to more schooling in North Carolina, and then at Dwight Moody's Institute for Home and Foreign Missions in Chicago. After finishing her studies, she learned there were "no openings for Negro missionaries in Africa."

Undeterred, she embarked on a career as an educator. On October 3, 1904, with $1.50 in cash—all the money she had—she opened the Daytona Literacy and Industrial School for Training Negro Girls in a cottage in Daytona Beach, Florida. The school started with five pupils. Bethune used crates for desks, made ink from elderberries, and sold sweet potato pies to raise funds. She convinced wealthy businessmen to support her efforts. "Invest in a human soul," she urged them. The school grew, and today it lives on as Bethune-Cookman University.

One night in 1920, eighty hooded Ku Klux Klansmen appeared outside the school, waving a burning cross. They had heard Bethune was registering black voters, and threatened to burn the school. If you do, we'll rebuild it, she answered. The Klansmen rode away, and the next day Bethune led a procession of blacks to the polls.

Her courage won the admiration of Franklin and Eleanor Roosevelt. In 1936, she became the first black woman to head a federal agency, the Division of Negro Affairs of the National Youth Administration. Bethune joined other prominent blacks to form FDR's "black cabinet," an informal committee that advised the president on racial issues. "There can be no divided democracy, no class government, no half-free county, under the Constitution," she wrote. Her life moved the country toward those ideals.

AMERICAN HISTORY PARADE

1899 John S. Thurman of St. Louis patents the first motor-driven vacuum cleaner, described as a "pneumatic carpet renovator."

1904 Mary McLeod Bethune opens the Daytona Literacy and Industrial School for Training Negro Girls.

1922 Rebecca L. Felton becomes the first woman to serve in the U.S. Senate when the governor of Georgia appoints her to fill a vacancy.

1955 *Captain Kangaroo* and *The Mickey Mouse Club* debut on TV.

1974 Frank Robinson of the Cleveland Indians becomes the first black manager in baseball's major leagues.

HIGH ON A GRANITE CLIFF in the Black Hills of South Dakota stand the massive carved images of four presidents who led the United States from colonial times into the twentieth century: George Washington, Thomas Jefferson, Abraham Lincoln, and Theodore Roosevelt. Rising more than 500 feet above the valley, the four heroes seem to gaze over an evergreen sea to the rim of the continent.

Danish-American sculptor Gutzon Borglum chose the site for Mount Rushmore National Memorial, declaring that "American history shall march along that skyline." The mountain itself had been named for Charles E. Rushmore, a New York lawyer who once owned mining property in the area.

On October 4, 1927, the job of carving the gigantic faces began. It lasted for fourteen years. About 400 workers toiled on the mountain, and many began each day by climbing 700 stair steps to the top and strapping themselves into swing seats before being lowered by cables over the mountain face. Dangling in the air, they blasted and drilled away nearly a half million tons of stone, carving faces as tall as a five-story building.

Borglum's original vision was a sculpture depicting the four presidents to their waists, but time and money limited the carving to their heads. Borglum himself died before Roosevelt's head was finished, and his son Lincoln finished the work on October 31, 1941.

The great project reaffirmed Americans' dedication to democracy in a world increasingly threatened by bloody dictators. It reaffirms still. Mount Rushmore is not really a tribute to the leaders etched into South Dakota's Black Hills; it is a tribute to the people who chose such leaders—and continue to choose them time and time again. It is a breathtaking place.

AMERICAN HISTORY PARADE

1777   Patriot troops launch a failed assault on the British at Germantown, Pennsylvania.

1822   Rutherford B. Hayes, the nineteenth U.S. president, is born in Delaware, Ohio.

1830   Isaac Adams of Boston patents a motorized printing press that helps enable the mass publication of books.

1895   The first U.S. Open golf tournament is played in Newport, Rhode Island.

1927   Carving begins on Mount Rushmore National Memorial.

OCTOBER 5 IS THE BIRTHDAY of Jonathan Edwards, born in 1703 in East Windsor, Connecticut. The Congregational minister's preaching and writing made him one of the most important figures in colonial America. His famous sermon "Sinners in the Hands of an Angry God" threatened doom for the unrepentant ("The God that holds you over the pit of Hell, much as one holds a spider, or some loathsome insect, over the fire, abhors you, and is dreadfully provoked") but also emphasized the transforming power of Christ's love ("Christ has flung the door of mercy wide open, and stands in the door calling").

Edwards became an influential voice in the Great Awakening, the religious revival that swept the colonies in the 1730s and '40s. Ministers with powerful preaching styles, such as George Whitefield from England, attracted huge audiences. Many established religious authorities, including Church of England officials, rejected the emotion-filled gatherings, but thousands of Americans listened spellbound. Even Ben Franklin, a genial skeptic, was moved. "It was wonderful to see the change soon made in the manner of our inhabitants. . . . [O]ne could not walk through the town in an evening without hearing psalms sung in different families of every street," he wrote.

The Great Awakening was a religious movement, but it ultimately affected the politics of the era. It was the first truly mass movement in America, helping the colonists find a common identity. Many preachers emphasized democratic theories, such as that all people stand equal in the eyes of God, and that churches should be run by the people, not kings or bishops. As historians have noted, colonists who had already rejected the authority of a powerful clergy tied to the British monarchy were more likely to reject as well the power of royal officials.

AMERICAN HISTORY PARADE

1703   Theologian Jonathan Edwards is born in East Windsor, Connecticut.

1829   Chester A. Arthur, the twenty-first U.S. president, is born in Fairfield, Vermont.

1877   Nez Perce leader Chief Joseph surrenders to the U.S. Army in the Bear Paw Mountains of Montana after a long-fought retreat.

1931   Clyde Pangborn and Hugh Herndon land at Wenatchee, Washington, to complete the first nonstop flight across the Pacific, having flown from Japan.

1947   In the first televised White House address, President Truman urges Americans to conserve meat and poultry to help save grain for a hungry Europe.

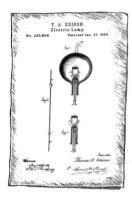

T. A. EDISON.
Electric-Lamp.
No. 223,898. Patented Jan. 27, 1880.

ON OCTOBER 6, 1942, inventor Chester Carlson patented xerography, the process that led to the development of modern photocopying machines. Ever since Benjamin Franklin invented the lightning rod and bifocal lenses, Americans have been busy coming up with one amazing idea after another. The *London Times* once wrote that "the American invents as the Greek sculpted and the Italian painted. It is genius." Here are just a few of the many American inventions that have changed billions of lives.

mechanical reaper	1834	**Cyrus McCormick**
sewing machine	1846	**Elias Howe**
telephone	1876	**Alexander Graham Bell**
incandescent lamp	1879	**Thomas Edison**
photographic roll film	1884	**George Eastman, Hannibal Goodwin**
modern submarine	1898	**John P. Holland**
air conditioning	1902	**Willis H. Carrier**
airplane	1903	**Orville and Wilbur Wright**
television	1920s	**Philo T. Farnsworth, Vladimir Zworykin**
rocket engine	1926	**Robert H. Goddard**
nylon	1937	**Du Pont Laboratories**
electronic computer	1942	**John V. Atanasoff, Clifford Berry**
microwave oven	1947	**Percy Spencer**
transistor	1947	**J. Bardeen, W. Brattain, W. Shockley**
integrated circuit	1959	**Jack Kilby, Robert Noyce**
laser	1960	**Gordon Gould, Theodore H. Maiman**
microprocessor	1971	**Intel Corp.**
cell phone	1973	**Martin Cooper**
Internet	1960s–1980s	**Scientists all over the country**

AMERICAN HISTORY PARADE

1780 Patriot Henry Laurens of South Carolina, captured at sea, is imprisoned in the Tower of London; after Yorktown, he is exchanged for British general Charles Cornwallis.

1866 In Indiana, brothers John and Simeon Reno stage the first robbery of a moving train in the United States.

1927 The *Jazz Singer*, the first feature-length "talking picture," opens in New York.

1979 Pope John Paul II becomes the first pontiff to visit the White House.

OCTOBER 7, 1780, brought the Battle of Kings Mountain, a fight Thomas Jefferson called the "turn of the tide of success" in the Revolutionary War.

By late summer 1780, British victories had convinced General Charles Cornwallis that the lower South lay under his control, and he marched north to subdue North Carolina. Along the way, he sent Major Patrick Ferguson, a hard-fighting Scot, toward the Carolina mountains to "keep alive the spirits of our friends." But "Bull Dog" Ferguson stirred up Patriot spirits when he warned uncooperative frontier settlers that he would "march over the mountains, hang their leaders, and lay their country waste with fire and sword."

Nine hundred men swarmed out of the mountains of present-day Tennessee, western North Carolina, and Virginia. Called the Overmountain Men because they lived "over the mountains," they were every bit as hard-fighting as Ferguson. And they had no intention of bowing to any king.

The Overmountain Men, along with other Patriots from the Carolinas and Georgia, caught up with Ferguson's Loyalist troops at Kings Mountain, a wooded ridge in South Carolina. Ferguson had the advantage of high ground, but the Patriots hid behind trees and rocks as they worked their way up the steep slopes. "I stood behind one tree and fired until the bark was nearly all knocked off," one recalled. At the end of the brutal fight, over 300 Loyalists had been killed or wounded, and 700 had been taken prisoner. Ferguson lay dead with eight bullets in his body.

Told of the defeat, a shaken Cornwallis retreated south. The Overmountain Men shouldered their rifles and headed home. Sir Henry Clinton, the British commander in chief in North America, later called Kings Mountain "the first link in a chain of evils that followed each other in regular succession until they at last ended in the total loss of America."

AMERICAN HISTORY PARADE

1765   The Stamp Act Congress meets in New York City to discuss colonial grievances against England.

1777   Patriots defeat the British at the Second Battle of Saratoga in New York.

1780   Patriot militia forces annihilate a Loyalist army at Kings Mountain in South Carolina.

1826   The Granite Railway, an early U.S. railroad, begins operation in Quincy, Massachusetts, with horse-drawn wagons hauling stone to build the Bunker Hill Monument.

1916   In Atlanta, Georgia Tech beats Cumberland College 222–0 in the most lopsided game in college football history.

2001   U.S. troops launch Operation Enduring Freedom, the campaign to destroy terrorist training camps in Afghanistan.

THE MOST FAMOUS AMERICAN WARRIOR of World War I was a reluctant hero. When drafted, he struggled with the idea of fighting. Thirty-year-old Alvin York, a backwoods Tennessee farmer, had only recently given up his "hog wild" days of drinking and carousing, and had asked his sweetheart to marry him. He had embraced the pacifist Christian faith of his widowed mother. "I loved and trusted old Uncle Sam and I have always believed he did the right thing," he later said. "But I was worried clean through. I didn't want to go and kill."

York spent weeks wrestling with his conscience, and finally decided that although he hated war, going was the right thing to do. He left for France convinced that "we were to be peacemakers. . . . We were to help make peace, the only way the Germans would understand."

He had grown up hunting, and the other soldiers soon discovered that he was an astonishing shot. On October 8, 1918, in the Argonne Forest, his marksmanship saved American lives when his patrol ran into a German machine-gun nest. "Our boys just went down like the long grass before the mowing machine at home," he recalled. He went on the attack, picking off 25 Germans with his rifle and pistol before their commander surrendered. By the time York and his companions got back to headquarters, they had a long line of prisoners. "Well, York, I hear you have captured the whole German army," an officer said. York replied that he had only 132.

Promoted to sergeant and awarded the Medal of Honor, he was greeted in New York City after the war with a ticker tape parade. But he declined to grow rich off his fame. He returned to Tennessee, married his fiancée, established a school for mountain children, and farmed the land as he had before.

AMERICAN HISTORY PARADE

1860   A telegraph line between Los Angeles and San Francisco opens.

1871   The Great Chicago Fire begins, reportedly when Mrs. O'Leary's cow kicks over a lantern; the blaze destroys downtown, kills 250, and leaves 90,000 homeless.

1871   A horrific forest fire burns a broad swath of Wisconsin and Michigan, killing 1,200 people.

1918   Alvin York almost single-handedly kills two dozen German soldiers and captures 132 prisoners in France's Argonne Forest.

OCTOBER 9 • JAMES FORTEN, FREEDOM FIGHTER

JAMES FORTEN, born in 1766 in Philadelphia, was the grandson of a slave but the son of free blacks. As a boy, he heard the Declaration of Independence read to the people of Philadelphia, and when he was fourteen, he went to sea to fight the British aboard a privateer named the *Royal Louis* under the command of Stephen Decatur.

In October 1781 the *Royal Louis* was captured by the British warship *Amphion*. Forten faced grave danger: the British often sold black prisoners of war to slave traders. But he befriended the British captain's son in a game of marbles, and the captain took such a liking to the young American that he offered to take him to England.

Forten would have none of that. "I have been taken prisoner for the liberties of my country, and never will prove a traitor to her interest!" he replied. So he spent the next seven months on a disease-ridden prison ship before being released in a prisoner exchange.

After the Revolution, Forten went to work for a Philadelphia sailmaker. Two years later he became foreman of the shop, and in 1798 he was able to buy the business. He invented a device that helped seamen handle sails, and his business prospered. In time he became a wealthy man.

What did Forten do with his success? He used it to protect and better his country. During the War of 1812, he recruited blacks to help defend Philadelphia. He later helped organize the American Anti-Slavery Society and contributed money to the abolitionist newspaper the *Liberator*. He aided runaway slaves on their way north, and extended a helping hand to all manner of people, black and white.

Forten did not live to see the end of slavery, but he believed it would come. He helped set his country on the road toward freedom for all Americans.

AMERICAN HISTORY PARADE

1635   Religious dissident Roger Williams is banished from the Massachusetts Bay Colony.

1781   James Forten is held aboard the British ship *Amphion*, where he refuses an offer of freedom if he will go to England with the captain's son.

1855   Joshua Stoddard of Worcester, Massachusetts, patents the calliope, a "new musical instrument to be played by the agency of steam or highly compressed air."

1876   Alexander Graham Bell, in Boston, and Thomas Watson, in Cambridge, Massachusetts, hold the first telephone conversation over outdoor wires.

1936   Boulder (now Hoover) Dam begins sending electricity across 266 miles of mountains and deserts to Los Angeles.

"AIR FORCE ONE" is not technically a plane—it's the radio call signal for any Air Force craft the president is aboard. The first aircraft made especially for the president and routinely called "Air Force One" was a Boeing 707 that entered service on October 10, 1962. That plane was also known as SAM 26000 (Special Air Mission, tail No. 26000). SAM 26000 served eight presidents: Kennedy, Johnson, Nixon, Ford, Carter, Reagan, George H. W. Bush, and Clinton. It flew Kennedy to Dallas, Texas, on November 22, 1963, the day he was assassinated. Vice President Lyndon B. Johnson took the oath of office as the new president on the plane, which then flew him and Kennedy's body back to Washington, D.C. In 1972 another Boeing 707 (SAM 27000) became the primary presidential aircraft, and SAM 26000 was used as a backup plane.

Today, two nearly identical, custom-built Boeing 747-200B jets (tail numbers 28000 and 29000) regularly carry the president. Both are based at Andrews Air Force Base in Maryland, ten miles from the White House. As soon as the president steps aboard one of these planes, it becomes *Air Force One*.

The presidential jet is as long as a city block and taller than a five-story building. It has an office, stateroom, and conference room for the president, as well as room for plenty of staff, Secret Service agents, reporters, and guests. Its communications network allows the president to contact virtually anyone from the air. The plane carries anti-missile devices, and shielding protects its electronics from interference caused by a nuclear blast.

This flying Oval Office can travel 630 miles per hour and halfway around the world without refueling. It can also be refueled in flight. *Air Force One* has a perfect flying record and is considered the safest plane in the world.

AMERICAN HISTORY PARADE

1845   The U.S. Naval Academy opens in Annapolis, Maryland, with 56 students.

1850   The Chesapeake & Ohio Canal is completed and opened along its entire 185-mile length from Washington, D.C., to Cumberland, Maryland.

1935   George Gershwin's opera *Porgy and Bess* opens on Broadway.

1962   The first aircraft commonly called *Air Force One* goes into service.

1973   Vice President Spiro T. Agnew pleads no contest to a charge of federal income tax evasion and resigns his office.

OCTOBER 11, 1986, brought the opening of a two-day summit in Reykjavik, Iceland, between President Ronald Reagan and Soviet leader Mikhail Gorbachev—a turning point in a four-decade-old Cold War with a Communist empire that threatened the liberty of the world.

Gorbachev, desperate to cut his ailing nation's military spending, offered major weapons cutbacks if the United States would do the same. Reagan was astounded and delighted. Previous Soviet leaders had answered *nyet* to serious proposals for nuclear arms reductions. The U.S. president responded by suggesting that both sides scrap all offensive missiles within ten years. Soon both leaders were trading breathtaking proposals to dismantle nuclear stockpiles. *We have negotiated the most massive weapons reductions in history,* an exultant Reagan told himself.

Then Gorbachev threw a curve: "This all depends, of course, on you giving up SDI." The demand angered Reagan. He had made it clear that the Strategic Defense Initiative—a U.S. research program to develop a defensive shield against incoming missiles—was not a bargaining chip. In his view, SDI would ultimately prove the best defense against foreign threats.

Reagan could have left Reykjavik hailed as a great statesman for making the deal. All he had to do was give up SDI. Instead, he ended the summit. "The price was high but I wouldn't sell," he wrote in his diary.

Critics accused the president of being too stubborn. But others believed that standing firm would pay off. "You just won the Cold War," an administration official predicted on the plane ride home. Reagan was confident that the bankrupt Soviet empire could not stand up to U.S. resolve. "I'm convinced he'll come around," he wrote of Gorbachev. Sure enough, the Soviets came back to the bargaining table, and the two countries soon reached historic agreements to reduce nuclear arms.

AMERICAN HISTORY PARADE

1776   In the Battle of Valcour Island on Lake Champlain, New York, American ships suffer defeat but thwart a British plan to cut the colonies in half.

1811   The world's first steam-powered ferryboat, the *Juliana*, designed by John Stevens, begins operation between New York City and Hoboken, New Jersey.

1890   The Daughters of the American Revolution is founded in Washington, D.C.

1968   *Apollo 7*, the first manned Apollo mission, launches carrying astronauts Wally Schirra, Donn Eisele, and Walter Cunningham.

1986   President Ronald Reagan and Soviet leader Mikhail S. Gorbachev open two days of arms-control talks in Reykjavik, Iceland.

CHRISTOPHER COLUMBUS had all kinds of trouble finding a crew to venture across the Atlantic. No one wanted to sail into that sea of darkness. Somehow he scraped together ninety men.

When the tiny *Nina, Pinta,* and *Santa Maria* finally set out, they passed an erupting volcano. The terrified sailors took the billowing smoke and flames as an evil omen. Columbus calmed their fears and persuaded them to sail on.

After several days the compass began to vacillate away from the North Star. The confused men fell into a panic, but their admiral convinced them to keep going.

The winds blew day after day to the west, pushing them across the sea. The crew began muttering. What if the winds always blew west? How could their ships ever sail back to Spain against them? They met thick stretches of green seaweed, which the men feared would entangle their rudders. Who knew what monsters lurked in these ocean forests? They cast dark scowls at Columbus.

Every so often someone cried, "Land!" But it was only low clouds hugging the horizon, a mirage of the sea. The crew plunged into despair. Columbus sailed on.

They saw birds overhead, which gave them hope. They tried following their direction—but saw nothing. The sullen crew neared mutiny. There was talk of throwing the admiral into the sea and forcing the pilots to turn around. Columbus, refusing to flinch, willed his vessels on. Then came the dawn that raised an island from the swells. Columbus reached a New World. The day was October 12, 1492.

Christopher Columbus has been subjected to criticism in recent years, some deserved, some not. Regardless, today is a good day to honor the courage and perseverance that once conquered fear of the unknown.

AMERICAN HISTORY PARADE

1492   Christopher Columbus makes landfall at an island he calls San Salvador, a part of today's Bahamas.

1892   In celebration of the 400th anniversary of Columbus's landing, American schoolchildren first recite the newly written Pledge of Allegiance.

1973   President Nixon nominates House Minority Leader Gerald R. Ford of Michigan to succeed Spiro T. Agnew, who had resigned as vice president.

1997   Singer John Denver dies when the small plane he is piloting crashes off the coast of California near Monterey.

2000   In Yemen, al-Qaeda suicide bombers in a small boat ram into the destroyer USS *Cole,* killing 17 sailors.

THE U.S. NAVY CELEBRATES its birthday on October 13, the day in 1775 that the Continental Congress authorized the outfitting of two armed vessels to cruise in search of British munitions ships. On that day, Congress also established a Naval Committee to oversee the new navy. John Adams was a member of the committee, and although the Massachusetts representative knew little of naval affairs, he got busy making himself expert. As historian David McCullough writes, the committee "met in a rented room at Tun Tavern [in Philadelphia], and it was Adams who drafted the first set of rules and regulations for the new navy, a point of pride with him for as long as he lived."

Throughout the Revolution, Adams urged support for the tiny American fleet, telling Congress that "a navy is our natural and only defense." Over the course of the war, the Continental Navy included about fifty ships of various sizes. After the Revolution, Congress disbanded the navy, then restarted it in 1794 when it ordered the construction of six frigates.

The U.S. Navy flag, adopted in 1959, is a dark blue flag that carries the image of a three-masted square-rigged ship underway before a fair breeze. A bald eagle and an anchor are shown in front of the ship. Navy ships do not fly the Navy flag from their masts. The banner is reserved for display purposes and is carried by honor guards during ceremonies.

AMERICAN HISTORY PARADE

1775   The Continental Congress authorizes an American naval force.

1792   The cornerstone of the White House is laid.

1843   B'nai B'rith, the world's oldest Jewish service organization, is founded in New York City.

1903   The Boston Americans beat the Pittsburgh Pirates 3–0 to win the first World Series, prevailing 5 games to 3.

1932   President Hoover lays the cornerstone of the Supreme Court Building.

UNTIL OCTOBER 14, 1947, no one knew if a plane could fly faster than the speed of sound. Aircraft approaching Mach 1 shook violently, as if hitting an invisible wall. Only a year earlier, British pilot Geoffrey De Havilland had died when his plane broke apart flying close to the speed of sound. Scientists theorized that as a plane reached high speeds, sound waves piled up around it, creating a "sound barrier" that held it back.

After World War II the U.S. military and Bell Aircraft developed the X-1, a "bullet with wings" designed to punch a hole through the sound barrier. The test pilot for the rocket-powered plane was 24-year-old Captain Chuck Yeager. A decorated combat ace, Yeager had cheated death more than once. During the war, he'd been shot down over France but eluded the Nazis with the help of the French Resistance, made it back to his squadron, and returned to the skies.

By mid-October 1947 Yeager had flown the X-1 several times over the Mojave Desert, edging closer to the sound barrier. On October 14 he climbed into the plane with two cracked ribs from a fall off a horse—an injury he kept secret so he wouldn't be grounded. A giant B-29 carried the X-1 to 20,000 feet and released it. The plane stalled and dropped 500 feet while Yeager struggled to bring it under control. He fired his rocket engines, climbed to 42,000 feet, leveled off, and fired a rocket again.

Then it happened. The shaking suddenly stopped. "I was so high and so remote, and the airplane was so very quiet that I might have been motionless," Yeager later recalled. But the needle on the speed gauge jumped off the scale. On the ground below, engineers heard the thunder of a sonic boom. Chuck Yeager had punched through the sound barrier.

AMERICAN HISTORY PARADE

1644   William Penn, founder of Pennsylvania, is born in London.

1774   The Continental Congress adopts a declaration of rights stating that colonists are entitled to "life, liberty, and property."

1890   Dwight David Eisenhower, the thirty-fourth U.S. president, is born in Denison, Texas.

1912   While campaigning for the presidency in Milwaukee, Theodore Roosevelt is shot in the chest but gives a speech anyway, proclaiming that "it takes more than a bullet to stop a bull moose."

1947   Air Force test pilot Chuck Yeager becomes the first person to fly faster than the speed of sound.

On October 15, 1860, young Grace Bedell of Westfield, New York, wrote the Republican nominee for president, a clean-shaven man, with some advice:

Dear Sir,

My father has just [come] home from the fair and brought home your picture. . . . I am a little girl only eleven years old, but want you should be President of the United States very much so I hope you wont think me very bold to write to such a great man as you are. Have you any little girls about as large as I am if so give them my love and tell her to write to me if you cannot answer this letter. I have got 4 brother's and part of them will vote for you any way and if you will let your whiskers grow I will try and get the rest of them to vote for you you would look a great deal better for your face is so thin. All the ladies like whiskers and they would tease their husband's to vote for you and then you would be President. . . . I must not write any more answer this letter right off Good bye. Grace Bedell

On October 19, the nominee wrote back:

My dear little Miss,

Your very agreeable letter of the 15th is received. I regret the necessity of saying I have no daughters. I have three sons—one seventeen, one nine, and one seven years of age. They, with their mother, constitute my whole family. As to the whiskers, having never worn any, do you not think people would call it a piece of silly affection if I were to begin it now? Your very sincere well-wisher, A. Lincoln

Despite his answer, Lincoln began growing a beard. The next year, on his way to the White House, he stopped in Westfield, gave Grace a kiss, and thanked her for her advice.

AMERICAN HISTORY PARADE

1860   Grace Bedell writes Abraham Lincoln, urging him to grow a beard.

1878   Thomas Edison incorporates the Edison Electric Light Company, the first electric company, to finance his work on the incandescent lamp.

1951   *I Love Lucy*, starring Lucille Ball, premieres on TV.

1976   In Houston, Democrat Walter F. Mondale and Republican Bob Dole square off in the first televised debate between vice-presidential nominees.

1989   Wayne Gretzky, while playing for the Los Angeles Kings, breaks a National Hockey League record when he scores his 1,851st career point.

OCTOBER 16 is the birthday of Noah Webster, born in 1758 in West Hartford, Connecticut. Generations of schoolchildren grew up studying his popular "Blue-Backed Speller," so called because of its blue cover. But his most famous work was the *American Dictionary of the English Language*, first published in 1828. At a time when even educated people spelled words however they wished, Webster's dictionary helped bring order and consistency to language. An ardent patriot, he tried to free the American language from British influences. For example, he "Americanized" the British spelling of *colour*, changing it to *color*. In his essay "On the Education of Youth in America," he argued that education in the young republic should promote love of country—an idea still good in the twenty-first century.

> But every child in America should be acquainted with his own country. He should read books that furnish him with ideas that will be useful to him in life and practice. As soon as he opens his lips, he should rehearse the history of his own country; he should lisp the praise of liberty, and of those illustrious heroes and statesmen who have wrought a revolution in her favor.
>
> A selection of essays, respecting the settlement and geography of America; the history of the late revolution and of the most remarkable characters and events that distinguished it, and a compendium of the principles of the federal and provincial governments, should be the principal school book in the United States. These are interesting objects to every man; they call home the minds of youth and fix them upon the interests of their own country, and they assist in forming attachments to it, as well as in enlarging the understanding.

AMERICAN HISTORY PARADE

1758   Lexicographer Noah Webster is born in West Hartford, Connecticut.

1829   The Tremont House, the first modern American hotel, opens in Boston with luxuries such as indoor plumbing and a key for each room.

1859   Abolitionist John Brown, hoping to start a slave rebellion, leads 21 men in a raid against the federal armory at Harper's Ferry, Virginia (now West Virginia).

1962   President John F. Kennedy learns that U.S. spy planes have detected missile bases in Cuba, triggering the Cuban Missile Crisis.

2002   President George W. Bush signs a congressional resolution authorizing the use of force against Saddam Hussein's regime in Iraq.

AMERICANS ASSOCIATE the USS *Arizona* with Pearl Harbor and World War II, but the forty-first battleship of the U.S. Navy was actually a World War I vintage ship, commissioned on October 17, 1916. During World War I, the *Arizona* served as a gunnery training ship and patrolled the U.S. eastern seaboard. In 1918, it escorted the ship carrying President Woodrow Wilson to the Paris Peace Conference. During the following decades, it operated in both the Atlantic and Pacific, helping to keep the peace and protect American shores.

The *Arizona* was docked at Pearl Harbor for repairs when the Japanese attacked on December 7, 1941. At 8:10 a.m., a 1,760-pound armor-piercing bomb slammed through her decks, and a few seconds later one of her ammunition magazines exploded, shredding the forward part of the ship. The *Arizona* sank in less than nine minutes, and 1,177 crewmen lost their lives—half of the casualties suffered at Pearl Harbor on that day of infamy.

Today the remains of the battleship rest on the harbor's bottom, in forty feet of water, with the bodies of about 1,000 men entombed aboard. The USS *Arizona* Memorial, dedicated in 1962, sits above the ship. Each year more than 1.4 million people visit the memorial, where the names of the crewmen who died are carved in marble. Overhead an American flag flies from a flagpole attached to the sunken ship's mainmast—a somber reminder of a terrible sacrifice for freedom.

AMERICAN HISTORY PARADE

1777   British forces surrender to Patriot troops at Saratoga, New York, an American victory that helps win France as an ally for the rest of the war.

1916   The USS *Arizona* is commissioned at the New York Naval Shipyard.

1933   Physicist Albert Einstein, fleeing Nazi Germany, arrives in the United States.

1973   OPEC announces it will cut oil exports to the United States and other nations supporting Israel during the Yom Kippur War.

1989   An earthquake measuring 7.1 on the Richter scale hits northern California, killing more than 60 people.

IN 1867, when word spread that William Seward, Andrew Johnson's secretary of state, had inked a deal for the United States to buy Alaska from the Russians, critics growled. They said that paying $7.2 million, or about two cents per acre, was too much for "a large lump of ice." They called Alaska "Seward's Folly," "Seward's Ice Box," and "Walrussia."

Seward was an old hand at politics. He had been Abraham Lincoln's secretary of state during the Civil War. (The night Lincoln was murdered, Seward survived an assassination attempt by one of John Wilkes Booth's accomplices, who broke into his bedroom and stabbed him.) When critics objected to the land deal, he refused to back down. After all, the tsar was eager to sell—his Alaskan fur-trading business had dried up, and he worried that the British would eventually seize the territory. After a week of debate, the U.S. Senate approved the agreement.

On October 18, 1867, the official transfer took place at Sitka, the last capital of Russian America. United States and Russian soldiers beat drums while a small crowd looked on, including the Russian governor, Prince Maksoutov, and his wife. As cannons boomed, the Russian flag started down a 90-foot pole. A sudden gust of wind wrapped the imperial double-eagle banner around the staff, and there it stuck. The harder anyone tugged, the more it refused to budge. Finally a seaman was hoisted up the pole to cut loose the flag, which fluttered down and landed on Russian bayonets. The Russian princess reportedly fainted. By the time she woke, the Stars and Stripes had been raised, and Alaska was U.S. soil.

In the late 1800s, prospectors found gold in the territory, and even critics decided that Seward had been pretty savvy after all. On January 3, 1959, Alaska entered the Union as the forty-ninth state.

AMERICAN HISTORY PARADE

1767   Charles Mason and Jeremiah Dixon complete their survey of the boundary between Pennsylvania and Maryland, the Mason-Dixon Line.

1842   In New York Harbor, Samuel Morse lays the first underwater telegraph cable.

1867   The United States takes possession of Alaska from Russia.

1898   U.S. troops fighting in the Spanish-American war raise the American flag in Puerto Rico, signaling U.S. authority over the former Spanish colony.

1989   The shuttle *Atlantis* releases the space probe *Galileo*, which begins a six-year journey to Jupiter.

AT 2:00 PM ON OCTOBER 19, 1781, British soldiers filed out of their trenches at Yorktown, Virginia, laid down their arms, and surrendered their flags. At that moment the American Revolution effectively ended.

British general Charles Cornwallis had taken his troops to Yorktown, on the Chesapeake Bay, because southern Patriots had worn down his army. He hoped to meet up with the British navy, which might either resupply his exhausted force or carry it away. But American and French troops laid siege to Cornwallis's lines, pounding them with cannon fire, and a French fleet cut off escape by sea. The British found themselves trapped.

Thomas Nelson, governor of Virginia and a signer of the Declaration of Independence, was with the American army at Yorktown. According to tradition, he directed an artilleryman to fire at a stately brick home. "It is my home," he explained, "the best one in town, and there you will be almost certain to find Lord Cornwallis and the British headquarters." According to legend, the first cannonball sailed through a window and landed on a table where several British officers had just sat to dine.

On October 19, as the redcoats marched forward to surrender, they could not help but notice how poorly dressed and equipped George Washington's troops were. Few had uniforms. Many wore rags and went barefooted. "Out of this rabble has risen a people who defy kings," one of King George's soldiers observed.

Bands played as the British troops filed between the French and American soldiers. The Americans played "Yankee Doodle." The British played a tune called "The World Turned Upside Down." After Yorktown the British realized there was no point in fighting the upstart colonists any longer. Americans had won their freedom.

AMERICAN HISTORY PARADE

1774   Colonists in Annapolis, Maryland, stage the Annapolis Tea Party by burning the tea ship *Peggy Stewart*.

1781   Lord Cornwallis surrenders his British army at Yorktown, Virginia, effectively ending the Revolutionary War.

1829   Baltimore's monument to George Washington, a 178-foot-high marble column, is completed.

1873   In New York City, representatives of Princeton, Yale, and Rutgers draw up the first set of intercollegiate football rules.

1987   On a day remembered as Black Monday on Wall Street, the Dow Jones Industrial Average drops 508 points, or 22.6 percent.

"THERE IS ON THE GLOBE ONE SINGLE SPOT, the possessor of which is our natural and habitual enemy," Thomas Jefferson wrote. "It is New Orleans, through which the produce of three-eighths of our territory must pass to market." The port city lay at the southern edge of Louisiana, the vast region named for French king Louis XIV that stretched from the Mississippi River to the Rocky Mountains, and from the Canadian border to the Gulf of Mexico. In 1801 President Jefferson instructed Robert Livingston, his envoy in Paris, to try to buy New Orleans from the French. Jefferson sent his good friend James Monroe to aid in the negotiations.

The Americans were in luck. Napoleon Bonaparte needed money to pay for expensive wars. And he didn't have much use for Louisiana, which he believed might be seized by the British or Americans at any moment anyway. Livingston and Monroe were stunned when Napoleon offered to sell not just New Orleans but the entire Louisiana Territory for $15 million.

The offer was too good to pass up. The envoys inked the treaty, and on October 20, 1803, the Senate quickly ratified it before Napoleon might change his mind. In one stroke Jefferson had more than doubled the size of the country for pennies an acre. It was, no doubt, one of the best land bargains in history.

The fact that no one had asked for the consent of the region's inhabitants, mainly Native Americans, went overlooked. Critics also insisted the Constitution gave the government no power to purchase territory. Yet the transaction set the United States on course to become a huge nation, with seemingly unlimited frontiers and possibilities. In the opinion of John Quincy Adams, the sixth president, the Louisiana Purchase would prove "next in historical importance to the Declaration of Independence and the adoption of the Constitution."

AMERICAN HISTORY PARADE

1629   In England, John Winthrop is elected first governor of the Massachusetts Bay Colony.

1803   The U.S. Senate ratifies the Louisiana Purchase.

1818   The United States and Great Britain fix the U.S.-Canadian border at the 49th Parallel between the Lake of the Woods and continental divide.

1944   During World War II, General Douglas MacArthur wades ashore at Leyte Island in the Philippines, fulfilling his promise of 1942: "I shall return."

1947   The House Un-American Activities Committee begins hearings on alleged Communist influence in Hollywood.

THE STORY OF THOMAS EDISON, born in 1847 in Milan, Ohio, is the stuff the American dream is made of. He dropped out of school when his teacher called him "addled," so his mother taught him at home, where he set up a chemical laboratory in his basement. Soon he was on his way to becoming the greatest inventor the world has known.

As a young man, Edison built an "invention factory" in New Jersey. It became America's first research laboratory for industry. He amazed a group of onlookers one day when he recited "Mary Had a Little Lamb" into a device and then turned a crank to make his voice come back out. Edison had invented the phonograph, the first machine for recording sounds. On October 21, 1879, he gave the world the invention for which he is best known—the electric lightbulb.

Edison worked eighteen hours a day and never feared failure. Once, he conducted experiment after experiment without getting the results he needed, and a friend said he was sorry the tests were failing. "Shucks, we haven't failed," Edison said. "Now we know a thousand things that won't work, so we're that much closer to finding what will."

One night in 1914 a tremendous fire destroyed his factories in West Orange, New Jersey. "We'll build bigger and better on the ruins," the 67-year-old inventor declared. And he did.

Thomas Edison patented more than one thousand inventions. He created new kinds of batteries, improved the telephone, invented a motion-picture machine, and helped found one of America's most famous industries: the movies.

Throughout his long career, Edison always insisted that hard work was the main reason for his success. "Genius is 1 percent inspiration, and 99 percent perspiration," he said. Americans have built a great nation by following that rule.

AMERICAN HISTORY PARADE

1797   The Navy frigate USS *Constitution*, "Old Ironsides," is launched in Boston.

1867   In Kansas, leaders of the Southern Plains Indians sign the Medicine Lodge Treaty, in which they give up their hunting grounds and agree to move to reservations in Oklahoma.

1879   Thomas Edison invents the first practical electric incandescent lamp.

1916   The first ROTC units are established at the University of Arkansas; University of Maine; St. John's College, Annapolis; Texas A&M; College of St. Thomas, St. Paul, Minnesota; and the Citadel, Charleston, South Carolina.

OCTOBER 22 • "THE GREATEST DANGER OF ALL WOULD BE TO DO NOTHING"

ON OCTOBER 22, 1962, President John F. Kennedy appeared on television to inform Americans that U.S. spy planes had uncovered a "clandestine, reckless, and provocative threat to world peace"—Soviet missile sites in Cuba, under construction but nearly complete, that could soon house nuclear missiles capable of striking the United States. Kennedy demanded the missiles' removal and announced a naval blockade of Cuba to stop Soviet ships from bringing more weapons to the island.

Thus began some of the tensest days of the twentieth century as the U.S. and U.S.S.R. stood at the brink of nuclear war. Soviet leader Nikita Khrushchev warned that his subs might sink U.S. Navy ships attempting to stop Soviet vessels. "If the U.S. insists on war, we'll all meet together in hell," he growled. Kennedy certainly did not want war, but he refused to back down. "The greatest danger of all would be to do nothing," he told the American people.

The world held its breath as Soviet ships approached the blockade line. The crisis deepened when a U.S. reconnaissance plane was shot down over Cuba and its pilot killed. Americans stockpiled emergency supplies and even fled large cities.

Meanwhile, U.S. and Soviet officials traded urgent proposals and counterproposals. On October 28, Khrushchev agreed to dismantle the sites in return for a U.S. pledge not to invade Cuba, as well as the removal of U.S. missiles in Turkey. "We were eyeball to eyeball, and the other guy just blinked," commented a relieved Secretary of State Dean Rusk.

Historians have debated who came out on top in the Cuban Missile Crisis, Kennedy or Khrushchev. But there is no doubt that in standing up to Soviet totalitarianism, the young president turned back a dangerous threat to the nation's security and to world peace.

AMERICAN HISTORY PARADE

1746   The College of New Jersey (present-day Princeton University) receives its charter.

1836   Sam Houston is inaugurated as president of the Republic of Texas.

1939   At Ebbets Field, the Brooklyn Dodgers defeat the Philadelphia Eagles 23–14 in the first pro-football game to be shown on television.

1962   John F. Kennedy announces a blockade of Cuba in response to the discovery of Soviet missile sites on the island.

1968   *Apollo 7*, the first manned Apollo mission, returns safely to Earth.

SHE'S NOT AS FAMOUS as the Statue of Liberty, but she's the crowning glory of a revered American symbol: the dome of the U.S. Capitol. 19½-foot bronze Statue of Freedom by Thomas Crawford depicts a woman in flowing draperies clasping a sheathed sword in her right hand. With her left hand she holds a thirteen-striped shield of the United States, along with a laurel wreath of victory. Her Roman helmet features an eagle's head, feathers, and talons, said to be a reference to Native American culture. (The original design included the Phrygian cap worn by freed Roman slaves as a sign of liberty, but Secretary of War Jefferson Davis objected that it might incite Southern slaves to rebel.)

The dome on which she stands appears to be stone but is really cast iron painted to look like white marble. Construction on the dome began in 1856 and continued for a decade, even during the Civil War. "If people see the Capitol going on," Abraham Lincoln said, "it is a sign we intend the Union shall go on." By 1863, the dome was far enough along to hoist the 15,000-pound statue in sections onto its perch, nearly 300 hundred feet high.

In 1993 the statue was temporarily removed for restoration. Preservation experts spent several months repairing cracks and corrosion. On October 23, 1993, with the aid of a helicopter, the Statue of Freedom soared to the top of the dome again, where she has remained since.

AMERICAN HISTORY PARADE

1824   Seventy-six-year-old John Stevens of Hoboken, New Jersey, completes the first U.S. steam locomotive to pull a train on a track.

1864   Union forces prevail in the Battle of Westport, near Kansas City, Missouri, one of the largest Civil War engagements west of the Mississippi.

1944   The three-day Battle of Leyte Gulf, the largest naval battle of WWII, begins in the Philippines; it ends in Allied victory.

1983   A suicide truck-bombing at the Marine Corps barracks in Beirut, Lebanon, believed to be the work of the terrorist group Hezbollah, kills 241 American servicemen.

1993   The Statue of Freedom returns to the top of the U.S. Capitol dome.

OCTOBER 24, 1861, brought the opening of the transcontinental telegraph and the advent of nationwide communication. Congress, anxious to connect distant California with the rest of the United States, had offered $40,000 a year to any company that could build and maintain a line across the rugged frontier. The Western Union Telegraph Company took up the challenge.

The obstacles were daunting. Wire, insulators, and other materials for the line's western portion would have to be shipped around Cape Horn to San Francisco. Supplies would have to be pulled by ox team over the Sierra Nevada and Rocky Mountains. Vast stretches of plains contained "not a stick of timber in sight," as one builder put it, so telegraph poles would have to be hauled hundreds of miles. On top of all that, the outbreak of the Civil War cast shadows of uncertainty on the project.

Building began in summer 1861. One crew worked eastward from Carson City, Nevada, the terminus of an existing line. The other crew worked westward from Omaha, Nebraska. The two lines would meet in Salt Lake City.

On average, they strung three to eight miles of wire a day, across mountains, plains, and desert. First came the men who measured and staked off the route, followed by the hole diggers, then the pole setters, and finally the wire party. When they ran out of poles, they trudged into the mountains to cut more. One day they built sixteen miles across the hot desert to reach a place with water.

On October 24, the work complete, Chief Justice of California Stephen J. Field, in San Francisco, sent the first transcontinental telegram to President Lincoln in Washington, D.C. The message assured Lincoln that the line "will be the means of strengthening the attachment which binds both the East and West to the Union."

AMERICAN HISTORY PARADE

1781   In Philadelphia, Congress hears a report of the American victory at Yorktown and processes to a nearby church to give thanks.

1836   Alonzo Phillips of Springfield, Massachusetts, receives a patent for safety matches.

1861   The first transcontinental telegraph message is sent from San Francisco to President Lincoln in Washington, D.C.

1901   A 63-year-old schoolteacher named Anna Edson Taylor becomes the first daredevil to go over Niagara Falls in a barrel.

1940   The 40-hour workweek goes into effect under the Fair Labor Standards Act of 1938.

ON OCTOBER 25, 1774, one of the first organized political actions by American women occurred in the town of Edenton, North Carolina, when fifty-one ladies gathered at the home of Mrs. Elizabeth King and signed a proclamation protesting the British tax on tea. Led by Penelope Barker, the patriots vowed to support resolves by the Provincial Deputies of North Carolina to boycott "the pernicious custom of drinking tea" and avoid British-made cloth until the tax was repealed.

The ladies of Edenton signed a resolution declaring that "we cannot be indifferent on any occasion that appears nearly to affect the peace and happiness of our country." The boycott was, they declared, "a duty that we owe, not only to our near and dear connections . . . but to ourselves."

It was a bold move in a time when it was considered unladylike for women to get involved in political matters. Unlike the participants of the famous Boston Tea Party, the Edenton women did not disguise themselves in costumes, but openly signed their names to their declaration "as a witness of our fixed intention and solemn determination."

At first the British sneered at the Edenton Tea Party. One Englishman wrote sarcastically, "The only security on our side . . . is the probability that there are but few places in America which possess so much female artillery as Edenton." They soon discovered otherwise.

AMERICAN HISTORY PARADE

1764   John Adams and Abigail Smith are married in Weymouth, Massachusetts.

1774   The ladies of Edenton, North Carolina, sign a resolution to boycott British tea.

1812   Captain Stephen Decatur becomes a national hero when his ship, the USS *United States*, defeats the British frigate *Macedonian* off the Moroccan coast.

1892   Caroline Harrison, wife of President Benjamin Harrison, dies in the White House.

1940   Benjamin O. Davis becomes the first black general in the U.S. Army.

1983   Troops from the United States and several Caribbean nations invade Grenada to halt a Communist takeover of the island.

ON OCTOBER 26, 1825, a floating parade led by the canal packet *Seneca Chief* left Buffalo, New York, in a grand opening of the newly finished, 363-mile Erie Canal. Cannons spaced an earshot's distance apart boomed the message east: the procession had begun. Cheering crowds lined the banks, with bands, speeches, and fireworks welcoming the flotilla at every town. "Our brightest, highest hopes are all consummated," the *Rochester Telegraph* proclaimed. "Let the shouts of triumph be heard from Erie to the Atlantic."

At Albany, the boats headed down the Hudson River to New York City, arriving on November 4. There Governor De Witt Clinton poured a keg of Lake Erie water into the harbor, symbolizing the "Wedding of the Waters" between the Great Lakes and the ocean.

The Erie Canal had taken nearly nine years to construct. Skeptics had called it Clinton's Ditch, after the governor who championed the most ambitious engineering feat yet attempted in the United States. Workers had felled thousands of trees, leveled hills, blasted rock, dredged mud, dug through earth. They built 83 locks to raise and lower boats a total of 565 feet between Albany and Buffalo, and 18 aqueducts to carry the waterway across rivers.

The canal proved a howling success, moving freight in thousands of mule-towed boats. The produce of the Midwest floated east, while immigrants and manufactured goods floated west, spurring the growth of the country. Along the canal, towns such as Syracuse and Rochester boomed, while New York City thrived as the busiest port in the nation.

Railroads brought an end to the canal's heyday. The waterway was enlarged several times, but business gradually fell off. Today it carries mostly recreational traffic and memories of a time when the Erie Canal was the nation's main street to the West.

AMERICAN HISTORY PARADE

1825   The Erie Canal opens its entire 363 miles from Buffalo to Albany, New York.

1858   Hamilton Smith of Philadelphia patents a hand-cranked, rotary washing machine.

1861   The Pony Express officially ceases operation two days after the Transcontinental Telegraph is completed.

1881   The Earp brothers and "Doc" Holliday confront the Clanton gang in the famous shootout at the OK Corral in Tombstone, Arizona.

1942   In the Battle of the Santa Cruz Islands, U.S. ships stop the Japanese from reinforcing Guadalcanal but lose the aircraft carrier *Hornet*.

OCTOBER 27, 1787, saw the publication of the first in a series of essays written by Alexander Hamilton, James Madison, and John Jay urging ratification of the Constitution. Written under the name "Publius," the eighty-five essays appeared mainly in New York newspapers and were later compiled in book form as *The Federalist*. They remain a brilliant explanation of the principles of American government. In "Federalist No. 1," Hamilton reminded Americans that for the first time, a nation's people would have the chance to freely decide what kind of government they want.

AFTER an unequivocal experience of the inefficacy of the subsisting federal government, you are called upon to deliberate on a new Constitution for the United States of America. The subject speaks its own importance; comprehending in its consequences nothing less than the existence of the Union, the safety and welfare of the parts of which it is composed, the fate of an empire in many respects the most interesting in the world. It has been frequently remarked that it seems to have been reserved to the people of this country, by their conduct and example, to decide the important question, whether societies of men are really capable or not of establishing good government from reflection and choice, or whether they are forever destined to depend for their political constitutions on accident and force. If there be any truth in the remark, the crisis at which we are arrived may with propriety be regarded as the era in which that decision is to be made; and a wrong election of the part we shall act may, in this view, deserve to be considered as the general misfortune of mankind. This idea will add the inducements of philanthropy to those of patriotism, to heighten the solicitude which all considerate and good men must feel for the event.

AMERICAN HISTORY PARADE

1682   Two months after leaving England, William Penn arrives at New Castle, Delaware.

1787   The first of *The Federalist Papers* is published in a New York newspaper.

1858   Theodore Roosevelt, the twenty-sixth U.S. president, is born in New York City.

1873   Illinois farmer Joseph Glidden applies for a patent on barbed wire, an innovation that helps fence the western plains, enabling large-scale farming.

1904   The nation's first rapid transit subway opens in New York City.

2002   Dallas Cowboys running back Emmitt Smith breaks Walter Payton's career rushing record of 16,726 yards to become the NFL's all-time rushing leader (Smith finishes his career with 18,355 yards rushing).

ON OCTOBER 28, 1886, President Grover Cleveland dedicated the Statue of Liberty on an island in New York Harbor, declaring, "We will not forget that Liberty has here made her home; nor shall her chosen altar be neglected."

A gift from France, the statue was designed by Frederic Auguste Bartholdi. The people of France raised money to build the statue itself, while the people of the United States raised funds to pay for its giant base. Construction on the statue began at a workshop in Paris in 1875 and took nearly a decade to complete. Lady Liberty was then disassembled into 350 pieces, packed into 214 crates, and sent by ship to America, where she was reassembled on her pedestal.

The statue, whose formal name is *Liberty Enlightening the World*, depicts a woman who has thrown off the chains of tyranny that lie at her feet. Her right hand holds up a torch symbolizing liberty. Her left hand holds a tablet containing the date July 4, 1776, in Roman numerals. The seven rays of her crown represent the light of liberty shining across the seven seas and continents.

Standing 305 feet high from the bottom of its base to the tip of the torch, the statue is one of the largest ever built. French engineer Gustave Eiffel, who built the Eiffel Tower in Paris, devised its iron skeleton. The exterior is sheathed with copper.

Millions of immigrants passed the Statue of Liberty over the years as they entered the harbor en route to the immigration station at Ellis Island. For them, it came to symbolize America's promise of opportunity. A tablet within the pedestal contains the famous words of poet Emma Lazarus: "Give me your tired, your poor, your huddled masses yearning to breathe free."

AMERICAN HISTORY PARADE

1636   The Massachusetts General Court establishes Harvard College.

1886   The Statue of Liberty is dedicated in New York Harbor.

1919   Congress passes the Volstead Act, which enforces Prohibition.

1942   The Alaska Highway, connecting Alaska to the Lower 48 states through Canada, is completed.

1965   The Gateway Arch in St. Louis, Missouri, is completed.

AFTER THE ATTACK ON PEARL HARBOR, a suspicious U.S. government ordered 110,000 people of Japanese descent into internment camps. Yet when offered the chance to join the Army, many Japanese Americans jumped at the opportunity to prove their loyalty. Hundreds ended up in the 100th Battalion/442nd Regimental Combat Team, a Japanese American unit that saw some of the hardest fighting of World War II.

Perhaps their finest hour came in October 1944 in the Vosges Mountains of France, where the Germans had surrounded 211 U.S. soldiers, many of them Texans, on a ridgetop. "Medical supplies low, no rations for three days . . . need ammunition," the desperate Americans radioed. News reports called the Texans the "Lost Battalion." The 100th/442nd got orders to save them.

The men started into the hills in darkness so thick, each grasped the man ahead to keep from losing the way. As they climbed the steep, forested slopes, the Germans opened fire. "I had never seen men get cut down so fast, so furiously," one GI remembered. They pushed forward a yard at a time.

Two days later, on October 29, the exhausted soldiers charged up the slope they dubbed "Suicide Hill" in a last effort to break the German line. "I didn't think about dying," a private later said. "I had a job to do." On October 30 the men of the Lost Battalion saw Americans where Germans had been. The 100th/442nd had arrived.

The 100th/442nd became one of the most decorated units in U.S. Army history. Its members received 9,486 Purple Hearts for battle wounds. Its twenty-one Medal of Honor recipients included Daniel K. Inouye of Hawaii. In 1959, when Inouye was told to "raise your right hand" to be sworn in as the first Japanese American member of Congress, a hushed awe came over the House of Representatives. Congressman, later Senator, Inouye had lost his right arm in service to America.

AMERICAN HISTORY PARADE

1796   The *Otter* of Boston, the first ship from the Atlantic coast to anchor in a California port, arrives at Monterey.

1858   The first store opens in the frontier town of Denver, selling goods to gold miners.

1929   Stock prices plunge on the New York Stock Exchange, marking the beginning of the Great Depression.

1944   In France, the 100th/442nd fights to rescue the "Lost Battalion."

1998   At age seventy-seven, John Glenn returns to space aboard the shuttle *Discovery*, 36 years after becoming the first American to orbit the earth.

TODAY IS THE BIRTHDAY OF JOHN ADAMS, born in 1735 in Quincy, Massachusetts. As this excerpt from his *Dissertation on the Cannon and Feudal Law* (1765) shows, Adams believed that the best way to guard the blessings of liberty is through education.

> Liberty cannot be preserved without a general knowledge among the people, who have a right, from the frame of their nature, to knowledge, as their great Creator, who does nothing in vain, has given them understandings, and a desire to know. . . .
>
> Let us dare to read, think, speak, and write. Let every order and degree among the people rouse their attention and animate their resolution. Let them all become attentive to the grounds and principles of government, ecclesiastical and civil. Let us study the law of nature; search into the spirit of the British constitution; read the histories of ancient ages; contemplate the great examples of Greece and Rome. . . .
>
> Let the pulpit resound with the doctrines and sentiments of religious liberty. . . . Let the bar proclaim "the laws, the rights, the generous plan of power" delivered down from remote antiquity—inform the world of the mighty struggles and numberless sacrifices made by our ancestors in defense of freedom. . . .
>
> Let the colleges join their harmony in the same delightful concert. Let every declamation turn upon the beauty of liberty and virtue, and the deformity, turpitude, and malignity, of slavery and vice. . . .
>
> In a word, let every sluice of knowledge be opened and set a-flowing.

AMERICAN HISTORY PARADE

1735   John Adams, the second U.S. president, is born in Braintree, Massachusetts.

1768   The first Methodist meetinghouse in America, the Wesley Chapel, is dedicated in New York City.

1938   Many listeners believe America is being invaded by Martians when Orson Welles broadcasts his *War of the Worlds* radio play.

1974   Muhammad Ali knocks out George Foreman in the eighth round in the "Rumble in the Jungle" boxing match in Zaire.

HALLOWEEN IS A HOLIDAY with ancient origins that has been gradually Americanized. Historians trace its roots back more than 2,000 years to Samhain, the first day of the Celtic New Year, observed around November 1. Samhain ("summer's end") was both a harvest festival and time when souls of the dead were believed to travel the earth.

In the ninth century, after Christianity spread to the British Isles, Pope Gregory IV designated November 1 as All Saints' Day to honor all the saints of the Church. All Saints' Day was also known as All Hallows' (*hallow* means holy one or saint). The evening before was called All Hallows' Eve—over time shortened to Halloween. As often happened, pagan customs mixed with Christian traditions, and Halloween remained a time associated with ghosts and wandering spirits.

Halloween celebrations weren't widespread in the United States until the great waves of Irish immigrants caused by the potato famine of the 1840s. The Catholic Irish brought both their observance of All Saints' Day and remnants of the older Celtic traditions. Their festivities mixed with other Americans' harvest customs to become Halloween as we know it today.

The American tradition of trick-or-treating echoes the ancient Celtic tradition of leaving food on doorsteps for the souls of the dead. In Britain, people went "souling" on All Hallows' Eve, walking from house to house asking for "soul cakes" in exchange for prayers for the dead.

In the Old World, people carved turnips and gourds into lanterns to scare away evil spirits. In America, they used pumpkins instead. Irish legend says a fellow named Jack was barred from hell for being too tricky, and had to walk the earth carrying a lantern lit with an ember the devil gave him. His name was Jack of the Lantern—or, as we say today, Jack-o'-Lantern.

AMERICAN HISTORY PARADE

1803   During the First Barbary War, the USS *Philadelphia* runs aground while blockading the port of Tripoli and is captured.

1864   Nevada becomes the thirty-sixth state.

1941   Work on Mount Rushmore comes to an end.

1950   Earl Lloyd, playing for the Washington Capitols, becomes the first African American to play in an NBA game.

1956   Rear Admiral George J. Dufek and six officers become the first Americans to set foot on the South Pole, and the first men ever to land a plane there.

Poems of American Patriotism

Columbus

Joaquin Miller

Joaquin Miller (1837–1913) was a colorful westerner known as the "Poet of the Sierras." His career included stints as a miner, lawyer, teacher, judge, cook, newspaperman, pony express rider, lecturer, and writer. His tribute to Christopher Columbus was memorized and recited by generations of American students.

> Behind him lay the gray Azores,
> > Behind the Gates of Hercules.
> Before him not the ghost of shores,
> > Before him only shoreless seas.
> The good mate said: "Now must we pray,
> > For lo! the very stars are gone.
> Brave Admiral, speak, what shall I say?"
> > "Why, say: 'Sail on! sail on! and on!'"

> "My men grow mutinous day by day.
> > My men grow ghastly wan and weak."
> The stout mate thought of home; a spray
> > Of salt wave washed his swarthy cheek.

"What shall I say, brave Admiral, say
    If we sight naught but seas at dawn?"
"Why, you shall say, at break of day:
    Sail on! sail on! and on!'"

They sailed and sailed, as winds might blow,
    Until at last the blanched mate said:
"Why, now not even God would know
    Should I and all my men fall dead.
These very winds forget their way,
    For God from these dread seas is gone.
Now speak, brave Admiral, and say—"
    He said: "Sail on! sail on! and on!"

They sailed. They sailed. Then spoke the mate:
    "This mad sea shows his teeth to-night,
He curls his lips, he lies in wait,
    With lifted teeth, as if to bite!
Brave Admiral, say but one good word.
    What shall we do when hope is gone?"
The words leapt like a leaping sword:
    "Sail on! sail on! sail on! and on!"

Then, pale and worn, he kept his deck,
    And peered through darkness. Ah, that night.
Of all dark nights! And then a speck—
    A light! A light! A light! A light!
It grew, a starlit flag unfurled!
    It grew to be Time's burst of dawn.
He gained a world; he gave that world
    Its grandest theme: "On! sail on!"

The Landing of the Pilgrim Fathers

Felicia Dorothea Hemans

Felicia Dorothea Hemans (1793–1835) was an English poet, but this poem could not be more American. It's still a good reminder of why many settlers came to these shores.

> The breaking waves dashed high
>   On a stern and rock-bound coast,
> And the woods against a stormy sky,
>   Their giant branches tossed,
>
> And the heavy night hung dark
>   The hills and waters o'er
> When a band of exiles moored their bark
>   On a wild New England shore.
>
> Not as the conqueror comes,
>   They, the true-hearted, came,
> Not with the roll of stirring drums,
>   And the trumpets that sing of fame;
>
> Not as the flying come,
>   In silence and in fear—
> They shook the depths of the desert's gloom
>   With their hymns of lofty cheer.
>
> Amidst the storm they sang,
>   And the stars heard, and the sea.
> And the sounding aisles of the dim woods rang
>   To the anthem of the free.

The ocean eagle soared
  From his nest by the white wave's foam,
And the rocking pines of the forest roared—
  This was their welcome home!

There were men with hoary hair
  Amidst that pilgrim band.
Why had they come to wither there,
  Away from their childhood's land?

There was woman's fearless eye,
  Lit by her deep love's truth.
There was manhood's brow serenely high,
  And the fiery heart of youth.

What sought they thus afar?
  Bright jewels of the mine?
The wealth of seas? The spoils of war?
  They sought a faith's pure shrine.

Aye, call it holy ground,
  The soil where first they trod.
They have left unstained what there they found—
  Freedom to worship God.

CONCORD HYMN

Ralph Waldo Emerson

Ralph Waldo Emerson (1803–82) wrote this poem as a tribute to Patriots who fought the British on April 19, 1775, at the Battles of Lexington and Concord. It was sung as a hymn on July 4, 1837, to celebrate the completion of a monument commemorating the battles.

> By the rude bridge that arched the flood,
>   Their flag to April's breeze unfurled,
> Here once the embattled farmers stood,
>   And fired the shot heard round the world.
>
> The foe long since in silence slept;
>   Alike the conqueror silent sleeps,
> And Time the ruined bridge has swept
>   Down the dark stream which seaward creeps.
>
> On this green bank, by this soft stream,
>   We set to-day a votive stone,
> That memory may their deed redeem,
>   When, like our sires, our sons are gone.
>
> Spirit, that made those heroes dare
>   To die, and leave their children free,
> Bid Time and Nature gently spare
>   The shaft we raise to them and thee.

The Bivouac of the Dead
Theodore O'Hara

Theodore O'Hara (1820–67) wrote "The Bivouac of the Dead" in memory of Kentucky troops killed during the Mexican-American War. This verse is inscribed in national cemeteries throughout the country.

> The muffled drum's sad roll has beat
> The soldier's last tattoo;
> No more on Life's parade shall meet
> That brave and fallen few.
> On Fame's eternal camping ground
> Their silent tents are spread,
> And Glory guards, with solemn round,
> The bivouac of the dead.

Sail On, O Ship of State!
Henry Wadsworth Longfellow

These lines are from Henry Wadsworth Longfellow's poem "The Building of the Ship." Published in 1849, a time of growing strife between North and South, they were intended as a plea for national unity. Abraham Lincoln was moved to tears as he listened to this verse. "It is a wonderful gift to be able to stir men like that," he said.

> Thou, too, sail on, O Ship of State!
> Sail on, O UNION, strong and great!
> Humanity with all its fears,
> With all the hopes of future years,
> Is hanging breathless on thy fate!

We know what Master laid thy keel,
What Workmen wrought thy ribs of steel,
Who made each mast, and sail, and rope,
What anvils rang, what hammers beat,
In what a forge and what a heat
Were shaped the anchors of thy hope!
Fear not each sudden sound and shock,
'Tis of the wave and not the rock;
'Tis but the flapping of the sail,
And not a rent made by the gale!
In spite of rock and tempest's roar,
In spite of false lights on the shore,
Sail on, nor fear to breast the sea
Our hearts, our hopes, are all with thee,
Our hearts, our hopes, our prayers, our tears,
Our faith triumphant o'er our fears,
Are all with thee—are all with thee!

I Hear America Singing

Walt Whitman

These lines come from Walt Whitman's poetry collection *Leaves of Grass*, first published in 1855. They have become a famous tribute to the vitality and variety of America.

I hear America singing, the varied carols I hear,
Those of mechanics, each one singing his as it should be, blithe and strong,
The carpenter singing his as he measures his plank or beam,
The mason singing his as he makes ready for work, or leaves off work,
The boatman singing what belongs to him in his boat,
    the deckhand singing on the steamboat deck,

The shoemaker singing as he sits on his bench, the hatter singing as he stands,

The wood-cutter's song, the ploughboy's on his way in the morning,
    or at the noon intermission or at sundown,

The delicious singing of the mother, or of the young wife at work,
    or of the girl sewing or washing—

Each singing what belongs to him or her, and to none else,
    The day what belongs to the day—at night the party of young fellows,
    robust, friendly,
    Singing with open mouths their strong melodious songs.

THE NEW COLOSSUS

Emma Lazarus

Emma Lazarus (1849–87) wrote "The New Colossus" in 1883 to help raise funds to build a pedestal for the Statue of Liberty, a gift from France. The poem's title refers to the Colossus of Rhodes, one of the seven wonders of the ancient world, a giant bronze statue of the god Helios that overlooked the Greek city's harbor. Lazarus's poem is engraved on a plaque inside the Statue of Liberty's base.

Not like the brazen giant of Greek fame,
With conquering limbs astride from land to land;
Here at our sea-washed, sunset gates shall stand
A mighty woman with a torch, whose flame
Is the imprisoned lightning, and her name
Mother of Exiles. From her beacon-hand
Glows world-wide welcome; her mild eyes command
The air-bridged harbor that twin cities frame.

"Keep, ancient lands, your storied pomp!" cries she
With silent lips. "Give me your tired, your poor,
Your huddled masses yearning to breathe free,
The wretched refuse of your teeming shore.
Send these, the homeless, tempest-tost to me.
I lift my lamp beside the golden door!"

THE FLAG GOES BY

Henry Holcomb Bennett

The U.S. Flag Code states that when the flag is passing in a parade or in a review, those not in uniform "should remove their headdress with their right hand and hold it at the left shoulder, the hand being over the heart."

Hats off!
Along the street there comes
A blare of bugles, a ruffle of drums,
A flash of color beneath the sky:
Hats off!
The flag is passing by.

Blue and crimson and white it shines,
Over the steel-tipped, ordered lines.
Hats off!
The colors before us fly,
But more than the flag is passing by:

Sea-fights and land-fights, grim and great,
Fought to make and to save the State,
Weary marches and sinking ships,
Cheers of victory on dying lips.

Days of plenty and years of peace,
March of a strong land's swift increase,
Equal justice, right, and law,
Stately honor and reverent awe.

Sign of a nation, great and strong
To ward her people from foreign wrong,
Pride and glory and honor—all
Live in the colors to stand or fall.

    Hats off!
Along the street there comes
A blare of bugles, a ruffle of drums,
And loyal hearts are beating high:
    Hats off!
The flag is passing by!

NOVEMBER

ON THE AFTERNOON OF NOVEMBER 1, 1800, an unannounced coach rolled to a stop before a grand but unfinished edifice in a weedy field in the new capital of Washington, D.C. John Adams climbed out and wandered inside the building, thus becoming the first president to occupy what we now call the White House. The next day, he wrote his wife: "I pray heaven to bestow the best of blessings on this house and all that shall hereafter inhabit it. May none but honest and wise men ever rule under this roof."

When Abigail arrived two weeks later, she was disappointed by the unready state of the home, but she made the best of it. "The great unfinished audience room I made a drying room of, to hang up the clothes in," she wrote her daughter.

In the republic's early days, people called the mansion the President's House. The name White House came into use after workers whitewashed its stone walls. (Today the building is painted white. It takes 570 gallons to cover the outside.) The mansion was badly damaged but rebuilt after the British burned it in 1814, during the War of 1812. It has been the home of every president except George Washington.

The White House is considered the First Family's private home, and each president has made a few changes. The Residence (the living-quarters portion of the White House) has 6 levels, 132 rooms, 35 bathrooms, 412 doors, and 28 fireplaces to accommodate all the people living, working, and visiting there. Recreation facilities include a movie theater, bowling lane, swimming pool, jogging track, and tennis court.

Thomas Jefferson, the third president, opened the White House for tours. Since then, except during wartime, the home of America's head of state has remained open to the public, free of charge.

AMERICAN HISTORY PARADE

1765   The much-despised Stamp Act goes into effect, a measure that American colonists view as taxation without representation.

1800   John Adams becomes the first president to move into the White House.

1900   The twelfth census reports that the United States has 76 million people at the outset of the twentieth century.

1913   Notre Dame uses the forward pass to beat Army, helping to popularize the play among football teams.

1938   In Baltimore, Seabiscuit upsets War Admiral in a horse race called "the match of the century."

1952   The United States explodes the first hydrogen bomb at Eniwetok Atoll in the Pacific.

HARDLY ANYONE gave President Harry Truman a prayer of a chance to win his 1948 reelection bid against Thomas Dewey of New York. All the pollsters predicted a win for Republican Dewey. Professional gamblers gave odds of fifteen to one against Democrat Truman. Reporters were writing stories about the upcoming Dewey administration.

Truman was about the only one who believed he could win. In September 1948 he left Washington, D.C., aboard a railroad car named the Ferdinand Magellan for a whistle-stop campaign across America. In speech after speech, town after town, he told people why they should reelect him while the crowds shouted back, "Give 'em hell, Harry!" The Ferdinand Magellan traveled nearly 22,000 miles in all. As historian David McCullough points out, never before had a president gone so far to take his case to the people.

Three weeks before the election, *Newsweek* magazine published a survey of 50 political writers. Every single one thought Truman would lose.

On election night, November 2, 1948, Truman went to bed at nine o'clock. He woke up around midnight, turned on the radio, and heard a commentator assure the nation that Dewey would win. Truman clicked him off and went back to sleep.

About four o'clock the next morning, an aide woke the president to tell him that he was ahead by 2 million votes. "We've got 'em beat," Truman said.

It was the biggest political upset in the nation's history. All the professional pundits were left scratching their heads. The voters had gone to the polls, elected the man who refused to quit, and reminded the experts that in this magical place called America, it's still the people who get to choose.

AMERICAN HISTORY PARADE

1795   James K. Polk, the eleventh U.S. president, is born in Mecklenburg County, North Carolina.

1865   Warren G. Harding, the 29th U.S. president, is born in Morrow County, Ohio.

1889   North Dakota and South Dakota become the 39th and 40th states.

1920   In one of the first radio reports of a presidential election, KDKA in Pittsburgh reports that Warren G. Harding has defeated James M. Cox.

1947   Howard Hughes pilots his gigantic wooden airplane, the *Spruce Goose*, on its only flight, lasting about a minute, near Long Beach, California.

ON NOVEMBER 3, 1924, President Calvin Coolidge took to the radio airwaves to remind Americans of a solemn duty:

All the opportunity for self-government through the rule of the people depends upon one single factor. That is the ballot box. . . . The people of our country are sovereign. If they do not vote they abdicate that sovereignty, and they may be entirely sure that if they relinquish it other forces will seize it, and if they fail to govern themselves some other power will rise up to govern them. The choice is always before them, whether they will be slaves or whether they will be free. The only way to be free is to exercise actively and energetically the privileges, and discharge faithfully the duties which make freedom. It is not to be secured by passive resistance. It is the result of energy and action. . . .

Persons who have the right to vote are trustees for the benefit of their country and their countrymen. They have no right to say they do not care. They must care! They have no right to say that whatever the result of the election they can get along. They must remember that their country and their countrymen cannot get along, cannot remain sound, cannot preserve its institutions, cannot protect its citizens, cannot maintain its place in the world, unless those who have the right to vote do sustain and do guide the course of public affairs by the thoughtful exercise of that right on election day.

AMERICAN HISTORY PARADE

1868   Republican Ulysses S. Grant defeats Democrat Horatio Seymour to become the eighteenth U.S. president.

1896   Republican William McKinley defeats Democrat William Jennings Bryan to become the twenty-fifth U.S. president.

1924   President Calvin Coolidge, in a radio address, reminds Americans of their duty to vote.

1948   The *Chicago Daily Tribune* announces "Dewey Defeats Truman" in a front-page headline (when, in fact, Truman had come from behind to win the presidential race).

1964   Incumbent president Lyndon B. Johnson defeats Republican challenger Barry Goldwater.

AT THE OUTSET OF THE REVOLUTIONARY WAR, America had no navy. Some colonies kept armed vessels, but the Continental government had no fighting ships. As the war got underway, Congress launched a small Continental Navy, voting to purchase and equip eight ships of war. On November 4, 1775, it acquired a swift, three-masted merchantman called the *Black Prince* and ordered that the vessel be converted into a warship with 30 cannons.

The *Black Prince* was soon rechristened the *Alfred*, named after Alfred the Great, the ninth-century British king regarded as the father of the Royal Navy. (In 1775, despite being at odds with the mother country, most colonists still considered themselves British and were proud to name a ship after an English king.) Many historians consider the *Alfred* the first ship in the U.S. Navy.

The *Alfred* was soon joined by the brigs *Columbus*, *Andrew Doria*, and *Cabot*, the schooners *Wasp* and *Fly*, and the sloops *Hornet* and *Providence*. In early 1776, with the *Alfred* serving as flagship, the little fleet sailed to the Bahamas and raided two British forts, seizing their cannons, mortars, and gunpowder.

Meanwhile, George Washington was one step ahead of Congress in realizing the need for a naval force that could intercept British ships sailing into Boston with supplies for the king's army. He chartered the armed schooner *Hannah* and on September 2, 1775, ordered it to sea in search of British cargo shipping. It became the first in a squadron of eleven vessels, known as "Washington's Navy," that the general commissioned to raid British supply ships. Some naval historians regard the *Hannah* as the first ship of the American navy.

AMERICAN HISTORY PARADE

1884   Democrat Grover Cleveland narrowly defeats Republican James G. Blaine in a presidential contest full of mudslinging.

1924   Nellie T. Ross of Wyoming is the first woman to be elected governor.

1939   In Detroit, the Packard Motor Car Company exhibits the first air-conditioned car.

1952   A computer called UNIVAC successfully predicts that Dwight D. Eisenhower will defeat Adlai Stevenson for president in a landslide.

1979   In Tehran, Iranian militants seize the U.S. embassy and 66 American hostages.

1980   Ronald Reagan defeats Jimmy Carter to become the fortieth U.S. president.

2008   Senator Barack Obama of Illinois becomes the first African American to be elected President of the United States.

"YOU WILL WRITE A LETTER to American pilots flying missions in the south. You will tell them it is wrong and they are criminals. You will tell them to protest to their government." With those words, Lt. Everett Alvarez's North Vietnamese captors led him into a room furnished with a wooden table, stick pen, bottle of ink, and blank paper. It was November 5, 1966. For the next several days, his jailors deprived him of sleep, kicked him, and then withheld food in an effort to get him to write a "confession." The ordeal was one of many Alvarez faced during his long captivity.

On August 5, 1964, while flying a mission against enemy torpedo boats, Alvarez had become the first American pilot shot down over North Vietnam. He soon found himself in the infamous prison known as the Hanoi Hilton. His starvation diet consisted of a chicken head floating in slimy stew, an animal hoof, or a blackbird lying feet up on a plate. Monstrous rats scurried across his tiny cell. More POWs arrived. The North Vietnamese often beat them, tied them up for days, or ratcheted handcuffs around their arms until it felt like hacksaws biting into their flesh. Not all survived.

Often held in isolation, the captives communicated by tapping a code on walls. "Contact with one another was essential," Alvarez wrote in his book *Chained Eagle*. "Without it, we were doomed." At the sound of pre-arranged taps, the POWs stood alone in their cells to whisper the Lord's Prayer in unison, then recited the Pledge of Allegiance with hand over heart.

At the war's end, after eight and a half years in the Hanoi Hilton and other prisons, Everett Alvarez came home. "Faith in God, in our president, and in our country—it was this faith that maintained our hope," he said. "God bless you, Mr. and Mrs. America. You did not forget us."

AMERICAN HISTORY PARADE

1862   Frustrated by Union troops' lack of success, Abraham Lincoln removes George McClellan from command of the Army of the Potomac.

1889   Wyoming citizens approve the first state constitution granting full voting rights to women.

1912   Woodrow Wilson defeats incumbent William Howard Taft and former president Theodore Roosevelt to become the twenty-eighth U.S. president.

1966   Everett Alvarez begins month 28 of what will eventually be 102 months as a POW in North Vietnam.

1994   Former president Ronald Reagan announces that he has Alzheimer's disease.

ON NOVEMBER 6, 1869, on a cold, windy day in New Brunswick, New Jersey, two teams from Rutgers and the College of New Jersey (now Princeton University) met in a contest often regarded as the first intercollegiate football game. Each team consisted of twenty-five men, and the only uniforms were scarlet scarves the Rutgers players wrapped around their heads. About a hundred spectators looked on, including a Rutgers professor who stayed only long enough to predict that "you men will come to no Christian end!"

That 1869 game was closer to soccer than modern American football. Players kicked the ball down the field and scored by sending it between two posts. Whichever team scored six goals first was to be the winner. Rutgers won 6–4.

Five years later, the game took a turn toward football as we know it when a team from McGill University in Montreal showed up in Cambridge, Massachusetts, to play some fellows from Harvard. The McGill team, it turned out, had come to play rugby, which permitted players to run with the ball and tackle. The Harvard team played a more soccerlike game. They decided to play two games, first by Harvard's rules, then by McGill's. Most of the Harvard boys had never heard of rugby, but they went wild over the sport and soon introduced it to other U.S. colleges.

During the next few years, players began to mix rugby with the American kicking game— and out of that came football. In the 1880s Yale coach and former player Walter Camp led the way in establishing rules about downs, yards to gain, snapping the ball to the quarterback, and tackling below the waist. Camp, more than anyone else, is remembered as the father of American football.

AMERICAN HISTORY PARADE

1789   John Carroll of Maryland is appointed as the first Roman Catholic bishop in the United States.

1860   Abraham Lincoln defeats three other candidates to become the sixteenth U.S. president.

1869   Rutgers defeats Princeton 6–4 in the first intercollegiate football game.

1888   Republican Benjamin Harrison receives fewer popular votes but more electoral votes to defeat incumbent Grover Cleveland and become the twenty-third U.S. president.

1928   Republican Herbert Hoover defeats Democrat Alfred E. Smith to become the thirty-first U.S. president.

NOVEMBER 7 • THE FIRST TUESDAY AFTER THE FIRST MONDAY

ON TUESDAY, NOVEMBER 7, 1848, Americans went to the polls and elected Zachary Taylor to the White House on the first nationwide presidential Election Day. Before then, Election Day varied from state to state. Federal law required only that states hold it sometime during a thirty-four-day period before the first Wednesday in December, when the Electoral College met.

As trains and telegraph wires brought speedier communication, officials grew concerned that people in late-voting states would be influenced by results in early-voting states. So Congress designated the first Tuesday after the first Monday in November, in years divisible by four, as the day for electing the president.

Why that particular time? According to the Federal Election Commission, November was a good month for voting in a mainly agrarian republic. The autumn harvest was over, so farmers had more time to go to the polls. In most places in early November, the weather was still mild enough to get over rough roads.

Why Tuesday? People often had to travel a good distance to reach the county seat where they voted. Monday did not make a good Election Day since it would require some people to begin traveling on Sunday, which would interfere with church activities. So lawmakers went with Tuesday.

Why the Tuesday after the first Monday? One explanation is that lawmakers wanted to make sure Election Day never fell on the first of November, All Saints Day, a holy day for Catholics. But the main reason was that in some years, the first Tuesday in November would fall more than thirty-four days before the first Wednesday in December, when the Electoral College met. Lawmakers therefore chose the first Tuesday after the first Monday in November, so as not to conflict with existing law.

AMERICAN HISTORY PARADE

1848   Zachary Taylor is elected the twelfth U.S. president on the first-ever nationwide Election Day.

1874   A cartoon by Thomas Nast in *Harper's Weekly* is the first to depict the Republican Party as an elephant.

1916   Republican Jeannette Rankin of Montana becomes the first woman elected to Congress.

1944   President Franklin D. Roosevelt defeats Thomas Dewey to win an unprecedented fourth term in office.

1989   In Virginia, Democrat Douglas Wilder becomes the first African American elected governor of a U.S. state.

WHICH PRESIDENT served two nonconsecutive terms? Hint: He was elected in 1884 and again in 1892, with Benjamin Harrison serving as president between his two terms. Answer below.

Which presidents signed the Declaration of Independence? *John Adams, Thomas Jefferson*

Which presidents signed the Constitution? *George Washington, James Madison*

Which president served the shortest time in office? *William H. Harrison,* 31 days

Which president served the longest? *Franklin D. Roosevelt,* 12 years, 39 days

Who was the youngest person to be elected president? *John F. Kennedy,* 43

Who was the youngest person to become president? *Theodore Roosevelt,* 42*

Who was the oldest person to become president? *Ronald Reagan,* 69

Who was the only president to resign? *Richard Nixon*

Which presidents were impeached? *Andrew Johnson, Bill Clinton*

Which president served two non-consecutive terms? *Grover Cleveland*

Which president was never elected either as president or vice president? *Gerald Ford*

Which presidents were elected even though their opponents received more popular votes? *J. Q. Adams,* 1824; *R. Hayes,* 1876; *B. Harrison,* 1888; *G. W. Bush,* 2000

* Theodore Roosevelt was forty-two in 1901 when he succeeded McKinley, who had been assassinated. John F. Kennedy was forty-three when elected president in 1960.

AMERICAN HISTORY PARADE

1889   Montana becomes the forty-first state.

1892   Former president Grover Cleveland defeats incumbent Benjamin Harrison to become the only president to serve two nonconsecutive terms.

1932   New York governor Franklin D. Roosevelt defeats incumbent Herbert Hoover to become the thirty-second U.S. president.

1942   U.S. and British forces land in French North Africa during World War II.

1960   Massachusetts senator John F. Kennedy defeats Vice President Richard M. Nixon to become the thirty-fifth U.S. president.

2000   Florida begins a statewide recount of ballots to decide the winner of the presidential race between George W. Bush and Vice President Al Gore.

To BENJAMIN BANNEKER, born this day in 1731 in Baltimore County, Maryland, the words "all men are created" had potent meaning. A free black and descendent of former slaves, Banneker had been limited to a few scattered months of education at a one-room Quaker school. But from an early age he exhibited a mathematical and scientific genius. As a young farmer, he decided to build a clock that struck the hours, even though he had never seen one before. He made it entirely from wood, carving the gears and wheels with a pocketknife, and it kept time for more than forty years.

At age fifty-seven, Banneker borrowed some books and a telescope from a neighbor, George Ellicott, and taught himself astronomical calculations that allowed him to predict a 1789 solar eclipse. In 1791 he helped lay out the boundaries of the nation's new capital, the District of Columbia.

From 1792 to 1797 he furnished the astronomical tables for *Benjamin Banneker's Pennsylvania, Delaware, Maryland and Virginia Almanack.* The yearly almanacs spread his fame as the "African astronomer," and abolitionists used them to fight antiblack stereotypes.

Banneker sent his first almanac to Secretary of State Thomas Jefferson, along with a letter reminding him of the ideals he'd expressed in the Declaration of Independence. He wrote Jefferson that he hoped "that your sentiments are concurrent with mine, which are, that one universal Father hath given being to us all; and that he hath . . . afforded us all the same sensations and endowed us all with the same faculties."

Jefferson's cordial reply expressed satisfaction "to see such proofs as you exhibit." A more cogent observation came from Maryland's James McHenry, a signer of the Constitution. Benjamin Banneker's work, he wrote, showed that "the powers of the mind are disconnected to the color of the skin."

AMERICAN HISTORY PARADE

1731   Mathematician and astronomer Benjamin Banneker is born near Baltimore.

1872   A three-day fire in Boston destroys 775 buildings.

1906   Theodore Roosevelt becomes the first president to leave the country while in office when he embarks on a trip to inspect construction of the Panama Canal.

1965   A massive power failure leaves much of the northeastern United States without electricity for up to 13½ hours.

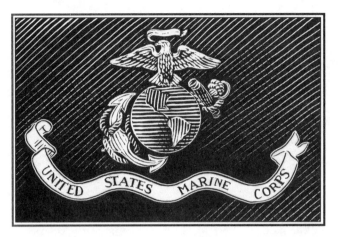

THE U.S. MARINE CORPS traces its origins to November 10, 1775, during the Revolutionary War, when the Continental Congress called for two battalions of Continental Marines to be raised. Their mission was to provide security onboard Navy ships, conduct ship-to-ship fighting, and serve as landing troops. Tradition has it that the Tun Tavern in Philadelphia served as the first Marines recruiting post. The Marines' first landing, led by Captain Samuel Nicholas, came in March 1776 at New Providence, in the Bahamas, where they seized British cannons, shells, and powder.

The Marines were disbanded after the Revolutionary War, then reformed in 1798. The U.S. Marine Corps has served in every major armed conflict in American history. As a "force in readiness," its missions range from amphibious assaults to counterterrorism operations.

The Marine Corps flag is a scarlet banner that carries a yellow and gray image of a globe (symbolizing service in any part of the world) and an anchor (a reminder of the amphibious nature of Marines' duties, and that the Marine Corps is a partner of the U.S. Navy). An eagle stands on the globe, holding in its beak a scroll inscribed with the Marine Corps motto, *Semper Fidelis* ("Always Faithful"). Below, a larger scroll reads, "United States Marine Corps." The flag's design dates to 1939.

AMERICAN HISTORY PARADE

1775   The Continental Congress founds the U.S. Marines Corps.

1871   *New York Herald* journalist Henry M. Stanley finds Scottish missionary David Livingstone at Lake Tanganyika, Africa, and greets him with the famous words: "Dr. Livingstone, I presume."

1928   Notre Dame football coach Knute Rockne tells his team, "Win one for the Gipper," and they do, beating Army 12–6.

1938   Kate Smith introduces Americans to Irving Berlin's "God Bless America," singing it for the first time on her network radio show.

1954   President Dwight D. Eisenhower dedicates the Marine Corps War Memorial (Iwo Jima Memorial) in Arlington, Virginia.

IN THE EARLY MORNING HOURS OF NOVEMBER 11, 1918, representatives of France, Britain, and Germany met in a railroad car near Compiègne, France, to sign an armistice ending World War I, or the Great War, as it was known at that time. The cease-fire took effect at 11:00 a.m. that day—the eleventh hour of the eleventh day of the eleventh month. Up and down the trenches, after four long years of the most horrific fighting the world had yet known, the guns fell silent. "The roar stopped like a motor car hitting a wall," one U.S. soldier wrote to his family. Soldiers on both sides slowly climbed out of the earthworks. Some danced; some cheered; some cried for joy; some stood numbed. The Great War had left some 9 million soldiers dead and another 21 million wounded. No one knows how many millions of civilians died. Much of Europe lay in ruins. But finally, with the armistice, it was "all quiet on the Western Front."

For many years November 11 was known as Armistice Day to honor those who fought in World War I. In 1954 Congress changed the name to Veterans Day to recognize all American veterans.

Every November 11 at 11:00 a.m., the nation pays tribute to its war dead with the laying of a presidential wreath at the Tomb of the Unknown Soldier in Arlington National Cemetery outside Washington, D.C.

But Veterans Day honors more than the dead. Memorial Day, observed in May, is for remembering soldiers who lost their lives in the service of their country. Veterans Day is set aside to honor and thank *all* who have served in the U.S. armed forces—particularly our 23 million living veterans.

AMERICAN HISTORY PARADE

1889   Washington becomes the forty-second state.

1918   World War I ends with the signing of an armistice in France.

1919   In the first Armistice Day ceremony, two California redwood trees are planted in Lafayette Square near the White House.

1921   President Warren G. Harding attends a burial ceremony at the Tomb of the Unknown Soldier in Arlington National Cemetery for an unidentified soldier killed in World War I.

WHEN FRENCH-AMERICAN J. Hector St. John de Crèvecoeur died on November 12, 1813, he left behind a vivid portrait of life on the eighteenth-century American frontier. Crèvecoeur had emigrated to the New World in 1755 and eventually settled on a farm in New York. His impressions, published in England in 1782 as *Letters from an American Farmer*, still offer insights about the American character:

> What then is the American, this new man? . . . He is an American who, leaving behind him all his ancient prejudices and manners, receives new ones from the new mode of life he has embraced, the new government he obeys, and the new rank he holds. He becomes an American by being received in the broad lap of our great Alma Mater. Here individuals of all nations are melted into a new race of men, whose labors and posterity will one day cause great changes in the world. Americans are the western pilgrims who are carrying along with them that great mass of arts, sciences, vigor, and industry which began long since in the East; they will finish the great circle. . . . The American ought therefore to love this country much better than that wherein either he or his forefathers were born. Here the rewards of his industry follow with equal steps the progress of his labor . . . without any part being claimed, either by a despotic prince, a rich abbot, or a mighty lord. . . . The American is a new man, who acts upon new principles; he must therefore entertain new ideas and form new opinions. From involuntary idleness, servile dependence, penury, and useless labor, he has passed to toils of a very different nature, rewarded by ample subsistence. This is an American.

AMERICAN HISTORY PARADE

1892   In Pittsburgh, William "Pudge" Heffelfinger becomes the first professional football player when he earns $500 playing for the Allegheny Athletic Association against the Pittsburgh Athletic Club.

1942   The Naval Battle of Guadalcanal begins, a pivotal Allied victory in the Pacific.

1954   Ellis Island closes after processing more than 12 million immigrants since opening in New York Harbor in 1892.

1981   The space shuttle *Columbia* becomes the first manned spacecraft ever to be launched twice when it lifts off at Cape Canaveral, Florida.

THE VIETNAM VETERANS MEMORIAL IN WASHINGTON, D.C., dedicated on November 13, 1982, honors American men and women who served in a long and controversial war. The main part of the memorial consists of a polished black granite wall that bears the names of more than 58,000 Americans who died in the war, or who are listed as missing in action. Every day, visitors leave flowers, pictures, and notes for loved ones lost in Vietnam. Many people make pencil rubbings of the name of someone special.

During a visit to the Wall, as it is known, President Ronald Reagan said this:

The memorial reflects as a mirror reflects, so that when you find the name you're searching for you find it in your own reflection. And as you touch it, from certain angles, you're touching, too, the reflection of the Washington Monument or the chair in which great Abe Lincoln sits. Those who fought in Vietnam are part of us, part of our history. They reflected the best in us. No number of wreaths, no amount of music and memorializing will ever do them justice, but it is good for us that we honor them and their sacrifice. And it's good that we do it in the reflected glow of the enduring symbols of our Republic.

When our soldiers returned from Vietnam, they sometimes met the scorn of fellow Americans who, as Reagan put it, "were unable to distinguish between our native distaste for war and the stainless patriotism of those who suffered its scars." In decades since, Americans have found renewed gratitude for those who served. The Vietnam Veterans Memorial is a place to remember the price of war *and* honor those who have answered the call of their country. As the poet Virgil wrote:

> Here, too, the honorable finds its due
> And there are tears for passing things;
> Here, too, things mortal touch the mind.

AMERICAN HISTORY PARADE

1775   During the American Revolution, Patriot troops under General Richard Montgomery capture Montreal.

1956   The Supreme Court strikes down laws requiring segregation on public buses.

1971   *Mariner 9* becomes the first satellite to orbit another planet, Mars.

1982   The Vietnam Veterans Memorial is dedicated in Washington, D.C.

NOVEMBER 14 • "When I go to sea, I go as a simple sailor"

NOVEMBER 14, 1851, brought the publication of Herman Melville's *Moby Dick*, a classic chock-full of American themes from its opening pages: the urge to strike out for frontiers, the dignity of the common man, and a democratic spirit of equality.

Call me Ishmael. Some years ago—never mind how long precisely—having little or no money in my purse, and nothing particular to interest me on shore, I thought I would sail about a little and see the watery part of the world. It is a way I have of driving off the spleen, and regulating the circulation. Whenever I find myself growing grim about the mouth; whenever it is a damp, drizzly November in my soul . . . I account it high time to get to sea as soon as I can. . . .

I never go as a passenger; nor, though I am something of a salt, do I ever go to sea as a Commodore, or a Captain, or a Cook. . . . No, when I go to sea, I go as a simple sailor, right before the mast, plumb down into the forecastle, aloft there to the royal mast-head. True, they rather order me about some, and make me jump from spar to spar, like a grasshopper in a May meadow. . . . [Yet] however the old sea-captains may order me about—however they may thump and punch me about, I have the satisfaction of knowing that it is all right; that everybody else is one way or other served in much the same way—either in a physical or metaphysical point of view, that is; and so the universal thump is passed round, and all hands should rub each other's shoulder-blades, and be content.

AMERICAN HISTORY PARADE

1851   Herman Melville's novel *Moby Dick* is published.

1910   Eugene Fly becomes the first pilot to take off from a ship, the USS *Birmingham*, anchored off Hampton Roads, Virginia.

1935   President Franklin D. Roosevelt declares the Philippine Islands to be a self-governing commonwealth (which gains full independence in 1946).

1972   The Dow Jones Industrial Average closes above 1,000 for the first time, ending the trading session at 1,003.16.

"AT TWO O'CLOCK IN THE AFTERNOON I thought I could distinguish a mountain to our right, which appeared like a small blue cloud," wrote Lieutenant Zebulon Pike, who on November 15, 1806, was leading an expedition toward the headwaters of the Arkansas River. A look through a spyglass seemed to confirm his conjecture, and as he rode forward the distant "cloud" turned into a majestic peak. His men gave three cheers when a "grand western chain of mountains" with snow-covered flanks appeared in full view. They had just become the first U.S. expedition to reach the Rocky Mountains in what is now Colorado.

Lieutenant Pike's journey was part exploration and part spy mission. His orders were to look over the southern portion of the Louisiana Purchase and find out what the Spanish were doing in the Mexican borderlands. His men were poorly trained and equipped, but Pike was determined to push as far as he could.

Several days later, he and three others set out to ascend the high peak he had spotted. They spent a day climbing rocks, "sometimes almost perpendicular," and shivered through a night in a cave. The next morning they climbed higher. Far below, clouds swept across the prairie "like the ocean in a storm, wave piled on wave." They hiked through waist-high snow to a summit, where Pike realized that the massive peak he'd seen still lay 15 miles away. Convinced that "no human being could have ascended to its pinnacle," the freezing men returned to their camp, and then continued their journey west.

In 1820 botanist Edwin James became the first man to conquer Pikes Peak. Today you can reach the top by highway, cog railway, or the old-fashioned way. Both authors have hiked to the summit for one of the most glorious views in America.

AMERICAN HISTORY PARADE

1777   The Continental Congress adopts the Articles of Confederation, the basic charter of government that preceded the U.S. Constitution.

1805   The Lewis and Clark expedition reaches the mouth of the Columbia River.

1806   Zebulon Pike spots the mountain now known as Pikes Peak.

1896   Streetlights in Buffalo, New York, switch on using power generated 25 miles away at Niagara Falls, the first such long-distance transmission of hydroelectricity.

1939   President Franklin D. Roosevelt lays the cornerstone of the Jefferson Memorial.

1969   A quarter million anti-Vietnam War protestors march in Washington, D.C.

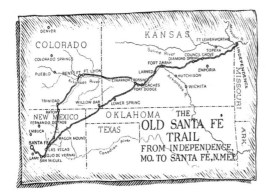

"EVERY MAN WILL FIT HIMSELF for the trip with a horse, a good rifle, and as much ammunition as the company may think necessary," William Becknell explained in a *Missouri Intelligencer* ad seeking men to accompany him west. "Every man will furnish an equal part of the fitting out for trade, and receive an equal part of the product."

Ever since Zebulon Pike wandered into Spanish territory during his explorations, Spanish officials had chased American traders out of New Mexico, which was said to be rich in silver, furs, and livestock. But in 1821, Becknell heard reports of Mexican independence from Spain, so he decided to risk a trading expedition. He set out from Franklin, Missouri, with a string of pack mules, and on November 16, 1821, after several weeks of "hardships and obstacles occurring almost daily," he arrived to a warm welcome in Santa Fe. When the traders got back to Franklin, they cut open saddlebags full of silver dollars that "clinking on the stone pavement rolled into the gutter."

Soon other exultant Missouri traders were heading west on the 900-mile Santa Fe Trail, their pack trains loaded with cottons, silks, woolens, hardware, and cutlery. They returned with pelts, hides, and Mexican silver. On the trail, they risked heat, thirst, hostile Indians, raging prairie fires, and storms that could tear wagons apart. While blazing a path across the Cimarron Desert, Becknell himself barely escaped dying of thirst by cutting open a buffalo and drinking the water in its stomach.

But the trade was good, so the traders kept coming. Pioneer families, gold-seekers, hunters, and adventurers followed along. For his role in opening the way in the Southwest, William Becknell is remembered as the Father of the Santa Fe Trail.

AMERICAN HISTORY PARADE

1700   Charleston, South Carolina, which had established the first library in the English colonies in 1698, passes an act allowing inhabitants to borrow its books.

1821   William Becknell reaches Santa Fe, an event that opens the Santa Fe Trail.

1864   Union general William T. Sherman leaves Atlanta in smoldering ruins as he begins his "March to the Sea."

1907   Oklahoma becomes the forty-sixth state.

WILLIAM COSBY, England's governor for the colony of New York, was a bully and a scoundrel. He tried to silence opponents, rig elections, and use his office to make himself rich. But Cosby had a problem: John Peter Zenger and his printing press.

Zenger, a German immigrant, began publishing his *New York Weekly Journal* in 1733, and he made it his business to publicize Cosby's greed and arrogance. No other paper had been so bold.

Cosby reacted by sending his henchmen to seize and burn copies of the paper. Zenger went right on printing his *Journal*. On November 17, 1734, the governor tried to silence Zenger for good by having him arrested for seditious libel.

At Cosby's request, bail was set much higher than Zenger could pay. For nearly nine months he sat in prison while his wife, Anna, helped publish the paper.

Finally Zenger got his day in court. But the governor's handpicked judges disbarred his lawyers, leaving him without counsel. Andrew Hamilton, one of the finest attorneys in the colonies, rose from his sickbed in Philadelphia and journeyed to New York City to defend the printer.

The court all but ordered the jurors to find Zenger guilty of libel. Hamilton reminded them that the printer's only crime was that he had dared to publish the truth. It did not take long for the jury to reach a decision. On August 4, 1735, it returned its verdict: not guilty.

The trial set a precedent for America's world-famous freedom of the press. Journalists sometimes abuse that freedom in pursuit of their own agendas. Still, the First Amendment remains an American bedrock. As Zenger's newspaper put it, "No nation ancient or modern has ever lost the liberty of freely speaking, writing or publishing their sentiments, but forthwith lost their liberty in general and became slaves."

AMERICAN HISTORY PARADE

1734   John Peter Zenger is arrested for criticizing Governor William Cosby in his *New York Weekly Journal*.

1800   Congress convenes for the first time in Washington, D.C., in the partially completed Capitol building.

1881   In Pittsburgh, Samuel Gompers helps found the Federation of Organized Trades and Labor Unions, forerunner of the American Federation of Labor.

1973   In Orlando, President Richard Nixon famously declares that "people have got to know whether or not their president is a crook. Well, I'm not a crook."

ON NOVEMBER 18, 1889, the Navy launched the battleship USS *Maine* at the Brooklyn Navy Yard. But the ship's beginning would turn out to be not nearly as famous as its ending—an explosion that sent it to the bottom of Havana's harbor in 1898, triggering the Spanish-American War and giving rise to the slogan, "Remember the *Maine!*"

The *Maine* was one of several battleships named after states. Over time, the Navy has developed a system (sometimes ignored) for naming vessels.

Aircraft carriers are often named for great Americans, such as the *Abraham Lincoln* and *Ronald Reagan*.

Amphibious assault ships are named for famous Navy ships, such as the *Wasp* and *Essex*.

Guided missile cruisers are usually named for famous battles, such as the *Ticonderoga* and *Gettysburg*.

Destroyers are named for naval leaders and heroes, such as the *Farragut* and *John Paul Jones*.

Frigates are named for heroes and distinguished members of the U.S. Navy, Marine Corps, and Coast Guard, such as the *Robert G. Bradley* and *John L. Hall*.

Ballistic missile submarines are named for states, such as the *Ohio* and *Alabama*.

Attack submarines are named for cities, such as the *Los Angeles* and *Norfolk* or states, such as the *Virginia* and *Texas*.

Other traditions include: mine countermeasures ships are given names representing strength and defense—*Avenger* and *Guardian*; dry cargo ships are named for famous explorers and pioneers—*Lewis and Clark*, *Sacagawea*; coastal patrol boats are often given storm-related names—*Typhoon*, *Thunderbolt*; hospital ships are given names indicating care—*Comfort*, *Mercy*.

AMERICAN HISTORY PARADE

1820   Captain Nathaniel Palmer becomes the first American to sight Antarctica.

1872   Susan B. Anthony is arrested in Rochester, New York, for trying to vote in the presidential election earlier in the month.

1883   At the urging of the railroads, the United States is divided into time zones.

1889   The battleship *Maine* is launched at the Brooklyn Navy Yard.

1928   *Steamboat Willie*, the first Mickey Mouse cartoon with sound, premieres.

IN THE AUTUMN OF 1863, President Abraham Lincoln received an invitation to give a speech at Gettysburg, Pennsylvania, where a few months earlier Americans had fought one of the bloodiest battles of the Civil War. The battlefield was being dedicated as a cemetery for soldiers who had died there. Would Lincoln come help honor the dead? The president accepted the invitation.

In the following weeks, Lincoln worked on his speech but did not get a chance to write it all down before the time came to travel to Gettysburg. He finished it there the night before the ceremony. The next morning, November 19, he made a few final changes and a clean copy.

A short time later, the president mounted a horse, joined a procession to the burial ground, and took his place on a wooden platform for the dedication. Thousands of people had gathered on the battlefield. The main speaker of the day, Edward Everett, spoke for two hours. When Everett was through, the president unfolded his single-page manuscript and approached the podium. He spoke for only two minutes. Many in the audience thought he was just getting going when he suddenly finished. Lincoln himself was unsure of the oration's success. ("Lamon, that speech won't scour!" he reportedly told a friend.) But with fewer than 300 words, Abraham Lincoln had given the greatest address ever delivered on American soil.

The Gettysburg Address still reminds us that thousands have died defending an ideal on which our country was founded—that *all* people are created equal. The dead can be honored only if the nation lives up to that ideal, Lincoln asserted. By devoting ourselves to it, and by defending it when necessary, Americans ensure that "government of the people, by the people, for the people, shall not perish from the earth."

The Gettysburg Address is reprinted on page 329.

AMERICAN HISTORY PARADE

1493   Christopher Columbus discovers Puerto Rico on his second voyage.

1831   James A. Garfield, the twentieth U.S. president, is born in Cuyahoga County, Ohio.

1863   Abraham Lincoln delivers the Gettysburg Address.

1919   The Senate rejects the Treaty of Versailles and U.S. participation in the League of Nations.

1969   *Apollo 12* astronauts Charles Conrad and Alan Bean make the second landing on the moon.

THE VARIOUS BRANCHES of the military and many military units have mottos that sum up their missions. The slogans speak volumes about the character of the men and women who serve in uniform. Here are a few of the mottos—some official, some unofficial—of those who defend us.

Army – This We'll Defend

Navy – *Non sibi sed patriae* (Not for self, but for country)

Air Force - Above All

Marine Corps – *Semper Fidelis* (Always Loyal)

Coast Guard – *Semper Paratus* (Always Prepared)

National Guard – Always ready, always there

U.S. Military Academy (West Point) – Duty, Honor, Country

U.S. Naval Academy – *Ex Scientia Tridens* (From Knowledge, Sea Power)

U.S. Coast Guard Academy – *Scientiae Cedit Mare* (The sea yields to knowledge)

Green Berets – *De Oppresso Liber* (To liberate the oppressed)

Army Rangers – *Sua Sponte* (Of Their Own Accord) and Rangers Lead the Way

Army Corps of Engineers - *Essayons* (Let us try)

Navy Seals – The only easy day was yesterday

Seabees – *Construimus, Batuimus* (We Build, We Fight) and Can Do!

AMERICAN HISTORY PARADE

1620   Peregrine White, the first child born of English parents in New England, is born aboard the *Mayflower* off Cape Cod.

1789   New Jersey becomes the first state to ratify the Bill of Rights.

1820   The Nantucket whaler *Essex* is attacked and sunk by a sperm whale in the South Pacific, an event that helps inspire Herman Melville to write *Moby Dick*.

1943   One of the bloodiest battles in Marines Corps history begins on Tarawa Atoll in the Pacific; the U.S. prevails, but at a cost of approximately 1,000 dead.

1953   Flying a Douglas Skyrocket at Edwards Air Force Base, California, Scott Crossfield becomes the first pilot to break Mach 2.

IN NOVEMBER 1620, after a stormy, two-month Atlantic voyage, the Pilgrims reached the coast of what is now Massachusetts. When they realized they had blown north of the region in which they had contracted to settle, some of the colonists announced they no longer felt bound by any legal authority, and that "none had power to command them." The Pilgrim leaders quickly solved the problem with a new contract.

On November 21 (November 11, by the Old Style calendar), as the *Mayflower* lay at anchor off Cape Cod, the settlers drew up an agreement to live together peacefully. They pledged to "enact, constitute and frame such just and equal Laws, Ordinances, Acts, Constitutions and Offices, from time to time, as shall be thought most meet and convenient for the general good of the Colony." After writing out the compact, forty-one adult males signed it, and then the signers agreed that John Carver would be their governor.

In essence, the Mayflower Compact was an agreement for self-government. It was not a forced bargain among unequals, such as a monarch and his subjects, or a lord and his vassals. Rather, it was a social contract between pioneers with a common purpose. Here was a group of people capable of forging a new society in a New World. In the coming years, as Pilgrim leader William Bradford wrote, "they met and consulted of laws and orders, both for their civil and military government as the necessity of their condition did require." Throughout the infant American colonies, settlers gained practice in something very rare for that time: government of the people and by the people.

AMERICAN HISTORY PARADE

1620   Pilgrim leaders frame the Mayflower Compact.

1789   North Carolina becomes the twelfth state to ratify the Constitution.

1877   Thomas Edison announces the invention of the phonograph.

1964   New York's Verrazano Narrows Bridge opens to traffic.

1980   Millions of TV viewers tune in to *Dallas* to find out "who shot J. R."

1995   The Dow Jones Industrial Average closes above 5,000 for the first time.

ON NOVEMBER 22, 1963, President John F. Kennedy was assassinated by Lee Harvey Oswald during a visit to Dallas, Texas. This somber anniversary is a good time to remember the stirring words the young president offered the nation in his inaugural address, less than three years before his death:

> Since this country was founded, each generation of Americans has been summoned to give testimony to its national loyalty. The graves of young Americans who answered the call to service surround the globe.
>
> Now the trumpet summons us again—not as a call to bear arms, though arms we need—not as a call to battle, though embattled we are—but a call to bear the burden of a long twilight struggle, year in and year out, "rejoicing in hope; patient in tribulation," a struggle against the common enemies of man: tyranny, poverty, disease, and war itself. . . .
>
> In the long history of the world, only a few generations have been granted the role of defending freedom in its hour of maximum danger. I do not shrink from this responsibility—I welcome it. I do not believe that any of us would exchange places with any other people or any other generation. The energy, the faith, the devotion which we bring to this endeavor will light our country and all who serve it. And the glow from that fire can truly light the world.
>
> And so, my fellow Americans, ask not what your country can do for you; ask what you can do for your country. . . .
>
> With a good conscience our only sure reward, with history the final judge of our deeds, let us go forth to lead the land we love, asking His blessing and His help, but knowing that here on earth God's work must truly be our own.

AMERICAN HISTORY PARADE

1718   Edward Teach, better known as Blackbeard, is killed off North Carolina's Outer Banks in a battle with ships sent from Virginia to hunt down the pirate.

1842   Mount St. Helens in Washington erupts during an active period lasting several years.

1935   Pan American Airways' *China Clipper* begins the first transpacific airmail service, from Alameda, California, to Manila, in the Philippines.

1943   President Franklin D. Roosevelt, Winston Churchill, and Chinese leader Chiang Kai-shek meet in Cairo to discuss World War II in Asia and the Pacific.

1963   John F. Kennedy is assassinated in Dallas, and Vice President Lyndon B. Johnson is sworn in as the thirty-sixth U.S. president.

FOR NEARLY A CENTURY AND A HALF, most First Ladies stayed out of the limelight, their public duties limited to greeting White House guests and hosting state dinners.

Eleanor Roosevelt changed that during the years her husband Franklin was president, from 1933 to 1945. She was the first First Lady to hold press conferences and address a national party convention. She gave scores of speeches, authored magazine articles, wrote a newspaper column, and captured the country's imagination.

Eleanor seemed to be everywhere, visiting coal miners in Appalachia, sharecroppers in cotton fields, and soldiers overseas. She was FDR's eyes and legs. Sometimes he would say in a meeting, "About that situation, my Missus told me . . ."

In November 1938 the outspoken First Lady attended a conference in Birmingham, Alabama, where segregation laws required blacks and whites to sit apart at public gatherings. She arrived at the auditorium, took one look at the whites sitting on one side of the aisle and blacks on the other, and took her seat on the black side.

After a few moments a police officer tapped her on the shoulder and said she would have to move. The chief of police had threatened to arrest anyone who broke the segregation laws. Move she did—by placing her chair in the aisle between both sections, managing to sit beside whites *and* blacks.

For the rest of the four-day conference, she carried a folding chair from meeting to meeting. In every room she sat in the middle, refusing to be segregated, a symbol of the need for all Americans to come together. "We are the leading democracy of the world," she told the conference, "and as such must prove to the world that democracy is possible and capable of living up to the principles upon which it was founded."

AMERICAN HISTORY PARADE

1804   Franklin Pierce, the fourteenth U.S. president, is born in Hillsboro, New Hampshire.

1863   The Battle of Chattanooga, Tennessee, begins, resulting in a critical Union victory.

1889   The first jukebox debuts at the Palais Royale Saloon in San Francisco.

1938   Eleanor Roosevelt attends the Southern Conference on Human Welfare in Birmingham.

1945   Most World War II food rationing ends in the United States.

IN 1863, when Abraham Lincoln was president, the cooks at the White House received a live turkey to fatten up for a holiday feast. The turkey's name was Jack, and it didn't take long for Lincoln's son Tad, age ten, to make friends with the bird. Soon Jack was following young Tad around the White House grounds like a pet.

One day, the story goes, Lincoln was in a Cabinet meeting when a tearful Tad burst into the room. He announced that Jack was about to be killed and begged his father to stop the execution.

"But Jack was sent here to be eaten," the president tried to explain.

"He's a good turkey, and we mustn't kill him," Tad sobbed back.

The president halted his meeting, took a piece of paper, and wrote out a reprieve. A joyful Tad raced away to show the presidential order to the executioner and save the life of Jack the turkey.

According to the White House, people sometimes gave live holiday turkeys to presidents in the years following the Lincoln administration, but it wasn't until 1947 that the first official National Thanksgiving Turkey was presented to Harry S. Truman, who followed Lincoln's example and pardoned the bird.

The reprieve has become an annual tradition. Each year, the National Turkey Federation chooses a plump bird and brings it to Washington. (Believe it or not, an alternate is also chosen in case the winner cannot fulfill its responsibilities.) Just before Thanksgiving, the president of the United States pardons the National Thanksgiving Turkey at the White House. The grateful bird then retires to a petting zoo or a resort such as Disney World, where it stays the remainder of its happy, natural life.

AMERICAN HISTORY PARADE

1784   Zachary Taylor, the twelfth U.S. president, is born in Orange County, Virginia.

1832   A South Carolina convention passes an ordinance to nullify the Federal Tariff Act, which placed duties on foreign imports.

1963   In Dallas, Jack Ruby fatally shoots Lee Harvey Oswald, the accused assassin of President John F. Kennedy.

1987   The U.S. and U.S.S.R. agree to dismantle medium- and shorter-range missiles in the first superpower treaty to ban an entire class of nuclear weapons.

2003   President George W. Bush pardons "Stars," the National Thanksgiving Turkey, and its alternate, "Stripes."

OUR NATION has inherited a long, rich tradition of thanking God for his blessings.

In 1541 Spanish explorer Francisco Vásquez de Coronado and his men conducted a service of thanksgiving for the abundant food and water they found along the Palo Duro Canyon in the Texas Panhandle.

In 1564 French Huguenot colonists settled in the area of Jacksonville, Florida, and "sang a psalm of Thanksgiving unto God."

In 1607, when the Jamestown colonists arrived in Virginia, they immediately erected a wooden cross and gave thanks for their safe passage across the ocean.

In 1619, English colonists at Berkeley Hundred in Virginia decreed that the day of their arrival, December 4, "shall be yearly and perpetually kept holy as a day of Thanksgiving to Almighty God."

In the autumn of 1621, the Pilgrims at Plymouth, Massachusetts, held a feast to celebrate the harvest and thank the Lord for his goodness—the feast we now remember as the "First Thanksgiving."

In 1777, during the Revolutionary War, the Continental Congress designated December 18 of that year a day "for solemn Thanksgiving and praise" for the Patriot army's victory at Saratoga—the first national day of thanksgiving.

In 1789 President George Washington proclaimed November 26 to be a day of thanksgiving for God's blessings and for the new United States Constitution.

It wasn't until 1863, in the midst of the Civil War, that the country got a regular national Thanksgiving Day. Abraham Lincoln proclaimed the last Thursday in November "a day of thanksgiving and praise to our beneficent Father." Succeeding presidents followed Lincoln's example. In 1941, Congress passed a law officially declaring the fourth Thursday in November as America's Thanksgiving Day.

AMERICAN HISTORY PARADE

1758   During the French and Indian War, the British troops defeat the French at Fort Duquesne in what is now Pittsburgh.

1783   The British withdraw from New York City, their last military stronghold in the United States during the Revolutionary War.

1920   In Philadelphia, Gimbels Department Stores begins what is now the nation's oldest annual Thanksgiving Day parade.

1963   President John F. Kennedy's body is laid to rest in Arlington National Cemetery.

1986   The Iran-Contra affair begins as President Reagan reveals that proceeds of secret arms sales to Iran had been used to aid Nicaraguan Contras.

THIS PRAYER is abridged from George Washington's Thanksgiving Proclamation of 1789.

May we all unite in rendering unto God our sincere and humble thanks—
For His kind care and protection of the people of this country,
For the great degree of tranquility, union, and plenty which we have enjoyed,
For the peaceable and rational manner in which we have been enabled to establish constitutions of government for our safety and happiness,
For the civil and religious liberty with which we are blessed, and the means we have of acquiring and diffusing useful knowledge, and in general for all the great and various favors which He hath been pleased to confer upon us.
And may we also unite in most humbly offering our prayers and supplications to the great Lord and Ruler of Nations and beseech Him—
To pardon our national and other transgressions,
To enable us all, whether in public or private stations, to perform our several and relative duties properly and punctually,
To render our national government a blessing to all the people, by constantly being a government of wise, just, and constitutional laws, discreetly and faithfully executed and obeyed,
To protect and guide all nations and to bless them with good government, peace, and concord,
To promote the knowledge and practice of true religion and virtue, and the increase of science,
And generally to grant unto all mankind such a degree of temporal prosperity as He alone knows to be best.

AMERICAN HISTORY PARADE

1778   Captain James Cook discovers Maui in the Hawaiian Islands.

1789   President George Washington proclaims this day a national day of thanksgiving.

1791   President Washington holds the first Cabinet meeting.

1863   President Abraham Lincoln begins the tradition of an annual national Thanksgiving Day.

1942   *Casablanca*, starring Humphrey Bogart and Ingrid Bergman, premieres in New York City.

WE KNOW VERY LITTLE about the first Thanksgiving the Pilgrims celebrated in Plymouth. We know it took place in 1621 sometime after the autumn harvest. William Bradford, long-time governor of the colony, reported that after a "sad and lamentable" first few months that brought much sickness and death, the first harvest left them with "all things in good plenty," including corn, "cod, bass, and other fish," waterfowl, venison, and a "great store of wild turkeys." Edward Winslow, one of the Pilgrims, left us the only other eyewitness account of the harvest feast in a letter he wrote on December 11, 1621. Though sparse in description, it conveys some sense of the joy and gratitude that must have marked the occasion:

Our harvest being gotten in, our governor sent four men on fowling, that so we might after a special manner rejoice together, after we had gathered the fruits of our labors; they four in one day killed as much fowl, as with a little help beside, served the company almost a week, at which time amongst other recreations, we exercised our arms, many of the Indians coming amongst us, and amongst the rest their greatest king Massasoit, with some ninety men, whom for three days we entertained and feasted, and they went out and killed five deer, which they brought to the plantation and bestowed on our governor, and upon the captain and others. And although it be not always so plentiful, as it was at this time with us, yet by the goodness of God, we are so far from want, that we often wish you partakers of our plenty.

AMERICAN HISTORY PARADE

1806   President Jefferson warns citizens of a conspiracy to make the western frontier a separate nation, a scheme that allegedly involves Aaron Burr.

1834   Thomas Davenport, a Vermont blacksmith, invents the electric motor.

1924   The first Macy's Thanksgiving Day Parade is held in New York City.

2003   President George W. Bush spends Thanksgiving with the troops fighting in Iraq.

ON NOVEMBER 28, 1942, during World War II, the assembly line at Ford Motor Company's huge Willow Run plant at Ypsilanti, Michigan, turned out its first production bomber, a B-24 Liberator. By the time the plant reached its peak, in summer 1944, it was producing a bomber an hour—thanks in no small part to Rosie the Riveter.

With so many men fighting overseas, war factories across the United States faced a critical labor shortage. Posters bearing slogans such as "Do the Job He Left Behind" and "Soldiers Without Guns" appealed for women workers. Millions of American women who had never worked outside the home traded aprons for overalls and went to work in the factories.

Soon they were tackling jobs only men had done before. They learned welding, drafting, and sheet-metal work to build airplanes, Jeeps, and ships. They packed ammo and tested guns, worked in lumber and steel mills, drove trucks, operated cranes, and more.

The women often worked six days a week, giving up vacations and holidays as long as the war dragged on. They put up with noisy, gritty working conditions and then, in the evening, many trudged home to take care of their children. All the while, they reminded themselves that their sacrifices would shorten the war and bring loved ones home.

An admiring public nicknamed the women defense workers "Rosie the Riveter." Their tough resourcefulness helped transform America into the arsenal of democracy.

AMERICAN HISTORY PARADE

1775   Captain Samuel Nicholas becomes the first officer commissioned in the Continental Marines (now the U.S. Marine Corps).

1895   The first auto race in the U.S. takes place, 52 miles between Chicago and Waukegan, Illinois, with winner Frank Duryea averaging a speed of 7.5 miles per hour.

1919   Lady Nancy Astor, born in Danville, Virginia, becomes the first woman elected to the British Parliament.

1925   The *Grand Ole Opry* makes its radio debut on WSM in Nashville.

1942   Ford's Willow Run plant in Michigan rolls out its first B-24 bomber.

HARRIET TUBMAN was born into slavery around 1822 on Maryland's Eastern Shore but refused to spend her life in bondage. One night in 1849, she began walking north until she reached freedom. Yet her own liberty wasn't enough. During the 1850s, she ventured again and again back into the South to guide slaves along the Underground Railroad to northern havens—even though she would face severe punishment if caught.

Tubman usually traveled at night, shepherding runaway slaves through dark woods, fields, and swamps as they followed the North Star to freedom. She often wore disguises, dressing as an old woman, and sang hymns to signal others along the way.

She moved just hours ahead of fugitive slave hunters. On one rescue mission, she saw a former master walking toward her. She was carrying some live chickens, so she pulled the string around their legs until they squawked, then stooped to attend to the fluttering birds while the man passed inches away. Another time when she was on a train, she spotted a former master, so she grabbed a newspaper and pretended to read. Since the man knew that Harriet Tubman was illiterate, he did not look closely at her, and she arrived at her destination unnoticed.

During the Civil War, Tubman went to South Carolina, where she acted as a nurse, cook, scout, and spy for the Union army. After the war she raised money for black schools and opened a home for elderly blacks.

Tubman was small in stature—only about five feet tall—but enormous in courage and faith. "I said to the Lord, I'm going to hold steady on to you, and I know you'll see me through," she said. Because of her determination to lead others to freedom, she came to be known by a name of old: Moses.

AMERICAN HISTORY PARADE

1853   In late fall, Harriet Tubman is engaged in a mission to rescue nine slaves from Maryland and conduct them north to Canada.

1890   The first Army-Navy football game is played at West Point (Navy wins 24–0).

1929   Navy lieutenant commander Richard E. Byrd and his crew make the first airplane flight over the South Pole.

1934   On Thanksgiving Day, the Chicago Bears beat the Detroit Lions 19–16 in the first NFL game to be broadcast nationally on radio.

MARK TWAIN, born November 30, 1835, was a loving critic of his country, usually with humor. ("There is no distinctly native American criminal class except Congress," he once observed.) But disdain for America by European snobs raised his hackles. In an 1890 address in Boston, he let loose.

If I look harried and worn, it is not from an ill conscience. It is from sitting up nights to worry about the foreign critic. He won't concede that we have a civilization—a "real" civilization. . . . [H]e said we had never contributed anything to the betterment of the world. . . .

What is a "real" civilization? [Let us suppose it is one without despotic government and near-universal inequality, ignorance, and poverty. In that case] there are some partial civilizations scattered around Europe—pretty lofty civilizations they are, but who begot them? What is the seed from which they sprang? Liberty and intelligence. What planted that seed? There are dates and statistics which suggest that it was the American Revolution that planted it. When that revolution began, monarchy had been on trial some thousands of years, over there, and was a distinct and convicted failure. . . . [W]e hoisted the banner of revolution and raised the first genuine shout for human liberty that had ever been heard. . . .

Who summoned the French slaves to rise and set the nation free? We did it. What resulted in England and on the Continent? Crippled liberty took up its bed and walked. From that day to this its march has not halted, and please God it never will. We are called the nation of inventors. And we are. We could still claim that title and wear its loftiest honors, if we had stopped with the first thing we ever invented—which was human liberty. . . . *We* have contributed nothing! Nothing hurts me like ingratitude.

AMERICAN HISTORY PARADE

1782   In Paris the British sign a preliminary treaty recognizing American independence.

1829   The First Welland Canal opens, connecting Lakes Erie and Ontario.

1835   Mark Twain (Samuel Clemens) is born in Florida, Missouri.

1864   Confederate troops suffer devastating losses at the Battle of Franklin, Tennessee.

1943   At the Tehran Conference, Franklin D. Roosevelt, Winston Churchill, and Joseph Stalin agree on an invasion of Europe, code-named Operation Overlord.

Prayers for the American People

I have been driven many times upon my knees by the overwhelming conviction that I had nowhere else to go. My own wisdom, and that of all about me, seemed insufficient for that day.

— Abraham Lincoln

Prayer for Our Country

Almighty God, Who has given us this good land for our heritage, we humbly beseech Thee that we may always prove ourselves a people mindful of Thy favor and glad to do Thy will. Bless our land with honorable industry, sound learning, and pure manners. Save us from violence, discord, and confusion, from pride and arrogance, and from every evil way. Defend our liberties, and fashion into one united people the multitude brought hither out of many kindreds and tongues. Endow with Thy spirit of wisdom those to whom in Thy name we entrust the authority of government, that there may be justice and peace at home, and that, through obedience to Thy law, we may show forth Thy praise among the nations of the earth. In time of prosperity fill our hearts with thankfulness, and in the day of trouble, suffer not our trust in Thee to fail.

— Traditional

DAILY PRAYER

Oh! Almighty and Everlasting God, Creator of heaven, earth and the universe, help me to be, to think, to act what is right, because it is right. Make me truthful, honest and honorable in all things. Make me intellectually honest for the sake of right and honor and without thought of reward to me. Give me the ability to be charitable, forgiving and patient with my fellowmen—help me to understand their motives and their shortcomings—even as Thou understandest mine! Amen, amen, amen.

— Daily prayer said
by Harry S. Truman

PRAYER FOR USE BY YOUNG AMERICANS

Oh God, our Father, Thou Searcher of human hearts, help us to draw near to Thee in sincerity and truth. May our religion be filled with gladness and may our worship of Thee be natural.

Strengthen and increase our admiration for honest dealing and clean thinking, and suffer not our hatred of hypocrisy and pretence ever to diminish. Encourage us in our endeavor to live above the common level of life. Make us to choose the harder right instead of the easier wrong, and never to be content with a half truth when the whole truth can be won. Endow us with courage that is born of loyalty to all that is noble and worthy, that scorns to compromise with vice and injustice and knows no fear when truth and right are in jeopardy. Guard us against flippancy and irreverence in the sacred things of life. Grant us new ties of friendship and new opportunities of service. Kindle our hearts in fellowship with those of a cheerful countenance, and soften our hearts with sympathy for those who sorrow and suffer. All of which we ask in the name of the Great Friend and Master of all.

— From the West Point Cadet
Prayer

Prayer for National Unity and Character

Almighty God, we make our earnest prayer that you will keep the United States in your holy protection, and that you will incline the hearts of the citizens to entertain a brotherly affection and love for one another. We pray that you will most graciously be pleased to dispose us all to do justice, to love mercy, and to demean ourselves with that charity, humility, and pacific temper of mind which were the characteristics of the Divine Author of our blessed religion, and without a humble imitation of whose example in these things, we can never hope to be a happy nation.

— adapted from George
Washington's Circular
Address to the States,
June 8, 1783

Prayer for Meeting the Obligations of Freedom

Our Father which art in heaven, we pray for all the people of our country, that we may learn to appreciate more the goodly heritage that is ours. We need to learn, in these challenging days, that to every right there is attached a duty and to every privilege an obligation. We believe that, in the eternal order of things, Thou hast so ordained it, and what Thou hast joined together let us not try to put asunder. Teach us what freedom is. May we all learn the lesson that it is not the right to do as we please, but the opportunity to please to do what is right. Above all, may we discover that wherever the Spirit of the Lord is, there is freedom. May we have that freedom now, in His presence here, to lead us and to help us keep this nation free.

— The Reverend Peter
Marshall, Chaplain of the
United States Senate,
1947–49

Prayer of Thanksgiving

Almighty God, we thank you for the many and great material blessings this nation has received. We know that material well-being is an indispensable foundation. But we also know the foundation avails nothing by itself, and that upon it must be raised the structure of the lofty life of the spirit, if this nation is properly to fulfill its great mission and to accomplish all that we so ardently hope and desire. The things of the body are good; the things of the intellect better; the best of all are the things of the soul.

Remembering these things, we set our faces resolutely against evil, and with broad charity, with kindliness and goodwill toward all men, but with unflinching determination to smite down wrong, we resolve to strive for righteousness in public and private life. We ask for the strength so to order our lives as to deserve a continuation of your great blessings.

— Adapted from Theodore Roosevelt's Proclamation of a National Day of Thanksgiving and Prayer, 1908

Prayer for All Peoples

We pray that peoples of all faiths, all races, all nations, may have their great human needs satisfied; that those now denied opportunity shall come to enjoy it to the full; that all who yearn for freedom may experience its spiritual blessings; that those who have freedom will understand, also, its heavy responsibilities; that all who are insensitive to the needs of others will learn charity; that the scourges of poverty, disease, and ignorance will be made to disappear from the earth, and that, in the goodness of time, all peoples will come to live together in a peace guaranteed by the binding force of mutual respect and love.

— Dwight D. Eisenhower (Farewell Address, January 17, 1961)

Prayer for Use by Those Serving in Office

Heavenly Father, we bow our heads and thank you for your love. Accept our thanks for the peace that yields this day and the shared faith that makes its continuance likely. Make us strong to do your work, willing to heed and hear your will, and write on our hearts these words: "Use power to help people." For we are given power not to advance our own purposes, nor to make a great show in the world, nor a name. There is but one just use of power, and it is to serve people. Help us to remember it, Lord.

— George H. W. Bush
(Inaugural Address,
January 20, 1989)

Prayer for the Armed Forces

Almighty God, we commend to your gracious care and keeping all the men and women of our armed forces at home and abroad. Defend them day by day with your heavenly grace; strengthen them in their trials and temptations; give them courage to face the perils which beset them; and grant them a sense of your abiding presence wherever they may be; through Jesus Christ our Lord.

— From *The Book
of Common Prayer*

Franklin D. Roosevelt's D-Day Prayer

President Franklin D. Roosevelt read this prayer on a national radio broadcast on the evening of June 6, 1944—D-Day, the day on which Allied troops stormed the beaches of Normandy.

Almighty God:

Our sons, pride of our nation, this day have set upon a mighty endeavor, a struggle to preserve our republic, our religion, and our civilization, and to set free a suffering humanity.

Lead them straight and true; give strength to their arms, stoutness to their hearts, steadfastness in their faith.

They will need Thy blessings. Their road will be long and hard. For the enemy is strong. He may hurl back our forces. Success may not come with rushing speed, but we shall return again and again; and we know that by Thy grace, and by the righteousness of our cause, our sons will triumph.

They will be sore tried, by night and by day, without rest, until the victory is won. The darkness will be rent by noise and flame. Men's souls will be shaken with the violences of war.

For these men are lately drawn from the ways of peace. They fight not for the lust of conquest. They fight to end conquest. They fight to liberate. They fight to let justice arise, and tolerance and good will among all Thy people. They yearn but for the end of battle, for their return to the haven of home.

Some will never return. Embrace these, Father, and receive them, Thy heroic servants, into Thy kingdom.

And for us at home—fathers, mothers, children, wives, sisters, and brothers of brave men overseas—whose thoughts and prayers are ever with them—help us, Almighty God, to rededicate ourselves in renewed faith in Thee in this hour of great sacrifice. . . .

Let our hearts be stout, to wait out the long travail, to bear sorrows that may come, to impart our courage unto our sons wheresoever they may be.

And, O Lord, give us faith. . . . Let not the keenness of our spirit ever be dulled. Let not the impacts of temporary events . . . deter us in our unconquerable purpose.

With Thy blessing, we shall prevail. . . . Lead us to the saving of our country, and with our sister nations into a world unity that will spell a sure peace, a peace invulnerable to the schemings of unworthy men. And a peace that will let all of men live in freedom, reaping the just rewards of their honest toil.

Thy will be done, Almighty God. Amen.

Prayer for Memorial Day

We pray for the sons and daughters of our land who have perished in the cause of liberty, country, and peace, the cause that has called Americans from generation to generation. We ask God to bless them and take them to Himself and reward their patriot's love. We pray for those who gave their lives in the hope of a future of freedom and peace for their countrymen. We pray for peace and for the devotion and strength of soul to build it and to protect it always. We pray and we resolve to keep holy the memory of those who have died for our country and to make their cause inseparably our own. We pray and we promise, so that one day Taps will sound never again for the young and the brave and the good.

— Ronald Reagan (abridged
from Memorial Day Prayer
for Peace, 1987)

Prayer for Times of National Grief

We come before God to pray for the missing and the dead, and for those who love them. . . . We ask almighty God to watch over our nation, and grant us patience and resolve in all that is to come. We pray that He will comfort and console those who now walk in sorrow. We thank Him for each life we now must mourn, and the promise of a life to come.

As we have been assured, neither death nor life, nor angels nor principalities nor powers, nor things present nor things to come, nor height nor depth, can separate us from God's love. May He bless the souls of the departed. May He comfort our own. And may He always guide our country. God bless America.

— George W. Bush
(at the National Cathedral,
September 14, 2001, after
the September 11 terrorist
attacks)

Prayer for Peace

Fondly do we hope, fervently do we pray, that this mighty scourge of war may speedily pass away. . . . With malice toward none, with charity for all, with firmness in the right as God gives us to see the right, let us strive on to finish the work we are in; to bind up the nation's wounds; to care for him who shall have borne the battle, and for his widow and his orphan—to do all which may achieve and cherish a just and a lasting peace among ourselves and with all nations.

— Abraham Lincoln
(Second Inaugural Address,
March 4, 1865)

December

LATE 1862 was a moment of grave danger for the republic. The nation had been torn in two by civil war, the outcome of which no one could predict. President Abraham Lincoln would soon sign the Emancipation Proclamation, and he was not sure what its effects might be. On December 1, in his annual message to Congress (a written equivalent of today's State of the Union Address), Lincoln reminded his fellow citizens of the stakes:

The dogmas of the quiet past are inadequate to the stormy present. The occasion is piled high with difficulty, and we must rise with the occasion. As our case is new, so we must think anew, and act anew. We must disenthrall our selves, and then we shall save our country.

Fellow citizens, we cannot escape history. We of this Congress and this administration will be remembered in spite of ourselves. No personal significance, or insignificance, can spare one or another of us. The fiery trial through which we pass will light us down, in honor or dishonor, to the latest generation. We say we are for the Union. The world will not forget that we say this. We know how to save the Union. The world knows we do know how to save it. We—even we here—hold the power, and bear the responsibility. In giving freedom to the slave, we assure freedom to the free—honorable alike in what we give, and what we preserve. We shall nobly save, or meanly lose, the last best hope of earth. Other means may succeed; this could not fail. The way is plain, peaceful, generous, just—a way which, if followed, the world will forever applaud, and God must forever bless.

AMERICAN HISTORY PARADE

1824   The presidential election goes to the U.S. House since neither John Quincy Adams, Andrew Jackson, William Crawford, or Henry Clay had won an electoral majority (Adams is eventually chosen).

1862   Abraham Lincoln reminds the nation that America is the "last best hope of earth."

1903   Thomas Edison's film company releases *The Great Train Robbery*, the first western movie.

1955   Rosa Parks is arrested after she refuses to give up her seat to a white man aboard a bus in Montgomery, Alabama, prompting a bus boycott by blacks.

1965   An airlift begins to bring thousands fleeing Castro's Communist Cuba to the United States.

ON DECEMBER 2, 1980, Congress created the world's largest continuously protected area when it expanded Denali National Park and Preserve in Alaska to more than 6 million acres (larger than the state of New Hampshire). The park's centerpiece is Mount McKinley, at 20,320 feet the highest peak in North America. The mountain is also known as Denali, which in the language of the Athabaskan Indians means "the high one."

Other famous U.S. peaks include:

Mountain	Alt (ft)	Notable Facts and Features
Mount Whitney, CA	14,494	Highest peak in the Lower 48 states
Mount Elbert, CO	14,433	Highest peak in the U.S. Rockies
Mount Rainier, WA	14,410	Highest peak in Cascades; covered with glaciers
Pikes Peak, CO	14,110	Inspired Katharine Lee Bates to pen "America the Beautiful"
Mauna Kea, HI	13,796	World's tallest mountain (33,476 ft.) from base on ocean floor to peak
Grand Teton, WY	13,770	One of America's most jagged, soaring peaks
Mauna Loa, HI	13,677	World's largest volcano
Mount St. Helens, WA	8,364	Killed 57 in violent 1980 eruption
Mount Mitchell, NC	6,684	Highest peak east of the Mississippi
Clingmans Dome, TN/NC	6,643	Highest peak in the Great Smoky Mountains
Mount Washington, NH	6,288	Highest peak in New England; famous for 200-mph winds
Mount Rushmore, SD	5,725	Site of Gutzon Borglum's giant sculpture of four presidents
Mount Marcy, NY	5,344	Highest peak in the Adirondacks
Mount Katahdin, ME	5,268	Northern terminus of the Appalachian Trail
Springer Mt., GA	3,782	Southern terminus of the Appalachian Trail

AMERICAN HISTORY PARADE

1763   The Jewish community of Newport, Rhode Island, dedicates the Touro Synagogue, the oldest synagogue in America.

1823   President James Monroe outlines his doctrine opposing European interference in the Western Hemisphere, known as the Monroe Doctrine.

1859   John Brown is hanged for his raid on the federal armory at Harpers Ferry.

1942   At the University of Chicago, Enrico Fermi and others give the first demonstration of a controlled nuclear chain reaction.

1980   Congress creates the 6-million-acre Denali National Park and Preserve.

1982   Doctors at the University of Utah Medical Center implant the first permanent artificial heart in a human; the patient, Barney Clark, lives 112 days.

"I MARKED MY NAME & the day of the month and year on a large Pine . . . 'Capt William Clark December 3rd 1805. By Land. U States in 1804 & 1805.'"

So wrote William Clark in his journal after nearly nineteen months of trekking across the West. Captains Clark and Meriwether Lewis, along with a band of about thirty explorers, had finally reached the Pacific.

They had set out from the St. Louis area on May 14, 1804, with instructions from President Jefferson: see what was out there. The explorers made their way up the Missouri River in boats, wide-eyed at a land filled with deer, turkeys, geese, and herds of buffalo. Lewis and Clark held councils with the Indians they met. They made maps of their route. They collected specimens—insects, animal skins, fossils, a prairie dog—and sent them back to the curious Jefferson.

The explorers spent about a month dragging their canoes around the Great Falls of the Missouri. When the river took them as far as it could, they traded with Shoshone Indians for horses and started over the Rockies. The horses often lost their footing on snow-covered trails. The explorers ran out of food and began to go hungry.

They finally stumbled out of the mountains, built canoes, and dashed down foaming waters to the Columbia River. The river widened, slowed, and lay shrouded with fog. When the fog lifted, they found that they had reached the Pacific.

As Jefferson said, the Lewis and Clark expedition was one "of courage undaunted, possessing a firmness and perseverance of purpose which nothing but impossibilities could divert from its direction." By the time they got back to St. Louis on September 23, 1806, they had traveled 8,000 miles. They brought back reports of a country grand enough to hold any dream.

AMERICAN HISTORY PARADE

1805   Lewis and Clark, having reached the Pacific coast, look for a spot to make winter camp.

1818   Illinois becomes the twenty-first state.

1828   Andrew Jackson is elected the seventh U.S. president.

1947   *A Streetcar Named Desire* by Tennessee Williams opens on Broadway.

1973   *Pioneer 10* obtains the first close-up images of Jupiter.

THE INDIANS SPOKE of a great river to the south, a "father of waters" that flowed all the way to the sea. Jacques Marquette, a Jesuit missionary from France, was determined to find the mysterious waterway. Perhaps it was the long-sought route to the Pacific. In the spring of 1673, he left northern Michigan with fur trader Louis Jolliet and five others in two canoes. In mid-June, the explorers shot down the Wisconsin River and reached the Mississippi.

They floated south through lands no Europeans had visited before, stopping to smoke the peace pipe with Indians they met. They passed the thundering mouth of the Missouri River in full flood and heard reports that it led to a western sea (reports that Lewis and Clark would later test). Buffalo with heads "a foot and a half wide between the horns" roamed the prairies. Marquette recorded that "from time to time we came upon monstrous fish, one of which struck our canoe with such violence that I thought that it was a great tree about to break the canoe to pieces."

They traveled 1,700 miles to the mouth of the Arkansas River. By that time, they realized the Mississippi must drain into the Gulf of Mexico, rather than the Pacific. Wary of being captured by Spaniards, they turned and headed home.

The next year, Marquette set out to found a mission among the Illinois Indians. On December 4, 1674, he and two companions became the first white men to build a dwelling at a site that would someday become Chicago. But the intrepid priest grew ill, his strength failed, and he died in 1675 near Ludington, Michigan.

Father Jacques Marquette never discovered the fabled route to the western sea. But his explorations turned vague rumors into known facts, and helped open the way to America's heartland.

AMERICAN HISTORY PARADE

1674   Jacques Marquette and two French traders build a hut at what is now Chicago.

1783   The Revolutionary War concluded, General George Washington bids his officers farewell at Fraunces Tavern in New York City.

1816   James Monroe of Virginia is elected the fifth U.S. president.

1833   The American Anti-Slavery Society is organized in Philadelphia.

1996   General Motors begins the first mass production of a U.S. electric car, the EV1.

"DON'T RIDE THE BUS TO WORK, to town, to school, or anywhere on Monday," read leaflets that spread through the black community of Montgomery, Alabama, in early December 1955. "If you work, take a cab, or walk."

An arrest had triggered the appeal. Rosa Parks, a black seamstress, was riding a crowded city bus home after a long day at work when the driver ordered her to give up her seat to a white man. Tired of being pushed around by segregation laws, Parks refused. The bus driver called the police, and Rosa Parks was arrested.

The city's black leaders called for a boycott of city buses on Monday, December 5. No one was sure if the protest would have much support. Many blacks in Montgomery depended on the buses to get to work. But when Monday morning came, city buses followed their routes carrying only handfuls of white riders.

The boycott organizers, led by a young pastor named Martin Luther King Jr., decided to keep the boycott going. Black taxi drivers lowered their fares for protesters. People loaned cars to help get others to school, work, or the store. Many blacks simply walked wherever they needed to go.

Tension rose as the boycott dragged on. Police harassed black taxi drivers and carpool drivers. King's home was bombed, but he and his family escaped harm. As news of the protest spread, support for the boycotters grew across the nation.

In November 1956 the Supreme Court struck down Alabama's bus segregation laws as unconstitutional. On December 21, 1956—381 days after it started—the boycott came to an end. Rosa Parks was one of the first to ride the desegregated buses. For her courage she is remembered as the mother of the modern-day civil rights movement.

AMERICAN HISTORY PARADE

1782   Martin Van Buren, the eighth U.S. president, is born in Kinderhook, New York.

1831   Former president John Quincy Adams takes his seat in the U.S. House as a representative of Massachusetts.

1848   President James K. Polk helps trigger the 1849 Gold Rush when he confirms the discovery of gold in California.

1933   The Twenty-first Amendment, ending Prohibition, is ratified.

1955   Prompted by the arrest of Rosa Parks, the Montgomery bus boycott begins.

THE WASHINGTON MONUMENT, built in memory of George Washington, is the focal point of our nation's capital and probably the world's most famous memorial dedicated to a national hero. Perhaps the most impressive thing about the monument is its simplicity. The majestic shaft of white marble, which towers 555 feet, 5⅛ inches into the sky, has the shape of an ancient Egyptian obelisk—a four-sided pillar that gradually tapers as it rises, ending with a pyramid on top.

Construction on the monument, which is covered with Maryland marble, began in 1848. The original design by architect Robert Mills called for the obelisk's base to be surrounded by a circular colonnade, which was never built. Delay after delay plagued the project, including the Civil War and a shortage of funds. On December 6, 1884, when workers finally set the capstone in place amid a howling wind, the Washington Monument was the tallest man-made structure on earth, a distinction it held until the Eiffel Tower was completed in Paris. It is still the world's tallest freestanding masonry structure, containing approximately 36,000 blocks of granite and marble.

Inside the monument, 897 steps lead to the top, but the stairwell is closed to the public. Instead, an elevator whisks tourists to the top for magnificent views of Washington, D.C., from eight small windows. Those who stand at the monument's base and gaze up at the giant white pillar gleaming against a blue sky never forget the sight.

AMERICAN HISTORY PARADE

1790   Congress moves from New York City to Philadelphia.

1865   The Thirteenth Amendment is ratified, officially abolishing slavery.

1884   Workers finish construction of the Washington Monument.

1907   In Monongah, West Virginia, 362 men and boys die in a coal mine explosion, the worst mining disaster in U.S. history.

1957   The U.S.'s first attempt to place a satellite in orbit fails when a Vanguard rocket explodes on the launchpad at Cape Canaveral.

2006   NASA announces that the *Mars Global Surveyor* has discovered indications of recent water flows on Mars.

SUNDAY, DECEMBER 7, 1941, began as a serene morning at the U.S. Navy base on the island of Oahu in Hawaii. The warships of America's Pacific Fleet rested at anchor. Many sailors were preparing for church or relaxing, and all was quiet at Pearl Harbor.

At about 7:55 a.m. a buzz from the sky broke the calm as a dive-bomber bearing the red symbol of the Rising Sun of Japan dropped out of the clouds. Seconds later, a swarm of Japanese warplanes followed. Sirens wailed as explosions sounded across the harbor and black smoke poured into the sky.

American sailors scrambled to battle stations while the Japanese planes screamed in for the kill. The main targets were several huge battleships moored in the harbor. Antiaircraft guns roared to life, but they did little good. Bombs and torpedoes hit ship after ship: the *Arizona*, the *Oklahoma*, the *California*, the *West Virginia*, the *Utah*, the *Maryland*, the *Pennsylvania*, the *Tennessee*, the *Nevada*.

Sailors fought to save their ships, their comrades, and their own lives. Much of the *California*'s crew abandoned ship after flames engulfed its stern. When the captain determined the battleship might be saved, Yeoman Durrell Conner hoisted the American flag from the stern. At the sight of the colors, the sailors returned to fight the fires and keep her afloat.

Despite such heroism, the attack reduced much of the fleet to smoldering wreckage. The Japanese planes disappeared into the sky, leaving 2,400 dead, 1,200 wounded, and 18 ships and more than 300 American planes destroyed or damaged.

News of the disaster left Americans stunned, but not for long. A remark attributed to Japanese admiral Isoroku Yamamoto, who planned the attack, sums up the result of Pearl Harbor: "I fear we have awakened a sleeping giant and instilled in him a terrible resolve."

AMERICAN HISTORY PARADE

1787   Delaware becomes the first state to ratify the U.S. Constitution.

1805   Lewis and Clark camp near the mouth of the Columbia River at a site that becomes Fort Clatsop, their winter quarters.

1917   During World War I, the United States declares war on Austria-Hungary.

1941   Japanese warplanes attack the U.S. Pacific Fleet at Pearl Harbor.

1963   An instant replay is shown on U.S. TV for the first time after a touchdown during an Army-Navy football game, prompting the announcer to scream, "This is a videotape! They did not score again! They did not score again!"

ON DECEMBER 8, 1941, the day after the attack on Pearl Harbor, a somber President Franklin Delano Roosevelt strapped his steel braces onto his legs and walked into the U.S. House chamber, leaning on his son Jimmy's arm. There he addressed a joint session of Congress and asked for a declaration of war against Japan:

> Yesterday, December 7, 1941, a date which will live in infamy, the United States of America was suddenly and deliberately attacked by naval and air forces of the Empire of Japan.
>
> The United States was at peace with that nation and, at the solicitation of Japan, was still in conversation with its government and its emperor looking toward the maintenance of peace in the Pacific. . . . The attack yesterday on the Hawaiian Islands has caused severe damage to American naval and military forces. Very many American lives have been lost. . . . As commander in chief of the Army and Navy I have directed that all measures be taken for our defense.
>
> Always will we remember the character of the onslaught against us.
>
> No matter how long it may take us to overcome this premeditated invasion, the American people, in their righteous might, will win through to absolute victory.
>
> I believe I interpret the will of the Congress and of the people when I assert that we will not only defend ourselves to the uttermost but will make very certain that this form of treachery shall never endanger us again.
>
> Hostilities exist. There is no blinking at the fact that our people, our territory, and our interests are in grave danger.
>
> With confidence in our armed forces, with the unbounded determination of our people, we will gain the inevitable triumph. So help us God.

AMERICAN HISTORY PARADE

1886 The American Federation of Labor is organized in Columbus, Ohio.

1940 The Chicago Bears demolish the Washington Redskins 73–0 in the most lopsided NFL championship game ever.

1941 A day after the Pearl Harbor attack, Congress declares war on Japan.

1987 In Washington, D.C., President Ronald Reagan and Soviet leader Mikhail Gorbachev sign an historic treaty to reduce stockpiles of nuclear missiles.

1992 U.S. Marines land in Somalia, leading an international effort to restore civil order and deliver food to starving refugees.

AS WITH MANY RECENT INNOVATIONS, the genesis of the Internet lies in U.S. technology developed during the Cold War. In the days when the U.S. and U.S.S.R. were racing to the moon, the Department of Defense created the Advanced Research Projects Agency (ARPA) to spearhead cutting-edge military research. Scientists at ARPA wanted to find a way to connect computers located hundreds or thousands of miles from each other. In 1969 the ARPANet was born, linking four computers at universities in California and Utah.

The ARPANet slowly grew during the 1970s, connecting computers at universities, research labs, and government agencies. By 1981 more than 200 computers were linked to the network. By that time it was no longer limited to military projects. The Defense Department and National Science Foundation opened access to the broader scientific and academic community.

Meanwhile, several corporations, universities, and agencies in the U.S. and Europe began building their own computer networks. Everyone realized these networks needed to trade information with each other. Building on ARPANet technology, scientists developed standards for an Internet—an *inter*connected *net*work of networks.

Then along came the personal computer. In the 1980s and '90s, millions of PCs appeared in homes and offices. In 1989 British computer scientist Tim Berners-Lee led the development of a system that allows people to navigate the Internet using "pages" of text and images on a computer screen—a creation he dubbed the World Wide Web. Corporations got busy connecting computers around the globe. By the dawn of the twenty-first century, an estimated 360 million people had access to the Internet. By 2008, that number had reached more than 1.3 billion.

AMERICAN HISTORY PARADE

1775   Patriots defeat a British and loyalist force at Great Bridge, Virginia, driving the British out of Virginia for the early part of the Revolutionary War.

1835   A Texan army captures San Antonio in the war for independence from Mexico.

1907   Christmas Seals first go on sale in Wilmington, Delaware, to help fight tuberculosis.

1970   By December 1970, the ARPANet connects eleven computer installations, mainly concentrated in the Boston and Los Angeles areas.

1993   The military blows up the first of 500 Minuteman II missiles designated for destruction under an arms-control treaty.

JOHN PHILIP SOUSA, the long-time leader of the U.S. Marine Band as well as his own concert band, was perhaps the most famous American musician of his day. He spent a lifetime as a musical ambassador for the United States, conducting thousands of concerts in cities around the country and world. His compositions ranged from waltzes to operas, but his most beloved tunes were his marches, including "Semper Fidelis," the "Washington Post," and his most famous, "Stars and Stripes Forever."

Sousa wrote "Stars and Stripes Forever" as a salute to his country. The music came to him in December 1896 as he steamed home from Europe after receiving word that the manager of his band had suddenly died. He later wrote:

> Here came one of the most vivid incidents of my career. As the vessel [the *Teutonic*] steamed out of the harbor I was pacing on the deck, absorbed in thoughts of my manager's death and the many duties and decisions which awaited me in New York. Suddenly, I began to sense a rhythmic beat of a band playing within my brain. Throughout the whole tense voyage, that imaginary band continued to unfold the same themes, echoing and re-echoing the most distinct melody. I did not transfer a note of that music to paper while I was on the steamer, but when we reached shore, I set down the measures that my brain-band had been playing for me, and not a note of it has ever changed.

Sousa died in 1932 at age seventy-seven. "Stars and Stripes Forever" was the last song he ever conducted. On December 10, 1987, the piece became America's official march. The U.S. Marine Band carries on the tradition of playing "Stars and Stripes Forever" in performances across the country.

AMERICAN HISTORY PARADE

1817   Mississippi becomes the twentieth state.

1864   General William T. Sherman reaches Savannah, Georgia, ending his "March to the Sea."

1869   The Territory of Wyoming grants women the right to vote.

1987   "Stars and Stripes Forever" is designated as the national march.

1998   Six crew members of the shuttle *Endeavor* become the first astronauts to enter the new International Space Station.

ON DECEMBER 11, 1816, Indiana became the nation's ninteenth state. It inherited its name from the old Indiana Territory, which Congress had created in 1800. *Indiana* means "land of the Indians." Here are several more origins of state and territory names:

Tennessee – from *Tanase*, the name of a Cherokee village in the region

Texas – from the Indian word *tejas*, meaning "friends"

Utah – for the Ute tribe, whose name means "people of the mountains"

Vermont – from the French *vert mont*, meaning "green mountain"

Virginia – in honor of Queen Elizabeth I of England, known as the "Virgin Queen"

Washington – in honor of George Washington (the only state named for a president)

West Virginia – separated from Virginia during the Civil War

Wisconsin – after the Wisconsin River, whose Indian name may have meant "gathering of the waters" or "river of red stone"

Wyoming – from the Delaware Indian words *mecheweami-ing*, meaning "at the big plains"

District of Columbia (Washington, D.C.) – "District of Columbia" in honor of Christopher Columbus; "Washington" in honor of George Washington

American Samoa – from *sa moa* meaning "sacred center" in the Samoan language

Guam – from the ancient Chamorro word *guahan* meaning "we have"

Northern Mariana Islands – in honor of Maria Anna, queen of Spain in the seventeenth century

Puerto Rico – Spanish for "rich port"

U.S. Virgin Islands – named by Christopher Columbus in honor of Saint Ursula, a British Christian saint of the fourth or fifth century, and her virgin followers

AMERICAN HISTORY PARADE

1816   Indiana becomes the nineteenth state.

1882   The Bijou Theater in Boston is the first theater lit by electricity.

1941   During World War II, Germany and Italy declare war on the U.S., which responds in kind.

1972   *Apollo 17* astronauts Eugene Cernan and Harrison Schmitt land on the moon during the last Apollo lunar landing mission.

"I CONFESS that in America I saw more than America; I sought the image of democracy itself, with its inclinations, its character, its prejudices, and its passions," wrote Alexis de Tocqueville, the Frenchman who traveled America in 1831–32 and published his impressions in his famous *Democracy in America.* His amused but admiring description of civic life in the young republic provides a wonderful yardstick:

> The political activity which pervades the United States must be seen in order to be understood. No sooner do you set foot upon the American soil than you are stunned by a kind of tumult. . . . Everything is in motion around you; here, the people of one quarter of a town are met to decide upon the building of a church; there, the election of a representative is going on; a little further the delegates of a district are posting to the town to consult upon some local improvements; or in another place the laborers of a village quit their plows to deliberate upon the project of a road or a public school. Meetings are called for the sole purpose of declaring their disapprobation of the line of conduct pursued by the government; while in other assemblies the citizens salute the authorities of the day as the fathers of their country. . . .
>
> The cares of political life engross a most prominent place in the occupation of a citizen in the United States. . . . An American cannot converse, but he can discuss; and when he attempts to talk he falls into a dissertation. He speaks to you as if he was addressing a meeting; and if he should chance to warm in the course of the discussion, he will infallibly say, "Gentlemen," to the person with whom he is conversing.

AMERICAN HISTORY PARADE

1787   Pennsylvania becomes the second state to ratify the U.S. Constitution.

1808   The first Bible society in the United States is organized in Philadelphia.

1831   Alexis de Tocqueville crosses the Tennessee River en route from Louisville to Memphis during his journey through America.

1870   Joseph Rainey of South Carolina is sworn in as the first black member of the U.S. House.

1925   The world's first motel, the Motel Inn, opens in San Luis Obispo, California.

THE NATIONAL GUARD is the oldest part of our nation's armed forces, tracing its roots to the time when the thirteen original English colonies required able-bodied male citizens to train and be ready to defend their communities. The Guard observes December 13 as its birthday because on that day in 1636, the Massachusetts Bay Colony organized scattered militia companies from villages around Boston into three regiments. Articles I and II of the U.S. Constitution lay down guidelines providing for the National Guard.

Today's Guard is made of more than 450,000 men and women—businessmen, factory workers, teachers, doctors, police officers—who volunteer on a part-time basis. Each state and territory, as well as the District of Columbia, has its own National Guard. Army National Guard units are part of the U.S. Army. Air National Guard units are part of the U.S. Air Force.

Guard members have a unique dual mission that requires them to swear an oath of allegiance to their state and to the federal government. In times of peace, the governor of each state commands its National Guard and can call it into action if needed. Guard members stand ready to battle fires or help communities deal with floods, tornadoes, hurricanes, earthquakes, and other crises.

The second part of the Guard's job is to defend America and respond to national emergencies. During times of war or national need, the president can call up the National Guard. In wartime Guard members constitute a large portion of the U.S. fighting force.

Guard personnel pour much time and energy into training. Units take part in efforts ranging from blood drives to the fight against terrorism. The motto of these citizen soldiers is "Always ready, always there."

AMERICAN HISTORY PARADE

1636   The Massachusetts Bay Colony organizes militia units into three regiments, an event the National Guard recognizes as its birthday.

1862   Confederate forces win a major victory at the Battle of Fredericksburg, Virginia.

1918   Woodrow Wilson becomes the first U.S. president in office to visit Europe when he arrives in France for the post–World War I peace conference.

2003   U.S. forces capture former Iraqi dictator Saddam Hussein, pulling him from a "spider hole" under a farmhouse near his hometown of Tikrit.

ON DECEMBER 14, 1799, George Washington died at Mount Vernon at age sixty-seven, two days after being caught out in sleet and snow while riding over his farms. Congress asked Virginia statesman Henry "Light-Horse Harry" Lee to eulogize the nation's hero. Lee's words about his friend have endured for over two centuries:

> First in war, first in peace and first in the hearts of his countrymen, he was second to none in the humble and endearing scenes of private life. Pious, just, humane, temperate and sincere—uniform, dignified and commanding—his example was as edifying to all around him as were the effects of that example lasting. . . . Correct throughout, vice shuddered in his presence and virtue always felt his fostering hand. The purity of his private character gave effulgence to his public virtues. . . . Such was the man for whom our nation mourns.

Fellow Virginian Thomas Jefferson wrote of George Washington's character:

> His mind was great and powerful, without being of the very first order; his penetration strong, though not so acute as that of a Newton, Bacon, or Locke; and as far as he saw, no judgment was ever sounder. . . . He was incapable of fear, meeting personal dangers with the calmest unconcern. Perhaps the strongest feature in his character was prudence, never acting until every circumstance, every consideration, was maturely weighed; refraining if he saw a doubt, but, when once decided, going through with his purpose, whatever obstacles opposed. His integrity was most pure, his justice the most inflexible I have ever known. . . . It may truly be said that never did nature and fortune combine more perfectly to make a great man.

AMERICAN HISTORY PARADE

1774   Four months before the Battle of Lexington, 400 Patriots attack Fort William and Mary at Portsmouth, New Hampshire, to capture powder and small arms.

1799   George Washington dies at Mount Vernon, his home in Virginia.

1902   A ship begins laying the first transpacific telegraph cable between San Francisco and Honolulu.

1947   NASCAR is founded in Daytona Beach, Florida.

1972   *Apollo 17* astronaut Eugene Cernan is the last person to walk on the moon during the twentieth century.

DURING THE BATTLE to ratify the U.S. Constitution, many Americans worried that the founding document failed to list specific rights to be protected against abuse of power. Thomas Jefferson, who generally approved of the new Constitution, put voice to that view when he wrote to James Madison: "A bill of rights is what the people are entitled to against every government on earth . . . and what no just government should refuse." To gain support for the Constitution, Federalists agreed to add amendments protecting personal liberties.

Madison was one of those who had considered a list of protected rights unnecessary. He believed the Constitution, as written, gave the federal government no power to violate citizens' liberties. He also worried that listing specific rights might imply that the government could limit rights *not* listed. Nevertheless, when the First Congress met in New York in 1789, he set about crafting a set of amendments. "If we can make the Constitution better in the opinion of those who are opposed to it," he said, "without weakening its frame, or abridging its usefulness in the judgment of those who are attached to it, we act the part of wise and liberal men to make such alterations as shall produce the effect."

Madison and a few colleagues sifted through scores of proposed amendments and winnowed them down to a brief list, using the Virginia Declaration of Rights and other precedents as guides. Congress sent twelve amendments to the states for approval. Ten were eventually ratified. On December 15, 1791, Virginia became the last state needed for ratification, and the Bill of Rights went into effect. Those first ten amendments to the U.S. Constitution, preserving such cherished rights as freedom of speech, press, and religion, lie at the heart of Americans' faith in limited government and the rule of law.

AMERICAN HISTORY PARADE

1791   The Bill of Rights is ratified.

1864   Union forces rout the Confederate Army of Tennessee in a two-day battle at Nashville.

1939   *Gone with the Wind* premieres in Atlanta, Georgia.

1944   An Army plane carrying bandleader Glenn Miller, who had joined the Army to play for troops during World War II, disappears over the English Channel.

1965   The *Gemini 6* and *Gemini 7* spacecraft maneuver to within a few feet of each other in orbit to achieve the first rendezvous in space.

ON THE COLD, DAMP NIGHT OF DECEMBER 16, 1773, a few dozen colonists wearing old clothing and blacked faces tramped through the streets of Boston toward three ships tied up at Griffin's Wharf. The Mohawks, as they called themselves, clambered aboard the *Dartmouth*, the *Eleanor*, and the *Beaver* and began hoisting chests of tea from the vessels' holds onto the decks. Working quietly and efficiently, they carried the chests to the rails, split them open, and dumped the tea into Boston Harbor.

The late-night raid came in response to the Tea Act passed by the British Parliament. That law gave the financially troubled East India Company, a British company, a virtual monopoly on the American tea trade. The Americans were already unhappy that Britain had placed a tax on their tea. Now, they told themselves, Parliament was dictating where they must buy their tea. In the colonists' eyes, tea had become a symbol of British oppression. So into the harbor went 342 chests.

In less than three hours, the Boston Tea Party was over. Their work done, the "Indians" swept the ships' decks, bid the crews farewell, and marched into the night whistling "Yankee Doodle." "Well, boys, you've had a fine pleasant evening for your Indian caper, haven't you?" a British admiral who had watched the entire episode called. "But mind, you have got to pay the fiddler yet!"

Indeed, Boston would be made to pay. George III was outraged at the act of defiance. "We must master them or totally leave them alone!" he declared. Parliament responded with the Intolerable Acts, which, among other measures, closed the port of Boston and required colonists to give lodging to British troops. Infuriated patriots viewed the reprisals as outright tyranny and turned their thoughts toward independence.

AMERICAN HISTORY PARADE

1773   Massachusetts colonists stage the Boston Tea Party.

1811   The first of the New Madrid earthquakes, a series of incredibly violent quakes centered near New Madrid, Missouri, occurs.

1835   Fire roars through New York City, destroying approximately 600 buildings.

1944   German forces launch a surprise attack in Belgium, beginning the Battle of the Bulge, Hitler's last major offensive on the Western Front.

1972   The Miami Dolphins become the first NFL team to go unbeaten and untied in a fourteen-game regular season; they go on to defeat the Redskins in Super Bowl VII.

TWELVE SECONDS. That's how long the world's first airplane flight lasted on December 17, 1903, above the wind-swept dunes of Kitty Hawk, North Carolina. Orville Wright was at the controls of the flimsy craft. He flew 120 feet.

Orville and his brother Wilbur had been interested in flight since childhood, when their father had given them a little toy helicopter powered by a rubber band. "We built a number of copies of the toy, which flew successfully," Orville later remembered. "But when we undertook to build the toy on a much larger scale it failed to work so well."

As young men, the Wright brothers went into business making and fixing bicycles in Dayton, Ohio, but they never forgot their dream of flying. They began building gliders, making hundreds of test flights, unmanned and manned. They chose Kitty Hawk for their trials because of its strong, steady winds.

Dissatisfied with their results, they used an old washtub, a fan, and a wooden box to construct a wind tunnel. They experimented with model wings and redesigned their glider. Then they built a gasoline engine to mount on the biplane.

Along the way they heard plenty of cracks about how they were wasting their time. One of the nation's leading scientists had shown by "unassailable logic" that human flight was impossible.

So on a frigid December morning at Kitty Hawk, the Wright brothers shook hands, Orville climbed into place, moved a lever that set the plane in motion—and did the impossible.

It took a while for the world to notice the achievement. But the handful of people who witnessed that first leap into the air knew what it meant. "They done it! They done it! Damn'd if they ain't flew!" one local exclaimed. The age of flight had begun.

AMERICAN HISTORY PARADE

1777　France, America's most valuable ally during the Revolutionary War, recognizes the young nation's independence.

1903　At Kitty Hawk, North Carolina, Orville and Wilbur Wright make the world's first successful motor-powered airplane flights.

1906　Oscar S. Straus becomes the first Jewish cabinet member as Theodore Roosevelt's secretary of commerce and labor.

1963　President Lyndon B. Johnson signs the Clean Air Act, the first important U.S. legislation designed to prevent air pollution.

DURING WORLD WAR II, the U.S. military had a policy of racial segregation. Blacks trained and fought in separate units from whites. Before 1941 blacks weren't allowed to serve as pilots. Many people said they weren't smart or disciplined enough to fly combat aircraft. But that year, under pressure from black leaders and Congress, the Army Air Corps opened an air base in Tuskegee, Alabama, and began to train black airmen.

The Tuskegee Army Air Base trained not only pilots but navigators, bombardiers, mechanics, and all the other personnel needed to keep planes in the air. Soon the Tuskegee Airmen were proving that they could fly aircraft as well as anyone else. Still, some people asked, "How will they do in combat?"

Beginning in 1943, the Army sent 450 Tuskegee pilots to North Africa and Europe to fight in the war. They flew fighters that escorted bombers over enemy territory. The Tuskegee Airmen painted the tails of their fighters red, and as their reputation for protecting planes grew, bomber crews started asking for the "Red Tail Angels" as escorts.

The Tuskegee Airmen flew hundreds of missions and rarely lost a bomber they were assigned to protect from enemy fire. Many became decorated war heroes. About 150 Tuskegee pilots lost their lives in combat or in accidents.

In 1946, after the war was over, training at Tuskegee ended. By then 992 pilots had graduated from the program. They had shown the world they could fly with the best, and their superb record paved the way for ending racial discrimination in the military.

AMERICAN HISTORY PARADE

1777   Americans observe the first national day of Thanksgiving to celebrate the surrender of a British army at Saratoga, New York, two months earlier.

1787   New Jersey becomes the third state to ratify the Constitution.

1813   During the War of 1812, the British capture Fort Niagara in New York.

1932   In Chicago, the Bears defeat the Portsmouth Spartans 9–0 in the first ever NFL playoff game, which was held indoors because of a blizzard.

1943   The 99th Fighter Squadron, a unit of the Tuskegee Airmen, flies almost every day during December 1943 in support of Allied bombers based in Italy.

FEW PEOPLE REALIZED IT AT THE TIME, but the issue of *Popular Electronics* magazine that hit the newsstands in late December 1974 marked the beginning of a modern revolution. On the cover, beneath the headline "World's First Minicomputer Kit," sat a photo of a plain-looking box covered with rows of switches and lights. The machine was the Altair 8800, and for about $400, anyone could buy the kit and assemble it themselves. It was the first truly personal computer to come to market, and thousands of hobbyists rushed to place orders.

In Boston a young computer programmer named Paul Allen picked up the magazine and ran to find his friend Bill Gates, a student at Harvard. The two had been computer enthusiasts since junior high school, and had dreamed of making their mark in the computer revolution. "Look, it's going to happen!" Allen said, waving the article. "I told you this was going to happen! And we're going to miss it!" Gates decided to leave Harvard and start a software company with Allen.* They wrote a program for the Altair, and Microsoft Corporation was born.

Meanwhile, in California, 20-year-old Steve Jobs and his friend Stephen Wozniak wanted to build their own small computers. Jobs sold his Volkswagen van and Wozniak sold his scientific calculator to raise funds to start Apple Computer, Inc., in 1976. They assembled their prototypes in the Jobs family's garage. Early Apples (like the one shown above) were among the first personal computers.

In 1981, industry giant IBM introduced its own personal computer, the IBM PC, run by Microsoft software. Other companies followed suit. By the mid-1980s, the American-bred personal computer revolution was poised to change the world.

---

* Several people advised Gates not to leave Harvard before completing his degree, including author W. J. Bennett. Gates's proctor, John Curnutte, asked Bennett to help convince the undergraduate not to drop out. "I think it's a mistake," Bennett told young Gates—an opinion that, fortunately, the latter did not share.

AMERICAN HISTORY PARADE

1732   In Philadelphia, Benjamin Franklin begins publishing *Poor Richard's Almanack*.

1777   George Washington's army enters winter camp at Valley Forge, Pennsylvania.

1871   Mark Twain receives the first of three patents for improved suspenders.

1974   The Altair 8800 kit is first put on sale, an event regarded by many as the beginning of the personal computer revolution.

1998   The U.S. House impeaches President Bill Clinton for perjury and obstruction of justice. (Andrew Johnson was the only other president to be impeached.)

JAMES NAISMITH, an instructor at the YMCA's School for Christian Workers in Springfield, Massachusetts, received a tough assignment in December 1891. The head of the school's physical education department asked him to come up with a new game that young men could play indoors during the cold winter months. Naismith had two weeks to think of something.

He tinkered with different ideas for several days, and then he remembered a game from his childhood called "duck on a rock," in which players tried to knock a small rock off a big rock by throwing stones at it. The memory of stones arching through the air at a target gave him just the inspiration he needed. He had the school custodian nail two peach baskets to the railing of a ten-foot-high balcony that ran around the school gymnasium. Since his class had eighteen students, he divided them into two teams of nine and explained that players scored by throwing a soccer ball into a basket.

"The first words were not very encouraging when one of the class made the remark, 'Humph, a new game,'" Naismith later said. "I asked the boys to try it once as a favor to me. They started, and after the ball was first thrown up there was no need of further coaxing."

The game was an instant hit. But it needed a name. One student suggested Naismithball, which the sport's inventor rejected. Then someone came up with "basketball"—since, after all, players threw the ball into peach baskets. In the early days the baskets had no holes in the bottoms, so someone had to climb up and get the ball out whenever anyone scored.

Basketball is now America's most popular indoor sport. James Naismith, who was born in Ontario, Canada, became a proud U.S. citizen in 1925.

AMERICAN HISTORY PARADE

1606   The Jamestown settlers set sail from England for Virginia.

1790   The first successful American cotton mill begins operating at Pawtucket, Rhode Island.

1803   The Louisiana Purchase is formally completed in New Orleans.

1860   South Carolina becomes the first state to secede from the Union.

1891   In late December, James Naismith works out the basics of basketball.

1951   An experimental reactor near Arco, Idaho, produces the first electricity ever generated by atomic power.

ON DECEMBER 21, 1620, the first landing party of Pilgrims came ashore in Massachusetts at the place they named Plymouth. There they founded the second successful English settlement in America. (The first was Jamestown, Virginia.) Tradition says that as they came ashore, the Pilgrims set foot on a granite boulder called Plymouth Rock, now a famous symbol of resolution and faith.

Nearly a century and a half later, in his *Dissertation on the Canon and Feudal Law,* John Adams of Massachusetts urged his countrymen not to forget the trials the early American colonists faced and the reasons they came to America:

> Let us read and recollect and impress upon our souls the views and ends of our . . .
> forefathers, in exchanging their native country for a dreary, inhospitable wilderness. . . .
> Recollect their amazing fortitude, their bitter sufferings—the hunger, the nakedness, the
> cold, which they patiently endured—the severe labors of clearing their grounds, building
> their houses, raising their provisions, amidst dangers from wild beasts and savage men, before
> they had time or money or materials for commerce. Recollect the civil and religious principles
> and hopes and expectations which constantly supported and carried them through all
> hardships with patience and resignation. Let us recollect it was liberty, the hope of liberty, for
> themselves and us and ours, which conquered all discouragements, dangers, and trials.

AMERICAN HISTORY PARADE

1620   The Pilgrims begin coming ashore at Plymouth, Massachusetts.

1861   Congress establishes the Medal of Honor, the highest U.S. military decoration.

1937   Disney's *Snow White and the Seven Dwarves,* one of the first feature-length animated movies, premieres in Los Angeles.

1968   *Apollo 8,* the first manned mission to orbit the moon, is launched.

1988   Libyan terrorists explode a bomb aboard Pan Am Flight 103, en route to New York City, when it is over Lockerbie, Scotland, killing 270 people.

IN DECEMBER 1944, during the late stages of World War II, German forces mounted a fierce surprise attack against Allied troops in the Ardennes Forest of Belgium. Powerful German tanks punched into the thinly stretched American line, creating a huge bulge in the U.S. defenses along the front. The fighting went down in history as the Battle of the Bulge.

American soldiers in the town of Bastogne found themselves surrounded, short on ammunition, and ill-equipped to fight in the heavy snows that began to fall. With bad weather grounding American supply planes, no relief was in sight.

On December 22 a group of Germans approached under a flag of truce. They handed the Americans a piece of paper demanding the surrender of the town within two hours. American officers took the ultimatum to their commander, General Anthony McAuliffe.

"Us surrender?" McAuliffe said. "Aw, nuts!"

That seemed as good a reply as any. McAuliffe grabbed a pencil and wrote, "To the German Commander: Nuts!" He sent the message back through the lines.

The Germans set out to obliterate Bastogne. Artillery bombarded the town while tanks attacked from every side. With no way to evacuate their wounded, and medical supplies now gone, the Americans hung on with grim determination.

Finally the weather cleared, and American bombers took to the skies. They came by the hundreds, driving back the German tanks. General George Patton's army arrived to reinforce Bastogne. By late January, the Allies had pushed the Germans back to their original position.

The Battle of the Bulge saw the last major German offensive and some of the most savage fighting of the war. The Allied line had bent, but it never broke. The Americans had stood their ground.

AMERICAN HISTORY PARADE

1864   Union general William T. Sherman sends a message to President Abraham Lincoln from Georgia: "I beg to present you as a Christmas gift the city of Savannah."

1882   Edward Johnson, an associate of Thomas Edison, displays the first electric Christmas tree lights in his home in New York City.

1894   The U.S. Golf Association is formed in New York City.

1941   Winston Churchill arrives in Washington for wartime meetings with President Franklin D. Roosevelt.

1944   During the Battle of the Bulge, General Anthony McAuliffe replies, "Nuts!" to a German demand for surrender.

THOMAS PAINE wrote these famous words in his pamphlet *The American Crisis*, dated December 23, 1776, a time when Patriot forces stood on the verge of losing the Revolutionary War. Paine implored Americans to not give up the fight. George Washington ordered that the pamphlet be read aloud to his troops on Christmas Eve 1776 before they crossed the Delaware River to launch a surprise attack at Trenton.

These are the times that try men's souls. The summer soldier and the sunshine patriot will, in this crisis, shrink from the service of his country; but he that stands it now deserves the love and thanks of man and woman. Tyranny, like hell, is not easily conquered. Yet we have this consolation with us, that the harder the conflict, the more glorious the triumph. What we obtain too cheap, we esteem too lightly: 'tis dearness only that gives every thing its value. Heaven knows how to put a proper price upon its goods, and it would be strange indeed if so celestial an article as freedom should not be highly rated. . . .

Let it be told to the future world, that in the depth of winter, when nothing but hope and virtue could survive, the city and the country, alarmed at one common danger, came forth to meet it and to repulse it. . . . I love the man that can smile in trouble, that can gather strength from distress, and grow brave by reflection. 'Tis the business of little minds to shrink; but he whose heart is firm, and whose conscience approves his conduct, will pursue his principles unto death.

AMERICAN HISTORY PARADE

1776   Thomas Paine's *The American Crisis* is published.

1783   George Washington resigns as general of the Army and retires to Mount Vernon.

1823   *'Twas the Night Before Christmas* by Clement C. Moore is published.

1947   At Bell Labs, researchers first demonstrate the transistor, a semiconductor device that becomes a building block for modern electronic equipment.

1986   Dick Rutan and Jeana Yeager land the experimental aircraft *Voyager* at Edwards Air Force Base, California, to complete the first nonstop, around-the-world flight without refueling.

THE YEAR 1968 was one of the most discouraging in modern U.S. history. The Vietnam War dragged on. Despite major civil rights bills, many people feared the country was turning "increasingly separate and unequal." The nation grieved over the assassinations of Martin Luther King Jr. and Robert Kennedy. Riots filled city streets.

At the end of this dismal year, a Saturn 5 rocket lifted off from Cape Canaveral on mankind's first attempt to reach the moon. On board were three *Apollo 8* astronauts: Frank Borman, Jim Lovell, and Bill Anders. Their mission was not to land on the moon, but to orbit it ten times. NASA told their wives that the men's chances of making it back to earth alive were about 50–50.

On Christmas Eve millions of enthralled TV viewers watched as the astronauts transmitted a blurry but miraculous image of the lunar surface. Then they heard the voice of Bill Anders: "We are now approaching lunar sunrise and, for all the people back on Earth, the crew of *Apollo 8* has a message that we would like to send to you. 'In the beginning God created the heaven and the earth. And the earth was without form, and void; and darkness was upon the face of the deep. And the Spirit of God moved upon the face of the waters. And God said, Let there be light, and there was light . . .'"

The astronauts took turns reading the first ten verses of Genesis. Then Frank Borman said, "And from the crew of *Apollo 8*, we close with good night, good luck, a Merry Christmas, and God bless all of you—all of you on the good earth."

After a year of death and destruction, the astronaut's brave journey and healing gesture were like a balm in Gilead. *Apollo 8* held the promise that a free people would not fail after all. Americans coming together could still achieve wonders.

AMERICAN HISTORY PARADE

1814   The United States and Britain sign a treaty in Ghent, Belgium, ending the War of 1812.

1906   Inventor Reginald Fessenden broadcasts the first radio entertainment program from Brant Rock, Massachusetts: a Bible reading and violin solo of "O Holy Night."

1923   President Coolidge presides over the first electric lighting of the National Christmas Tree on the White House grounds.

1946   A candlelight service at Grace Episcopal Church in New York City becomes the first religious service televised from a church.

1968   The *Apollo 8* astronauts read from the book of Genesis while orbiting the moon.

IN 1949, President Harry Truman sent Christmas greetings to the nation by radio from his home in Independence, Missouri:

Once more I have come out to Independence to celebrate Christmas with my family. We are back among old friends and neighbors around our own fireside. . . . Since returning home, I have been reading again in our family Bible some of the passages which foretold this night. It was that grand old seer Isaiah who prophesied in the Old Testament the sublime event which found fulfillment almost 2,000 years ago. Just as Isaiah foresaw the coming of Christ, so another battler for the Lord, St. Paul, summed up the law and the prophets in a glorification of love which he exalts even above both faith and hope.

We miss the spirit of Christmas if we consider the Incarnation as an indistinct and doubtful, far-off event unrelated to our present problems. We miss the purport of Christ's birth if we do not accept it as a living link which joins us together in spirit as children of the ever-living and true God. In love alone—the love of God and the love of man—will be found the solution of all the ills which afflict the world today. Slowly, sometimes painfully, but always with increasing purpose, emerges the great message of Christianity: only with wisdom comes joy, and with greatness comes love.

In the spirit of the Christ Child—as little children with joy in our hearts and peace in our souls—let us, as a nation, dedicate ourselves anew to the love of our fellowmen. In such a dedication we shall find the message of the Child of Bethlehem, the real meaning of Christmas.

AMERICAN HISTORY PARADE

1651   By order of Puritan lawmakers in Massachusetts, any colonist caught observing Christmas with feasts or other festivities is fined five shillings.

1776   George Washington's army crosses the Delaware River on Christmas night for a surprise attack against Hessian forces at Trenton, New Jersey, the next morning.

1830   In South Carolina, the *Best Friend of Charleston* becomes the first U.S. locomotive to begin regularly scheduled passenger service.

1868   President Andrew Johnson grants an unconditional pardon to all Confederates involved in the Civil War.

1896   John Philip Sousa completes his most famous march, "Stars and Stripes Forever."

LATE DECEMBER 1776 may have been the American Revolution's gloomiest hour. The Patriot army, which seemed unable to win a battle, lay shivering in Pennsylvania. The troops were hungry, sick, and exhausted. More and more men deserted every day. "I think the game is pretty near up," George Washington wrote.

Across the Delaware River in Trenton, New Jersey, 1,400 Hessian soldiers hired by King George of England sat snugly before their fires. Figuring that no army could move in such frozen winter weather, they were getting ready for a Christmas feast of roast goose and rum. George Washington's men, meanwhile, were searching the Pennsylvania banks of the river for every boat they could find.

The Patriots began crossing the river as dark fell on Christmas night. Chunks of floating ice crashed into their boats as they fought the currents. Rain, hail, and snow fell. "It will be a terrible night for the soldiers who have no shoes," wrote one of Washington's aides. "Some of them have tied old rags around their feet."

It was 3 a.m. before the last of the troops and equipment were across. The snow was stained with bloody footprints as the men stumbled nine miles toward Trenton. The wet weather had soaked much of their gunpowder, making it useless. Washington decided to push on.

The Americans attacked in the early light of December 26 in a blinding snow. The Hessians, stunned to discover an army appearing out of nowhere, had no chance to organize a defense. Within forty-five minutes, the fighting was over.

News of the American victory raced through the colonies. Perhaps the Patriot cause was not so hopeless. Weary soldiers began to talk of fighting on. With one bold move, George Washington had his countrymen believing that the fight for liberty might be winnable after all.

AMERICAN HISTORY PARADE

1776   After crossing the Delaware, George Washington's army defeats a Hessian force at Trenton, New Jersey.

1865   James Mason of Massachusetts wins the first U.S. patent, for a coffee percolator.

1933   Edwin H. Armstrong patents FM radio, which he developed at Columbia University in New York City.

1941   Winston Churchill becomes the first British prime minister to address Congress, calling for "courage and untiring exertion" to defeat the Axis powers.

THE WHOLE EFFORT STARTED BY MISTAKE. Several days after the Japanese attack on Pearl Harbor, people in North Platte, Nebraska, heard that their own Company D of the Nebraska National Guard would be passing through town on its way from an Arkansas training camp to the West Coast. A crowd gathered at the Union Pacific train station to greet the boys with cookies, candy, and small gifts. When the train arrived, it turned out it was transporting a Company D from *Kansas*, not Nebraska. After a moment of disappointment, someone in the crowd asked, "Well, what are we waiting for?" And they began handing their gifts to the war-bound soldiers.

The next day, Miss Rae Wilson wrote the North Platte *Daily Bulletin* to suggest that the town open a canteen to greet all troop trains stopping there. "Let's do something and do it in a hurry!" she wrote.

Beginning on Christmas Day 1941 and continuing through World War II, the town offered itself as the North Platte Canteen. For 365 days a year, volunteers from the remote community of 12,000 and surrounding hamlets provided hot coffee, donuts, sandwiches, and encouragement for young soldiers passing through. Hundreds of families, churches, schools, businesses, and clubs pitched in to help raise money, buy supplies, and make food. They greeted every soldier on every train with gifts and good wishes. By April 1, 1946, its last day, the North Platte Canteen had served more than *6 million* GIs.

"You don't forget that when you're overseas," one veteran told Bob Greene, author of *Once Upon a Town: The Miracle of the North Platte Canteen.* "There was no place I ever knew of, or ever heard about, that went to that great effort. A lot of people might be *willing* to do it. Or at least they might say they would be willing. But in North Platte, they *did* it."

AMERICAN HISTORY PARADE

1900   Prohibitionist Carry Nation begins her campaign of destroying saloons when she smashes the bar at the Carey Hotel in Wichita, Kansas.

1927   *Showboat,* a play that revolutionized musical theater, opens at the Ziegfeld Theater in New York City.

1932   Radio City Music Hall opens in New York City.

1941   The newly opened North Platte Canteen serves war-bound troops.

1947   The children's TV program *Howdy Doody* premieres.

1968   *Apollo 8,* the first spaceflight to reach the moon's orbit, returns to Earth.

ON DECEMBER 28, 1945, Congress made the Pledge of Allegiance the official national pledge to the U.S. flag. Noted clergyman Henry Ward Beecher (1813–87) reminded us what our flag means:

> If one asks the meaning of our flag, I say it means just what Concord and Lexington meant, what Bunker Hill meant. It means the whole glorious Revolutionary War. It means all that the Declaration of Independence meant. It means all that the Constitution of our people, organizing for justice, for liberty, and for happiness, meant.
>
> Under this banner rode Washington and his armies. . . . It waved on the highlands at West Point. . . . This banner streamed in light over the soldiers' heads at Valley Forge. . . . It crossed the waters rolling with ice at Trenton. . . .
>
> Our flag carries American ideas, American history, and American feelings. Beginning with the colonies, and coming down to our time, in its sacred heraldry, in its glorious insignia, it has gathered and stored chiefly this supreme idea: Divine right of liberty in man. Every color means liberty. Every thread means liberty. Every form of star and beam or stripe of light means liberty. Not lawlessness, not license, but organized, institutional liberty— liberty through law, and laws for liberty.
>
> This American flag was the safeguard of liberty. Not an atom of crown was allowed to go into its insignia. Not a symbol of authority in the ruler was permitted to go into it. It was an ordinance of liberty by the people, for the people. That it meant, that it means, and, by the blessing of God, that it shall mean to the end of time.

AMERICAN HISTORY PARADE

1832   John C. Calhoun becomes the first vice president to resign, leaving office over political differences with President Andrew Jackson.

1846   Iowa becomes the twenty-ninth state.

1856   Thomas Woodrow Wilson, the twenty-eighth president, is born in Staunton, Virginia.

1945   Congress formally recognizes the Pledge of Allegiance as the national pledge.

DECEMBER 29 • "WE MUST BE THE GREAT ARSENAL OF DEMOCRACY"

ON THE NIGHT OF DECEMBER 29, 1940, theaters and restaurants across the country emptied as Americans gathered around radios to hear President Franklin Delano Roosevelt deliver one of the most famous of his beloved fireside chats. His topic was a somber one for the holidays. "Never before since Jamestown and Plymouth Rock has our American civilization been in such danger as now," the president said.

World War II was underway, though America had not yet entered the fight. Germany and its allies had overrun much of Europe and Asia. The British, Greeks, Chinese, and a few other nations struggled to hold back the Axis assault. If Great Britain fell, FDR predicted, Americans "would be living at the point of a gun." (That very night, German bombs fell on London, engulfing many buildings in flames.)

"There can be no appeasement with ruthlessness," Roosevelt warned. "There can be no reasoning with an incendiary bomb. We know now that a nation can have peace with the Nazis only at the price of total surrender."

The president explained that America had no choice but to use its industrial might to arm nations battling the Axis powers. "We must be the great arsenal of democracy," he said. "We must apply ourselves to our task with the same resolution, the same sense of urgency, the same spirit of patriotism and sacrifice as we would show were we at war."

In the following months, American factories began pumping out planes, tanks, guns, and ships to aid the Allies. Between 1940 and 1943, the United States increased its war output by a stunning 25 times. As the British journalist Alistair Cooke wrote, "The Allies would not have won the war . . . without the way the American people, with amazing speed, created an arsenal no coalition of nations could come close to matching."

AMERICAN HISTORY PARADE

1808   Andrew Johnson, the seventeenth U.S. president, is born in Raleigh, North Carolina.

1845   Texas becomes the twenty-eighth state.

1851   The first Young Men's Christian Association (YMCA) in the United States is organized in Boston.

1890   The U.S. Cavalry massacres up to 300 Lakota Sioux at Wounded Knee, South Dakota.

1913   Filming begins on *The Squaw Man*, about a British officer's adventures in the American West, reputedly the first feature-length movie made in Hollywood.

1940   FDR calls on the United States to become "the great arsenal of democracy."

PRESIDENT DWIGHT D. EISENHOWER offered the following words to the nation during the Christmas season of 1956. His closing quote, "with charity for all, with firmness in the right," comes from Abraham Lincoln's second inaugural address.

"Peace on earth, good will to men." These are hallowed words. Through ages they have heartened and moved mankind, even though their message of peace is far too often drowned by the strident voices of the fearful or the arrogant, who fill our minds with doubt and pessimism. . . .

The spirit of Christmas returns, yet again, to enable us to gain understanding of each other; to help each other; to obey the elemental precepts of justice; to practice good will toward all men of every tongue and color and creed; to remember that we are all identical in our aspirations for a peaceful, a decent, a rewarding life.

In the warm glow of the Christmas tree, it is easy to say these things, but when the trees come down and the lights are put away—as they always are—then we have a true testing of the spirit. That testing will be answered, throughout the year ahead, by the success each of us experiences in keeping alive the inspiration and exultation of this moment.

We must proceed by faith, knowing the light of Christmas is eternal, though we cannot always see it. We must believe that the truth of Christmas is constant; that men can live together in peace as Lincoln said, "with charity for all, with firmness in the right."

AMERICAN HISTORY PARADE

1853   James Gadsden, minister to Mexico, signs the Gadsden Purchase, in which the United States buys nearly 30,000 square miles of land from Mexico.

1862   The ironclad USS *Monitor* sinks in a storm off Cape Hatteras, North Carolina.

1924   Astronomer Edwin Hubble announces evidence of the existence of a galaxy outside our own.

1940   California opens its first freeway, the Arroyo Seco Parkway, connecting Los Angeles and Pasadena.

1951   The TV western *The Roy Rogers Show* debuts.

IN 1974, then Governor Ronald Reagan of California gave one of his most famous speeches, known as his "City upon a Hill" speech because of his allusion to those words by John Winthrop, governor of the Massachusetts Bay Colony. These are good words with which to end a year and begin a new one:

> You can call it mysticism if you want to, but I have always believed that there was some divine plan that placed this great continent between two oceans to be sought out by those who were possessed of an abiding love of freedom and a special kind of courage. This was true of those who pioneered the great wilderness in the beginning of this country, as it is also true of those later immigrants who were willing to leave the land of their birth and come to a land where even the language was unknown to them. . . .
>
> Standing on the tiny deck of the *Arabella* in 1630 off the Massachusetts coast, John Winthrop said, "We will be as a city upon a hill. The eyes of all people are upon us. . . ."
>
> We cannot escape our destiny, nor should we try to do so. The leadership of the free world was thrust upon us two centuries ago in that little hall of Philadelphia. In the days following World War II, when the economic strength and power of America was all that stood between the world and the return to the dark ages, Pope Pius XII said, "The American people have a great genius for splendid and unselfish actions. Into the hands of America God has placed the destinies of an afflicted mankind."
>
> We are indeed, and we are today, the last best hope of man on earth.

AMERICAN HISTORY PARADE

1879 Thomas Edison gives the first public demonstration of his incandescent lightbulbs by lighting up a street in Menlo Park, New Jersey.

1907 A giant ball is first dropped in Times Square to bring in the New Year.

1929 In New York City, Guy Lombardo and his Royal Canadians introduce Americans to the custom of playing "Auld Lang Syne" on New Year's Eve.

1935 Charles Darrow of Pennsylvania patents the board game Monopoly.

1999 The U.S. transfers full control of the Panama Canal to Panama.

Acknowledgments

WE COULD NOT HAVE WRITTEN this book without the help of others. The first debt goes to the historians, scholars, authors, and statisticians—too numerous to name—whose works have informed this one. Creating this almanac meant depending on literally centuries of research. We consulted hundreds of books, magazine articles, and Web sites. We are grateful that so many lovers of history have done so much to preserve our nation's heritage.

We also had the help of many knowledgeable people who answered questions on topics ranging from Revolutionary War battles to America's space program. We are grateful for their kind assistance.

We owe thanks to a few people in particular who gave indispensable aid.

Our friend Seth Leibsohn always supplied excellent advice and shared his wisdom. Likewise, Noreen Burns kept the caissons rolling along over all sorts of bumps, large and small, throughout this project, as she always does.

When this book was barely more than an idea, the invaluable Bob Barnett recognized its potential and went to bat for it. He never ceases to amaze. His colleague Jackie Davies offered wise counsel and helped work out many important details.

Joel Miller, our editor at Thomas Nelson, immediately grasped our intent, offered guidance to make the book better, and worked tirelessly to bring it all together. Thom Chittom made the process of moving from manuscript to finished almanac a pleasure. Dave Schroeder brings contagious enthusiasm to his work. Many thanks to the entire Thomas Nelson team.

Finally, endless thanks to Elayne Bennett and Kirsten Cribb. Their love, support, and judgment have been the anchors, ballast, and mainstays of this work. We're grateful also for the love and support of our children—John and Joe Bennett, and Molly and Sarah Cribb. With young patriots such as these, this country's future looks bright indeed.

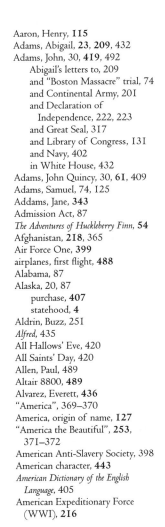

INDEX

About the Authors

DR. WILLIAM J. BENNETT is one of America's most important, influential, and respected voices on cultural, political, and educational issues. A Brooklyn native, Bill Bennett studied philosophy at Williams College (B.A.) and the University of Texas (Ph.D.) and earned a law degree from Harvard. Host of the top-ten nationally syndicated radio show *Bill Bennett's Morning in America*, he is also the Washington Fellow of the Claremont Institute. Former chairman of the National Endowment for the Humanities (1981-1985), and Secretary of Education (1985-1988), and first director of the Office of National Drug Control Policy (1989-1990), Bennett is a regular contributor to CNN and has contributed to America's leading newspapers, magazines, and television shows. He is the author and editor of seventeen books, two of which—*The Book of Virtues* and *The Children's Book of Virtues*—rank among the most successful of the past decade. He, his wife Elayne, and their two sons, John and Joseph, live in Maryland.

JOHN T.E. CRIBB is a writer and president of the Palmetto Creative Group, a communications firm. A native of Spartanburg, S.C., he studied literature at Vanderbilt University in Nashville, Tennessee. His previous work includes coauthoring *The Educated Child* (with William J. Bennett and Chester E. Finn), coediting *The Human Odyssey*, a three-volume world history text, and developing online history courses. During the Reagan administration, he served at the Department of Justice, the Department of Education, and the National Endowment for the Humanities. He is also a cofounder of BulletinNews, an electronic publishing company. He lives in Spartanburg, S.C., with his wife Kirsten and his daughters Molly and Sarah.